Books of Merit

ALSO BY TOM HARPUR

Harpur's Heaven and Hell
Always on Sunday
For Christ's Sake
Life After Death
God Help Us
The Uncommon Touch
Would You Believe?
Prayer: The Hidden Fire
Finding the Still Point
The Pagan Christ
The Spirituality of Wine
Living Waters
Water into Wine
Born Again

TOM HARPUR

THERE IS LIFE AFTER DEATH

Thomas Allen Publishers
Toronto

Library and Archives Canada Cataloguing in Publication

Harpur, Tom
There is life after death / Tom Harpur.

Rev. ed. of: Life after death.
ISBN 978-0-88762-740-8

1. Immortality. I. Title.

BL530.H37 2011   202'.3   C2010-907343-6

Editor: Patrick Crean
Cover and text design: Gordon Robertson
Cover image: Benjamin Rondel / First Light

Published by Thomas Allen Publishers,
a division of Thomas Allen & Son Limited,
390 Steelcase Road East,
Markham, Ontario L3R 1G2 Canada

www.thomasallen.ca

The publisher gratefully acknowledges the support of
The Ontario Arts Council for its publishing program.

We acknowledge the support of the Canada Council for the Arts, which
last year invested $20.1 million in writing and publishing throughout Canada.

We acknowledge the Government of Ontario through the
Ontario Media Development Corporation's Ontario Book Initiative.

We acknowledge the financial support of the Government of Canada
through the Canada Book Fund for our publishing activities.

1 2 3 4 5   15 14 13 12 11

Printed and bound in Canada
Text printed on a 100% PCW recycled stock

To all those dear ones
whom we have "loved long
since and lost awhile"

Contents

PART I

THE SECULAR EVIDENCE

INTRODUCTION

An Urgent Question

WHEN IN THE SPRING of 2004 *The Pagan Christ* was launched onto the Canadian scene and quickly became a major controversial bestseller, what initially captured most of the headlines was the way the book cast doubt on the actual existence of a historical Jesus. However, those who read the book soon realized that this was not its main message. Their overwhelmingly positive response was to its real message—the reality of the spiritual presence of the Divine spark (for Christians, the Inner Christ) within us all. Still, because my whole approach to and understanding of my own faith has publicly evolved into something to me and to many thousands of others so much more intellectually and spiritually satisfying than what it was when I was first ordained, or even since *Life After Death* was first published in 1991, I am repeatedly asked today whether I still believe in a future life. Do I today believe in a life beyond the grave, one that transcends this present sphere of being, one that offers a lively hope for oneself and for loved ones—everyone, in fact, on the "other side"? Answering that insistent and ultimate query with a resounding, reasoned "yes" is the major reason for this new fully revised and much enriched version of the original work. With that said, we can begin the story.

The Fountain of Youth

In 1513 when the Spanish explorer Ponce de Leon made landfall at what is today St. Augustine, Florida, North America's oldest city, he believed he had discovered the spring of eternal life. Thousands of visitors visit the site annually and sip from this slightly sulphuric-tasting would-be elixir. However, like everybody else on this planet, all those who have ever drunk from that source still have to face the blunt truth confronting each of us: nobody is getting out of here alive. But is that the whole story or is it only the beginning of an infinitely more complex and liberating story?

That's what this investigation is about. Is death the final reality? Is the grave the ultimate end of human hopes or is there, as billions have believed since the dawning of self-reflective consciousness in our earliest ancestors, a more glorious future yet ahead? Is there, in short, life after or beyond our final hour on earth?

A headline in a major newspaper a short time ago trumpeted: "Eternal life, here—scientists are making some amazing finds." The story dealt with humanity's age-old, universal dream of discovering the secret of immortality, or some magical talisman to stave off the hour of our death. While carefully documenting the latest research into the ageing process, however, in the end the account had very little to say about the headline. The best it could offer was the hope that future scientific progress in this field will increasingly ensure that people "die 'young' as late as possible."

Not long after the newspaper article quoted above appeared, the same paper ran a story billed "Advocates of Cryonics Defy Death."[1] It told of the American Cryonic Society's ventures in freezing recently dead bodies and brains as a logical step "toward immortality." At the rather sparsely furnished Trans-Time warehouse in West Oakland, California, two human bodies, two heads, one brain and a dog and cat are "on ice" in cryonic suspension inside shiny, stainless-steel containers that resemble giant silver thermos bottles. They have been frozen, with instructions that they be thawed some time in the next couple of centuries and, with luck and presumed scientific advances, brought back to life. Altogether, about seventy members of this society have made similar arrangements to be frozen when they die. One of them, Art Quaife, has reportedly arranged for his freezing to be paid for through life insurance. "Fifty cents a day for immortality," he was quoted as saying. "I like the deal."

All of this gives further emphasis to the ancient truth that there is indeed nothing new under the sun. It's just that today, at least in the West, we tend more and more to rely on technology in what was once the exclusive territory of God and religion. We now know that the graves of Neanderthal man, dating to some fifty thousand years ago, contained spherical stones and other ritual objects, including food and weapons, that strongly suggest they believed in a life after death. On October 21, 1987, newspapers everywhere carried the story of how American and Egyptian scientists, using space age technology, discovered a five-thousand-year-old pharaoh's funeral boat at the Cheops pyramid near Cairo. The team, coordinated by the National Geographic Society, lowered cameras through a hole some four inches in diameter into a pit sealed by the Egyptians in or about 2600 BCE. They took a picture of this "solar boat" and found it to be similar to one found nearby in 1954. Under the ancient Egyptian custom of the solar cult, a cedar boat was left in the tomb to transport the soul of the dead king to the afterworld.[2]

In the Egyptian Book of the Dead, dating from about 1500 to 1400 BCE, the chief features of the myth of Osiris and his divine son, Horus, are elaborated. But the story existed orally for many centuries before it was written down—probably back to 2500 or 3000 BCE Osiris/Horus was the "king of eternity" and the Egyptian doctrine of eternal life was based upon the story of his resurrection in a transformed body after an unjust and cruel death. Since Osiris was the mythical way of speaking of the fate or destiny of

every person, the way to eternal life was described in terms of identification with him, just as Christians speak of their identification
with a crucified and resurrected Lord. Just as happened to Osiris
and Horus (or to Jesus Christ, according to St. Paul) at death, the
body of every individual germinates or is transformed into a spiritual, glorified body. The Egyptian Book of the Dead says that,
when a person enters heaven, he becomes "God" or the "Son of
God." He or she receives a crown, feeds upon the Word of God as
"bread," is clothed in white raiment and eats of the tree of life.[3]

In this book I am more interested in current phenomena and
thought than I am with the distant past. But unless we can see the
matter in its proper context, unless we sense the longevity and the
universality of the question Is there life after death?, we are des-
tined to go badly astray.

There is today a major paradox in the fact that, while more people than ever are concerned about dying and what may lie beyond,
fewer and fewer are turning to traditional religion to find the answers
they seek. Little of what traditional religions teach today about
life after death—and my research suggests that many clergy avoid
the topic completely—makes much sense to many people. To the
increasing number of those outside the Church, Western teaching
on life after death often seems childish, a boring prospect and the
product of mere wishful thinking. Yet there has seldom been a time
in history when more men and women held some form of belief in
survival beyond the grave. Indeed, in many ways, the present spiritual searching in our culture is a rebuke to organized religion and
suggests that its essential message has failed to communicate reasonable answers to life's most basic and most urgent concerns.

Surely the most momentous personal question of our day—or
indeed any other—is, having died, is that the end or do we somehow live again? Moreover, if the answer is in the affirmative, what
kind of life can we expect? While, for obvious reasons, this is not an
area where categorical finality of thought or utterance will ever

be possible, nevertheless there is an extraordinary need for some clear thinking and analysis. This book is an attempt to provide that. What is the evidence, if any, for life after death? What are we to make of the contemporary surge of interest in near-death experiences? Is there any truth in the New Age insistence upon reincarnation, with all the tales of past lives that now appear so frequently in the popular press and other media? Have we really lived before and have we already died a thousand times? What is the teaching of Christianity and of other major world religions about life after death? Is there a flaming hell for sinners and a heaven above the stars for all the redeemed? Has modern science anything to say to all of this? After reviewing and sifting this material, what is left for an intelligent modern man or woman to believe? It is to these issues that we now must turn.

Before we do so, however, it is important that we make some initial, basic distinctions. Evidence for the belief in a life after death has to be sharply distinguished from evidence for life after death itself. Humans have always and nearly everywhere held some form of belief that life does not end with the grave or funeral pyre. Anthropology, sociology and the history of world religions all provide ample evidence of the extent to which our species has expressed its solid, near-universal faith that death is not the last word. But evidence of such a faith, however abundant or moving, is not the same thing as evidence for the reality of a life beyond.

This doesn't mean we must simply discount faith or ignore it altogether. That would be highly unscientific to say the least. The fact that something is obviously very widely believed must itself be accounted for. The inherent conviction in the human psyche that there is some kind of eternal life or survival after death has to be explained. It may be a form of indirect evidence of the truth of what is believed. In other words, such an effect could testify to such a cause. But, in and by itself, it doesn't necessarily do so. When I speak of evidence for life after death itself I have in mind material—

whether historical documents or recent experiences—that bears directly upon the subject. Yet, it must be said, even this evidence, however solid and weighty, or even at times sensational, does not establish absolute certainty.

This brings us to the second important clarification. Evidence and proof are by no means one and the same thing. For example, I am fully convinced that there is considerable evidence to be taken into account when trying to answer the question Is there a God or not? But, because of the very nature of the inquiry, there can be no proof of God's existence in the normal, scientific use of the word "proof." This should not, however, discourage us or make us think that any discussion of what we call metaphysical (beyond the physical or material) concepts is a matter of "Your guess is as good as mine." In science, as in courts of law, those areas where absolute empirical proof is possible are far more limited than many of us imagine. With regard to many important and far-reaching scientific theories or legal cases, the best one can do is to gather all the available evidence, weigh it judiciously and then make a decision based on a reasonable conclusion about where the evidence leads. I propose to follow the same principle here.

One final brief observation—a personal one. Most married couples have a very vivid memory of their first date. I certainly do. It was the spring of 1979, and Susan and I went for a picnic lunch beside Lake Ontario, not far from the *Toronto Star* offices where we both worked at the time. When we had eaten, we decided not just to talk but to have a discussion. I asked Susan: "What would you most like to talk about?" She replied very calmly, "Let's talk about death. What do you really believe about death?" Considering it was our first time alone together and that it was a simply glorious day, I could tell this was no ordinary woman! This book now wholly revised and updated is my best effort at answering her profound request.

1

STRANGE ENCOUNTERS

"Oh, their eyes, their eyes are so beautiful!"

CHARLES TEMPLETON, a one-time associate of Billy Graham, was a leading light in Canadian media for many years. He began as a charismatic, evangelistic star with Youth for Christ (an independent Christian youth organization) and then made headlines when he announced in 1957 that he had lost his faith and was leaving the ministry forever. Active as a politician for a time, then as a radio and television commentator, newspaper editor and a novelist, he quickly gained a reputation as the country's most articulate agnostic. In his 1996 book, *Farewell to God*, he set out myriad reasons why he found it impossible to be a believer. Yet, as I watched his career and got to know him personally—we worked together on his earlier book, *Jesus*, and he would often call me at home on Sundays to discuss my column—he always seemed to me a God-haunted man. Templeton, whom I had visited in his home not long before his death from Alzheimer's disease, June 7, 2001, had a remarkable visionary experience on his deathbed. He saw a vision of angels "waiting for me on the other side." Madeleine, his wife, was alone with him in the hospital room when it occurred and she called me the day following his funeral to tell me what had happened. She asked whether I'd be interested in hearing of Charles's encounter with "something quite transcendent and wonderful." Although I had already sent off a tribute to Charles to the paper, this was too interesting to miss and I wrote the following account that appeared in a front-page *Toronto Star* story a day later:

"Charles had been ill for seven years when his condition suddenly worsened and he required full-time hospital care. There were times when he seemed 'very sweet' and others when he had furious rages. He had grown worse in the three weeks leading up to his death, even fighting with the nurses at times.

"He always quieted down when his wife was there and this was the case when she visited him on the afternoon of June 6, about 24 hours before he died. He'd had a terrible, rage-ridden morning but became quite calm as she kissed and soothed his forehead.

"Suddenly he became very animated and alive, looking intensely towards the ceiling of the room, with his blue eyes 'shining more blue than I'd ever seen before.' He cried out: 'Look at them, look at them . . . they're so beautiful . . . they're waiting for me.' Then with great joy in his voice, he said: 'Oh, their eyes, their eyes are so beautiful! . . . I'm coming!'

"Madeleine Templeton describes herself as 'somewhere between an atheist and a deist' but she spoke with deep emotion as she described what happened. 'It's such a surprise and such a tremendous comfort,' she said."

Recent polls in North America reveal a remarkable upsurge in the number of people reporting that they have had one or more paranormal experiences. For example, priest-sociologist Father Andrew Greeley has done several major surveys showing that millions of Americans undergo psychic and mystical experiences, from extrasensory perception (67 percent of all adults) to being in some form of contact with the dead (42 percent). In all, Greeley and his associates have discovered that 74 percent of Americans believe in a life after death where they will be reunited with their loved ones.[1] In a special survey of Canadian beliefs about life after death, published in 1983 as *Death and Beyond: A Canadian Profile*, University of Lethbridge sociologist Reginald Bibby found that 40 percent of the population believed it might be possible to communicate with the dead. Only one in three ruled it out as a total impossibility. Some 70 percent said they believe in "something after death." A 1990 Gallup poll of Canadians had almost identical findings. Slightly over 70 percent of those interviewed stated they "believe in heaven."[2]

Greeley, whom I got to know in Rome during the year of the three Popes, 1978, says he first became interested in what are generally referred to as "paranormal" experiences in the early 1970s when he began to be aware of just how many people have them "even if they don't tell anyone." He found that in the case of those North American adults who now believe they have had experiences of contact with someone who has died, the dead person is usually a spouse or sibling. Studies were conducted in 1973 and 1986 at the University of Chicago's National Opinion Research Council. Greeley's data show that there had been a marked increase in the number of people claiming to have had contact with the dead—from 27 percent in 1973 up to 42 percent in 1986. Among widows alone, the figures are 51 percent in 1973 and 67 percent in 1986. What is perhaps most striking is that there seems to be a split between scientific belief and personal realities. Greeley stated, "For example, 26 percent of the 30 percent of Americans who do *not* believe in life after death still say they've been in personal contact with the dead."

Belief in a hereafter appears to be increasing among North Americans. A 2000 Harris poll showed that 86 percent believe in the survival of the soul after death and another 9 percent say simply they don't know. A 2003 Barna Group poll reported that eight out of ten Americans believe in an afterlife of some sort—over 80 percent, in fact—while again approximately 9 percent say it may be true but they're not certain.

At the same time (2003) www.religioustolerance.org, which tracks religious trends, recorded that 51 percent or roughly half of Americans believe that ghosts exist. Those between 25 and 29 years of age were more likely (65 percent) to say they believed than their seniors—persons 64 and over. The figure for the latter group was 27 percent. One interesting statistic was reported in a *Washington Post* special feature on religious trends on April 24, 2000. The story by Washington polling director Richard Morin said that even Americans who say they have "no religious preference" are expressing greater belief in the hereafter, 63 percent of them today compared with 44 percent three decades ago. Overall, the proportion of people who believe in life after death rose from 77 percent in 1973 to 82 percent in 1998, Morin says.

Greeley has quoted a theologian friend, Father John Shea, who says encounters with the deceased may well be real and the cause, not the result, of man's tenacious belief in life after death. One argument in support of this thesis is that Greeley and his colleagues found that many of the widows who reported contact with a dead spouse said they had not believed in life after death before their experience. Another important finding in this study was that the people making such reports were "anything but religious nuts or psychiatric cases." In fact, Greeley maintained, "They are . . . ordinary Americans, somewhat above the norm in education and intelligence and somewhat less than average in religious involvement." Subsequent studies bear out these findings.

Other researchers have confirmed the vividness of these experiences. At the University of North Carolina, a team led by an associate professor of family medicine, P. Richard Olson, found that nearly two-thirds (64 percent) of widows at two Asheville nursing homes felt they had been in touch with a dead person at least once or twice. Of those reporting such contact, 78 percent said they saw the deceased. Some 50 percent said they heard, 21 percent touched, 32 percent felt the presence, 18 percent talked with the departed one and 46 percent had some combination of these experiences. Most found the contact "helpful" and not one had mentioned it to her doctor! Greeley himself did another survey in 1984, which, among widows and widowers in the general population, just about replicated Olson's findings in North Carolina.[3]

In England, Oxford biologist David Hay, director of the Alister Hardy Research Centre, conducts scientific research in religion. In one large survey of English nurses, he discovered that two-thirds of them reported mystical events, "brought on mainly by close involvement with people in dire and dying moments."[4] In the spring issue (1990) of the Oxford University magazine *Oxford Today*, Peter Snow reports that the Alister Hardy Centre has recorded thousands of mystical experiences by ordinary Britons as well. Visions, out-of-body "trips" and transcendental dreams have been coded for computerization by the centre. One staggering statistic emerges, he says: Nearly 40 percent of the British population will have a profound religious or spiritual experience at some time in their lives. "Clearly there is something in us struggling to get out," Snow concludes.

Colin Wilson cites similar results obtained by Dr. Karlis Osis of the New York Parapsychology Foundation. In 1960, Osis sent out ten thousand questionnaires to nurses asking about their patients' deathbed visions, and found that in a large number of cases, at the moment of death, the dying believed they saw a dead relative. The same discovery was made, Wilson relates, when Sir William Barrett, founder of the Society for Psychical Research, was gathering materials for his own book, *Death-bed Visions*. For a modern and insightful look at how the dying often communicate their feelings, read *Final Gifts*, written by two hospice nurses, Maggie Callanan and Patricia Kelley.

Before reading further, I want to make one thing clear. Although I was raised in an intensely religious home and have not just studied but have experienced the spiritual dimension of reality all my life, I have never had what I would label a paranormal experience of any kind. One doesn't go around looking for such experiences. They either happen or they don't and, in my case, it seems they don't. In other words, there is no hidden agenda here.

At the same time, however, when I was a parish priest I've had first-hand encounters with some seemingly extraordinary phenomena. Several times when attending the deathbed of a parishioner, something was either said or observed to lead me to the conclusion that the dying person had had a vision or foretaste of a glory to come. One such incident stands out in my memory and illustrates what I mean.

One day in June, many years ago, I was leaving the hospital closest to my church, St. Margaret's-in-the-Pines, in West Hill, Ontario, when a young couple stopped me in the entrance. They had spotted my Roman collar and, not knowing a minister themselves, suddenly asked me for help. They said the woman's mother was in a coma suffering from a terminal illness. They asked me whether I would mind paying her a brief visit. We went up to a private room, one of those reserved for the dying, and I saw the patient, a woman in her mid-sixties, lying unconscious under an oxygen tent. I said a brief prayer at her bedside and, because I had learned that even when in a coma our sense of hearing can often still be operative, I read a brief passage to her from the New Testament. It is the one that speaks eloquently of the fact that nothing can ever separate us from the love of God, not even death itself. Then I put my hand through the opening of the tent and placed it on her forehead as I said a final blessing.

Two days later, the daughter called me to say that, to their complete surprise, her mother had regained consciousness for a brief time the following day and had told her in great detail about my visit. "She said she heard the prayer and the reading and that suddenly her whole being had been flooded with an incredible sense of light," the daughter said. "It seemed to envelop her and give her an assurance of wholeness and peace she had never known before. She had a kind of radiance about her face that was quite wonderful to see." The dying woman relapsed into the coma shortly afterwards and died peacefully later that evening.

Since I had been only too aware of my own limitations on that occasion—it had been a very hot day, I was tired and looking forward to getting home and there seemed to be nothing anyone could do for her at that point—I am certain that whatever happened had absolutely nothing to do with me. Yet I know that something strange and spiritually healing did occur.

Because of my university background in the classics, particularly in ancient history, coupled with my training in journalism, I have always been reluctant to accept things on the basis of secondhand evidence. A couple of times over the past few years, most recently in June 2005, I decided to test the life-after-death-poll experiences with the readers of my syndicated *Toronto Star* column. In a brief footnote to the column, I said simply: "I am doing some research and would like to hear from you on the following: Do you believe in life beyond death? Have you ever experienced anything that amounts to solid evidence for this *as far as you yourself are concerned*? Please write briefly . . ."[5] I was quite aware it was not a scientific poll. It wasn't intended to be; there was little point in duplicating the many that had already been done by qualified researchers. What I wanted was a live sample, as it were, to get the flavour or feel of this phenomenon for myself.

I received hundreds of letters in answer to my requests. While some were brief, most ran to several pages. They came from people of all ages, all walks of life and from various regions of the country. Roughly 3 percent of the respondents said they did not believe in a life after death. Typical of these was the man from a small Ontario town who concluded his articulate rebuttal with the words "What is after your life is what was before your life—nothing. Sorry, but at times the truth hurts." Another skeptic wrote as follows: "I find it sad that so many people's grip on their life is so precarious that rather than face the bleak truth of their mortality they will embrace any preposterous delusion promising them immortality." To cover all his bases, though, he added, "In any case, from what I have read and heard of heaven I am sure I would find it incredibly boring and unpleasant existing under the critical eye of a humourless dictator whose compassion is all too capricious and fleeting."

For illumination on how paranormal experiences that are not properly understood can be a risk to one's mental and emotional health, I refer the reader to Dr. Yvonne Kason's book, *A Farther Shore*, mentioned in the bibliography. Dr. Kason discusses how millions of people today who have undergone religious experiences are greatly at risk of slipping into mental illnesses or of being misdiagnosed because psychiatrists and clergy tend to be the least skilled at helping people in spiritual crisis.

The overwhelming majority, however, obviously wrote because they now feel positively about a future life. Several themes or characteristics stood out sharply as I read and reread what they had to say. Most of those who described one or more mystical experiences involving some form of "contact" with a deceased person said that this was the first time they had ever told anyone else about it. They expressed sincere relief not only at the opportunity to share this with somebody else, but also at learning that they were not going to be looked upon as eccentric or even deranged for talking about such intimate and unusual psychic happenings. I was also greatly impressed by the number of respondents who prefaced their story with the observation that they had not previously held strong convictions about an afterlife. In other words, it seems that it was an unusual experience that awakened belief in them, rather than the other way around. Greeley's research has uncovered the same phenomenon. Closely related to this was the way in which the psychic event, in most instances, came unexpectedly as to place and time, as well as content. There were certain similarities, on the one hand, but there was a striking range of variables on the other. To tell the truth, I was surprised by the originality or creativity involved in whatever it is that is going on at such times. As you will see, people report a wide variety of visual and auditory experiences. At times, a fragrance is the vehicle; often electrical disturbances seem to occur with no explanation.

One final word about the methodology. The content of the letters described several stages. The process was admittedly a subjective one. While nearly every letter was interesting, some were obviously more interesting than others. All I can say is that, using whatever critical powers I have, I gradually sifted them down to a final score or so. The overriding criterion was believability: Does this account have about it the ring of authenticity and of truth-telling? This is what Colin Wilson refers to as the "boggle threshold"—how far do we feel or intuit we can trust the person concerned? The credibility of any witness, whether in a court of law or elsewhere, has much to do with how sane and balanced they seem in other ways. None of this, of course, makes any prejudgment about the status of such reports as hard evidence of a life to come. More on that later.

- M.B. is a widow whose husband died in 1984. They were "always very happy together" and his death has left a great void. She writes: "I have had the feeling many times that my husband was there in the room with me, but it is one particular experience that I wish to tell you about. I had stretched out on the chesterfield for a nap before watching a program due to come on TV in an hour. I fell sound asleep but soon the presence of someone standing beside me caused me to wake up. I knew it was Jack, my husband. There he was. He bent over and offered me a bottle of beer. I remember thinking 'Oh yes, he's taken the cap off and he wants to pour it into two glasses for us' (we had always done this and really consumed very little; in fact, I haven't bought any since I've been alone). I reached out to touch him but, in a flash, he was gone! But I actually saw him. And I had a warm feeling for days after. I know it must have been an apparition—but it was the most realistic one I have ever known. I speak to him and feel he guides me in many things."

- F.P.'s father who died at the age of ninety-six remained completely lucid and alert to the very end. She had visited him the day before, a Sunday, and they had talked about Christmas plans and the new house his son had bought. He wanted to see it "when the weather gets better." Out of the blue, the old man asked her: "What do you know about double vision?" When she asked if he had some problem with his eyes, he said: "Not really, but this morning when I came into my room there was a woman sitting on my bed." She asked him whether he knew the woman (there were no women in the wing of the seniors' home where he lived) and he answered that she had had her back to the doorway. He turned to leave the room and, glancing back as he did so, noticed the woman "was gone." F.P. felt intuitively that it had been the spirit-form "of my mother who died long ago." When she went home, she told her husband she had a strange feeling her father's death was not too far away. Although her father seemed normal for the rest of the day, after he went to bed that night his heart began to fail and he was rushed to the hospital for oxygen. A few hours later, he died. His daughter comments: "While his death came as a surprise, since he was normal when I left him, it wasn't the shock it might have been because of what he told me he had seen. I can't explain it, but I accept what happened as a real event."

- S.J. writes: "One day I received a call and was told that my beloved grandmother, who was in the final stages of ALS, was near death. Earlier that day, I was told she had spoken about 'going home' repeatedly, an expression that I found unsettling as she had never used it before. She had turned against God and did not spend much time worrying about her eternal soul. Yet in the last three weeks of her life, she had spoken at length about seeing her long-dead mother, being surrounded by unknown children and conversing with people who had long since left this world. Late that night, I was alone with her. I climbed into the chair with her, placed her head into the crook of my arm and wrapped myself around her. I wanted to comfort her, to cradle her; I thought that even catatonic as she was, she would feel me there and be comforted by it. I did not close my eyes, and was just being still, when everything changed. My vision blurred and I felt energy all around me, an energy so great it caused a visual disturbance in the room. My entire body felt electrified and, although I had never felt it before, it was so purely alive, so strong, that I knew what I was feeling was a different energy, another form of life, in the room. In my arms, Nan seemed to still and settle and I knew, as well, that in that moment her soul had gone forward and away from me. She died six minutes later—her breath just sputtered, and then stopped. It was so peaceful and natural that it changed every opinion I had ever formed about life and death. I was only left to wonder where she had gone, and wait for the day when that wonderful energy comes for me."

- M.H. begins her letter with the terse statement "I doubt a lot. I'm not superstitious; I'm fairly intelligent." She then relates how on Mother's Day a few years ago she was with her grandmother, holding her hand as the old lady was dying. She says she told her over and over, even though she seemed unconscious, that she would help her with dying and that she would soon see her mother and sister, to be with them as she had longed to be. "She died at about 4 P.M. After about ten minutes, while I was looking at her, not touching, I felt a sudden and very powerful aura in the room. It felt as though my grandmother was all around me, in the air of the room, and as though she was most intensely projecting her personality toward me. I have never felt anyone, ever, as strongly as then. It was one of the happiest moments of my life. I have tried to analyze it, tried to be objective, but those few minutes were so incredible, so very happy, and the world all around was brilliant, jubilant, everything in super-Technicolor. I can't begin to explain how powerful it was."

- J.D. was devastated at losing her father a few years ago. She writes: "He had a treasured pocket watch that, after he died, I kept on a shelf near where I watch TV. I wound it carefully each night and still do. Several times while I was looking through our album of his pictures or reading his letters from the past and feeling very sad, I would become aware that the watch was ticking more loudly than usual. These spells of enhanced ticking went on for about five months and I wavered between thinking my father was present and thinking something was wrong mechanically with the watch. It then stopped. This past Father's Day, I was relaxing in the TV room, involved in a program. The watch began to tick loudly. Without thinking, I said: 'Oh, are you here? Then please show me—flick the lights on and off or do something with the lights to show me you're here,'—not my exact words but close. Nothing happened immediately and I really didn't expect it to. I became interested in my program again. About two minutes later, I was stunned when the lamp that my daughter had given her grandfather flicked on. I sat frozen for a minute. I ran upstairs to tell my husband, then went back downstairs and turned it off. The lamp had a trilight bulb in it. By the time I had sat down, it flicked on again, flicked up to the strongest light level, then flicked off! I feel that something otherworldly happened, but my rational mind has trouble with this. I don't know how it's possible, but this light had never done this before or since. I have only told my family and a close friend about this since they know I'm not given to imaginings."

- A.G. lost his wife five years ago. The day after her sudden death, he was alone in the house thinking how glad he was that her will, which they had often discussed, had been finally drawn up only a couple of days before she died. "I spoke her name and said I had fulfilled all her wishes. The room was suddenly filled with her perfume and looking up I saw a form all in white which gradually faded away. I knew then that she knew what I had said. I firmly believe that my wife's spirit remained in the house for some time afterwards. This has been on my mind a lot and I am very glad to write to you about it because when I mentioned the above to anyone I got funny looks. But, I'm certain I did not just imagine it."

- S.H. writes: "My grandmother, who died ten years ago, wore an uncommon type of perfume that had a way of completely enveloping one in a sense of calm, serenity and peace. Five years ago, my mother became terminally ill. During one of several heart-to-heart talks, she stated that it would be so good to see her mother (my grandmother) again because she had missed her terribly. She said my grandmother had told her that when it was my mother's time to pass the veil, Grandmother would be waiting there to show her the way. When my mother neared the end, my sisters, brother and father were in her bedroom, telling her to let go, that we wanted her to be at peace and that we would promise to be there for each other as she had been for us. Suddenly the room became incredibly still and filled with the unmistakable aroma of my grandmother's perfume. I had not smelled that smell in ten years, but never forgot it . . . that unmistakable aroma of love and peace. My mother died at that very instant, but I knew my grandmother had kept her promise. My father, brother and sisters all smelled the presence."

- J.P. writes: "When other people close to me had died I quite often smelled something unusual, such as cigarette smoke, or natural gas, shortly after the time of their death. There was never any logical explanation for the scent. One night after my mother died I could smell the gas fireplace. I went downstairs to make sure everything was okay and lay down on the couch. I was just beginning to fall asleep when I was awakened by a light and an indescribable sensation. The light was amazingly brilliant and the feeling was one of complete love. I had the sensation of being held very close. Even that description seems grossly inadequate. Words cannot describe the experience. And my mother spoke to me. I don't even know how to describe how she spoke to me. She was not in a human or physical form. But I could hear her voice and feel her embrace through the embrace of light."

- R.B., an Anglican priest, who says he feels somewhat "ridiculous and exposed" in recounting several paranormal experiences of his own and of his immediate family, tells the following: "My maternal grandfather died in 1965. My mother often thought of him and wondered 'how he was.' About 1968–69, she answered the telephone one day only to hear his voice faintly at the other end, as through static. She was deeply traumatized and asked: 'Dad, where are you?' He replied: 'You know where I am. I'm OK.' Then the phone went dead. It was years before I heard that story because, of course, my mother thought everyone would think she was crazy. My eldest sister was greatly relieved, however, because, as she explained to us, she 'knew' she had seen my grandfather about 1971 but had been afraid to speak of it to anyone else."

- G.C. writes: "My father was in the palliative unit, dying. The room was lit by the light on the wall, over the head of his bed, shining toward the ceiling. I was standing close to his head when there appeared a spiral of 'smoke' from his head. I looked to the others in the room for confirmation that this was happening, but no one else was registering the surprise and excitement that I was feeling. The ribbon of 'smoke' was pure white and dense and absolutely exquisite. It was 1.5 to 2 inches wide, and moved slowly in a spiral, disappearing about 15 inches from where it began. After about half a minute it wasn't there anymore. Dad died about 45 minutes later. My niece and I are both trained in Radiance Technique, a therapy similar to Reike, which helps people reveal and neutralize difficult energy life patterns. As a point of interest, about a half hour before the smoke occurred, we were gently touching Dad's abdomen while doing Radiance."

- H.B. describes a "vision" she had the night after her mother died: "My mother stood before me, smiling, and told me not to grieve for her, that we would eventually be together again. Even before I woke from it, I was surprised that I had had no difficulty recognizing her. She appeared to be about seventeen or eighteen. She was wearing a long garment of a beautiful mulberry shade, and she had a radiance as if, as I thought later, she had seen God. My mother was forty-one when I was born so I never knew her except as a middle-aged and then elderly woman. Her favourite colour was a shade of mulberry, but I had never seen her wear it. Then, as now, it is a most difficult dye to achieve. I told my husband about the experience and, while he was very kind and sympathetic, he thought I had become unstrung by grief and was raving. Until now, I have never told anyone else about it but remain convinced that it was what it seemed to be: a genuine message from my mother who had gone on to a higher life. The memory has not faded but remains as vivid as when I experienced it some thirty years ago."

- D.W. lived in Owen Sound, Ontario, and his mother was quite ill in hospital in London, over 150 kilometres away. He was driving down to visit her and stopped overnight at his aunt's home in Goderich. In the middle of the night he was awakened to see his mother as a younger woman standing at the foot of the bed. She told him she had come to say goodbye. In the morning, when he got up, his aunt informed him that his mother had died during the night. He knew that "it hadn't been a dream; it had really been her."

- R.M. writes: "My son passed away in August of 2001. In November of that year my husband and I many times both heard the phone ring once and then stop. When we would answer there was no one there. My husband heard the doorbell ring several times and again there was no one there. He even walked all around the outside of the house to make sure it wasn't just neighbour children playing a prank. Then around 3 A.M. one morning I again heard the phone ring and then stop. I lay pondering the realization that perhaps it really wasn't the phone when I clearly heard my son's voice say "Hi!" We heard this ring many times after and it was reassuring to know that he could be with us wherever we went. One morning I was awakened by the ring and as my bed faces out into the hallway I was surprised and intrigued to see what I can describe best as a small 'dance of fire' taking place in front of the door to my son's bedroom. This only lasted about one minute and then disappeared. The surest and most amazing sign of his presence happened last summer on the anniversary of his death. I went to his room and talked to him for a short time and then was looking in his closet for some photographs which I had stored there. I couldn't see well and was just thinking to myself I should turn the light on, when suddenly the light on his desk turned on. It was amazing how that changed my mood from feeling very sad to feeling much better. I had to run downstairs to find my husband and tell him. We have also had some strange coincidences happen—one being that his budgie bird died last year on his birthday."

- A baptist minister, T.B., was away at college in Evanston, Illinois, when he got word that his father had died. He came back to Canada for the funeral feeling very badly that he had been away and had not seen his father in over a year. "We had always been close in a quiet, empathetic way." Life went on, and that summer he and his wife were vacationing at a small lake in Wisconsin. T.B. got up at six o'clock one morning and wandered down to the deserted shore. "As I stood gazing across the water, I suddenly became aware of my father's presence. I simply cannot describe the sensation. There was nothing visual or auditory—just a 'spirit' awareness that he was there. I never moved a muscle. It lasted for maybe five minutes and left as quickly as it came. I believe God allowed Dad's spirit to return to communicate with me since I had been away at the time of his death . . . I have never had a similar experience nor sought one. Whatever the explanation, I know beyond all doubt that my father was there with me."

- J.W. writes: "I live in an apartment on a very busy and noisy street, but I always slept soundly through the noise. Recently, I was awakened by an unusual swishing sound. For a while I lay listening, trying to identify it and it seemed to me that it was in my bedroom. Just as I realized this, the sound stopped and I felt a nudge and a warm, solid body slid in behind me. I felt the weight of his arm over my shoulder. I knew of a certainty it was my first husband who had died thirty-one years ago! For a moment he put his cheek against mine (and I felt the after-shave stubble) then he rested his head beside mine. I cannot describe the happiness I felt for around twelve to fifteen seconds before I felt his arm grow lighter as did his body and I was alone. I looked at the clock, it was 11:50 P.M., and I went back to sleep. In the morning I asked myself many questions: How is it that I was so accepting and without fear or surprise? It never happened again."

- W.K. had what could be described as an "auditory" experience some three and a half years after the death of her mother. She describes herself as having been "fairly neutral" on the subject of life after death prior to this. The death of her mother came after she had been living with W.K. for four years, and the two were very close. At the time of the event, W.K. had been having a series of medical tests and had an appointment to go into hospital for more. Her mother was the furthest thing from her thoughts as she wrestled with her growing reluctance to go to the hospital. "Much to my surprise, since I wasn't even thinking of her, my mother's voice came into my head and all she said was: 'Go on, you can do it!' It was definitely her voice and not a thought—she had an English accent which I could never imitate. I want to stress I know the difference between a voice and a thought! At the same time it wasn't coming in my ear but inside my head." She concludes her letter, "I am not a religious person and would love to hear an explanation as I'm sure nobody believes me."

- B.R. writes: "My wife's father suffered from cancer and died at our home several years ago. That evening, a light bulb in the kitchen, which had been changed recently, started to mysteriously 'blink.' My wife is convinced that this was her father's way of communicating to us that all was well. It continued for some time. Another incident happened a few years ago when my mother passed away in her 97th year. We were living in Muskoka at the time, and had visited my mother in Toronto the day before she died. After the telephone call from her retirement residence, we were discussing funeral plans when all of a sudden a heavy fridge magnet detached itself and flew across the room. For years she was always critical of my enjoyment of beer, so my wife and I were especially amused, thinking it was more than significant that the hurling fridge magnet was a beer stein!"

- F.N. writes: "We lived in Kent, not far from London, during World War II. Many enemy bombers flew over Kent on their way to London, and indeed Kent was hit very hard. My sister was a nurse in St. Mary's in Paddington, London. There was a bombing at the hospital and my sister received serious injuries while trying to help move patients to a safer wing. She was very ill and in a great deal of pain for several months, eventually going into a coma and dying just before Christmas in 1943. During the war it was common to put a blanket over the windows at night to ensure that no light could be seen on the outside, to ensure safety from the bombs. One night in the summer following my sister's death, when I was seven, an air-raid warning sounded. We had become used to them but we would go down and sit under the stairs, known as the safest place in a house. During this raid, my mother, father, two brothers and myself, heard my sister Rita's voice say: 'Mum, the blanket on the window is down at the corner, quick— the planes are coming.' Sure enough, the blanket had fallen away, leaving an area where light would have shone through."

- S.B. describes a time she was on a bus with some friends in London, England: "A woman opened a car door on the wrong side and a man on a bicycle swerved violently to avoid a collision. So did the bus driver. The bus hit the cyclist and dragged him some distance before coming to a stop on the sidewalk. We were all pretty shaken and everybody was staring, not doing anything. I got off the bus and tried to help the young man. Someone ran to call an ambulance and I covered him with my coat. He was fully conscious, so I sat on the curb amid all the glass and the blood and tried to console him. Later that night I was in bed reading—at about 2 A.M.—when this man appeared. I was scared at first, but all he did was to mouth 'Thank you.' There was no sound. I was still shaking the next day when the papers reported the accident and said he had died at 2 A.M."

- M.F-E. writes: "A few nights after my father died, I was awakened by a brilliant golden light coming in under the curtain. It moved across the floor and up the wall and became a glowing oval. Inside this shape a door frame appeared and a dark silhouette moved from a great distance beyond and, on reaching the frame, waved, and then receded. Then the mandala shape moved down the wall, across the floor, and out under the curtain. To be sure I wasn't dreaming, I turned on the light and checked the time—4:15 A.M., twenty-four hours after his death. I had definitely felt his presence."

- A.G. wrote to tell of an unexplained happening just after his wife died on July 15, 1986. Attached to his letter is a sworn affidavit signed by the nurse who was in attendance at the time of his wife's death. A.G.'s wife fell ill with cancer in January 1986. During her illness he took care of her and, although they had been childhood sweethearts, marrying soon after leaving school, they became even closer as they discussed every aspect of dying. "My wife helped me plan the life I would lead after she died and I asked her to try to find a way of letting me know if there was indeed a life after death and if there was, was she happy." Sometime between one and three hours after his wife ceased breathing and had been pronounced dead by the coroner, "she closed her mouth and smiled with unmistakable bliss. Her face that was so drawn and haggard due to the stress leading to her death became once again full and happy in appearance. Her colour returned and her countenance took on a look that I can only describe as the appearance I remember when she was about fifteen to twenty years younger. I felt I was witnessing a miracle." The nurse confirms the "miracle" in her statement, noting that the woman was indeed smiling and that she "looked twenty years younger." A.G. discussed the case with the undertaker and two attending physicians. "They know that it actually happened but they stated that it is impossible. For the body's mouth to close and for a smile to appear, the brain would have to be alive. This, of course, is not possible after hours of not breathing." As far as A.G. is concerned, what happened was his wife's way of assuring him she was still alive, although in a new mode, and that she was happy. He concludes: "I have written to you because I feel that not to record this event in some form is wrong. It did happen."

- M.M. says that her husband, who was a "total disbeliever in God," died in 1982 after being ill for some time. She says they both knew he was leaving her but that they never spoke of this. When she reached her doorstep, still stunned and in shock after coming from the hospital and seeing his dead body, M.M. felt a sudden sense of desolation. "Where is this Comforter Jesus spoke of?" she asked herself. Immediately she felt a powerful presence at her left shoulder. "It was so strong that I even turned to see who it was; and my heart was touched by something which seemed to say 'You will be alright!'" She was able to carry through all the arrangements for the funeral and to care for the needs of her family "almost as though someone were guiding me." About a week later, she accidentally locked herself out of the house. (She could see her keys inside on the kitchen table.) It took her about forty-five minutes to open a basement window that her husband had previously nailed shut. "And I would take an oath he was there watching me and laughing, his presence was so strong." M.M. goes on to say that the whole experience has taught her there is a "centre where we can 'radio' for help when we get beyond our depth in this life." She admits her friends wouldn't understand her if she related any of this to them, "but I felt compelled to pass this along to you."

- A.M. writes that fifteen years ago she was very ill at home. One day she awoke to find a tall, well-dressed man standing just outside her bedroom door. When she looked at him, he asked, "Are you ready?" "I quickly said 'No,'" she relates. For many years, she supposed she had dreamed this odd incident. Seven years ago, her husband was diagnosed with terminal cancer. Near the end, she brought him home from hospital, as he had expressed a deep wish to die at home. "As our two sons helped the ambulance men carry my husband to the bedroom, my husband pointed to the same spot where I had seen the stranger and asked me, 'Who is he?' When I asked him later who was who, he described the same well-dressed man I had seen years before. I have never told anyone about this, but felt I had to write. No, I do not know who this man was, and as we bought the house new thirty years ago no one else had lived here. I still wonder who this stranger was." (This theme of a friendly stranger, sometimes male, sometimes female, who comes at the hour of approaching death and in some way helps the dying person, appeared in several of the responses I received.)

- B.Y., who says he was raised in the United Church of Canada but always felt very skeptical about such beliefs as those concerning life after death, had been very close to his grand-mother as a boy. He was in his early twenties and recently married, when he learned that she was quite ill in hospital in a northern town many miles away. One morning, he awoke very early and saw his grandmother standing at the entrance to his bedroom. "She was wearing the mauve suit that I always recognized as one of her favourites. Her face was very taut and sunken and would have looked terrible had it not been for the fact that she looked joyful at the same time. She just stood there silently. I closed my eyes before taking another look. She was gone but the phone began to ring. It woke my wife—it was on her side of the bed—and as she reached for it, I told her 'Grandma is dead.' She picked the phone up and my aunt told her what I already knew." (I received several other letters corroborating this kind of telepathic awareness, sometimes with apparitions, sometimes not, communicating the fact of a loved one's demise.)

- R.H. of Toronto had never given much thought to what happens at or after death. Her mother, to whom she was devoted, had once told her, "When we die, that's the end," and she had mentally agreed. Mother and daughter had been through great times of crisis and difficulty together, first as refugees in Europe and then as immigrants in Canada. Her mother died during the night of June 25, 1977, and was buried on Monday, June 27. A few weeks later, in obedience to something her mother had said a few days before she died—"When this is all over, you must take a holiday"—R.H. and her husband were travelling by train down the beautiful Agawa Canyon in northwestern Ontario. She was thinking how sad it was that her mother wouldn't be able to see "all this" anymore when, "Suddenly, she spoke to me, but not with a voice one hears with one's ears. It came right through my heart some way and Mother had reverted to her native tongue, German. Translated, what she said went like this: You can't do anything for me anymore. Don't grieve so. We will be together again. Please look after yourself!" All the words, she says, seemed underlined as though to emphasize their importance. As the train moved on, "It was not as though we were moving from her, but as if she was moving away from me as she seemed to float away, unable to stay. This experience gave me strength. My plucky, courageous mother . . . had to let me know that we will be together again one day." She concludes that while skeptics may not see this as "solid evidence" of anything, it was "proof enough" for her.

- The final example in this mini-review of phenomena is perhaps the strangest of all. E.M. of Oakville, Ontario, had lost her son some years before she wrote me her story: "We were a young family that had just moved into our new home in Oakville. Our street was the last one bordering farmland between Oakville and Bronte. We drove past these old farms on our way to church each Sunday. In one field we passed, an old grey horse spent the days of his retirement watching the traffic go past. Our son, Bobby, almost seven, was delighted by that horse. We had Sunday conversations about it over many months. Bobby would say, 'That horse is lonely. I could be his friend. Can we take him home?' I would have to answer, 'No, dear. You can't just take somebody else's horse.' He once replied, 'I have four dollars saved up. I could buy him from the farmer.' But, of course, even if he had had more money we didn't have a stable, etc. Bobby insisted he could build a small house, cut grass and feed him: 'He really is my horse,' he argued. Ten weeks later, Bobby was dead. He drowned while playing with some friends. My spirit silently screamed, 'Where are you, my little one? I know where your body is, but where are you?' Now our street is a crescent shape with about fifty homes on it. We live near the middle of the crescent. The horse's field was almost a mile from us with orchards, lanes and old farms between us. The Sunday following Bobby's burial, when we were getting ready to drive to church, we looked out and there on our front lawn, peacefully cropping the grass, was the old grey horse. Only the spirit that never dies, the spirit of Bobby, could have known the perfect assurance this meant for us that there is, without doubt, a life of the spirit after bodily death. Thank you for letting me tell this reality. It is true."

Ghosts and Apparitions

The following experience of one of my correspondents, S.D., does not involve anyone she knows personally: "Twenty years ago we bought a lovely old historic home in a small Ontario town. At the time of the move I was studying for my Ph.D. orals. Several events transpired after we moved in. I used to read in a bright sunroom at the back of the house. Every day about 3 P.M. I'd hear someone open the front door and climb the stairs to the second floor. The first few times I went into the front foyer and yelled up the stairs to my daughter, asking, 'What are you doing home from school so early?' Of course, there was never an answer. (My husband often heard this same sound of the front door opening and footsteps on the stairs.) One day I went up to the third floor and found all my Ph.D. reading materials strewn around the room and the dresser moved. I was quick to blame a family member for this, but they were all adamant that they'd had nothing to do with this phenomenon and I finally had to accept that fact. The interesting thing is this: the dresser had been placed against a wall in front of a curled lip of old linoleum; the large piece of furniture had to be picked up, lifted over the curled lip, and could not have been slid along, thus requiring two fairly strong people."

There are a number of responses we can make to such testimonials. The determined skeptic will naturally scoff at all of this and dismiss it out of hand. The true believer will tend to take it all as some kind of proof positive that humans survive death in some mysterious way. Both responses, I believe, are inadequate. In spite of every attempt to be as scientific as possible in methodology and outlook, none of the results of the surveys—either my own or those of the experts—can claim to be scientific proof. About that, we must be very clear. These experiences cannot be repeated in a laboratory under scientific conditions; they cannot be verified by any normal, empirical methods. They are, by their very nature, highly subjective.

Having said that, however, it should once more be pointed out that simply to dismiss them on those grounds as nonsense would in itself be highly unscientific. Something major, something highly significant, clearly is going on here, and it would be irresponsible to try to ignore it or brush it away. The fact that intelligent, non-religious people, as well as those with faith in life after death, have had such experiences, together with the vividness and unexpectedness of the happenings themselves, combine to suggest there is much more to all of this than wishful thinking or projection. Whatever else we may say, these experiences are intensely real to the millions who have them. The possibility, even the probability that they witness an objective reality "out there" has to be taken with full seriousness. I was personally enormously intrigued by what my readers had to say, and this was what led me to look further into the topic for the next chapter: the near-death experience. For those interested in reading more on this subject, I would recommend the book *Hello From Heaven* mentioned in the bibliography.

Lack of Communication

A friend of mine wrote: "As you know, my father died twenty-three years ago. I adored him and we were very emotionally close. And, he was a Christian with a great faith. He and I had a sort of pact, which we mentioned from time to time. He promised me that wherever he was in the afterlife, he would let me know that 'all was well' by moving or shaking whatever dining room fixture was in my home, wherever that happened to be. Well, I have seen and heard nothing! I know you likely have some explanation, that it was a promise made which should not, or could not, be kept. In my heart he is still very much with me always, and I know I should be content with that. But nonetheless, I'm disappointed."

During the interval between the first edition of *Life after Death* and this revised and updated version, I have heard from several people writing variations on the same theme. Loved ones have solemnly undertaken to "come through" or give a sign of some kind that all was well and that they were fully alive on the other side. But, they have felt, heard or seen nothing to confirm that promised message. On the other hand, most of those who have reported meaningful evidence of contact of some kind were not expecting it or, in many cases, didn't believe it was even a remote possibility.

Total honesty leaves one little choice here other than to confess there is no obvious answer. I certainly don't have a ready, easy explanation. I am aware of hundreds of cases where a sign was undertaken and where the person concerned is fully convinced that some form of it has actually been made manifest. I must add, though, that hardly ever has it been exactly as promised or forecast. A sense of the quixotic, or a wry humour, often seems to slant the phenomenon in some way. It's almost as though some higher intelligence were saying: "You can't command these things, you know." Some of us perhaps may need to learn more trust, more confidence, in God's ultimate caring and comfort. Perhaps, in some cases, it's really a very positive thing. Our loved one may be so caught up in amazing, new creative tasks or learning untold heavenly mysteries as to be wholly occupied with "things above." In truth, I do not know.

One final story before we move on. When the bishop gave me my first parish, out in the wilds of Scarborough, Ontario, he sent me a young priest from the Church of South India, who was studying at Wycliffe College, to be my Sunday assistant. His name was T.K. George, a small, gentle man of deep faith and intelligence. Just as I was writing this chapter a letter came from a former parishioner of mine saying that she had just heard from T.K.'s wife. She wrote that my former associate had died very peacefully at his home in India after a long illness. What she particularly wanted to share with those who had known him was that, just before the moment of his last breath, he told his wife he could see "[his] spiritual body coming to meet [him]."[6]

2

THE
NEAR-DEATH
EXPERIENCE

THERE ARE MILLIONS of people today—well over eight million in the United States alone—who claim to know what death is like. They have "died" in the sense that they have suffered cardiac arrest or have been otherwise declared clinically dead and then have regained consciousness. Others, under the influence of various anaesthetics, in the throes of giving birth, at moments of extreme crisis and danger, or simply in a "natural" out-of-body event, report curiously similar perceptions of a transitional state of being between this world and another. All have come back from this experience remarkably changed and with an amazing story to tell.

For many people, ever since Dr. Raymond Moody described this phenomenon in his trendsetting, pivotal book *Life After Life*, published in 1975, the near-death experience (NDE) is the final proof they have been waiting for that life goes on beyond the grave.[1] The skeptics and serious critics disagree. So much more has been written on this subject in the period since that first book by Moody, and so much invaluable research has been done by doctors and scientists, among others, that we must now attempt to come to terms with the possibilities and problems raised. What light does the NDE throw upon the belief in life after death? The fact that the experience does occur on an extraordinarily vast scale in all cultures and climes is not in doubt. Researchers who are officers of the International Association for Near-Death Studies (IANDS), of which I was for some years a member, report that as many as 35 to 40 percent of all those who have almost died can recall a near-death experience.[2]

Moody must be given credit for having given a name to the phenomenon and for having brought it dramatically to the forefront of public consciousness, but he certainly did not invent the NDE. Plato wrote about it. In his classic dialogue, *The Republic*, which focuses on the theme of the true nature of justice and the ideal state, Plato tells the mythos or story of a man called Er. There was a great battle in which Er was grievously wounded and ended up being tossed on a funeral pyre because he was presumed dead. However, as the fire was about to consume him and his dead comrades, it was discovered he was still alive. Plucked from the burning pyre just before it was too late, he was given proper care and was soon able to talk. He then told his rescuers of an extraordinary "journey" he had just taken. It is obvious to the modern reader that Er is describing a more or less typical NDE. The date of *The Republic* is nearly five centuries BCE.

Current research shows that the NDE has appeared in various forms since the dawn of literature.[3] But does the NDE really constitute evidence that there is some kind of afterlife, a state of blissful existence beyond "the valley of the shadow of death"? It is to this question that we now must turn.

Since all of the basic data about the NDE phenomenon is of necessity highly personal and anecdotal—flowing as it does from first-hand accounts of the experiences of ordinary people—it is essential to make this chapter as personal as possible. Let me begin, then, by saying that, while the statistical evidence for the prevalence of the NDE is quite arresting and should not be underplayed (some NDE researchers have used a figure as high as 60 percent of all those who experience clinical "death"), it is by no means true that everyone who comes close to death, has a narrow escape, endures cardiac arrest or is declared clinically or even brain-dead and then survives has some kind of mystical revelation of a life beyond. I haven't. But, I have, however, had several uncomfortably close brushes with death.

In the summer of 1949 while still in my teens, I was teaching school on a Cree reserve in the remotest corner of northwestern Ontario, about a thousand miles from Toronto. I was struck down with a violent fever and acute dysentery and had to be flown out in a single-engine float plane to Sioux Lookout, a tiny frontier town. For about two weeks I hovered in and out of consciousness while the two doctors at the rudimentary hospital debated whether or not to perform surgery on my seriously ulcerated intestines. In all, I was in hospital for six weeks and finally emerged a pale, skinny vestige of my former self. I was told I had had a severe case of amoebic dysentery and that neither nurses nor doctors had expected I would leave the place alive. All I remember of the crisis part of the illness was that, while I might have been able to utter a few, brief mental prayers at moments of lucidity, my chief awareness was of not having the strength to care whether I lived or not. I just wanted to be left alone. There were no mystical overtones whatever, although, naturally, once it was all over I felt extremely grateful to be alive and on the road to recovery.

A second close encounter happened in 1979 on a hazardous trek over very rugged terrain in the interior of Nepal. My photographer and I were on assignment for the *Toronto Star*. The project was for a newspaper series called "Christmas in Asia." We had spent a week in Calcutta visiting and interviewing Mother Teresa, who had just been awarded the Nobel Peace Prize for her outstanding work among "the poorest of the poor." After visiting her orphanage and the House of the Dying, we also spent some time with a remarkable Canadian minister, Rev. Mark Buntain, who had built a modern hospital and ran schools both in Calcutta and in the surrounding countryside, including one near the city dump where abandoned children tried to make a living from scouring the rubbish for saleable scraps of metal and glass. He was called "St. Mark of Calcutta." From Calcutta we flew north to Kathmandu, hired a car to take us over a single-track, treacherous road (built by the Chinese) into the foothills of the Himalayas. We were dropped off in the middle of nowhere and had to hike the final 40 kilometres into a jungle hospital near a mountain village called Amp Pipal. We were on our way to visit a Canadian missionary doctor, Helen Huston, who was known in some circles as "the doctor on the roof of the world." It was growing dark as we wound our way up a steep path that our Sherpa guide—a bronzed, wiry man who, though almost half my size, had the strength of a lion—said was the final ascent to the Huston clinic. Suddenly, at a sharp turn in the path, I felt myself stepping into nothingness. I fell hard against the lip of the cliff face and started to slip towards the yawning abyss below. Fortunately, the frame of my large backpack caught on a root and I lay there on my back afraid to move. I heard Bob, the photographer, call my name and then there was a crash as he too took a misstep and landed in a bush just above me. It seemed an eternity, but it was actually a short time before the Sherpa reached down and pulled us both to safety. The following day we walked back down to where our near miss occurred and were horrified by the awesome, sheer drop into the canyon that lay only a couple of feet from where we had hung so precariously. I will remember the feelings and thoughts I had during the moments lying on my back on the edge of that precipice, where the least movement could have ended in tragedy, for the rest of my life. But, there was no hint of any life review; no memory of anything other than fear and the kind of praying only extreme danger can provoke.

During my research, I have found many people who have had cardiac arrest while in intensive care or during surgery, or who have had close encounters with death such as I have described, but who have had nothing dramatic to report. My own father-in-law is a case in point. Some years ago he suffered a severe heart attack while undergoing kidney surgery. A few months later, he had open-heart surgery to remove the scarring caused by the attack and was in a coronary intensive care unit for several days. While he had some mild hallucinations as a result of the medication he was on, there was nothing he could identify as truly mystical, nothing approaching an NDE.

Leading figures in NDE research admit they don't know why some have the experience and others do not. In an interview, Dr. Bruce Greyson, a psychiatrist at the University of Connecticut's Medical Center and one of the best-known researchers in this field, told me he considers it quite possible that all those who "die" and come back have an NDE, but that for unknown reasons some of them repress it. Greyson said, "It could be either that they didn't actually come close enough to really dying or that some other factor, say, the medication, interfered in some way. In situations like this, people are under extreme stress, so it's hard to calculate all the variables."

Intrigued, I followed this up by interviewing three anaesthetists, including Dr. Richard Cooper, assistant professor in the Department of Anaesthesia at the University of Toronto Medical School. They told me that there are usually three components in any general anaesthetic: analgesics to prevent pain, muscle relaxants to prevent bodily movement during the surgery or other procedure and amnesics to ensure the experience is forgotten. As Cooper explained, the amnesics are to erase or prevent the formation of memories of the operation. "People don't want to be aware of what has gone on," he said. Those rare few who do manage some recall generally are plagued by a sense that "something has gone wrong." They can even have recurring nightmares in which they sense danger or risk of death but are unable to move to avoid it. The amount of amnesic given (usually one of the benzodiazepines) varies with each patient, and the effects vary as well, depending on other drugs being administered at the same time. Some surgery, the doctors said, is done without the use of amnesics if it is thought they might interfere with, for example, the heartbeat of cardiac patients. However, given the wide use of memory suppressants in most serious operations, I find it noteworthy, not that many who experience clinical death during surgery don't have an NDE, but that so many appear to remember so clearly that they did.

Kenneth Ring, whose first book, *Heading Toward Omega* (1984), examines the transformative effects of NDEs on those who experience them—including the temporary heightening of perceptual abilities—is today one of the leading authorities on this entire phenomenon. Particularly striking and persuasive are his ongoing studies of blind people who have had either NDEs, out-of-body experiences or, in many cases, both. The first results of this research came in a 1997 article in the International Association for Near-Death Studies' official *Journal of Near-Death Studies*. Those wishing to follow this aspect further should read also Ring's 1999 book, *Mindsight*, written with co-researcher E. Valarino. The blind subjects interviewed ranged from those congenitally blind from birth to those who lost their sight because of accidents or disease later in life. Ring and his associates are unequivocal in their conviction, based on the evidence presented by this group of NDErs, that the blind do have visual perception, that is, they can see in a clear and detailed fashion during their experience—even those who are blind from birth.

In his first book on near-death experiences, *Life After Life*, Moody analysed the "otherworld journeys" of those who have been to the brink of death and have reported "miraculous" glimpses of a world beyond. They found a plane of existence glowing with love and understanding, a place of bliss and light that can apparently be reached only "by an exciting trip through a tunnel or passageway." In his later book, *The Light Beyond*, he summarizes the characteristics of these "near-death visions" in this way: "NDErs experience some or all of the following events—a sense of being dead, peace and painlessness even during 'painful' experience, bodily separation, entering a dark region or tunnel, rising rapidly into the heavens, meeting deceased friends and relatives who are bathed in light, encountering a Supreme Being, reviewing one's life, and feeling reluctance to return to the world of the living."[4]

By chance, a few days after I had read *Life After Life*, I noticed a brief story in the *Toronto Star* about a man who had been critically wounded in the abdomen by a shotgun blast at close range. He was a night watchman at a Canadian Tire store outlet in the west end of Mississauga, Ontario, and had surprised two thieves in the act. What caught my eye was the statement in the story that this security guard had "died" twice during the many hours of surgery required to save him. I kept the clipping for three months and then tracked him down by phone. He was by then well on the road to a near-miraculous recovery and was willing to give me an interview. I told him nothing in advance of my area of interest. I spent several hours with him and discovered that, although he was reluctant to talk about it at first, he had had an experience that he described as "a kind of religious conversion." It turned out that during the moments or minutes when his vital signs had totally flattened out on the monitor and the doctors were certain they had lost him, he had in fact had an NDE.

It was my first direct encounter with anything of the sort, and it gave me a strange feeling to hear him describe roughly the same phenomenon outlined in *Life After Life*. Incidentally, at that time he had not read the book and had been afraid to speak to anyone else about his experience for fear of being thought strange. Not every detail matched the complete profile of an NDE given above, but there were enough of the major traits—the tunnel, the sense of shining light and the reluctance to "go back"—to make me realize he was talking about essentially the same thing. I wrote the story and it gained a considerable response from readers and other media.

I was not the first *Toronto Star* journalist, however, to have reported such a case. In my first months at the paper, well before Moody set off the NDE floodtide with *Life After Life*, a colleague of mine at the newspaper, Sidney Katz, wrote the strange story of Leslie Sharpe. Sharpe, who at that time headed a successful Toronto-based printing firm, had never concerned himself with the ultimate mystery of life after death. But, as Katz told it, ". . . late one spring afternoon a year ago, Sharpe, sixty-eight, had an experience that changed all that. He died." Katz, basing his account on an article by Sharpe that had just been published in the *Canadian Medical Association Journal*, told how the man had gone to Toronto General Hospital complaining of sharp pains in his chest and left arm.[5] Once in bed, his symptoms vanished and blood pressure, heart sounds, everything, seemed completely normal. Later that same day, however, at two minutes to four in the afternoon, he looked at his watch. A few seconds afterwards, he gave a very deep sigh and his head flopped over to the right.

He reported: "I remember wondering why my head flopped over, because I hadn't moved it. I figured I must be going to sleep. That was my last conscious thought." Immediately, Sharpe was looking down at his own body from the waist up. "Almost at once, I saw myself leave my body, coming out through my head and shoulders. The body was somewhat transparent, although not exactly in vapour form. Watching, I thought, 'So this is what happens when you die.'" Next, the businessman found himself sitting on a small object, tilted at a forty-five-degree angle, and travelling through a blue-grey sky at great speed. He had the feeling he didn't know where he was or where he was going but that this was "one journey I must take alone." He felt safe and that everything was "being taken care of."

Then he began to feel a "delightful" floating sensation as he was bathed in a bright yellow light.

He wrote: "I have a scar on my right leg, the result of an old injury. Although at the time I was not conscious of having any lower limbs, I felt the scar being torn away and I thought, 'They have always said your body is made whole out here. I wonder if my scars are gone?'" Continuing to float, he tried unsuccessfully to locate his legs. The sensation of tranquility and joy engulfed him so fully that he could only describe it afterwards as "something beyond words to tell." Just then, a series of hard blows to his left side brought him back to consciousness. His heart had been restarted by means of shocks from an electric paddle. Looking up, he could see the doctors and nurses. He heard someone say that he'd taken "a bad turn." In the article he wrote in the medical journal and in his interview with Katz, Sharpe said he then told the medical team not to resuscitate him if he suffered another relapse. He wanted the experience to "go on and on. If that was eternity, I wanted to stay there. I was annoyed at being brought back to earth."

Some facts given in Katz's article are important. Sharpe was not a member of any religious group and had not been to church for many years. In his own mind, he had "long ago reached the conclusion that death was the final end and that beyond that there was nothing." He had, according to the hospital staff, received only Demerol and was not on any hallucinogenic chemical. (Demerol, a strong narcotic, normally produces extreme drowsiness and some confusion of mind as it numbs pain. In rare cases it can contribute to hallucinatory experiences of a confused nature, quite unlike the highly structured account that Sharpe describes.) Having "returned from death," he had lost any fear of it he previously had. "I've had the rare privilege of seeing behind a closed door that's never opened. I'm no longer afraid to go." Finally, Sharpe wrote his story for the *Canadian Medical Association Journal* at the urging of his physicians, Drs. Robert L. MacMillan and Kenneth W.G. Brown of Toronto

General's coronary care unit. It bore the very conservative title "Cardiac Arrest Remembered."

Those familiar with the writings of Dr. Carl Jung will be aware that the great psychoanalyst, at first a colleague and then a critic of Sigmund Freud, had a very similar experience to that of Sharpe, one which he later said ranked among the most meaningful of his eventful life. During a brief clinical "death" after a heart attack, he said, "It seemed to me I was high up in space. Far below I saw the globe of earth bathed in a glorious blue light. Ahead of me I saw a shining temple and was drawn towards it. As I approached, a strange thing happened. I had the certainty I was about to enter an illuminated room and meet there all those people to whom I was beloved in reality. There I would understand at last the meaning of my life." Jung then realized he was being pulled back into his physical body. It happened at the same moment his doctor injected him with a strong heart stimulant.[6]

Of the hundreds of readers who responded to the requests in my column to describe briefly any experience they had had which for them constituted evidence of an afterlife, about forty responded with a story of an NDE. What was significant, in my view, is the fact that no two of them were exactly the same and none was a replica of the full, classical NDE that is regularly discussed in the media. That, plus the way in which most respondents stressed that this was the first time they had ever told anyone outside their immediate family circle about the experience, gives considerable credibility, I believe, to the conviction that what they describe did actually happen.

- R.H.D., of Burlington, Ontario, wrote: "Prior to quadruple bypass surgery in 1979, I experienced cardiac arrest while in the intensive care unit at Joseph Brant Hospital. The arrest occurred during sleep but I was brought 'back to life,' as it were, by a very alert and able nursing staff. I have retained a very vivid recollection of the few minutes that I was 'dead.'

Whether it was a dream or a temporary entrance into eternity
I will obviously never know. However, just prior to administration of electric shock by the staff, I travelled through a long
and misty-white tunnel, the end of which I never reached and
the surroundings of which were immensely peaceful. I can
remember no other details but it was an experience which I
can never forget. It was not just a matter of imagination."

- P.W.L. is a physicist with one of the largest public utilities in
  Canada. He had an NDE in 1965, a decade before *Life After
  Life* appeared. P.W.L. only realized that other people had had
  a similar experience when he happened upon the condensa-
  tion of Moody's book in *Reader's Digest* in 1976. He never
  spoke of it to others until 1989, when he took an introductory
  course on the New Testament at the Toronto School of Theology. Early on a Saturday in January 1965, he was involved in
  a serious car accident on the Gardiner Expressway, the major
  arterial roadway running along the Toronto waterfront. The
  police closed the Gardiner immediately afterwards and the
  story was carried in the final edition of the *Toronto Star* the
  same day. His memory of the actual crash was "wiped out," he
  says. He was not wearing a seat belt and only learned later that
  he had been battered between the two doors and the steer-
  ing wheel and then thrown clear. He does remember lying
  waiting for the ambulance and giving his girlfriend's phone
  number to some bystanders. He was rushed to St. Joseph's
  Hospital where, in emergency surgery, his ruptured liver was
  sutured and repairs done to a series of tears in his lower intes-
  tine. While unconscious on the operating table, P.W.L. had
  "an amazing experience." He became aware of a bright, round,
  yellow light overhead. "Then, I was up there beside the yellow light, watching the operation from the vicinity of the ceiling. I could see myself in the yellow illumination, in sharp focus

on the operating table below. There was medical equipment above my body but it didn't impede my view in any way. I had the feeling that I was in the arms of God. An overwhelming sense of unconditional love and concern and support completely saturated me, in direct mind-to-mind contact, and it persisted for an indefinite duration. There was no dialogue involved. And then I woke up in the recovery room. My immediate reaction was, 'So *that* is what God is like!'" Having graduated from university in physics not all that long before, he says he was a "nominal Christian" with considerable skepticism prior to his NDE. He is aware that what happened to him is not firm proof of anything, but it changed his religious outlook completely. "Before, I could only hope, but now I know what God is like and that God loves each of us, whether we deserve it or not." One immediate result of the NDE, he says, is that he proposed to Jean, his girlfriend, while he was still in hospital, and they were married nine months later. I met with this man not long ago at the close of a lecture I had just given. We discussed his NDE briefly and I must say that I have seldom met anyone whom I would judge to be less given to hallucinations or flights of fancy than this particular scientist.

- Several women wrote about NDEs or out-of-body experiences they had had during the process of giving birth. Two of these were instances where the baby was either born dead or died during the delivery. P.R., for example, relates that on August 1, 1947, she had the following "unforgettable experience." She was in the delivery room of the local hospital. "Something had gone wrong with the way the baby was being born. Suddenly, I remember, I found myself walking up a path in a beautiful garden. The scent of the flowers was overpowering. I was walking towards a figure dressed in white, surrounded by a bright light. This person was holding a baby in his left arm and holding his right hand out to me. I heard someone calling me from what seemed a long distance away and suddenly I was out of the garden and back in the delivery room. One of the nurses, who happened to be a friend of mine, told me that the baby had died. I have not been able to talk about this very much but have told members of my prayer group."

- J.C.S. writes: "On my father's deathbed, but while he could still speak, he told my husband and me that he had nothing to fear now that the end of this life was drawing to a close. Then he told us about his bout with pneumonia in 1939 or 1940, pre-antibiotics, at home. He said he had never felt so ill before or since. Then he 'died.' He was at the ceiling of his bedroom looking down at the doctor seated by his bed shaking his head at his body, with his parents standing arm-in-arm behind the doctor. His father was grim-faced clutching his wife who was sobbing gently. Dad was met by a being of pure, warm inviting light. No words were spoken, but there was clear communication. This being was to be his guide. The ceiling 'disappeared' and he found himself, with his guide, on the edge of a shining path. He was gently told that he had died to the life of that body below. Seeing his parents' obvious distress, my father asked if he could make them happy. His guide told him that he had a choice to make. The path that led to the next life beckoned, but he could return to his body. He was warned that much physical pain might ensue. Even as Dad watched the doctor begin to pull up the sheet to cover his face, Dad chose this life. He felt a wave of approval and then he was back in his body looking up at the shocked face of the doctor. After Dad had finished speaking, his countenance was beaming and he appeared to be other-worldly. Visiting hours were over. Dad kissed both of us and said that this was likely his final 'good bye' to us. He slipped into a coma that night and died a couple of days later without speaking again."

- One of the replies I received came from the Reverend Ken Martin, pastor of Siloam United Church in London, Ontario. Martin wrote to me on August 22, 1989, to say he had recently had a remarkable out-of-body experience during a "silent heart attack." It was the first of two attacks, and Martin, who is forty-eight, had been feeling tired and overworked. He told me he had made notes in his diary the same night he had his NDE and offered to share them. I spoke with him on the phone, discovered that the NDE had had a profound effect upon him, and invited him to send me his account. Here it is, verbatim: "I was sleeping earlier tonight with my wife, Beverley, when suddenly I awoke. There was an incredible pain in my chest and I was suddenly aware of being lifted up from the bed into the air. I took a fleeting, backward glance at the bed and saw Beverley sleeping, and then I was transported right out of the room into the sky. The sky was very dark in the background and yet there were swirls of very bright lights. I found myself caught up in one of these swirls. It was like being at the small end of a long funnel that was opening wider and wider. I was rushing through the funnel in a fast-moving swirl of light. It was incredibly bright. It was also warm and I felt very much at peace and extremely contented. It was as if there was a great strength lifting me and pulling me forward. I experienced the feeling that I was going home. There was no pain, no depression, and no worries about finishing my thesis, earning a living, or whether or not I would be able to return to work. It was as if these things were gone forever. I had a very definite feeling that I was coming home from someplace I had left a long time ago. Then I saw an extremely bright light ahead of me. All was so peaceful, warm, and well. I was rushing faster and faster into this ever-widening swirl of blazing light. It was as if someone was summoning me to come home but I heard no voice. The overwhelming feeling was one of incredible peace. Then, abruptly, I was yanked back and found myself in my bed again. I felt deeply disappointed and cried out: 'Oh no, not this again!' I guess that was a terrible thing to think and voice. Although there had been a few seconds as I first had felt myself being lifted into the dark sky when I felt disappointment at leaving my family, that feeling had quickly left me, overwhelmed by the sense of peace. Now I was back in bed with all the pain and depression and worry. I wept because I had come back. I now have a deep feeling that 'home' is somewhere else and would like to go back. When will I resume my journey? It was incredible!" Martin has now lost forty pounds—he had been up to 195—is swimming regularly on his doctor's orders, and is back at work in a busy parish. In his accompanying letter to me, he says he now knows first-hand that "there is nothing to be afraid of after death." He is also convinced that there is so much more to life than what we have known on earth. "Yet, I am also convinced that we Christians are in for a big surprise and that we have certainly made our God far too small." He added that, apart from his wife, he has told nobody else about his experience. He has not, at the time of my writing this, shared this experience with his congregation. "Why not?" he queries. "Likely because I'm afraid of being called eccentric, crazy, or worse."

It is impossible to do more than skim the surface of my flood of mail on this and related subjects, never mind describing in any adequate way all of what is now available on near-death experience. Letters have come from the educated and the uneducated, from the religious and the non-religious, from those who believe in life after death and those who previously were total skeptics. Many of those who wrote to me were not at death's door when their "glimpse of eternity" or their sense of being able to "look down on my body" from some other vantage point occurred. Nearly all of them spoke of the "light," of feelings of a peace beyond understanding, and of seeing loved ones or supernatural beings—God, Christ, Krishna, angels, or others—aware that they were using symbolic language to express what had happened to them. Most say their attitudes to both life and death were changed in the process. One man wrote to say that he now feels as though he is living "with one foot in each of two different worlds." While there is generally some regret at not having passed on to the other side, there is, paradoxically, a greater commitment to this life, a desire to learn more, to love more. While those who have the experience do not necessarily become suddenly more religious, they invariably become more spiritual, more concerned with the depth dimension of living. All fear of death and dying, they say, is gone.[7]

"Hellish" Near-Death Experiences

One of my correspondents wrote me: "In 1992 I had a brain aneurysm bleed, and was given very little chance to live. Unfortunately I didn't have the wonderful experience of going to the light. I went to the darkness and it was an experience that was both terrifying and life altering. If this is a glimpse of hell it is not at all the fire and demons—it is total isolation. I often wondered if there are others who have had this experience and if they see it as a warning or as a prophetic experience. I have never discussed this with anyone as it seems to be outside the bounds of what we all desire. Thank God I don't think it lasted long. But it is as clear today as if it happened this morning."

It is tempting, given the overwhelmingly positive nature of the NDE portrayed in the bulk of both popular and scientific literature, to assume that, whatever is signified by this phenomenon, its main thrust is extremely good news about dying and death. However, there is another side to the story, one that has not yet been fully studied and assimilated by NDE researchers. That some people who come close to the gates of death experience a reality that is anything but reassuring was first fully discussed by Dr. Maurice Rawlings in his 1978 book, *Beyond Death's Door*.[8] Rawlings, an evangelical, fundamentalist Christian, argued from his medical experience that some people who have an NDE feel themselves to be in hell. *Beyond Death's Door* is not a particularly good book in my opinion, as Rawlings only manages to adduce a very tiny number of such stories, and one has the feeling throughout that he had already decided on his conclusions before he began his research. But at least Rawlings has raised the issue that possibly all is not light and bliss during the near-death experience.

When George Gallup Jr. published his 1982 book, *Adventures in Immortality: A Look Beyond the Threshold of Death*, he too referred to respondents who said they had had a "hellish" experience while close to death. For the most recent and the most insightful look at this aspect of the NDE, though, one must look at Margot Grey's *Return From Death: An Exploration of the Near-Death Experience*.[9] Grey, a humanistic psychologist, based her research on interviews with thirty-eight people claiming near-death experiences and many more patients she later worked with in her practice. Grey herself had an NDE when she had a close brush with death while travelling in India. She reports she too had an encounter with light accompanied by a "feeling of being very close to the source of light and love, which seemed to be one." Grey, who has no religious ties, states quite categorically that her studies have brought her to the conclusion that "conscious awareness survives physical death."[10]

Her chapter on negative experiences breaks some new ground. She bases her remarks here on five of her own cases and nine negative cases from the general literature, together with information gleaned from interviews with cardiologists who have been on the lookout for NDE reports from their patients. Like Rawlings, these doctors stressed that negative NDEs are only made known *very shortly after* the episodes happen. In other words, such experiences tend to be quickly repressed. Grey found that those who experience this type of NDE feel a sense of guilt or shame at hellish experiences and would rather not admit to them. She also concludes that they may indeed have had some terrible deed in their background that they felt accounted for their sense of being in or going to hell. In his review of her book, Karlis Osis says that in this finding Grey "has put her finger on the right spot. We might need to rethink our methods. Maybe we have relied too much on the self-reports of the patients and have failed to ascertain observations made through the cooler eyes of doctors and nurses who were around when the patients started to talk about the NDEs that were still fresh in their memories."[11]

Grey was able to come up with some quite significant similarities between the pattern of positive NDEs and that of the negative ones. In the negative NDE, instead of peace and a sense of well-being, there is a feeling of fear and panic. The sense of being out of the body is similar in both types. Instead of entering a tunnel, however, in the negative NDE one enters a black void. There is no light, but rather the sense of an evil force, and one enters what can only be described as a hell-like environment. In the negative cases, there are after-effects, too. "Like those respondents who had positive experiences, the people in this category returned from their encounters with an increased conviction that life continues after death. They also felt a strong urge radically to modify their former way of life."[12]

In all, about one-eighth of Grey's interviewees reported experiences that were hell-like. None of this, of course, means that such imagery has to be taken in a literal fashion or that there is such a place or state as a literal hell. But, it is clearly an area of research that still needs much more careful examination. As Osis remarks,

"If this pattern is replicated and sound, it would require nothing less than considering the positive and negative NDEs as one integrated whole—a sweeping reorganization of our views."

Problems with the Near-Death Experience

According to the International Association for Near-Death Studies, "An NDE may occur when a person is considered clinically dead, or even to one not close to death but who is under some biological and/or psychological stress. Somehow, the experience appears to be a biologically-based trigger for a spiritual event." For me, one of the most exhaustive and fascinating attempts to understand just what is going on in this event is a book by Carol Zaleski, *Otherworld Journeys: Accounts of Near-Death Experience in Medieval and Modern Times*. Zaleski, who wrote this work initially as her doctoral thesis in religious studies at Harvard, gives us a sparkling overview of the NDE and sets it in a more universal perspective by analyzing examples from sources as diverse as the epic of Gilgamesh, Plato, St. Paul and Dante's *Divine Comedy*. Her main focus, however, as the title says, is a comparison of medieval otherworld journeys with those described in the NDE literature of today. In addition, she reviews the modern scientific debate between the advocates of the NDE as a real glimpse of eternity and the hard-nosed skeptics who pour cascades of cold water over such "imaginative flights of fancy."

Zaleski finds amazing parallels between the experiences of medieval saints, mystics and ordinary folk, and those relayed on talk shows or in the books of the NDE researchers of today. But she also finds some remarkable differences: "Gone are the bad deaths, harsh judgment scenes, purgatorial torments, and infernal terrors of medieval visions; by comparison, the modern other world is a congenial place, a democracy, a school for continuing education, and a garden of unearthly delights."[13] In other words, there is something very western about the terms in which the modern otherworld traveller conceptualizes his or her vision.

This brings us to one of the first observations I want to make about the NDE. The experience, though obviously universal in the sense that we can find examples of it at every time period and in every culture, is nevertheless culture specific. That is, it is expressed in forms of thought and language peculiar to its historical context. While those who have had the experience may all, or nearly all, see beings of light, these will be described variously as Jesus, Buddha or Krishna depending on who is doing the seeing and where. Zaleski points out, for example, that Dante's heaven is much more hierarchical than any heaven in modern NDE experience. But the social order of Dante's time was itself a hierarchical one: "For medieval audiences, the ranking of the blessed in a series of concentric but ascending heavens . . . derived its plausibility—or rather its imaginative power—from the fact that it reflected and affirmed the social order and provided an emblem for the structure of human intelligence." What this cultural component indicates is that, whatever is happening in the NDE, there is certainly a subjective element provided by the individual concerned. If someone is indeed viewing a reality of some kind, it is a reality shaped by a particular background, conditioning and life situation. This, of course, does not automatically mean that the NDE itself can be dismissed as totally subjective. Being human, it is impossible for us to apprehend any reality in this world or the next without bringing to it whatever we ourselves are, and shaping it accordingly. It is possible intellectually to conceive of a totally objective reality *in the abstract*, but in practice there is no such thing as the "unobserved observer." Even in science, allowance has to be made for the contribution we make in describing the "real" world.

A second problem faced by Zaleski and admitted in varying degrees by even the most enthusiastic of the NDE proponents is that of defining death itself. No matter how moving some of the descriptions of journeying into this other realm may be, we have to keep reminding ourselves that the operative word in "near-death experience" is "near." All of these visionaries were near death; they were not actually dead, because, by definition, to be dead is to be at that point from which any kind of physical return is ruled out. Zaleski quotes from an article in the British medical journal *The Lancet*: "Death is just beyond the point from which anyone can return to tell us anything." As she goes on to say, the "popular appeal of return-from-death stories rests partly on the assumption that temporary absence of vital signs is equivalent to death."[14]

The difficulty here is that it is now very hard, even for ethicists and medical experts, to agree on what constitutes death. What's more, as medical technology and skills advance and ever more amazing rescues of the dying are possible, even tentative definitions have to be constantly reexamined and updated. It should be remembered too, in this connection, that even NDE researchers themselves do not want to restrict the NDE too closely to death because they have documented so many cases where the same experience was encountered not near death but during meditation, in the face of extreme danger, while on a drug or during childbirth. Even allowing for all of this, however, I agree with Moody that while those who experience NDEs are not really dead in the full sense of the word, they have come very much closer to this ultimate experience than the rest of us. Or, as Zaleski puts it, "Whether NDEs occur in the grip of death or only in the face of death, they may still constitute a revelatory encounter with death." These experiences are certainly not proof of a life after death, or of the other realities and entities reported. But, it is argued, they could well supply at the minimum some evidence upon which a belief in life after death could reasonably take its stand.

The critics, as one would expect, have come up with a wide variety of natural explanations to account for what the proponents of the NDE claim is a vision of another world or plane of reality. Certainly, as both Zaleski and Moody admit—along with a host of other responsible researchers in this field—it is essential to look hard at the question of whether any sufficient, natural causes exist to explain the phenomenon before leaping to any transcendental conclusions. In *The Light Beyond*, Moody devotes his final chapter, "Explanations," to a detailed refutation of a range of natural possibilities. Zaleski, too, in an even more thorough manner, considers the critical literature and explanations ranging from the effects of stress on the body to drugs or sensory deprivation. Her chapter is called "Explanations and Counterexplanations." There is no need to repeat here everything that has been said pro and con. Instead, I propose to look at the most obvious alternative, the hallucination theory.

Since a large majority of those who have experienced near-death were on various medications at the time of their brush with death and since altered states of consciousness can be produced by such physiological factors as an acute lack of oxygen (hypoxia or anoxia) or a sudden rush of endorphins, enkephalins or other as yet unknown chemicals secreted by the brain when stress, pain or fear occur, many skeptical scientists have argued that what we are dealing with here is some form of hallucination. As Zaleski says, as far as the debunkers are concerned, these "endogenous opiates are a neurochemical equivalent for and an answer to grace."[15]

I believe this theory deserves further consideration. There can be no doubt that the human mind is capable of quite extraordinary thoughts and visions under the right stimuli. Visionary experiences can be produced by extended fasting, by extremes of physical exhaustion or by hallucinogenic substances. As I have already made clear, I am not personally subject to mystical visions or visitations of any kind. However, I do know what it is like to hallucinate on a chemical substance.

Let me explain. In the summer of 1962 I took a year's leave of absence from my parish in Scarborough, Ontario, to return to Oxford, England, for some postgraduate studies in patristics, the writings of the early fathers of the Church. In February 1963, Dr. Frank Lake, a British psychiatrist from Nottingham, came to the university for a series of lectures. Lake was one of the earliest pioneers in the use of lysergic acid diethylamide (LSD) in the treatment of the mentally ill. He had been a missionary doctor in India for a number of years, and had spent almost all of his time as a psychiatrist dealing with people heavily involved in organized religion. At his invitation, following one of his lectures, I joined a small group of other clergy who volunteered to assist in a research project. Lake had become discouraged by the difficulty and length of time required for traditional analysis and counselling and was experimenting with LSD as a psychiatric shortcut. (I would remind the reader that this was well before LSD appeared in North America and became part of the drug scene in any way. At this point, none of us had even heard of it before.) I hitchhiked up to Nottingham one weekend that spring and joined Lake and the others at his centre, a place called Lingwood. An Anglican priest came and, along with four other priests, one of whom had been a distinguished Spitfire pilot in the Battle of Britain, I received Holy Communion and then was administered some LSD. Each of us had been assigned to a room of his own and the doctor dropped by frequently to monitor what was going on.

Although it happened many years ago, the experience remains perfectly vivid in all its details. I had known nothing like it before and have never since. At first, it was like seeing Technicolor movies run at a very high speed inside my head. The speeded-up images were mainly of various family members, often doing extremely funny things. A tremendous sense of exaltation flooded me and it seemed nothing would ever be impossible—writing a world bestselling novel, rivalling the greatest artists who had ever painted, or composing music as great as Mozart's or Beethoven's. There were sensations of glorious light, and then visions of great beauty, both of the human form and of natural landscapes.

Suddenly, the mood changed, and with a growing sense of dread I approached a tunnel, which was as arid and dry as dust. The sensation of drawing a fingernail over a slate blackboard is the closest I can get to describe the feeling on my skin as I was forced through. From that point on, the trip became much worse. Spider-like monsters threatened my very being. Even with my eyes open it seemed as though the room was filled with horrific presences with sinister intent. Quite frankly, it was terrifying until I felt myself growing increasingly angry and wanting to fight back. I imagined myself wielding a short, sharp sword and plunging it into the belly of the enemy creatures, much like Frodo did with Shelob in Tolkien's *The Lord of the Rings*. This was followed by a renewed sense of exaltation and awareness of a beauty I had never dreamed existed.

All of this went on for at least two hours, and even much later, when I was able to leave the centre and go for a walk in a nearby park, the flashbacks continued. One moment I was in the park watching the children playing and some adults busy with a cricket game, the next I was back in my own inner world with its exaggerated fears and glories. I remember looking across the park at some slum-like houses in the distance. Caught in the rays of the westering sun, they seemed to stand out with a glory that utterly transformed them.

I'm not sure what help any of us were to Dr. Lake in his research. The memory of the experience stands out much more sharply for me today than his conclusions with all of us afterwards. Although I gained no personal insights that could not have been acquired by other means, there was certainly a revelation of a kind. What was instructive was the glimpse into the incredible capacity of the brain to invent or recall suppressed material and to put it together in totally unexpected and original ways. There was, however—and this is in marked and important contrast with the NDE—no specifically religious content that I can remember, no visions of God or of Christ, no feeling of being in another realm of existence. Yet, while I would never care to repeat it, nor would I ever recommend it to anyone else, the experience was spiritual in that it further convinced me of dimensions of beauty or wider "doors of perception" only hinted at in ordinary life. Significantly, I felt no urge to stay there and no deep sense of peace.

It is tempting to infer from this personal account that perhaps the skeptics are right after all. In the NDE some kind of hallucination—possibly nature's way of softening the moment of death—is taking place. Moody himself counters this argument with substantial evidence that a large number of recorded NDEs have taken place when there was a completely flat EEG.[16] "The sheer number of these cases tells me that in some people NDEs have happened when they were technically dead. Had these been hallucinations, they would have shown up on the EEG." The difficulty with this solution, however, is that at the current level of technology an EEG does not always give a precise reading in every instance. As Moody himself concedes, "Brain activity can be going on at such a deep level that surface electrodes don't pick it up." What impresses me much more is the remarkable fact that while NDEs vary widely in their tone and content, as we have seen, there is nevertheless a *common core* of experience running through them all regardless of time or place. It strains credulity in my view to suppose that hundreds of thousands of experiences, all of them hallucinatory, would still manage unanimously to convey such a profound sense of other-worldliness and of having somehow transcended death. I find this all the more cogent when the results of such experiences are almost uniformly positive—loss of the fear of death, commitment to greater love and understanding and commitment to a greater spiritual, although not necessarily religious, awareness and lifestyle. One other significant point should be made. As Zaleski makes clear, "for every pathological condition presumed [by the critics] to cause near-death visions, one can find subjects who were demonstrably free of its influence; therefore no single psychological or physiological syndrome can account for near-death experience."[17]

In *How to Know God*, Deepak Chopra, the prominent doctor-writer, correctly notes that researchers today have found that many of the experiences summed up under the letters NDE can be reproduced if the right temporal lobe of the brain has been deprived of oxygen for a few moments. There can be a sense of going into the light or having visions of departed souls or angels welcoming one into the light. But, he wisely comments that "inducing the experience isn't the same as having it; there is no spiritual meaning . . . to oxygen loss." He observes, as we have already said, that people who have experienced near-death episodes report profound spiritual changes.[18]

In the years since Zaleski's ground-breaking book, a lot of research has been done around the world. Particularly important is the work of Britain's leading clinical authority on the NDE, Dr. Peter Fenwick, and his scientist wife, Elizabeth. Fenwick himself is a Fellow of the Royal College of Psychiatrists and an internationally known neuropsychiatrist—a specialist in the mind/brain interface and consciousness studies. Together the Fenwicks have written *The Truth in the Light—An Investigation of Over 300 Near-Death Experiences* (1996). Indeed, Elizabeth began her research convinced that NDEs could all be explained away scientifically. But, after confronting the full evidence, she concluded: "While you may be able to find scientific reasons for bits of the Near-Death experience, I can't find any explanation which covers the whole thing. You have to account for it as a package and sceptics . . . simply don't do that. None of the purely physical explanations will do; (sceptics) vastly underestimate the extent to which near-death experiences are not just a set of random things happening, but a highly organized and detailed affair." Dr. Peter Fenwick is scathing in his critique of the professional skeptics' arguments and systematically destroys the entire range of objections made—from the one about the NDE being the natural product of a "dying brain" to the ever-present theory of wish fulfillment. He has a list of questions that he challenges the skeptics to answer. They are incisive, tough-minded and, in my view, utterly convincing. He accuses skeptical psychologists in particular of writing "absolute rubbish" about the NDE because they're venturing into territory—the study of brain function—where they have no training at all. The Fenwick book is one all doubters should be required to read.

There is one final objection I want to look at before summarizing our findings. It deserves attention both because of the prestige and popularity of its chief proponent and because, at first sight, it has about it an aura of great plausibility. I'm referring to the views of astronomer and keen debunker of all paranormal phenomena the late Carl Sagan. In the concluding chapter of his book *Broca's Brain*, titled "The Amniotic Universe," Sagan uses the symbolism that has gathered around the universal experience of birth to explain away the cluster of experiences reported by those who have had an NDE.

In his view, not only the NDE but almost every major religious concept, from death and rebirth to the primal Eden and the Fall, derives from our unconscious memories of the womb, the birth passage, the emergence into light and being swaddled and nursed. Religion, from his extremely polemical point of view, is nothing but the vague recollection of profound experiences at a time when we are utterly helpless and inarticulate.

As noted, there is an immediate surface appearance of verisimilitude about this. Yet, to coin a phrase, the more you scratch the surface of it the more there is to scratch. Without attempting to deal with Sagan's theory as it affects the whole of religion, let me simply set out the problems I have with it vis-à-vis the topic in hand, the NDE.

First, birth, unlike the classical NDE, is an experience of moving from a place of safety, warmth and total intimacy out into the exposed and separated world of individual existence. However dependent and close to the mother, the baby begins to experience the pain of existence right from the start. With the first breath often comes a cry. Any accounts of birth experiences I have encountered in the relevant literature all stress the element of trauma and pain that attends the moments of our leaving what Sagan calls "the amniotic universe." This is not what the NDE is about.

Second, so far from being "blurred perceptions" or "vague premonitions," as Sagan describes our perinatal memories, reports of the NDE describe a great sense of clarity surrounding both perceptions and the recall of them later. In fact, as we have seen, many liken normal, waking perception to "dreaming" compared with the reality and vividness of what they have gone through.

Third, Sagan deliberately ignores or plays down the extraordinary transformational power of the NDE. Nothing he says, in my view, comes close to explaining why it is that the majority of people who've had a near-death experience find themselves so profoundly moved and changed by the events of their NDE. Something numinous or totally "other" seems to have happened to them.

Sagan, a media-wise, militant skeptic, may have been a scientist, but he can hardly be viewed as completely objective in his claims at this point. He was a leading member of the American Committee for the Scientific Investigation of Claims of the Paranormal. It was founded in 1976 by Sagan, Isaac Asimov and others to combat media promotion of anything purporting to be mysterious or unexplained—from the Bermuda Triangle to Von Daniken's alien astronauts. There is nothing wrong with any of that except that, in their enthusiasm to expose "pseudo-science," Sagan and company sometimes have been carried away and have swept with too wide a broom. They end up at times espousing not science but scientism, the view that *only* the empirical, scientific method can yield true knowledge. There are few things less scientific than that!

Obviously, if death is indeed a kind of new "birth" into an entirely different dimension of reality and being, it would not be surprising if attempts to describe it were to parallel those attendant on our emergence into the light of this world as infants. But the differences, at least to this investigator, seem to be much greater than the similarities.

The one overwhelmingly important aspect of the NDE none of these critics have ever really been able to deal with is the life-changing impact on the vast majority of subjects experiencing it.

After his NDE, Carl Jung wrote: "What happens after death is so unspeakably glorious that our imaginations and our feelings do not suffice to form even an approximate conception of it."[19] This view is almost universally held by both those who experience NDEs and the positive NDE researchers. But, of course, we are here still in the arena of faith and not of absolute scientific proof. In her review of Moody's *The Light Beyond* in the IANDS *Journal of Near-Death Studies*, Judith Miller, Ph.D., chided Moody for not stating his faith in more positive terms and for not challenging traditional scientific paradigms.[20] Moody, the acknowledged "leader on the cutting edge of this field," began the book by saying: "We are no closer to answering the basic question of the afterlife now than we were thousands of years ago when it was first pondered by ancient man." In other words, since the evidence provided by NDEs can't be replicated on demand in a scientific laboratory, none of the amazing stories is firm proof of life after death. What the matter comes down to in the end is the authority or weight we give to mystical glimpses or visions of realities other than the empirical world we live in.

Zaleski argues that, like the arguments for the existence of God, the realities attested to by people who have had an NDE belong to a totally different sphere where the question is not so much can they be proven to be true as, do NDEs give insights which can be verified in one's own experience? She concludes: "We may find no difficulty in respecting the testimony of those whose lives have been transformed by a near-death vision, but we can verify their discoveries only if, in some sense, we experience them for ourselves."

I find the whole expanding exploration and research in this field and of consciousness studies to be one of the most exciting developments of our time. In my own thinking and research I find myself increasingly (though cautiously) positive about the validity of the NDE as a strong witness to invisible realities beyond. What carries most weight with me, as I have already suggested, is the consistency and clarity of the stories themselves, together with the undeniable evidence of dramatically changed lives. I know from my own pastoral experience the truth of what researcher Dr. Bruce Greyson has said. Psychiatry or therapeutic counselling often takes years to bring about only slight changes in people's outlook and behaviour, but "the NDE regularly brings about a total transformation almost overnight."

One final point. Mark Fox in his 2003 book, *Religion, Spirituality and the Near-Death Experience*, raises the question clearly and persuasively: Why have the churches and religious leaders in general paid so little attention to what, after all, lies very near to the heart of what they are all about? The NDE raises sharply the issues of the nature of the soul, the afterlife, our personal destiny and, ultimately, the very meaning of life itself. Like Fox, my personal belief is that this entire phenomenon offers a bridge between religion and the modern world that church leaders should be rushing to cross. It affords a common language today in a crucial area where meaningful communication has virtually broken down.

3

THE SPIRIT MEDIUMS

"Mediums claim the stimuli are there for all to perceive but they're low level and subtle, and most of us are too distracted by the outside world as well as our own thoughts and feelings to sense them."

— GARY SCHWARTZ, Ph.D.

The Afterlife Experiments

HISTORY WAS MADE on North American television in 1967 when the American medium, or psychic, the Reverend Arthur Ford, held a séance on TV. The affair made headlines across the continent because Ford's participant, or "seeker," was none other than Bishop James A. Pike, unquestionably the most controversial bishop in the Anglican communion in modern times. Because he had publicly announced his doubts about the Virgin Birth, the Holy Trinity and other orthodox teachings of his Episcopal Church, Pike had come close to facing a heresy trial, and in 1965 he was forced to resign as leader of the Episcopal Diocese of California. He remained a bishop, however, and continued to make news as he probed Christian origins and leaned increasingly towards interest in the paranormal.

In February 1966, Pike's son Jim, aged twenty-two, committed suicide in a hotel room in New York. Pike was studying at Cambridge University in England at the time and, filled with remorse at having neglected the young man and his problems, he began consulting mediums.

The famous public séance, arranged by my predecessor as religion editor of the *Toronto Star*, Allen Spraggett, author of several books on paranormal phenomena, took place in the studios of CFTO-TV in Scarborough, Ontario. It was taped as part of a special two-hour program on Pike's ideas and stormy career and aired on September 17. Ford went into a trance and professed to make contact with Pike's son, Jim Jr., through his own habitual "spirit control," who went by the name of Fletcher. (Fletcher had been a childhood playmate of Ford's who had died at an early age.)[1]

Ford, wearing a blindfold, mentioned several persons from Pike's past, including his son's grandfather who "was with [him] on the other side." Not only did the son speak to Pike, but there were also brief messages from the others—most notably from Pike's predecessor as Bishop of California, the Right Reverend Karl Block. Pike told Block how much he admired him and added that he hoped Block had not been too upset by some of the changes he had introduced. Block told him: "No . . . You did a magnificent job and you have magnificent work yet to do." The key point of the affair, however, was the statement, purportedly from Jim Jr., assuring Pike that he was in no way to blame for what had happened.

Voice: "Jim says he wants you to definitely understand that neither you nor any other member of the family have any right to feel any sense of guilt or have any feeling that you failed him in any way."[2]

This most reassuring message, accompanied by some bits of information that the medium, in the bishop's view, "could not have possibly known," persuaded Pike that Ford had really conversed with the dead youth, and in subsequent interviews he gave great credence to the belief that bona fide mediums could indeed make use of spiritual entities to bridge the gap between the dead and the living. *The New York Times* and other papers quoted him as saying he truly believed he had spoken with his son: "To me, this is the most plausible explanation of the phenomena that occurred."

When Arthur Ford died at the age of seventy-five, however, the secret of his ability to cite dates, names and obscure bits of information about those whom he was allegedly contacting was finally revealed. Among his belongings were vast files of obituary notices and other clippings on the relatives of the people he gave sittings for. He always took a briefcase filled with such material along with him when travelling to see new clients. Spraggett, who initially had been completely taken in by Ford himself, later wrote a book describing how Ford used this research in the Pike séance and other similar frauds.

The unfortunate bishop, one of the brightest and most colourful churchmen of his or any other day (he was the only bishop in church history known to have had two ex-wives and his current wife all mourn him at his funeral), did not have the magnificent future predicted by Ford. He died horribly, not long after the séance, of thirst and exposure in the Judean wilderness while trying to reach the Dead Sea caves. His third wife, Diane, who accompanied him, escaped the tragedy. Several mediums were consulted, but were unable to throw light on the bishop's whereabouts. The search for Pike went on for several days and made headlines around the world. He was eventually found dead at the foot of a cliff over which he had fallen in a heat- and thirst-induced delirium. In death as in life he made front-page news.

The sad truth is that it would take almost a library of books to contain the full accounts of all the past deceptions and frauds perpetrated by would-be spiritualists and psychics. Their number is legion. Most of them, of course, have not had the panache—or the publicity—of an Arthur Ford. Significantly, considering the staggering nature of their claims, one is almost always struck by the extraordinary triviality and triteness of a great deal of what they report. I agree with Colin Wilson's comment that most of this stuff is banal, "oddly boring and disappointing." It's not just that what the spirits have to say is so inconsequential, he notes, it's that it usually "sounds like the ramblings of an uninspired Sunday School teacher."[3]

For the origins of spiritualism, Wilson's treatment in his book, *Afterlife*, is as good as any. For our purposes here, we can be fairly brief. Necromancy, as it is called by scholars, the belief system that has as its chief focus the establishment of communication with the dead, existed among most primitive peoples, and there is evidence of it in the Hebrew Bible, where it is repeatedly condemned. In its modern form it dates from the occult experiences of the Fox family in 1848 in the United States, from where it soon spread to England and Europe.

The Fox affair began with some poltergeist-like rappings and knockings at the Fox home in Hydesville Township, near Rochester, New York, in March of that year. At first, it was the two girls, Margaretta, fourteen, and Kate, twelve, who found they could get the spirit behind the knocking to imitate their commands and rap on cue. Then Mrs. Fox, joined eventually by curious neighbours, found it was possible to ask questions by means of a kind of code—rap twice if the answer is yes, once for no. By this means it was established that the house was haunted by one Charles Rosma, a peddler who claimed he had been robbed and murdered there by an earlier tenant. Curiously, the sounds only happened when the children were in the home. The children were then separated and sent to stay with relatives, but the allegedly supernatural noises followed them and, later, when the Fox family reunited and moved to Rochester, the manifestations began to occur there as well. Publicity grew apace, and very soon many others began to report similar phenomena. Séances multiplied and before long mediums were popping up everywhere across the country. "Table-moving" or "table-turning" became a common form of social activity both in the United States and in Britain and France. By 1888, however, both the Fox girls, whose antics had sparked the entire movement, publicly confessed that the whole thing—at least as far as their part in it was concerned—had been a gigantic hoax.4

Today's mediums and channellers may or may not know the historical background, but they are the psychics of the past under a fresh name. There are, however, slight but significant differences. For example, many channellers are concerned not so much with contacting dead persons as with dispensing arcane wisdom and guidance from other planes. While they claim to make use of various spirit guides or "entities"—sometimes a single name is given to a cluster of entities—many of them hold that their ultimate inspiration is the spirit of God or of "the gods," and that they provide ways to understand one's relationship to the divine Mind.5 Others claim simply to have unusual psychic gifts that enable them to contact the spirits of dead loved ones. They will provide comforting messages for a fee.

When I first began to research this topic some time ago, it was largely because of Shirley MacLaine's books, media appearances and multiplying seminars, that channelling and mediumship had become so popular. Today you can even take night-school courses in it at otherwise staid, academic institutions. While MacLaine herself never claimed to be a channeller, she promoted the whole process and reportedly made a small fortune from her seminars alone, which were regularly attended by 1,000 participants at $300 a head. Channelling has since become an even bigger business, and not just for the leading figures in the New Age movement, but for hundreds of lesser lights in every city and town on the continent. People seem to flock to channellers for the kind of comfort and reassurance they once looked to doctors, clergy or psychiatrists to give.

Today the big names in this field are no longer MacLaine and her contacts, but John Edward, James Van Praagh, Sylvia Browne,

Anne Gehman, Suzane Northrop and several others. Edward, Van Praagh and Browne appeared on *Larry King Live*, March 6, 2001, and have been guests off and on ever since. Anyone who searches "medium" on Google will find close to three million hits listing everything from online counselling sessions to the promise of actual contact with dead loved ones. All, of course, for a fee. It is reported that the waiting list for a private session with James Van Praagh is now about three years.

Freaks or Frauds?

One might be tempted to dismiss the whole phenomenon as relatively harmless on the grounds that if people want this kind of thing and are willing to pay for it, it's nobody's business but their own. However, since we are engaged in an inquiry into whether there is any reason to believe in life after death, the matter cannot simply be left there. Two questions stand out: Are these channellers or mediums actually in genuine contact with the deceased or other spirit beings? And what kind of messages are being conveyed to the eager and often very vulnerable people who are the recipients of this information or advice?

There are usually so many obvious distortions and little regard for evidence or documentation that it is easy to come to the conclusion than that many of these people, in spite of claims to the contrary, have very little passion for objectivity and truth. This is evident in, for example, the wholly uncritical acceptance of such unproven legends as that of the lost civilization of Atlantis, the belief that the whole human race is the result of genetic experiments by extraterrestrials from uncharted planets, the certainty that UFOs exist and so on.

Shirley MacLaine's bestselling books are filled with wild assertions about what the Bible says, what Einstein and other scientists say, yet there are no solid facts or references to back up any of it. Anyone trying to check these alleged quotations or statements will find that they either don't exist or have been so wrenched from their context as to be totally different. We get a real clue to the kind of approach I'm referring to when we read her own words in *Out on a Limb*.[6] On information received from channellers: "Wherever the information came from didn't matter as much to me as the sense it made. Maybe it was a psychic's subconscious talking; maybe they were just good actors. But even if that were true, the morality of their message was unmistakable." MacLaine's most characteristic reply when questioned about any of her New Age beliefs, from UFO sightings to clairvoyance, is: "We all create our own reality." Or, "That's my reality anyway." As Henry Gordon noted in his 1988 exposé book, *Channeling into the New Age, The Teachings of Shirley MacLaine and Other Such Gurus*, who can reason or argue with this kind of lack-logic? Once we all create our own realities, all discourse about what is or is not true becomes totally meaningless. Anyone can say whatever far-out or ridiculous thing that takes their fancy and not fear rebuttal.

There was a time when I was convinced that mediumship presented far more problems than it solved. However, since that time much work has been done in this field. I have revised my thinking somewhat and, in full integrity, realize the need to put right one or two earlier opinions and conclusions. In retrospect, I realize that my original treatment of mediums or channellers was somewhat skewed and overly skeptical on several points, even though I still remain very critical of many features of this burgeoning field.

Two experiences have occurred in the intervening years to help bring about significant changes in my thinking. One was a deep moment of self-examination and awareness about six years ago that revealed to me the full extent of my own built-in religious prejudice against even entertaining the idea that there was anything solid whatever to the claims of psychics, mediums and others to be able to establish contact with the deceased. I will describe how dramatically this bias was challenged and vanquished shortly. The second step came as I opened myself to more of the literature on the subject and especially when I encountered the benchmark book *The Afterlife Experiments*, by two Ph.D.s, Professor Gary E. Schwartz, assisted by clinical psychologist Linda Russek. The subtitle was: *Breakthrough Scientific Evidence of Life After Death*. Schwartz has taught at both Harvard and Yale. His Ph.D. is from Harvard and he has written over four hundred peer-reviewed papers for various medical and other scientific journals. Neither he nor Russek can be written off as flakes.

The absolutely rigorous, double-blind experiments they conducted with a select team of well-known mediums including John Edwards, Rev. Anne Gehman, George Anderson and others at the University of Arizona presented me with the kind of evidence I could no longer simply dismiss with my former habitual skepticism. I ended up, to quote Marcel Proust, "seeing with new eyes." *Publisher's Weekly* praised *The Afterlife Experiments'* "consummate authority." Dr. Richard Powell, vice-president for research and graduate studies at the University of Arizona, hailed the book as "an important milestone in the scientific research on the survival of consciousness after death." More about Schwartz and Russek shortly.

Here I'll explain the basis of my previous antagonism. In general, it flowed in part from a high respect for concrete evidence and a natural as well as a professional habit of asking for proof where claims affecting people's lives and pocketbooks are being made. I make no apologies for that. However, my own religious upbringing in a strictly evangelical home where we went to church three times every Sunday—my father was always a Sunday school superintendent—set my mind at a very early age in direct opposition to anything that even vaguely suggested necromancy, spiritualism or mediums. Even at such an early age I knew the Bible, at a surface level, from cover to cover. I knew the story of King Saul's consultation with the witch of Endor as he tried (successfully) to conjure up the deceased prophet Samuel. This was a forbidden act for which he paid the price in the end. I knew that in our family's biblically correct circles it was strictly taboo to have anything to do with fortune-telling or with "familiar spirits." This was all so deeply engrained in my psyche that even much later as the religion editor for Canada's largest newspaper I never once visited a spiritualist church or investigated the claims of local or national channellers or psychics. I welcomed any media evidence of psychic fakery since it validated my pre-existing prejudice.

All this was to change. In the spring of 2000, an old friend from an evangelical Anglican church we had attended as a family for many years when I was growing up—it was in downtown Toronto and my parents had been married there in 1928 after emigrating from Northern Ireland—wrote me a lengthy letter. In it she described all the many twists and turns of her spiritual journey over the years. It turned out she had followed my career through my writing and had noticed that I had always kept clear of the topic of spiritualism and the possibility of communication with the souls or spirits of the dead. She wanted to present me with a challenge to examine the roots of my reluctance in this area and at least give the matter an open and fair hearing. We then exchanged a couple of letters and as a result my wife Susan and I decided to take up my friend's invitation to attend a week-long series of lectures that June at the small resort village of Lily Dale in southwestern New York State, about 90 kilometres south of Buffalo. The lectures were to be given by the Rev. Anne Gehman, pastor of the Center for Spiritual Enlightenment in Washington and a leading member of the National Spiritualist Association of Churches. Though we didn't realize it at the time, we were to meet Anne not just at Lily Dale, but later were to read about her in the afterlife experiments described in the book by that title by Dr. Gary Schwartz. Experience was to prove my old friend's prediction true: "You'll find Anne Gehman to be one of the sanest, most logical persons you are ever likely to meet."

Lily Dale was unlike anything we had ever experienced before. Called by the media the "town that talks to the dead," the brightly painted cottages clustered by the shore of a lovely lake house what during the summer months constitutes the world's largest collection of mediums, psychics and other spiritualists. Established in 1879, today Lily Dale's assembly of about 450 registered mediums sees about 20,000 visitors annually. If you don't think a medium really delivers during a sitting you can complain and get your money back. We found Gehman to be extraordinarily open, reasonable, even gently persuasive in her lectures on spiritualism and thoroughly enjoyed the sessions, especially the very frank exchanges during question periods. In general, apart from the segments where we were urged to meditate in silence and keep ourselves open to possible "signs" from "the other side," it seemed to us that spiritualism closely resembled most of the mainline Protestant churches with which we had long been familiar. They were like Pentecostals in the way they stressed the New Testament's teachings about the "gifts of the Spirit."

We had not come to Lily Dale, however, just to hear lectures. Both Susan and I made appointments for readings with two of the mediums-in-residence. One was Anne Gehman herself; the other was an unknown (to us) Canadian psychic. Susan had recently experienced the deaths of three very close family members: both parents and her brother, and so was strongly motivated to be as open as possible without abdicating in any way her strong common-sense habit of judging all would-be evidence fairly. Nevertheless, in both instances, the sessions Susan had proved less than illuminating. Little of the material allegedly "coming through" or being suggested corresponded directly with anything or anyone she was able to recognize. There was a subtle suggestion as each session ended in a frank admission by the mediums that "it's not working"—that she may have been "trying too hard" or have been too intense. But, anybody in the same situation would have been eager for a positive result of some kind, or they wouldn't be motivated to be there in the first place. In both instances, part or all of the fee was waived.

In total fairness, it should be said that both of our readings with Anne Gehman, came at the end of the week's lectures when she would most likely have been totally exhausted. In mine, apart from a few generalities which could have applied to anyone, nothing of note really happened. Since this outcome was very unusual for Anne, she strongly urged us to try another session at a better time, but we have not yet had the opportunity to cross paths again.

The other reading I had, however, proved to be somewhat remarkable—even in retrospect some years later. I had never heard of, nor even seen, the psychic before the moment we sat across from each other in a porch of his sunlit cottage that summer afternoon. After a brief period of silence, he said: "You have the feel of a minister about you, Tom." I was surprised, but thought he might well have recognized me from my newspaper columns or an old television series I had done. He then described various details about my Irish background and spoke about my father and the major role he had played in my life. He noted correctly that my father had been a minister also. This all had a ring of truth, but there was little that he could not have learned through normal channels. But then he said he was being told that I would shortly receive some kind of unusual manuscripts or hidden documents which he described as a "gospel" or good news, that I would ignore them for a while, putting them aside on a shelf or in a closet, but that eventually they would be read by me and would burst into my life with some fresh light or insights.

He gave me a tape of the session and it is still in a drawer of my desk. I was mildly excited by his words at that moment, but soon forgot them in the welter and rush of life on our return home. Lily Dale receded to the overall memories of a pleasant summer.

It was some months later that I realized I needed to deal with a growing pile of monographs being sent to me by a previously unknown United Church cleric. When you have been writing in the field of religion for as long as I have—I left teaching at the seminary in May 1971, to become religion editor of the *Toronto Star*—people constantly send you material on spiritual matters that they have either written themselves or collected elsewhere. It's a major task to cope with it. Most eventually is put in the recycling bin. But something had made me keep this material on the shelf. It was entirely made up of the work of an American scholar of comparative religion, Dr. Alvin Boyd Kuhn. One day, during a pause in my own writing, I took one of the monographs down and read it. It was stunning in its impact and I reached for another one when that one was finished. I was hooked and not only read everything in the pile, but wrote to the minister in question asking for more. Eventually, I read all of Kuhn's books, then all those of his major sources and the basic research for my book, *The Pagan Christ*, was well underway. The book was named the "number one bestseller for 2004" by the *Toronto Star* and has been published in several languages around the world. Those who have read it know how the experience helped to totally transform my understanding of the origins of Christianity and the vision I now hold of a rebirth of not only it, but all religions in our time. Was this "prophecy" simply a lucky guess? I don't know for a certainty, but honesty compels me to say that I feel it could have been something more. We listened to the tape of that sitting just the other day and it still gives us a sense of amazement at its accuracy on that one point, even though the rest of it was pretty banal. However, it could be argued that, if anything, it is evidence of clairvoyance rather than communication with the deceased.

Notable as this experience seems, then, it certainly does not of itself prove that mediums can actually communicate with the dead. It shook my skepticism to be sure, but I wanted something more scientific, more open to testing and verification if possible. That was when I discovered the remarkable book by Professor Gary E. Schwartz already cited. In *The Afterlife Experiments*, he describes in measured detail a lengthy, scrupulously scientific series of experiments, using some of the top mediums in North America, in which he and his colleague, Dr. Linda Russek, claim to have established beyond a reasonable doubt that the soul is an eternal living reality and that communication with those "on the other side" is possible. In a previous book, *The Living Universe: A Fundamental Discovery that Transforms Science and Medicine*, the pair had explained how contemporary science is leading to the conclusion that everything in the universe is eternal, alive and evolving. In *The Afterlife Experiments* they apply that thesis to human consciousness. The hypothesis they set out to prove is that, like all other forms of energy, consciousness too is never lost—it simply is transformed as it evolves into a new kind of being. Schwartz, who was once a professor of psychology and psychiatry at Yale and later a professor of psychology, medicine, neurology and psychiatry at the University of Arizona, has presented hundreds of papers at scientific meetings in the United States and abroad.

Both he and Russek know how science proceeds when trying to sift out opinion from fact and fraud from truth. They not only used the now universally accepted double blind protocol where the mediums didn't know who the "sitter" was and vice versa, they invited veteran skeptics as well as psychics skilled in "cold" sittings, where the person seeking to contact loved ones is simply led along by clever suggestions and tricks of the trade, to critique their methodology and help them hone it even more sharply.

In the most impressive of these trials, the sitters were wholly masked from view and never spoke, hence the accuracy rate of the positive hits thus obtained was all the more striking. In the case of one of the mediums, Laurie Campbell (not as well known as John Edward and the others), her rate of accuracy with one of the sitters, George Dalzell, ranged between 90 and 100 percent per deceased person "contacted." The striking thing about his particular reading was that the medium and the sitter were in two different parts of the United States with no contact other than that they were connected by a muted telephone.

The bottom line of Schwartz and Russek's books is that the mediums tested were able to establish a rate of success well over triple that of ordinary lay folk making their best guesses. The score was only wholly perfect once as cited, but so strikingly high in almost every instance as to point to survival of consciousness as the most obvious explanation. The two scientists conclude that as with all other energy systems, "the soul and spirit of a living person will continue after death as a 'living info-energy system' in the vacuum of space." According to their conclusions, the subtle info-energy patterns that surround us at all times in this life continue after physical death and can be read or tuned into by those sufficiently gifted and aware of their presence.

Schwartz adds an interesting observation relating to ghosts or apparitions: "History tells us that they typically appear in dreams, during meditation, or in the darkness when the light is dim. These are precisely the stimulus conditions, predicted by contemporary physics, that would allow us to potentially detect the subtle but nonetheless persistent info-energy patterns of the history of the universe that literally surrounds each and every one of us."[7]

The hypothesis of ghosts using energy systems terminology is really not different from the concept of far-distant stars in astrophysical terms. Although we may only see these stars—or ghosts—under quite special conditions, the theory requires that their patterns of info-energy are still there whether seen or unseen. As Schwartz puts it, mind is not the same as the physical brain: "Mind extends like the light from distant stars. This single fact is more shattering than the discovery that the earth is round" and not flat.[8]

One of the things I liked most about the Schwartz-Russek approach is that at all times they had a volunteer devil's advocate committee to query every aspect of the exercise. There is no question that anyone has ever had regarding this whole issue that is not tackled at some point in the discussion. For example, why is it that dead people always seem to give such Sunday-school-like messages about love and the like? Why is there no word about new science or cures? It seems they tell clients what they most want to hear. Here's what the book says. Suppose a deceased person, a mother or a father has long awaited an opportunity to communicate with a son or daughter. His time with a high-priced medium is perhaps five minutes, or even fifteen. There may be other deceased relatives who wish to communicate too. Schwartz asks: "What will he tell him or her? The latest scientific discoveries? The great books he's been reading in the afterlife? That's not what his daughter (or son) came to hear." The reason for being with the medium is to give and receive love and reassurance. The deceased parent wants to prove to the living relative that he or she still exists, is truly at peace and still cares very much for those temporarily left behind. That approach makes sense, I believe, but I commend his whole section, "Answering the Sceptics," to those who want to read more.[9]

However, I must warn that channelling misused can easily end by messing up people's minds and actually destroying families. When MacLaine was a guest on the *Larry King Live* TV show on September 17, 1987, a caller complained that his family had been "blown apart." He said his wife had been suffering acute depression and went to a channeller, who, by means of her "entity," told the woman that her husband had murdered her in a past life and then had run off with their teenage daughter. She immediately left her husband and disappeared. He hadn't seen her in two years. He went on to comment that he thought his wife "was looking for a crutch to avoid dealing with the realities of life."

I could match this story with many similar ones that readers have shared with me in response to my newspaper columns on reincarnation and hypnotic regression into alleged past lives. In fairness, it must also be said that the misuse or overly fanatical pursuit of almost any set of ideas, religious or otherwise, can readily result in personal or social harm.

What I find most dangerous in the beliefs that often go along with channelling, however, is the New Age theory, based upon a misunderstanding of the teaching of Dr. Carl Jung about evil, that the truly spiritual person is beyond good and evil. This argument for amorality cropped up often in the channelling material I examined. It is highly erroneous and hence should be shunned.

There is no doubt in my mind that channelling works in the sense that certain individuals can and do sometimes find a new sense of worth, meaning and self-confidence when they consult a channeller or medium. A great spiritual search is going on at this moment in history and there would be no such thing as the channelling explosion if it were not addressing specific needs with some genuine measure of success.

A study of the current, massive upswing in the number of people consulting psychics and mediums shows that the vast majority are in search of comfort and resolution of deep issues both of grief and, in many cases, guilt. They want to be reassured that the loved one is OK, that family members have been reunited, that they themselves have been forgiven for past sins of omission or commission concerning the deceased (for example, that the suicide of a loved one was not their fault or that love truly can reach across to "the other side). James Van Praagh puts it starkly when he says it is the mission of the medium to "heal" while that of the professional skeptic is simply "to destroy."

Here is a letter received in my May 2005 poll of the readers of my *Toronto Star* column. It is unique, yet typical, in its sincerity and simplicity. You sense the eagerness of the recipient of the "other-side" information to be reassured. But, there is also the mystery of the medium's knowledge concerning the green dressing gown.

G.C. writes: "My husband, David, died three and a half years ago. About six months later I was in England and arranged a visit with a spiritual medium. Many things that came out were telling, but two things convinced me that this was genuine. 'Why does he keep showing himself to me in a green dressing gown,' asked the medium. The answer to that is that, because we had chosen a closed casket, I had David dressed in warm pyjamas and his big, soft *green* dressing gown. It still makes me smile when I think of that acknowl-edgement. While getting ready for that appointment, I felt like I was going on a date (very odd!) and was careful with hair and makeup. I thought to myself, 'I wonder what Mum thinks of my hair.' Mum had died the previous year and hadn't lived to see me transform from a white-haired woman to blonde. Right off the bat, I was told by the medium that my mother was telling me that she'd leave the session solely for David himself and would 'speak' with my sister who had the next session. But, she wanted me to know that she really liked my hair! She repeated it as the reading was coming to a close. It was most reassuring."

In a confusing and confused world, where traditional faiths seem under fire and unable to bridge the gap between their dogma and the needs of ordinary people, where the individual can so eas-ily get lost in the shuffling of forces beyond his or her control, where materialism seems to exclude all else, to believe one has been addressed by voices or guides from the other side can be of considerable solace. One is given a sort of instant spirituality, an appropriate remedy from a culture that has an instant solution for everything else. One is assured of an infinity of possibilities for one's future, of wider dimensions than mundane living and of the certainty of bliss to come. In fact, channelling today functions rather like the spiritualism of the last century; it is a kind of protest against a secularist world view. It operates as a substitute religion, one that is very personal and much easier than traditional spiritual disciplines. This is far from establishing that it is based upon reality and I would urge great caution for the unwary. However, I believe the traditional faiths could learn a great deal about themselves and their own failure to speak meaningfully to contemporary men and women by paying greater attention to this aspect of the whole channelling phenomenon, instead of simply criticizing or condemning it.

4

REINCARNATION

I hold that when a person dies
His soul returns again to earth;
Arrayed in some new flesh-disguise,
Another mother gives him birth.
With sturdier limbs and brighter brain
The old soul takes the road again.

Such is my own belief and trust;
This hand, this hand that holds the pen,
Has many a hundred times been dust
And turned, as dust to dust again;
These eyes of mine have blinked and shone
In Thebes, in Troy, in Babylon.

All that I rightly think or do,
Or make, or spoil, or bless, or blast,
Is curse or blessing justly due
For sloth or effort in the past.
My life's a statement of the sum
Of vice indulged, or overcome . . .

And as I wander on the roads
I shall be helped and healed and blessed;
Kind words shall cheer and be as goads
To urge to heights before unguessed.
My road shall be the road I made,
All that I gave shall be repaid.

So shall I fight, so shall I tread,
In this long war beneath the stars;
So shall a glory wreathe my head,
So shall I faint and show the scars,
Until this case, this clogging mould
Be smithied all to kingly gold.

—JOHN MASEFIELD, Poet Laureate

The Creed

"YOU CAN RELIVE your past lives" the tabloid's three-inch black headline screams. "Expert gives step-by-step instructions . . ." One of the most popular features of New Age thinking is the very widespread ancient theory that we have already lived many lives and will continue to do so in the future. This process, it is believed, goes on until we have learned all the lessons God (or life itself) has to teach us and are sufficiently enlightened to be released from the cycle of rebirth. We are then fit for the Presence of God, union with universal Mind or the oblivion of nirvanic bliss. The law of karma, the spiritual equivalent of physical cause and effect in the scientific world, governs the kind of sufferings or blessings experienced in each successive life. Free will enters into it, of course. According to the mainstream theory in the West—and there are many variations depending upon the particular religious or philosophical approach taken—there is free choice about how one deals with specific aspects of our karma. The matter of where, to which parents and in what circumstances one is reborn is widely believed to be a matter of choice. Advice, however, may be given by exalted masters or other higher spiritual beings in the plane between lives, called in Tibetan Buddhism, the Bardo.

Until quite recently, it was possible to think of belief in reincarnation as something rather exotic, belonging to the great religious traditions of the East but foreign to western thought. A visit to the nearest bookstore or a glance at the tabloids at the neighbourhood supermarket will quickly dispel such a notion. Recent public opinion polls reveal some quite remarkable statistics. According to the 1981 Gallup poll on religion in the United States, some 38 million Americans (then 23 percent) professed to be believers in reincarnation.[1] But, a more recent Gallup poll of Canadian views on an afterlife shows that nearly one-third of the population (29 percent) believe you are reborn into another life here on earth after death.[2] Indeed, belief in life after death overall showed a marked upswing well through the 1990s. According to a 2003 poll by www.religious-tolerance.org,[3] 40 percent of young adults twenty-five to twenty-nine years of age in North America believe in reincarnation. Most of this can be seen as the result of the enormous impact over the past three decades of eastern religious ideas upon western society. But there are deeper causes, too. The decline of Christianity in the West and the spiritual vacuum created by this have provided a fertile ground for alternative answers to the most basic questions of all.

Belief in some form of reincarnation or in the transmigration of souls is one of the oldest, most universal religious phenomena known. It came to the West originally from India by way of Pythagoras and Plato, but it is found in almost every culture on earth, from the Inuit of the Arctic to the Aborigines of Australia. Since a significant portion of the whole of humanity throughout history has held it, including some of the best minds, ancient and modern, ever to address the mysteries of human existence, reincarnation is not something to be lightly dismissed. I have sympathy with those, for example, who have criticized Hans Küng, the renowned Roman Catholic theologian, for doing precisely this in his otherwise clever book *Eternal Life?*[4] On the other hand, the fact that many millions of people still believe in reincarnation—or any other doctrine— or that celebrities such as Shirley MacLaine and others cite it as a definite ingredient in their obviously successful life philosophies doesn't prove it to be true either.

Speaking of proof, or at any rate evidence, for reincarnation, one of the things that makes this whole matter particularly interesting at this time is the large number of people coming forward to report that under hypnosis they have actually revisited and relived their past lives. Serious hypnotherapists as well as innumerable quacks make a lucrative living by counselling and guiding people today on the basis of what is alleged to have happened to them in previous existences. In response to invitations in my column, readers by the score have written to me giving first-hand accounts of their own experiences in this regard. For example, a hypnotherapist, who says this story is only one of more than thirty cases he has on record, wrote the following:

A young married woman once came to see him about her dread of sleeping in the dark. She had been to many doctors but to no avail. Under hypnosis she regressed to a previous life where she was known as Anna. She lived at a specific address in Heidelberg, Germany. She was then thirteen years old. The year was 1943 and her family was Jewish. She vividly recalled the Nazis coming, putting her in a van with many others, then pushing her along a narrow corridor into a very dark room. "She became hysterical under hypnosis and cried bitterly saying, 'What are they going to do with us?'" The therapist was then able to assure her that although she had been killed and her body destroyed, her soul was indestructible. She would soon be living in another body. She described her in-between life as very peaceful, surrounded by angelic beings of light.

The therapist went on to write: "Having found the ground of her fear of darkness, I suggested that this fear belonged to Anna, Anna was in the past, and the past was no longer with her. She was then able to sleep in the dark with no further fears." Incidentally, this same hypnotherapist claims to have written to the Heidelberg address and to have confirmed that a Jewish family had indeed once lived there. The father was a music teacher, there were children, and the teacher's name was Arthur, just as the patient (as Anna) had said.

The occult or New Age sections of bookstores now overflow with books detailing similar narratives. However, although one is assured, as in the case of Anna, that proper research was done and that the record confirms things were exactly as described in the trance, a truly objective outsider may find nothing but endless frustration in trying to pin any of it down satisfactorily. I have read and examined as many of these as I could, and while one encounters some quite unusual stories I have seen nothing yet personally that amounts to completely convincing evidence or proof.

Certainly the work of Dr. Ian Stevenson, Carlson Professor of Psychiatry at the University of Virginia Medical School, must be mentioned wherever reincarnation is discussed today because of what he has to say about contemporary hypnotic regression into past lives. For an enthusiastic review of his research one of the best and most concise sources is the 1984 book, *Reincarnation: A New Horizon in Science, Religion, and Society*, by Sylvia Cranston and Carey Williams.[5]

Cranston and Williams, to their credit, quote some remarks of Dr. Stevenson's from the October 1976 newsletter of the American Society for Psychical Research.[6] Stevenson notes that many people write to him asking for hypnotic regression to previous lives or to investigate material arising from such experiences. He then comments: "Many persons who attach no importance whatever to their dreams . . . nevertheless believe that whatever emerges during hypnosis can invariably be taken at face value. In fact, the state of a hypnotized person resembles in many ways—though not in all—that of a person dreaming. The subconscious parts of the mind are released from ordinary inhibitions, and they may then present in dramatic form a new 'personality.' If the person has been told by the hypnotist, either explicitly or implicitly, to 'go back to another time and place,' the 'new personality' may be extremely plausible both to the person having the experience and to others watching . . . In fact, however, nearly all such hypnotically evoked 'previous personalities' are *entirely imaginary* [italics mine], just as are the contents of most dreams."

Stevenson goes on to say that such experiences may include some accurate historical details, but these are usually derived from information the person has acquired through reading, from radio and television programs or from other sources. "He may not remember where he obtained the information, but sometimes this can be brought out in other hypnotic sessions designed to search for the sources of the information used in making up the 'previous personality.'"

Coming from such a prestigious source and from one who himself seems convinced, for other reasons, of the reality of reincarnation, this is a powerful antidote to many of the often bizarre claims made in the name of past-life regression. It should be noted as well that Stevenson has some words of caution for those who experiment with this kind of hypnosis: "There are some hazards in this procedure of regression to 'previous lives.' In a few instances, the previous personality has not gone away when instructed to do so, and the subject in such cases has been left in an altered state of personality for several days or longer before restoration of his normal personality."

The late Geddes MacGregor, professor emeritus of philosophy at the University of Southern California and an Anglican (Episcopalian) priest for over forty years, believed firmly in reincarnation.

His 1978 book, *Reincarnation in Christianity*, is still by far one of the most reasonable and persuasive I have read on the subject. However, MacGregor, though friendly to the doctrine, also has major reservations about using alleged past-life recall as a proof. He notes that many such cases have turned out to be completely bogus and says, "The literature on the subject is considerable; the results, though they leave many unsolved puzzles, are inconclusive."7

More and more doctors and psychologists are expressing concern over the uncritical acceptance by some members of the healing professions of alleged past-life recall as a means of healing. Mark Albrecht, in *Reincarnation, A Christian Critique of a New Age Doctrine*, quotes Alexander Rogawski, former chief of the Los Angeles County Medical Association's psychiatry section: "Indeed, the past-lives movement is cashing in on the disillusionment with conventional therapies, fear of death and the current interest in the occult. But all the therapy's popularity proves is that suckers are born every minute and customers can be found for anything."8

The doctor's blunt words were originally spoken to reporters from *Time* magazine, and appeared in the October 3, 1977, issue. In the same article, Dr. Lucille Forer, a member of the board of directors of the Los Angeles County Psychological Association, said that most of her contemporaries were skeptical about hypnotic regression to past lives as a therapy. She warned that a good therapist may be able to use material brought up from a patient's subconscious, but that leading a person to believe that past lives were being tapped could be dangerous: "A person could develop psychosis if the fantasy material was extreme. He could feel guilt about what he thought were past acts. I would warn anyone who wants to do this sort of thing to do it with a trained person who can handle any problems that might arise . . . People are looking for shortcuts that don't exist."

Professor Ernest Hilgard, director of the Hypnosis Research Laboratory at Stanford University, views past-life regression as complete nonsense. He is on record saying that hypnosis is a very dangerous tool in the hands of amateurs. He adds: "New identities claimed during trance are not uncommon and are very easy to produce. Invariably they're related to long buried memories, and anybody who makes claims to the contrary has not based them on scholarly judgments."9

One possible explanation for those cases where the contents of the hypnotic trance do seem particularly vivid or can be checked out in some detail is the phenomenon of cryptoamnesia. There are millions of details stored in our subconscious minds and many, if not the majority, became stored there without our having been aware of them. The British psychiatrist Anthony Storr contends that recall of past lives is actually an example of this cryptoamnesia, a purely imaginary construction using subconscious memories of some long-forgotten historical novel, film or magazine article. He comments that "most of us have a grade B movie running in our heads most of the time."10

The famous, or if you prefer notorious, Bridey Murphy affair of the 1950s still stands as an additional caveat to those who uncritically wish to gallop off in this particular direction. For a full account of this apparent hoax I refer the reader to Colin Wilson's book, *Afterlife*.11 It is a long, complicated and in many ways fascinating story. In essence, Virginia Tighe, the wife of an insurance salesman in Pueblo, Colorado, was persuaded to undergo hypnotic regression by Morey Bernstein, a Pueblo businessman who had found he was naturally proficient at putting people into a hypnotic trance. Under hypnosis, Tighe began to speak in Gaelic and said she was Bridey Murphy, born near Cork, Ireland, in 1798. In a series of tape-recorded sessions, she talked in great detail of her life as the wife of a Belfast lawyer who taught at Queen's University in that city. She had died in 1864. Bernstein wrote a book, *The Search for Bridey Murphy*, and it became front-page news. Mrs. Tighe appeared on national television in the United States.

Various events then occurred to debunk her story, not the least of which was the coming forward of Tighe's Irish nanny who had helped care for her to about age two. She recognized the baby-game songs she had sung to Mrs. Tighe as an infant, some even including the name "Bridey."

As we have already had occasion to observe, there is nothing stronger than the will to believe, which is such a prominent characteristic of our time. Far from being an age of unbelief, this is an age of unmatched credulity and willingness to accept almost anything, from the significance of numbers in one's life (numerology) to healing with crystals to contact with aliens on UFOs. Evidence is the last thing on many people's minds.

I had a remarkable example of this recently in a lengthy interview with a successful businessman. This was a man who told himself at the age of twenty that he would be a millionaire by the time he was thirty-five. He is now just over fifty and a millionaire several times over. However, over the past few years he has developed a strong belief in reincarnation and now believes he has had a succession of past lives. Even though he is aware of the warnings of Stevenson and others in the field, he nevertheless remains unshaken in his conviction that, for example, he was a young man in Jerusalem at the time of Christ, that Christ once touched his head as he stood at the front of a crowd as He passed by and that he was crucified soon after Jesus himself. This person is totally reasonable in every other way, yet he is adamant in his belief that every major figure in his life today—both friend and foe—has been connected to him in a repeated cycle of previous lives. In this respect, he is typical of many hundreds of thousands of North Americans.

Stevenson, who is, as we have seen, extremely skeptical of claims about most hypnosis-induced, past-life experience, nevertheless is impressed by the phenomenon of children who suddenly and quite spontaneously speak in some language other than that spoken in their home or immediate background. He is equally impressed by the more than two thousand cases he has investigated of young children in both the East and West who seem to have spontaneous and fairly precise recall of places, people and even incidents they could not have experienced. This phenomenon seems to defy normal explanation.[12]

There is little to be gained by reproducing specific examples of this from Stevenson. Some of the cases he relates are quite extraordinary and I have no reason to doubt the authenticity of what he reports. But, as with the case of that common experience called déjà vu, or the case of child prodigies such as Mozart, who wrote a sonata when he was four and an opera when he was seven, the theory of past lives is by no means the most obvious or most plausible explanation. There is a whole range of possibilities.

Dr. Stevenson himself admits that in addition to reincarnation there could be several other explanations for the detailed, spontaneous recall he has been able to observe in the children he has studied. For example, it could be caused by telepathy, clairvoyance or even spirit possession—the influence of some discarnate personality. This has been suggested by none other than an orthodox Hindu swami, Sri Sri Somasundara Desika Paramachariya of south India. The swami, a believer in reincarnation, has written an open letter to Stevenson denying that the hundreds of cases from India the doctor cites are any proof whatever of the reincarnation doctrine. He wrote: "All the 300-odd cases reported by you do not in fact support the theory of reincarnation . . . They are all spirit possessions, ignored by the learned in south India."[13]

Whatever one may think of that particular approach, it is undoubtedly true that the full mysteries of the human mind, particularly human memory, remain largely uncharted territory. Some of the most recent discoveries of neurologists and other researchers, however, point to the probability that memories reside in the "soft disks" of our DNA (deoxyribonucleic acid). In other words, perhaps tracks or imprints of experiences of the family, clan or tribe are stored along with the rest of our genetic coding. These DNA impressions, especially in our youth, can flash into consciousness much as the images of dreams do.

There is also the matter of RNA (ribonucleic acid), which our DNA uses to direct the activities of individual cells. One thoughtful reader of my weekly columns responded to the incident of "Anna," which I have already quoted, with an interesting letter. She is a registered nurse and not long ago attended a conference on prenatal psychology. At one lecture, a professor who has been studying the nature of our inherited RNA and its role in long-term memory storage put forward a theory. "Nobody," he said, "knows where long-term memory, body memory of movements needed to perform tasks, or a baby's pre-verbal memories are stored." Using the analogy of silicon chips and their use in computers, he suggested that "protein chips" in the RNA could hold much more information, extending back through one's ancestors and eventually linking all humanity in a unified family. Bits would be inherited from all sides—some verbal, some visual, some perhaps pre-verbal—which might explain those times when we experience déjà vu—vague feelings of having been somewhere before but are unable to express where or when. Perhaps just hearing or seeing a certain sound or image or smelling a particular scent could trigger this information and bring it to consciousness.

For a refreshingly different approach to reincarnation in terms of quantum theory and expanded awareness, see the section called "Memories of Former Lifetimes" in Deepak Chopra's *How to Know God*. He says:

Time and space could just be convenient concepts that hold true in the material world but dissolve gradually as you approach the quantum level. That is what I believe reincarnation is about. Former lives fall into the unexplored territory of expanded awareness. It isn't absolutely necessary to decide whether they are "real" or not.[14]

Other explanations for what now seems to masquerade as past-life recall would include Carl Jung's concept of the "collective unconscious," which, he postulated, is common to us all and holds the great archetypes of our memories as humans. And then there is the whole phenomenon of extrasensory perception, ESP, with which some seem more endowed than others but which may well at times operate unconsciously in us all. Jung himself was strongly attracted to the idea of rebirth but never gave it his wholly undivided assent. He described it as "one of the primordial affirmations of mankind."

Reincarnation in the Bible

New Age thinkers have made a number of assertions concerning the doctrine of reincarnation and its alleged confirmation in the pages of the Bible. Some of these statements appear contradictory, as we shall see. Others are based upon "facts of history" that, on closer examination, turn out to have no foundation. Since, however, the stature of some of these experts is beyond dispute and the mass appeal of others is established through the media, it is essential to examine the matter more closely.

In Shirley MacLaine's bestselling book *Out on a Limb*, a character called David is explaining the theory of reincarnation to her:

"'But David,' she said, 'why aren't these teachings recorded in the Bible?'

"'They are,' he said. 'The theory of reincarnation is recorded in the Bible. But the proper interpretations were struck from it during an ecumenical council meeting of the Catholic Church in Constantinople sometime around 553 CE called the Council of Nicea. The council members voted to strike those teachings from the Bible in order to solidify Church control.'"[15]

This passage and its sentiments are repeated in MacLaine's writings, and crop up continuously wherever the New Age gospel is proclaimed. But it simply bristles with problems. The Council of Nicea, of course, was held in Nicea in Asia Minor and not at Constantinople. It was in the year 325 CE, not 553. There was a council held in Constantinople in 553 called the Second Council of Constantinople. However, in my research, neither at Nicea nor Constantinople—nor indeed at any other ecumenical council— were passages relating to the doctrine of reincarnation or any other theory expurgated from the Biblical text. That there was some tampering with various New Testament texts during the early centuries is a fact not to be denied. But, I have found no evidence that any passage relating to reincarnation has been dropped.

Without question there were early Christians—most notably the Gnostics—who believed in the doctrine of reincarnation, and pronouncements were made condemning it by theologians and several councils. One of the reasons that the brilliant Alexandrian Origen (*c.*185–*c.*254 CE) was driven from the priesthood and regarded as a heretic was his espousal of a form of this doctrine. But arguments based upon a supposed deliberate attempt to conceal the "true" teachings of Moses or Jesus on this theory, are as far as I can discover, simply false. Since the most influential (and by far the easiest to read) exposition of the grounds for believing in reincarnation today is Sylvia Cranston and Carey Williams's 1984 book, *Reincarnation, A New Horizon in Science, Religion, and Society*, I propose to look now at the case set forth there for the presence of reincarnational thinking in the Old and New Testaments.

The Old Testament

Cranston and Williams say that none of the three main branches of Judaism today "openly" teach reincarnation. They point out as well that the doctrine of the rebirth of souls is not developed in a systematic fashion in most traditional Jewish writings. They do, however, document fairly fully the indisputable fact that esoteric or kabbalistic Judaism—an ancient and important strain of mysticism and interest in the occult—has always believed in the doctrine. The most important modern figure in the revival of this movement was Gershom Scholem (1897–1982), the late professor of mysticism and Kabbalah at the Hebrew University of Jerusalem. His book, *Major Trends in Jewish Mysticism*, remains a classic for those who wish to pursue this aspect of Jewish tradition more deeply. Today it is within the Hasidic movement, which originated in Poland in the eighteenth century, that this particular teaching finds a central place.[16] It can be found everywhere in Hasidic writings but is nowhere more movingly expressed than in Martin Buber's book *For the Sake of Heaven*.

When this has been said, however, Cranston and Williams themselves concede that all this flows from extra-canonical literature, from Jewish mystical writings and not from the Old Testament itself. In fact, they are unable to produce a single text in support of the teaching of reincarnation. As a matter of fact, explicit evidence for a belief of any kind in life after death is extremely scant and undeveloped in the Old Testament. When it comes to the migration or the rebirth of souls there is total silence. The best that our two authors can say is that "nowhere in the Old Testament is reincarnation denied. In the Book of Job, Job plaintively asks 'If a man dies will he live again?' but receives no answer." This, of course, is an argument from silence, which carries little or no weight at all.[17]

The New Testament

In asking "Does the New Testament believe in reincarnation?" it has to be made quite clear that it is different from the question "Are there leading Christians today who hold this theory and who believe that Jesus and his earliest disciples did also?" The answer to the latter is a very firm yes. Undoubtedly there have been, and are today, many, including some notable scholars, who remain Church members while adhering to such a view. Cranston and Williams cite in particular the already mentioned Anglican theologian Geddes MacGregor, author of several books on the subject, including *Reincarnation in Christianity*.[18] But what about the New Testament evidence itself? It is one thing to believe in a doctrine personally; it is another to claim that this or that document actually teaches or upholds it.

At the outset, our two authors again propose the argument from silence: "It can be stated without qualification that Jesus in the four Gospels and St. Paul in the books of the New Testament attributed to him say not one word against the teaching of reincarnation."[19] But then they go further and proclaim that in the Gospels "there are a number of places where reincarnation seems clearly expressed" (a position taken by nearly all New Age exponents, even though they paradoxically also hold that all references to reincarnation were purged by early councils). The reason the record is not more "expansive," we are told, is because Christ's disciples misunderstood him and supposed the world was about to end shortly. The fact that some ultraconservatives today hold that a historical Jesus was the source of this expectation of an imminent doomsday is either ignored or unknown to Cranston and Williams. Indeed, much of the urgency that characterized all Bible teaching would have completely evaporated if the authors had believed that there were countless lives ahead and that this present life was not "the accepted time" for a decision for God.

Our two authors, however, go on to a type of *a fortiori* argument that goes like this: If Christ is really the Son of God then he presumably has all powers, so why would he not have the power to be reborn again and again to save the world? This is unworthy of the generally quite intelligent and careful approach the pair use. There is practically no limit to what one can "prove" taking such a tack. They argue that Jesus himself implied he had such power and indeed would use it when he said in the Gospel of John, "I lay down my life for the sheep. And I have other sheep, that are not of this fold; I must bring them also . . . So there shall be one flock and one shepherd . . . No one takes it from me, but I lay it down of my own accord. I have power to lay it down and I have power to take it again."[20]

But there is not one word in any of this to confirm a belief in reincarnation. In John's Gospel, which is late (90–100 CE), we are reading not what a putative historical Jesus actually said, but what post-Resurrection theologizing of the early Church put into his mouth. In any case, his character is simply saying that he seeks not just the "sheep" of the House of Israel (Jews), but gentiles as well. In saying he has power to lay his life down and to take it again, the author simply has Jesus affirm his sovereignty and his control over the events of the Passion and Crucifixion.

As further evidence of their contention that Jesus himself taught that he had appeared on earth in previous ages and might do so again, Cranston and Williams then adduce another passage from John where Jesus is being taunted as setting himself up above "our father, Abraham." Jesus tells his adversaries, "Your father Abraham rejoiced to see my day and was glad." Surprised, they respond, "You are not yet fifty years old and hast thou seen Abraham?"[21] Jesus replies: "Truly, truly I say to you, before Abraham was, I am." Unfortunately, however, even if one were to take a fundamentalist view and hold that these are the exact words of a historical Jesus, they cannot be said to be valid evidence for reincarnational thinking. What is being claimed by the speaker is pre-existence as the Divine

Son of God. This is in keeping with the opening verses of the Gospel about the Logos (Word of God) being "in the beginning with God." It has no reference to repeated rebirths. And there is no suggestion whatever that this pre-existent state is one shared with all humanity. Quite the opposite. It is the Son's uniqueness that is being stressed by the evangelist.

Admitting that, even if their arguments to this point were solid, they would still not necessarily apply to ourselves, our authors then ask whether the New Testament gives any indication that anyone other than Jesus has the power (or necessity) to be reborn. They believe it does. Returning to John, they quote the case of the man born blind.[22] Walking along with his disciples Jesus sees a blind man. His disciples ask him: "Rabbi, who sinned, this man or his parents, that he was born blind?" At first sight it does seem that the question indicates "there were only two explanations . . . either he had sinned before he was born, suggesting he had lived previously, or that his parents had been guilty of some transgression."[23] The two go on to build on this, saying that the fact the idea of pre-existence and possible reincarnation had entered the disciples' minds "appears to indicate it was a prevalent theory among the Jews at that time." But there is no evidence whatever that it *was* a prevalent theory. What is more, any evidence I have been able to discover points in quite another direction.

Certainly the Jews of that period believed that disease was the direct result of punishment for sin. The man was blind, therefore someone must have done wrong. We can understand this reasoning in the case of parental sin, but what are we to make of the suggestion that the man might have sinned prenatally? The truth is that in Jewish thought of the time it was quite possible to think of a person sinning prenatally as a fetus in utero. Commentaries on specific Old Testament passages of that era reveal it was believed that when, for example, a pregnant Jewish woman worshipped in a heathen temple the fetus also was guilty of the sin of idolatry! All the disciples are querying, then, is whether there was this type of prenatal sin by the man or whether his parents alone were to blame.

Incidentally, in his reply to the disciples' question, Jesus is made to reject explicitly the disease-as-a-result-of-sin doctrine. I can find nothing in the words here to suggest reincarnational views.

This brings us to what Cranston and Williams call "The Case of Elijah and John the Baptist." The prophet Elijah, who is held by many to have lived in the ninth century BCE, went up to heaven in a chariot of fire instead of dying in the normal manner, according to the Old Testament record. Much later, the prophet Malachi proclaimed that God would send Elijah back to earth before the final "Day of the Lord"—the end of all things. This was widely interpreted as meaning that before the Messiah came, Elijah would return to presage his arrival. The followers of Jesus, believing him to be the Messiah, naturally then were concerned to know what had happened to the forerunner.

Indeed, in the passage known as Peter's Confession, where Christ asks his disciples, "Whom do men say that I am?" the reply comes, "Some say John the Baptist, others say Elijah, and others Jeremiah or one of the prophets."[24] In other words, some of his contemporaries took Jesus to be Elijah, come back from the dead.

The issue becomes explicit in Matthew, chapter 11. Here Jesus tells his disciples that John the Baptist is indeed "Elijah who is to come." Interestingly, according to John's Gospel, when John the Baptist himself was asked whether or not he was Elijah he denied it quite abruptly. What are we to make of the Elijah references? Cranston and Williams—in agreement with their sources—have no doubts. They are convinced that Jesus explicitly believed there is such a thing as reincarnation and that the words about Elijah and John confirm this.

But there are two overwhelming difficulties with their reasoning. In the first place, the belief in the return of Elijah was never thought of in terms of the orthodox reincarnational position that the spirit keeps coming back but as someone else. What the Jews believed was that Elijah would come back *as himself*. He had not died as other humans do and therefore God could send him back, not as a child, but as the fully mature adult he was when he died. Second, there is a literalist reading of the text here that betrays a complete ignorance of Semitic thinking and of the Biblical use of typology. For a full understanding of this one should read Northrop Frye's *The Great Code*.[25] For our purposes, however, it is sufficient to point out that when the Gospels speak of John the Baptist as "Elijah who is to come," they are in no way making a direct, one-to-one identification. This is not how typology works. What was being said was that John the Baptist was playing the role of an Elijah, that he represented or stood for what was meant in the symbolism of a returning Elijah. To say "John is Elijah" is to speak in the same way as Paul does when he says Christ is a second Adam, or as Christ himself reportedly did at the Last Supper when he took bread and wine and said, "This is my body . . . this is my blood."

I am surprised that such a scholar as Professor MacGregor would strain the text to the point where he takes all references to returning prophets as evidence that the theory of reincarnation was commonplace among the first Christians. He says these questions "were characteristic of the way people were thinking at the time of Jesus."[26] Nobody doubts that it was held that great saints—and in the case of Nero, great sinners—might return, but there was no suggestion of a belief that they might be reborn as somebody new and different.

The story of the Transfiguration in Mark, chapter 9, with parallel accounts in Luke and Matthew, is also used by the authors as evidence for reincarnation in the New Testament. This time both Elijah and Moses are involved. The narrative is a familiar one. Jesus leads his inner circle of disciples, Peter, James and John, up a high mountain. There he is transfigured before them and is seen talking with Moses and Elijah. It seems obvious to me that this whole passage is mythical. Liberal scholars would argue that the entire meaning of the event is theological. In other words, it is inserted into the text by the evangelist to express the early Church's deep conviction that Christ's teaching was in full accord with and in fulfillment of both the law (Moses) and the prophets (Elijah).

Undoubtedly, supposing it was historical, the theological import given to it would have been the same. But even if it actually happened just as it is described—and there are modern accounts of Indian and other holy men that come amazingly close—does it provide evidence for reincarnation from the New Testament? The enthusiasts think so, but similar arguments to those I have used above apply. Moses and Elijah are not reborn here, nor do they appear as entities other than they originally were. After the descent from the mountain, when they ask about the coming of Elijah to precede the Messiah, they are told that Elijah, that is, John the Baptist, has come already and they (Herod) have done to him "what they wished."

In his book *Mystical Christianity*, the Reverend Thomas Strong, a contender for Christian belief in reincarnation, calls this incident "interesting" because it "indicates that reincarnation was accepted by the disciples, and Christ's reply confirms he also believes it."[27] My conclusions, after much study and thought, run totally contrary to his. You can only get reincarnation out of the New Testament if you have already determined to find it there before you start. This doesn't mean that the doctrine itself is not true; it does mean we should beware of those who too glibly assert that it's all there "in the Book" if you're willing to read between the lines.

I have spent some time on this because, as a former professor of the New Testament, I have direct knowledge and expertise in this field and because so many unfounded claims have been and are still being made by New Agers about what the Bible "says" on this matter. The time for an honest appraisal and rebuttal of such glibly inaccurate affirmations is long overdue.

Some Problems with Reincarnation

Despite what may be said by either the supporters or the opponents of reincarnation in general, there is absolutely no way of proving or disproving the theory at this time. One can simply look at all the various arguments for and against and come to a reasoned stance of acceptance, disbelief or open-minded skepticism. If it is true, then of course there obviously is life after death—many lives in fact. If it is not, we would have to look elsewhere in our search for clues. Having given it much thought ever since first encountering the theory while reading Plato at Oxford as an undergraduate, having read as widely as possible in the current literature and having had time since first writing about it to weigh the responses of a wide range of critics of my views, I feel more open to the theory of reincarnation than I did twenty years ago and am still working towards a deeper understanding of the subject. Some questions I have had about the theory, however, continue to make the truth unclear:

1. The argument that the law of karma—"As a man soweth so shall he surely reap"—explains all the manifest injustices of life is one that is made repeatedly in the reincarnational literature I have studied. We keep coming back, or rather our souls do, in dozens of rebirths until all the necessary lessons are learned. The good news, in this view, is, presumably, that this one life here and now is not our only chance. Each of us gets another, and another—in fact, as many chances as we need to "get it right." Nobody will ever be lost or damned because there are endless opportunities to atone for past misdeeds and to learn true virtues.

    There is a surface appearance of plausibility about this that has attracted many, including some very bright people. I think in particular of the late Reverend Leslie Weatherhead, of London, England (1893–1976), who to my mind was one of the greatest preachers of the twentieth century and who came to accept reincarnation in his later years. (The serious reader may want to read chapter 14, "Reincarnation and Renewed Chances," in his book *The Christian Agnostic*.) When you think about it at length, however, it seems that some rather large contradictions arise.

In spite of all the recent emphasis on past-life recall, it is central to the orthodox theory of reincarnation that one forgets one's previous lives. "The cumulative pain might be too great otherwise," we are told. In the Platonic myth, for example, souls drink from the river of forgetfulness (Lethe) before they can be reborn. But if the vast majority of us cannot remember our previous incarnations, where is the justice in having to suffer for mistakes committed in them, or in benefitting from good deeds we cannot know? If I have absolutely no memory of a particular action, punishing me or rewarding me for it accomplishes little, I believe.

The problem is made worse by the fact that in certain versions of reincarnation the personality of the individual does not survive each death and rebirth; only the soul goes on from body to body. But if there is no memory and no continuity of personality, what sense does it make to say that any one of us actually survives death at all? If you die as one person and come back as another, why should the second have to pay for the sins of the first? If Hitler, for example, were to come back as John Jones the farmer, with no memory of his abominations and a wholly different personality, how is justice served by the said John Jones having to endure untold hardships or horrors?

I have serious doubts about the value of a belief that tells me I have lived many times before when I haven't the slightest glimmering of a memory of any of it. It's fine to say we're in a kind of cosmic school, where we learn successive lessons about life and gradually purify ourselves. That may well be so. But if I can't remember a single thing from all of this, of what use are these lessons and who is the "I" who is supposed to be the student? I know it is argued that while we forget the details of past lives (unless there is a hypnotist around) the really important lessons are retained as changes in the inner nature of our souls themselves. But since memory is an essential part of what makes me me and you you, I have difficulty seeing in what sense we remain the same person through repeated reincarnations, or what possible good it does us to be told that we have lived before.

I spoke about this criticism to Dr. Joel Whitton, a noted Toronto psychiatrist and author of the popular book *Life Between Life*, a study of the Bardo.[28] Dr. Whitton noted there are various views of karma, all the way from the older "an eye for an eye" belief, where one gets back in successive lives exactly what one has handed out, to that of the alchemists who taught that it simply refers to the process whereby the point of any given event or experience in each incarnation is: What am I supposed to learn from it for my overall growth? Whitton subscribes to the view that for the most part the lack of memory of previous lives is a good thing because "with an average of twenty or so lives behind us, as some authorities hold, there would be just too much pain involved in remembering it all." He added that most exponents of reincarnation in the West—and the Lamaist Buddhists of Tibet—believe that while names, outward circumstances and so forth do change, the essential person remains throughout each life lived. "Tom," he said, "would continue to be recognizable as Tom for those with the proper discernment."

2. I am quite aware that in the great world religions that hold reincarnation as a key doctrine it is accepted not because it

suits their fancy but because of deep insights and convictions
that this is the way the universe operates. But I must confess
that the working out, over countless millions of years, of this
cold, impersonal force called karma seems to me to reduce
the cosmos and the "wheel of life" to a chilling, heartless kind
of machine. Since it will all end one day in an equilibrium of
the universe leading inevitably to another cycle of cosmic
rebirth, one has to ask: What is the point of it all? If we have
done it all and seen it all before, not once but perhaps a myriad of times, ultimately can anything be more meaningless?
One can agree with the advocates of reincarnation when they
argue that surely one lifetime is too short to learn all the spiritual truth of which the human soul is capable. But that does
not constitute proof of reincarnation. It only adds to the evidence already before us that belief in some form of existence
beyond our life span on earth is truly universal.

However, in spite of the problems, I'm certainly keeping
an open mind on the subject. With my more mythological
approach to the Gospel story as given in 2004 in *The Pagan
Christ*, my understanding of our evolution and human destiny
has undergone a sea change. I now firmly believe that in spite
of all the evils currently present in our world, we are indeed
moving forward to what the renowned Catholic scientist
Teilhard de Chardin called "the Omega Point," a consummation of our spiritual potential.[29] Or, to use the phrase from
Masefield's poem with which this chapter began, there will
come a day for each and every one of us when "this clogging
mould" of our present state will by the divine alchemy "be
smithied all to kingly gold." It is possible, it now seems to
me, that some process of reincarnation, perhaps in worlds or
other dimensions far beyond this, could be the instrument
to bring this final miracle of resurrection to fulfillment.

5

DREAMS
OF DEATH
AND DYING

M Y FIRST ACQUAINTANCE with the remarkable Dr. Marie-Louise von Franz came when I attended a two-day symposium in Toronto, in the summer of 1987, at which we viewed a unique series of films called *The Way of the Dream*. The films, a documentary series produced and directed by Fraser Boa, a Canadian Jungian dream analyst, featured Dr. von Franz in her Zurich consulting room commenting on and interpreting the dreams of a wide range of people, from California surfers to skinheads in London and business executives in New York.

Like the many thousands who have given this series standing ovations in most of the major cities of Europe and North America, I was captivated by the depth of wisdom and insight displayed. Dr. von Franz, now deceased, was the foremost living successor of the Swiss psychiatrist Dr. Carl Jung, who pioneered research into the world of dreams. "He discovered that dreams attempt to regulate and balance both our physical and mental energies," said Boa. "They not only reveal the root cause of inner disharmony and emotional distress, but also indicate the latent potential for life within the individual." Dreams offer innovative solutions to problems of daily life and creative directions for the individual in his or her life journey. Jung came to realize that it is often in our dreams that we gradually discover our own true identity.[1] Dr. von Franz worked directly with Jung for over thirty years, collaborating on at least two of his books. Like Jung, she believes that our dreams are the "voice of nature within us" and so cannot be manipulated. If one can see the meaning of their symbolism—for the language of dreams is always symbolic—one can get an objective view of the psychic reality within. Having analysed more than sixty-five thousand dreams in a lifetime devoted to this approach to healing the soul, she then wrote what in my opinion is one of the most important books ever written as far as the question of life after death is concerned, *On Dreams and Death, a Jungian Interpretation.*[2]

In her introduction, Dr. von Franz notes that in the incredible outpouring of books about death and dying that began soon after the 1976 publication of Raymond Moody's *Life After Life* and has gone on apace ever since, very little of a scientific nature has been said about dreams. Yet, as her patients have revealed to her over the years, the unconscious, through dreams, speaks often and eloquently about death, especially in the second half of life. In fact, she noted, compared with near-death experiences, dreams are much more graphic, varied and detailed. The imagery is much richer: "Compared with dreams, near-death experiences appear schematic and more specifically culture-formed. It seems to me that the individuals experience something inexpressible in the death experiences which they then elaborate in culture-specific images."[3]

We have already seen just how true this is in our discussion of the NDE phenomenon. What the doctor is talking about is the way in which there is a certain set pattern now expected in the recounting of an NDE, and why someone from the American Bible Belt, for example, will talk about "seeing" Jesus or angels where a Hindu from India will "see" the Lord Krishna or some other deity.

Dr. von Franz says that her analysis of the dreams of older people has provided a wealth of dream symbols that "psychically prepare the dreamers for impending death." Nature, or God, it seems, has a concern to prepare the individual for the ultimate and inevitable end of physical life. Yet, she notes, Jung himself emphasized strongly that the unconscious psyche very obviously "believes" in a life after death. The dream symbols seem to indicate certain basic, archetypal structures existing in the very depths of the soul that behave "as if the psychic life of the individual . . . will simply continue." There are indeed dreams, as examples will demonstrate, that use vivid symbols to show "the end of bodily life *and the explicit continuation of psychic life after death* [italics mine]."4

Of course, von Franz was aware that skeptics will immediately pounce upon such statements and say that what we are dealing with here is the projection in dreams of our own lust for immortality. She refutes this objection by pointing out that Jung himself has shown quite clearly how dreams much more often portray a wholly objective psychic "natural event" that is quite uninfluenced by the desires of the ego. The best example of this, she says, is the case where the dreamer won't accept the truth of his or her impending death or is utterly unaware how close it is: "Dreams may even indicate this fact quite brutally and mercilessly, as, for instance, in the motif of the dreamer's clock which has stopped and cannot be started again, or the theme of the life-tree, which has been hewn down and is lying on the ground."5 This point is of such great importance it is impossible to overemphasize it. The evidence which follows here cannot simply be shrugged off with the kind of easy criticism I myself so often hear whenever I mention life after death in my columns— "That's just wish-fulfillment speaking."

No healthy person wishes to die, either physically or psychically. As Dr. von Franz remarks, "The comforting message of the unconscious—that death is a 'cure' and that there is an afterlife—

obviously cannot be interpreted here as a wish-fulfillment dream, for at the same time the end of physical existence is also predicted, quite brutally and unequivocally." She says that many people begin to dream of death from middle age on. "Such dreams do not indicate an immediately impending death, but are rather to be understood as a *memento mori*." They are reminders, particularly when the individual has an "overly youthful attitude towards life," that death is a reality, and they call the dreamer to think about it seriously.[6]

The Dreams

The entire literature about death and dying from the dawn of history is filled with references to plants—grass, grain or trees, for example—as symbols of the continuity of life after death. This theme runs all through the myths of the ancient Egyptians, the Greeks and the Druids. In the Gospels, it speaks of the natural law that a kernel of wheat must fall to the ground and die if the wheat is to spring up to renewed, transformed life. The plain reference is to the spiritual truth of the need for the death of the individual as the gateway to rising again.[7] In the Book of Revelation, which we will examine later, the seer's vision of the next world is filled with images of trees. There is the tree of life whose leaves are "for the healing of the nations." Similarly in the Qur'an we find that in the Islamic paradise there are many trees of precious stones, especially the *tula* tree which has "its roots in the sky and its light reaches into every corner of the world." From her many thousands of dream analyses, Dr. von Franz testifies to the recurrence of such vegetation imagery in the dreams of the dying. In each case, the meaning clearly denotes the deep-seated belief of the unconscious mind that life goes on beyond the grave.

Here is the dream of a dying seventy-five-year-old man: "I see an old, gnarled tree high up on a steep bluff. It is only half-rooted in the earth, the remainder of the roots reaching into the empty air . . .

Then it becomes separated from the earth altogether, loses its support, and falls. My heart misses a beat. But then, something wonderful happens: the tree floats, it does not fall, it floats. Where to? Into the sea? I do not know." The tree, which here clearly symbolizes the dying man, his life and his potential for growth or what Jung called "individuation," teeters on the brink of the abyss and then falls. In other words, death is frankly faced and admitted. But then to his utter surprise, the tree floats. It is not destroyed but exists in an entirely new way.

The doctor then cites the dream of another man who died a few days later. He sees himself as on or in a sky-blue "air-liquid" that seems shaped like an egg. Then he feels he is "falling into the blue, into the universe." But suddenly he is caught and carried by what appears to be a little blue cloth. The feeling of falling into the universe is repeated, and part of him welcomes this, but again he feels himself "caught by cloths and by people who speak to me." The small cloths surround him and he sees a red staircase which then becomes a Christmas tree.

At first, the dream seems an insolvable enigma or sheer fantasy. But for one experienced in dream symbolism and the archetypes of the unconscious mind, it speaks lucidly of his psyche's belief in a continuing life beyond the grave. The dreamer feels he is about to fall into nothingness, to disintegrate. The cloths or "honorary garments" protect him from destruction. People reassure him of ongoing community. The tree—a Christmas tree, with all the lights and celebration that go with this image—symbolizes growth towards fuller spiritual or inner maturity. Thus, Dr. von Franz concludes, "The dream seems to say to the dreamer that in the Beyond he will continue to grow and to develop toward a higher degree of awareness."

The following dream is that of a young woman whose body had been taken over by cancer. Once it reached the brain, she was unconscious most of the time. The therapist, a colleague of Dr. von

Franz's, continued to visit her regularly, sitting at her bedside in silence. Some twenty-four hours before she died, the patient suddenly opened her eyes and told of a dream she had just had:

"I am standing beside my bed in the hospital room and I feel strong and healthy. Sunshine flows in at the window. The doctor is there and says, 'Well, Miss X, you are unexpectedly completely cured. You may get dressed and leave the hospital.' At that moment I turn around and see, lying in the bed—my own dead body!"

Dr. von Franz's comments are significant. She says that while the unconscious is clearly stating that death is a form of cure and that the young woman's life will go on renewed beyond the grave, at the same time it is not indulging in mere wishful thinking. It announces the impending physical death of the patient with a brutal clarity.

An old woman, earlier in the day on which she died, had a dream in which she sees a candle lit on the windowsill of her hospital room. Quite suddenly the candle goes out. "Fear and anxiety ensue as the darkness envelops her. Suddenly the candle lights on the other side of the window and she awakens."[8] The woman died wholly at peace because she was helped to see the dream's meaning. The candle in some mysterious way dematerializes and then materializes on the other side of the closed window. The meaning being communicated by her unconscious mind, according to von Franz, is that the "light" of the individual goes out at death but is miraculously renewed *on the other side*.

The dream of another elderly European woman, just before her death, reaches the same conclusion through different imagery. In this case, she has packed two suitcases for a journey. One has her working clothes; the other contains her diaries, her photographs and her jewellery. She is aware that the first is for the "mainland" but the other is "for America." Dr. von Franz comments that the old lady's unconscious is making her aware that in dying she is on a journey where she will not be able to take along her everyday attitudes and her physical body, "But she can take along her inner psychic treasures." Obviously America is the symbol for "the Beyond," or life in the hereafter.9

Another dream, this one sent to Jung himself by an elderly man, recalls something of the dream of the man who felt himself falling into the universe and then being caught and given the vision of the Christmas tree:

"He meets two . . . guides who lead him to a building where he finds many people, among them his father . . . and his mother who give him a kiss of welcome. He has to go on a long climb ending at the edge of a deep precipice. A voice commands him to leap; after several desperate refusals he obeys and finds himself swimming 'deliciously into the blue of eternity.'" Jung saw this dream as a preparation for coming death and wrote to the man to point out the Hindu belief that the dying rise upwards to the cosmic *Atman* where they find "allness" or "increasing completeness."10

Thus far, we have examined specific examples of dreams to show how they can illustrate the belief of our deepest natures in some kind of ongoing life after death. As Dr. von Franz notes, all such dreams of people facing death "indicate that the unconscious, that is our instinct world, prepares consciousness not for a definite end but for a profound transformation and for a kind of continuation of the life process which, however, is unimaginable to everyday consciousness."11 What's more, her research shows beyond dispute that the symbols that appear in dreams to convey this message, while greatly varied, "present a thematic or structural harmony with the teachings of the various religions about life after death." They use mythical images drawn not just from the world's great religions but from religions and cults going back to the earliest stages of civilization. None of this by itself proves beyond a shadow of a doubt that there is a life after death, but it is a fascinating, new and, it seems to me, strong piece of evidence pointing in that direction.

Dreams of Ordinary, Healthy People

Over the years many readers have written to describe vivid, highly meaningful dreams they have had either of loved ones who have died recently or of those who were very soon to make the transition to "the other side." In cultures we often wrongly describe as primitive, such dreams are taken seriously as a form of communication. Difficult though it might be, it seems to me an area in need of more research and analysis following the path already pioneered by Dr. von Franz. Here are some of these dreams:

- A.U. writes: "I dreamed that I was in that familiar tunnel spinning towards an ever brighter light; ahead of me there were a man and a woman who vanished in the light. I was on the brink of entering into the light when I awoke. It was a dream, pure and simple, except for one very remarkable thing. Upon awakening, I was bathed in a state of peace and love which defies description. It was that peace that 'transcends all understanding.' I only wanted to return to the light. During that time I was very much involved in meditation at a Sri Chinmoy Centre. My experience was relayed to a Sri Chinmoy guru in New York. He believed that I must have had a 'health incident' but it was not my time to go. I had no health problems then and I don't now. I do not believe in an afterlife and I am a lifelong atheist, albeit one with an open mind. If there is some form of awareness after death and it is accompanied by such feelings as I had, then I am more than ready to kick the bucket. I believe that the lowliest microbe to the highest life forms are nothing more than organisms striving to exist on a hospitable planet. Upon death—eternal nothingness. Then again, there is that dream I had . . ."

- A.S. writes: "The saddest day of my life came when my wife of forty-seven years died of Alzheimer's disease. But before then, I had four or five unusual dreams of her, all similar. In these dreams, I was walking on country terrain when a voice called my name, always from behind me. I turn around, and there's my wife, looking radiantly healthy and wearing a lovely coloured, very bright dress. I cry out, 'Is that really you?' and she answers, 'Yes, yes, it's me!' 'Are you alright?' I exclaim, 'Is everything okay?' Again comes her cheerful answer, 'Yes, I am fine and well.' Since her demise these dreams have ceased altogether."

- S.C. had a dream a few days after her father died. In the dream, although she knew her father had died, he appeared before her. She was very concerned about how he was feeling, but he said his health problems were gone, and he felt well. She asked what he was doing, and he said he was doing the same things he did here, i.e., reading, gardening, painting, etc. The dream was so strong it woke her up. She recognized the difference in the intensity of this dream from others because she had had a similar experience on the death of her brother. In that dream, he called her name three times and on the third time she awoke with the feeling of a powerful explosion coming from her chest. As with the previous letter writer, she had also had dreams of her brother in the months preceding his death from a long illness and in these dreams he was healthy and young, looking vibrant.

- E.L. writes: "As a young man I left my home in B.C. and went to Australia. In December 1965 I had been away for a little more than five years and was preparing to take a meandering journey back home. One day, while I was at work, my landlord called to say that a telegram had arrived. I asked him to open it and read the contents to me. My father had died suddenly. I was shocked but then remembered that I had had a dream the night before. In my dream I had gone to visit some friends. While there, a knock came to the front door, which was odd because everybody who knew these people always came to the back door. I was in the living room so I opened the door. My dad was standing there and he gave me a big hug. I had never felt particularly close to my dad—I was the oldest child and not exactly a 'chip off of the old block.' Ever since, the memory of that dream has warmed and encouraged me. And I am convinced that the spirit of my father came across the ocean to wish me 'Goodbye!'"

- R.H. writes: "I believe I had a spiritual visit from my deceased father sixteen years after his death. I was thirty-four at the time and a very heavy smoker. My father came to me in a dream and told me to stop smoking. In the dream, only his face appeared. The image was in vivid colour. I had never had such an extremely clear dream before nor since that occurrence. The image has never left me. Anytime I've thought about it in the ensuing years I see the vision as clearly as the night that it happened, and I'm now seventy-eight. Needless to say, I quit smoking a few days later and have never smoked since. I'm sure I'm alive today as a result of that visit by my father's spirit forty-four years ago."

We must turn now to some equally intriguing material from neurology and physics.

6

NEW LIGHT
FROM SCIENCE

*"What is one to say to the assertion that brain machinery
has accounted for the mind, the spirit of man, and the idea
of God? . . . It is a basic tenet of materialism. But, I find no
evidence to support it in [my] studies of the human brain."*

— DR. WILDER PENFIELD, neurosurgeon and author[1]

IN POLLING READERS of my column about their views and
experiences with regard to an afterlife, I have over the years
received a number of skeptical letters on the topic ranging all
the way from an agnostic position—"I simply don't know"—to
adamant denial of any such possibility. The following excerpt is
typical of the view put forward by the most rigidly and rigorously
opposed. It comes from a Bramalea, Ontario, businessman: "If you
would just step outside your thoughts and look at the question logically you would quickly see that the belief in an afterlife is simply
wishful thinking . . . No, Mr. Harpur, there is no life after death . . .
When we die we are just as dead and gone as the cow that provided
the roast beef for lunch. The cow has simply returned to its ele-
mental parts and that is what will happen to both you and me when
we depart this life. Our thoughts are just so much electrochemical
reaction and they will be gone too . . . Sorry to be such a wet blanket
but that's the way it is."

I am tempted to stop here and critique the dogmatism and blind faith aspects of "that's the way it is" and to ask this respondent how, if our thoughts are "just so much electrochemical reaction," he can ask me to "step outside them." I mean, who is it who is doing the "stepping outside"? But I'll let that pass for the moment because I want to show that this reader has more or less stated the classical position of rationalistic, humanist doubters. The simplest way to do that is to quote the brilliant agnostic Lord Bertrand Russell from his book *Why I Am Not a Christian*:

"All the evidence goes to show that what we regard as our mental life is bound up with brain structure and organized bodily energy. Therefore it is rational to suppose that mental life ceases when body life ceases."[2]

The nineteenth-century biologist Thomas H. Huxley made a similar point when he said, "The thoughts to which I am giving utterance and your thoughts regarding them are the expression of molecular exchanges."[3]

Russell devotes a complete chapter, "Do We Survive Death?" to the question of life after death, but his chief argument against the proposition is the materialistic one that the mind or consciousness is merely a function of brain "machinery" and so must perforce cease when the brain dies. Because of his total acceptance of what is now called "The Old Story of Science," Russell believed we are nothing but the result of purely mechanical, chance causes, "the outcome of accidental collocations of atoms." Thus he was able to say that "no fire, no heroism, no intensity of thought and feeling, can preserve an individual life beyond the grave." This led to his now-famous, if somewhat mournful, dictum: "Only on the scaffolding of these truths, only on the firm foundation of unyielding despair, can the soul's habitation henceforth be safely built."[4]

There is a major problem, however, for this kind of objection to the belief in an afterlife today: it is based on a scientific world view that has now been completely transformed. People like Russell and many others who still argue that the mind is simply a matter of brain function or that matter is the sole and ultimate reality are wholly out of touch with recent developments in physics, neurophysiology, the study of the human brain and nervous system, and the new cosmology. The best, brief introduction to this area of knowledge is the striking work *The New Story of Science*, with a preface by the great neurosurgeon Sir John Eccles. It's written by two Americans, Robert M. Augros and George N. Stanciu. I can do no more here than to sketch the main outline of the argument, but its importance cannot be overemphasized. Scientists are obviously not in the business of attempting to "prove" a life after death. What is significant is that, because of their new insights, the old, so-called scientific or rationalistic "proofs" that the grave is the final end no longer bear close scrutiny.

Here's why I say this. The old view of science held, with Newton, that atoms were the ultimate particles of matter—hard, impenetrable and, as the original Greek behind the word suggests, uncuttable or indivisible into smaller particles. Matter, space, time— these are the Newtonian ingredients of the cosmos, all of them obeying unalterable laws, such as gravity. The scientist, as observer, stood, as it were, outside looking on as he did his measurements and experiments. But since 1903, when Russell first penned the words quoted above from *Why I Am Not a Christian*, incredible changes have taken place. First of all, Einstein's theory of relativity led physics to abandon the ideas of both absolute space and absolute time. The observer is not apart from, but is *a part of*, the world of physics. Time and space are relative to the point at which the observer takes his or her stand. "Einstein showed that space-time and the laws of motion can be defined only by reference to an observer and his physical conditions."[5]

Then a similar revolution occurred in the realm of particle physics. Instead of being a hard, ultimate piece of matter, it was established by Ernest Rutherford in 1911 that an atom consists of an inner nucleus surrounded by a host of invisible electrons. This led eventually to the overthrow of Newtonian atomic theory and the development of quantum mechanics by thinkers such as Niels Bohr and Werner Heisenberg in the 1920s. Two things happened here. In quantum mechanics it was realized that the old idea of the scientist as unobserved observer "looking on," already put in question by Einstein's theory of relativity, had to be completely scrapped. The mere act of observing electrons, for example, was found to interfere with their behaviour. The observer becomes a participant in the world he is trying to observe. As Augros and Stanciu remark, "In some strange sense, this is a participatory universe." Now in science there is what is called the anthropic cosmological principle. Humans are essential to understanding the whole of the cosmos.

The second significant aspect of this discovery that atoms are balls of energy rather than bits of indestructible matter is that it led to the current view of material reality by physicists as "a cosmic dance of energy" rather than as some kind of stuff or substance.[6] That's why modern physicists often come close to the language of mysticism when they try to describe the underlying basis of the cosmos. This is a theme we will return to in a moment. For now, we turn to look more closely at the role played by the human mind or consciousness vis-à-vis the universe.

In the Newtonian model, mind played no important part in the physical realities of the universe. With relativity and quantum mechanics, however, it is an essential part of the whole. Thus, Augros and Stanciu can state: "Physics in the twentieth century has gradually replaced materialism with the affirmation that mind plays an essential role in the universe."[7] This raises immediately the question of the nature of mind. As we have seen, in the old view, mind was nothing more than a function of the physical brain. To be wholly made up of matter meant to be totally subject to mortality and decay, as both my respondent above and Bertrand Russell made clear. The only thing that is eternal in that view, as the pre-Socratic philosopher Democritus noted over two millennia ago, is matter itself.

But it is at this point that twentieth-century neurophysiology comes in. Sir Charles Sherrington (1857–1952), who was in many ways the founder of contemporary neurophysiology, said that, as a result of his research on the human nervous system and the brain, he had to conclude that "a radical distinction has . . . arisen between [physical] life and mind. The former is a matter of physics and chemistry; the latter escapes chemistry and physics."[8] Sherrington came to the conviction that our humanity has two fundamental elements, matter and mind. Sir John Eccles agrees: "Conscious experiences . . . are quite different from any goings-on in the neuronal machinery."[9] The biologist Adolf Portmann, in his book *New Pathways in Biology*, puts it this way: "No amount of research along physical or chemical lines can ever give us a full picture of psychological, spiritual or intellectual processes."[10] In other words, while the mind depends on the physical brain as its tool or base in this life, it is nevertheless something different from and greater than the brain itself. In his watershed book, *The Mystery of the Mind, A Critical Study of Consciousness and the Human Brain*, the distinguished Canadian neurosurgeon Dr. Wilder Penfield noted that the mind seems to act with an energy all its own. It makes decisions and puts them into action by employing the various mechanisms of the brain, but it is something more than these mechanisms themselves.[11] Thus, as the authors of *The New Story of Science* point out, "expecting the mind to be found in some part of the brain, or in the whole brain, is like expecting the programmer to be a part of the computer."[12]

If the mind is not simply a matter of "electrochemical reaction," as our Bramalea businessman insists, the whole basis of his argument falls to pieces. What the neuroscientists are now saying reveals that the mind, as Penfield put it, "may be a distinct and different essence" from the body altogether.[13] Reading Penfield's reflections, not just in *The Mystery of the Mind* but in his essay "Science, the Arts and the Spirit," in his book *Second Thoughts*, as well as in his other numerous articles and books, one is struck by a remarkable irony or paradox. Penfield admits quite candidly that he began his career and struggled for years to fulfill his intention of proving that "the brain accounts for the mind." All his research, however, brought him to the inescapable conclusion that the materialistic view of the mind was wholly untenable. "The physical basis of the mind is the brain action in each individual. It accompanies the activity of his spirit. But the spirit is free . . . No brain mechanism has yet been demonstrated that directs the action of the mind."[14] Carrying the logical consequences of this kind of finding into the realm of our special interest, Eccles says: "What a thrill it is to discover that the scientist too can legitimately believe in spirit." Since the mind and will are non-material, it then becomes possible for such scientists to argue that they are "*not subject in death to the disintegration that affects both the body and the brain* [italics mine]."[15]

The American neurophysiologist Candace Pert, whom many predict will shortly be a prime candidate for a Nobel Prize in science for her work on neuropeptides—the agents of messages from the central nervous system to all parts of the body—has built upon this earlier research. She believes the mind is not located spatially in the cranium but is present throughout the entire body. She has gone on record with her belief that when a person dies, something akin to the spirit or soul leaves the physical body of the deceased.

In my view, Christian theologians and those of most other faiths still at the beginning of this new millennium have not taken these new developments in physics and neuroscience as seriously as they ought. Those interested in a rational approach to the belief in life after death will get more insight in this area from the work of Carl Jung and his disciple, Marie-Louise von Franz, than from official religious sources. In *On Dreams and Death*, von Franz has a chapter on the "subtle" or astral body and one on Jung's "new hypothesis," in which she introduces these new findings of physics and neuroscience to a rationale for an afterlife. She discusses the widespread belief in China, wherever Hinduism has spread, among primitive peoples, in ancient Egypt and among the great majority of Christians who believe in a resurrection of the body, that each person has not just a physical body but also a subtle body that survives death. In theory this body, which has many names—a spiritual body, a sidereal or "star" body—is made up of a finer, more intense energy than the physical body. (For a credible explanation of soul in scientific terms, see *The Seat of the Soul* by Gary Zukav.) Given the way physics now sees that even the coarsest of material substances is ultimately made up of a "cosmic dance of energy," von Franz argues that it may one day be shown that the psychic energy of the soul or mind-spirit is part of a continuum that underlies all three aspects of our humanity—mind, subtle body and physical body. She goes on to point out that Jung himself formulated this kind of hypothesis in a letter to a friend.[16]

Jung defined the psyche or inner self thus: "Psyche = highest intensity [of energy] in the smallest space." He likened the human brain to a kind of "transformer station" in which the exceedingly intense energy of the mind—"transcending, for instance, the velocity of light"—is changed or transformed into frequencies or "extensions" suitable for our use in our earthly, space-time mode. This seems to me to be an even more potent analogy for mind-brain relationship than that of the computer as brain and mind as the programmer.

The point being made by Jung and von Franz is that we may be dealing here with a form of energy that gradually changes or moves from the *physically* measurable—as in the measuring of brainwaves by an EEG—to the *psychically* immeasurable. Von Franz concludes: "The subtle body in this sense would then be a form of the psyche that would indeed remain close to the body but would also possess a certain minimal mass and extension in time-space." She quotes the physicist Frithjof Capra to underline the point already made that to speak of mass and extension can no longer be thought of in the crude terms of the "Old Story of Science": "In modern physics, mass is no longer associated with a material substance, and hence particles are not seen as consisting of any basic 'stuff,' but as bundles of energy."[17]

Once you conceive of matter in this way, von Franz rightly says, the idea of a body that is transformed into an intensity that is no longer visible in space and time becomes quite a rational concept. This whole mode of thinking has, it seems to me, not just enormous relevance to the renewal of religious thinking about the resurrection of the body, it also offers a radically new approach to the rationalization or understanding of such paranormal phenomena as apparitions or ghosts.

In our normal human condition, light is the highest perceivable form of energy intensity. It constitutes our ultimate limit. That is why near-death experiences, as well as the language of all religions, are filled with references to light. "*Deus illuminatio mea*, the Lord is my light," says the Psalmist. All early religions were almost obsessed with the solar orb, the sun, as the ultimate symbol of the divine in us and in the cosmos. The phrase "Light of Light" is one of humanity's highest attempts to describe or define the Deity. But today we know of energies more subtle and more powerful than light. Many modern physicists, Frithjof Capra, for instance, have gone so far as to postulate vast universes of energies of other frequencies that not only underlie our own but in a sense interlock with it. The work of physicist David Bohm, in particular, comes at once to mind. There are, in this view, many dimensions of reality or being going on simultaneously around us. We experience one, the physical, empirically; another, the psychic, through imagination, intuition and insight. But there may be others as well that we do not have either the "eyes" or "ears" to discern. It's a little like knowing that the air all around us is filled with transmissions of dozens of channels of television and radio programming—a veritable mael-strom of sounds and images—and yet, without a radio or a television, we are unaware of any signal whatsoever.

The material or physical universe, on this new scientific line of reasoning, could be a double of a subtler, psychic universe. The latter, Jung believed, is possessed of a transpersonal knowledge that he sums up in his idea of a collective unconscious from which the various great archetypes of our human unconscious arise. Considering all of this, in my view God would be the author and source of the eternal universe behind, beneath and through all the others, the ultimate consciousness and energy of the whole: the Circle whose centre is everywhere, whose circumference is everywhere as well.

What is truly exciting today is the way in which new studies in human consciousness, coupled with those in physics—take, for example, the ground-breaking research of Rupert Sheldrake of Cambridge with his theories of morphic resonance, as well as chaos theory—are deeply challenging all the nostrums of the materialistic, mechanistic philosophies of the first half of the twentieth century. The tables have been turned on those who once resorted to the name-calling of "wishful thinking" whenever the subject of life beyond death was raised. Today's wishful thinkers are increasingly those who deny belief in immortality because they deeply resent the notion that they may not be total masters of their own fate; that indeed they, and all of us, live *sub specie aeternitatis*, under the aegis of eternity. The ancient sages believed you will never be more dead than you are right now. This life, they argued, is a kind of death, and at what we mortals call death, the soul is truly resurrected to its real life in the light. Science is daily providing more evidence that they could well have been right. What is urgently needed right now is for scientists and theologians together to take this whole area of research far more seriously than ever before. It is of urgent importance for our understanding of the nature, purpose and destiny of the human organism. Fortunately, a distinguished, international group of scientists, philosophers and other experts in the field have now organized around the theme Survival of Bodily Death. Their purpose is to encourage and correlate scholarly research in this field and make it available to the public through their website, presently under construction. Readers can watch for it by searching "survival of bodily death."[18]

The single most important book on the whole subject of science, the brain and the nature of near-death experiences is *The Spiritual Brain*, published in 2007 and written by Dr. Mario Beauregard and journalist Denyse O'Leary. Beauregard, a Montreal neurosurgeon selected by the World Media Net to be among the "One Hundred Pioneers of the 21st Century," gives the fullest and most compelling rebuttal of the positions taken by Richard Dawkins (*The God Delusion*) and the many other vocal skeptics and atheists that I have read to date. Beauregard makes a powerful and convincing "neuroscientist's case for the existence of the soul" and debunks the entire line of reasoning that argues for a "God spot" or "God Gene" that is simply an evolutionary plus-factor—a neuronal survival feature fashioned by nature. His critique is a must read at a time when the materialist/mechanistic approach is receiving so much coverage in all the media. Most importantly, he has issued an urgent call for a new scientific frame of reference for studying the great questions of human existenc—life and death and the nature of the soul. Such a frame, he argues, "will recognize that dogmatic materialist scientism is not synonymous with science" (page 294). One would have to say Amen to that!

Given all of the above, it is now time to look more closely at the religious and spiritual dimensions of belief in what one of the Christian creeds calls "the life of the world [or age] to come." The question before us in Part 2 is: Since the ultimate issue addressed by all religions since the dawn of recorded time has been that of some form of survival beyond the grave, what do the major faiths have to say? How compelling or persuasive is it?

THE WITNESS
OF RELIGION

CHRISTIANITY

The Witness of St. Paul

THOSE WHO HAVE little or no acquaintance with formal New Testament studies may be unaware that the letters of Paul were written before any of the four Gospels. In fact, the earliest letter of Paul was written at the very least fifteen or twenty years before the earliest Gospel, Mark. Thus, the first written account of the Resurrection of Jesus comes not in the Gospels but in Paul's first letter to the young Christians at Corinth, about 50 CE.

For the purpose of our study it is of great importance to recognize that in chapter 15 of I Corinthians, Paul is setting out what is regarded as the most primitive form of the tradition about witnesses to the Risen Christ. He adds the aura of authenticity to his account, not just by using the technical words of his time for the careful handing on of an oral tradition, but by noting that the majority of those witnesses cited are apparently still living at the time of writing. In other words, he is inviting the readers not simply to take his word for it; they can check it out with those who claimed to have been there when the various appearances occurred. He believes his claims can be verified. Added to all of this, he tells us, is his own personal, mystical encounter with Jesus on the road to Damascus.

For Paul, this life-changing experience, turning him from an arch-persecutor to a leading protagonist in the Church, was the clincher. Because this whole chapter is the strongest documentation for the belief in the Resurrection of Jesus, and because it sets out in very vivid detail Paul's thinking about the nature of a "bodily" resurrection for humanity, it ought to be much more familiar to the general public, Christian and non-Christian, than it has been or is. For this reason, and since I will be commenting on parts of it to clarify my own views on authentic Christian teaching about a future life, I want to let readers see for themselves just what it is Paul had to say. I must add that in the intervening years since the first version of this book was published my understanding and interpretation of this key passage have changed considerably. It is decidedly not the plain and simple testimony to a historical happening it once seemed to me to be.

When Paul says he "handed onto you at the beginning the tradition which I myself had received . . ." it sounds as though there was a specific set of teachings that had been given to him by other apostles or the tiny Christian community as a group. Many scholars have taken this as the clear meaning. However, such a view directly contradicts what Paul says elsewhere in his letters. For example, in his very personal letter to the Galatians he goes to great lengths to instill in them the awareness that he owes nothing to anyone of the message he preaches. He opens the letter with "Paul, an apostle, not from men nor through (other) men but through Jesus Christ and God the father who raised him from the dead." As explained earlier in *The Pagan Christ*, Paul's Jesus Christ is a spiritual, mythic being, not a historical person. All his knowledge about him, including his meeting with him as risen Lord, comes by "revelation," that is, by mystical experiences.

He makes this point with singular clarity a few verses later in Galatians I, chapter 11–12, where he almost raises his voice, so to speak, as he says: "I make it known to you, brothers, that the Gospel which I preach is not according to human sources, because I did not receive it [using the technical verb to receive a tradition] from humans, nor was I taught it. It came [to me] by revelation [that is, in a vision of some sort]." The rest of the chapter hammers home this same point. For example, in verse 16, he says it had pleased God "to reveal his son in me"—again a clear reference to the visionary, mystical nature of his encounters with the Risen Christ.[1]

Paul was a deeply mystical, intuitive person open to a whole range of paranormal experiences and no sound scholar will deny this. Deep study of such passages as II Corinthians 12 where he speaks of being caught up to Paradise and of "hearing things which cannot be spoken of," as in the mystery religions of his day, as well as of the accounts of his conversion in Acts, have made it more than clear to me that Paul did not know a Jesus "after the flesh" at all, but one wholly "after the spirit"—the Spiritual Christ of the Mythos.

It should also be noted that Paul's list as given in I Corinthians 15 not only does not match any other given in the New Testament, it directly contradicts the later Gospel testimony that the women were the first at the tomb and the first to encounter a (visionary) experience of the resurrected Christ. John, chapter 20, gives Mary Magdalene as the first to "see" him.

Also worth commenting on in passing is the obvious error contained in Paul's list of witnesses. He says the Risen Christ was seen by the Twelve (apostles). But, according to the Gospel records, Judas had already committed suicide by hanging (a part of the pre-Christian myth also) and he had not yet been replaced by Matthias. In conclusion, notice that this, if anywhere, was the logical point at which Paul ought to have cited the empty tomb. He says nothing about it at all, not here, not anywhere, because he obviously knew nothing whatever about it. It was a later tradition unknown to the very first believers.

What follows is my own translation of the original Greek text:

"Brothers [and sisters], I am making known to you the Gospel which I once preached to you, which you received, and in which you stand; through which also you are being saved—that is, if you are indeed holding my words steadfastly and have not simply believed in a reckless fashion.

"For, I handed on to you at the beginning the tradition which I myself had received: that Christ died for our sins, according to the Scriptures, that he was buried, and that he was raised on the third day according to the Scriptures. And that he was seen by Cephas [Peter], then by the Twelve. Then, he was seen by more than five hundred of the brethren at one time, of whom some have died but the majority are alive to this day. Then, he was seen by James, then by all the apostles. Last of all, he was seen by me also; it is as if I were somebody who had an untimely birth. My reason for saying this is that I am the least of all the apostles. I am not worthy to be called an apostle because I was a persecutor of the church of God.

"But, I am what I am by the Grace of God. For, his Grace towards me has not been in vain. I have toiled more vigorously than all the rest—yet not I, but the Grace of God that was with me. However, whether it was I or the others, so we go on preaching, and so you came to faith.

"If Christ is being proclaimed as one who was raised from the dead, how is it certain dissenters among you are saying that there is no resurrection of the dead? If there is no resurrection of the dead, then Christ was not raised up either. And it follows that if Christ was not raised up, then our preaching is empty and your faith is in vain, too. We are discovered to be false witnesses of God because we have borne testimony that God raised Christ—whom he did not raise up if indeed the dead are not raised. For, if the dead are not raised, Christ has not been raised either. And, if Christ be not raised, your faith is void and you are still in your sins. What's more, those who have died in Christ have perished utterly. If we have hope in Christ only in this life, we are more pitiable than all others!

"But now has Christ been raised from the dead as the first-fruits of those who have died. For since death came by a man [Adam], so too the Resurrection comes by a man [Jesus]. For, as in Adam all die, so too in Christ shall all be made alive, but each in his own order; Christ is the leader in this, then those who belong to Christ at his coming again.

"Then comes the consummation when he will hand over the kingdom to the Father; when he has abolished all rule, authority, and power. For he must reign until he has put all his enemies under his feet. The last enemy to be destroyed is death itself. 'For He has put all things under his feet,' the Scripture says. But when it says that all things have been subordinated to him, it is manifest that He who is the Agent of this subordination [God] is not included. When He has subjected all things unto him, then the Son himself will be made subordinate to Him that has made all things subject to him—in order that God may be All in All.

"Otherwise, what will they do who are having themselves baptized on behalf of their dead [loved ones]? If there is no way the dead are raised, why are they being baptized on their behalf? And why do we live in danger [as Christians] hour by hour? I swear to you as you are my pride in Christ Jesus, I die daily. If, humanly speaking, I fought with wild beasts when I was at Ephesus, what good did it do me if the dead are not raised? 'Let us eat, drink, and be merry, for tomorrow we die!'

"Don't be made to err: bad companions corrupt good character. Wake up to righteousness and don't go on in sin; for, some [there in Corinth] are ignorant of God's ways. I say this to shame you."

Paul then goes on to explain how resurrection is possible:

"But, someone will say: 'How are the dead raised? With what kind of body do they come?' Foolish person! Whatever you sow is not made to live unless it dies first. And what you sow is not the body that will come into being but a naked seed—perhaps of wheat or of some other plant. But, God gives it a body according to His will, and to each seed a body of its own. All flesh is not the same; there is human flesh, a flesh of beasts, of birds, and of fish. And there are heavenly bodies just as there are earthly bodies. But the glory of the heavenly is one thing; the glory of the earthly is another. There is one glory of the sun, but another of the moon, and another of the stars. For one star differs from another in brilliance.

"So, too, with the resurrection of the dead. It is sown in decay, it is raised up in immortality; it is sown in dishonour, it is raised up in glory; it is sown in weakness, it is raised up in power. What is 'sown' is an earthly or animal body, it is raised up as a spiritual body. There is a natural body and there is a spiritual [or psychic] body. Thus, it is written: 'The first man, Adam, became a living creature; the last Adam [Christ] became a life-giving spirit.' But the spiritual body is not first; rather, the natural body is first, and then comes the spiritual. The first man was of the earth, earthy; the second man was from heaven [the spiritual sphere]. Such as was the earthy, so too are those that are earthy. As was the heavenly, so too shall the heavenly be. And, just as we have borne the appearance of the earthy, so too shall we bear the likeness of the heavenly.

"I tell you this my friends: Flesh and blood cannot inherit the Kingdom of God. Nor can decay inherit immortality. Look, I am declaring a mystery to you: We shall not all die, but we shall all of us be changed, in a moment, in the twinkling of an eye, at the final trumpet sound. For the trumpet shall sound and the dead shall be raised up immortal, and we shall be changed. For this perishable body must be clothed with that which does not perish, and this mortal body must put on immortality. Then shall come to pass the saying that is written: Death is swallowed up in victory. Where, oh death, is thy victory? Death, where is thy sting?

"The sting of death is sin; and the power of sin comes from the law. But thanks be to God who keeps giving us the victory through our Lord, Jesus Christ. So, beloved brethren, be steadfast, immovable, always abounding in the work of the Lord. For you know that your labour is never in vain in the Lord."

The Resurrection of the Body

I do not believe that Paul was infallible; it is certainly not something he ever claimed for himself. In fact, he has a habit of making a sharp differentiation between those occasions when he has a specific "word of the Lord" to back what he is saying and when he is simply speaking on his own. There are many places where a modern understanding of issues (for example, the role and calling of women in the Church) is more spiritual than his culturally conditioned approach. But, granting his enormous intellect and his obvious, balancing, mystical insights, I believe that what he has to say about resurrection commands the greatest respect.

On a personal note, I remember well how as a student of the humanities and particularly philosophy at Oxford I went through a long, dry period when I simply could not say certain parts of the Creeds. My philosophy don, an avowed atheist, had been giving me a difficult time in tutorials as he echoed the kind of mocking sentiments about life after death that we see Paul contending with in the Book of Acts. Thus, when it came to the statement in the Creeds about believing in the resurrection of the body I simply stood mute. It was only when I found myself in my rooms one evening

rereading this passage from I Corinthians that I really understood
for the first time what was being said.

Paul is not talking about the physical resuscitation of corpses
when he speaks either of Jesus's resurrection or of any other persons. All the nitpicking objections of my tutor and similar skeptics
were totally beside the point, I discovered. It didn't matter whether
or not we were talking about those who have been tragically lost at
sea, blown to smithereens in war, consumed by the flames of cremation or hacked to pieces in the obscenity of murder. The fate of the
actual physical body, according to Paul, is irrelevant to the resurrection of the body—or, as I prefer to render it, a bodily resurrection.

Paul meets the query about what kind of body the risen dead
will have by the metaphor of the dying and rising wheat. The seed
(our physical body) dies and rots away. But new life appears and
springs up because "God gives it a body according to his will . . .
to each seed a body of its own." In the case of humans, he says, our
physical body decays in the grave, but we are raised in a spiritual
body. The Greek is instructive here. Paul calls our physical body the
psychikon soma (a psychic or natural body), while the new resurrection
body is called the *pneumatikon soma* (a pneumatic or spirit body). His
logic is unassailable because he notes correctly that ordinary flesh
and blood, which is corruptible, cannot inherit immortality. God,
who remains the prime actor in Jesus's resurrection, giving him a
new and glorious body fit for eternal life, similarly acts to clothe us
with the spiritual body needed for the life to come.

What is particularly interesting in this account is that it so
closely parallels what modern investigators of the paranormal insist
upon. They have various ways of expressing it, but such terms as
"astral body," "sidereal body," "subtle body" or "etheric body" are
all attempts to distinguish between our physical selves and a bodily
reality that transcends them. It is a body still recognizably ours and
intimately connected with what has gone before, but, exactly as in
the case of the stories of the resurrection body of Jesus, it is freed

from earthly limitations. It is precisely the sort of subtle body one would need to move into a more spiritual world—the world of not just many but of infinite dimensions. Anyone familiar with contemporary physics and the writings of such scientists as David Bohm or Niels Bohr will realize at once that past "impossibilities" have now vanished in a holographic world of parallel universes and implicate and explicate orders.

Treasure in Earthen Vessels

Paul did not know any historical Jesus, but his conviction that at his famous conversion on the road to Damascus he had a real encounter with the spiritual, Risen Christ is absolutely fundamental to his writing. What actually happened at that time, as with any profoundly moving, mystical experience, is difficult to describe with any hope of precision. But that something momentous occurred there cannot be doubt. When a man as brilliant and passionate as Paul changes suddenly from persecuting Christians to witnessing at great personal cost to the resurrection of a crucified "Lord," there has to be a sufficient cause.

Paul, we know, belonged to the group within Judaism that believed in the doctrine of bodily resurrection. He was a Pharisee, and resurrection was a major point of difference between Pharisees and the other major religious party, the Sadducees. In fact, he occasionally made use of this contentious difference to set the two groups at loggerheads and thus deflect their attacks on himself. But it is a far cry from a general belief in this doctrine to an acceptance of Christian claims that God raised up Jesus from the dead.

Paul's encounter with the Risen Christ is described three times in the Book of Acts. Interestingly, each of these accounts differs in some minor details, and there are one or two major contradictions. For example, in Acts 9:1ff, Paul says those travelling with him heard the voice that spoke, saying, "I am Jesus, whom you are persecuting," but that they saw nothing. In Acts 22 verses 6–16, Paul says the others saw the bright light that shone "from heaven" but that they "did not hear the voice of him that spoke." Thus, the question can be raised rather sharply as to whether this experience was objective, that is, exterior to Paul, or whether it was subjective, an inner happening. That it was somehow different from the earlier appearances of the Resurrected Jesus is evident. We have already seen how he refers to his experience as unusual: "Last of all, he was seen by me also; it is as if I were somebody who had an untimely birth."

The whole episode has to be understood, however, as we have seen in the context of Paul's extraordinary psychic and extrasensory gifts. Scholar and rationalist though he was, he was more than at home with the so-called paranormal, whether it was non-medical healing, speaking in tongues (glossolalia) or out-of-body experiences. He tells us himself that he was given "a plethora of mystical revelations." Speaking of various "visions and revelations," he describes that curious out-of-body event just cited that, if one didn't know its source, could well seem like something from the *National Enquirer*:

"I knew a man in Christ more than fourteen years ago [he obviously means himself]—whether in the body or out of the body I cannot tell, God knows—who was snatched up into the third heaven. And I know that this man—whether in the body or out of it I don't know, God knows—was snatched up into paradise and heard unutterable words which it is not permitted for humans to speak."[2]

Unlike the tabloid articles of today, however, Paul does not go on to give us any details. In fact, he tends to bring these experiences up only to play them down again as if they were a source of embarrassment. But, I have no doubt personally that Paul's total certainty about the future bliss that lies beyond the grave is based, at least in part, upon his own experience of what he terms paradise. This throws light upon his eloquent and emphatic Creed-like affirmation: "As it is written, 'Eye has not seen nor ear heard, neither has it entered into the heart of man, the things which God has prepared for them that love Him.'"[3] It may also lie behind his other soaring passage, which has meant so much to so many down the centuries. Here it is in my translation from the Greek: "For now we see as it were riddles reflected in a mirror; but then face to face. Now I have partial knowledge; but then I shall know even as also I am known."[4]

While Paul never takes an escapist view of life, one in which we can let this world and its problems or our personal conduct go to hell because heavenly rewards are all that matter, there can be little doubt that it is eternal life in the realm beyond death that constitutes for him the fulfillment of human existence. Our present body is a clay pot or vessel into which the treasure of God's light has been poured. This outer man grows older daily, but our true inner, or higher, self is daily renewed. "For we keep looking not at the things which are seen but at the things which cannot be seen. For the things that can be seen are for a moment, but the things unseen are forever."[5]

Changing the imagery, he likens our physical body to a tent and says that when it is destroyed we "have a building from God"—an eternal body "in the heavens." At times, he says, we feel the burden of our mortality weighing us down and we groan or sigh as we look forward to a life to come. It's not, he rushes to state, that we are anxious to escape this life, but that we yearn for the day when the physical body with all its weaknesses will be "utterly swallowed up by life."[6] Unlike some of the Platonists and their successors, he doesn't conceive of a pure state of being for the soul or higher self. He remains much closer to the originators of the eternal Christ mythos, the Egyptians, who from millennia earlier based a similar faith upon the Osiris–Horus myth of death and resurrection. Always he insists upon our being "clothed" by a new, spiritual body. "For, having been clothed, we shall not be found naked." The same thought is powerfully conveyed in Paul's letter to the Philippians, where he seems to come close to the Platonic idea of this world versus the real world of the eternal, but where he again insists upon the fact that any future life will be an embodied one: "For our citizenship is in heaven whence we await our Saviour . . . who will transform our lowly body into the likeness of his glorious body."7

While there are some basic constants in Paul's thinking about life after death, the biggest mistake anyone can make is to try to impose an overall, totally consistent theology or schema upon what he has to say. He really lacks what we would call an elaborated eschatology or doctrine. In one of his earliest letters, his first one to the Thessalonians, he seems to be expecting the imminent return of Christ and talks about those who "sleep" (meaning the dead) being raised first, and then "those who still remain alive" will be snatched up to meet the Lord. This seems to imply a belief in a waiting period for those already dead and so, presumably, a kind of intermediate state where the deceased exist without a body. But later, in II Corinthians, he states quite boldly that there is no waiting period at all because "to be absent from the body [is] to be present with the Lord."8 This latter position, that the day of resurrection is always *now* because it is outside space and time, is the one I have always felt makes the most sense.

One final note: In Paul's letters, the ultimate fate of the unrepentant is death in the sense of complete annihilation or nothingness. As in the Gospel and letters attributed to John, there is absolutely no fiery hell or torment. In several places he suggests that those who persist in not wanting God and in saying no to His grace and mercy are ultimately let go and simply perish. But, at the same time, however paradoxical it may seem, he frequently expresses his conviction that the whole of creation will one day be reconciled to God. The kind of loving God experienced and trusted by Paul will, in the end, let none of his creatures be lost.

The Teachings of Jesus

Anyone who reads the New Testament or searches elsewhere for a consistent body of doctrine that could readily be packaged and labelled "Jesus's Doctrine of Survival Beyond the Grave" is in for complete disappointment. The wise reader will do well to beware of those who profess to have discovered such a neat set of teachings. The Bible as a whole offers no tidy, logical theory of life after death, and the sayings attributed to the persona of Jesus in the Gospels are part of the Bible's overall, at times openly contradictory, mélange of messages.

However else one understands the role played by Jesus, not only was he often addressed as a rabbi, but also he is portrayed for the most part as if he were a rabbi, using pithy aphorisms, paradoxes, similes and parables. But, though the language and style used were not those normally associated with Greek philosophy or religion—where the immortality of the soul was taken as a given—the hidden theme in all of it is that of incarnation. The meaning of the symbolism and allegory beneath the surface of the text is that pertaining to the central truth that we are each of us a spark of the Divine. As this is described in detail in *The Pagan Christ*, I refer the reader to the full discussion there. As in the case of the parable of the prodigal son, we are exiles in "a far country" who need to come to our true selves as he did, and one day return to the "the father's house."

In any case, the Gospel taught by imagery and not by following the linear, left-brain thinking so typical of our western world since Gutenberg and the invention of printing. From our point of view, the content of this kind of communication often seems inconsistent, but it stems from a wholly different way of coming at truth—a belief that spiritual truth is hammered out between paradoxes, that it is best illustrated by means of stories, that it is something to be grasped as much or more with the heart (intuition, imagination and emotion) than with our purely rational mind. Nevertheless, having said all that, it is still possible to discern some very basic directions in the four Gospels. Like the Pharisees, Jesus is shown as believing in the resurrection of the body and in a life after death in the presence of God. To elucidate this further, we need to look at two key concepts.

The Kingdom of God

As related in *For Christ's Sake*, I can never forget the sense of illumination and of liberation that came when I fully realized for the first time that in the Jesus story, Jesus's main message and sense of mission had very little to do with saving us from sin and with proclaiming himself as a third person of the Trinity (that is, as absolute Deity) and everything to do with proclaiming the reality of the Kingdom of God. The opening verses of Mark, the earliest of the four Gospels, make this absolutely clear. Jesus there came preaching the *euaggelion* or "good news" of God's Kingdom. The entire focus of the parables and other sayings is upon the Kingdom of God, also known by the pious synonym "the Kingdom of Heaven." (Pious Jews used "heaven" as a way to avoid saying the name of God.) Jesus announced by word and deed that no matter what outward appearances may seem, God is in complete and ultimate control of human affairs. God reigns, nurtures, heals and, finally, delivers humanity into an entirely fresh dimension of being and wholeness.

It is essential to notice that the primary emphasis of this teaching about the Kingdom is not about some kind of escape from this present world with its great joys, its grievous sufferings and its enormous challenges. Rather, the call is for a radical trust in God now, in the present moment. The Kingdom is the challenge of claiming God's loving presence with and within us today. "The Kingdom of God is within you or in your midst," he said. It is a reality inside us and in any human community where right relationships or justice prevail; it is present in the form of a judgment and a challenge to action wherever injustice exists, as for example it did for so long in South Africa or in Central America, or indeed in the midst of the homelessness and poverty in our great cities as well as around the globe.

Belonging to the Kingdom is not a matter of trusting some deity "above all things" or somehow "out there." It is about a God who is the ground and depth of the entire cosmos, and hence of every one of us. This Kingdom or Presence of God in power is both a current reality and a future or "eschatological" event. In the Jesus teaching, one realizes this Kingdom now by childlike trust—not in dusty dogma or in rigid creeds, but in the living God. Yet, at the same time, because of the very trustworthiness of this Presence, there is the assurance that one day the Kingdom will come in all its fullness. What Jesus taught his followers to pray for—"Thy will be done on earth as in heaven"—will indeed be done. Sickness, pain and death will have no more reign over humanity in this teaching. Significantly, the most prevalent metaphor of this future bliss is that of a great wedding feast. The truth described in this image is that life in the future Kingdom (itself a metaphor) will be richly celebrative, communal and filled with all the sense of newness, adventure and creativity that only a wedding can signify. Already we can get a foretaste here of what that heaven will be like.

Eternal Life

The first three Gospels, while constantly using the image of the Kingdom of God when Jesus is presented as speaking of God's presence and our relationship to the spiritual order, have one other important way of expressing this same reality. Although they use it rather sparsely, it becomes the dominant note in the fourth Gospel, that attributed to John. I'm referring, of course, to the phrase "eternal life." When the rich young man, in Mark 10:17ff, comes running to Jesus, we are told that he fell at his feet and asked him excitedly, "What must I do to inherit eternal life?" This expression, which occurs only a couple of times in Matthew, Mark and Luke, appears some fourteen or fifteen times in John. The reason for this is not hard to find. Scholars believe that the fourth Gospel was aimed at sophisticated, Hellenistic Jews and gentiles. For these readers, the phrase "the Kingdom of God," with all its Hebraic background, would have had a very unfamiliar ring, so John uses it only a couple of times. Paul totally avoids its use in his own writings for the very same reason. He too uses the term "eternal life"—for example in Romans 2 verse 7—but he has other more mystical ways of expressing the same concept. Anyone interested in good communication obviously has to speak the language of the intended audience. The early Christians thus felt no inhibitions about dropping the imagery attributed to Jesus and replacing it with their own. The phrase "eternal life" made perfectly good sense in Greek, and John fills it with all the meaning that he was convinced flows from a right relationship with God, oneself and others through Christ. John's Jesus (who is in so many striking ways different from the Jesus of the first three Gospels) teaches that to follow him, to trust in his revelation of the nature of God, to keep his sayings, is to be at one with God—as he knows himself to be. All of this is to have eternal life.

The Problem

The great difficulty about such an expression in English, however, is that while it appears self-explanatory it doesn't quite get the meaning of the original Greek and, consequently, has done more, in my view, to put intelligent people in our culture off the Christian view of life after death than any other single thing! The same can be said of the synonym often used in the King James Version, "everlasting life." Both expressions strongly suggest a life very much like this one only going on and on ad infinitum. Coupled with a literal understanding of other Bible imagery about celestial choirs, harps without number and streets paved with gold, it has conjured up a mental image attended by colossal boredom, if not outright horror. If that is what the afterlife is going to be like, a great many people would like the opportunity of saying, "No, thanks all the same." As Robert Service said in the last line of his poem against the concept of immortality, "Please God, spare me your great hereafter."

But the Greek words *aionios zoe* mean literally "life of the age," that is, of the age to come. In other words, the New Testament at this point is not talking about an infinite extension of temporal life but a wholly different quality of life—life as it was meant to be, life as we have known it in rare glimpses, perhaps, not so much life going on forever but rather the life of an eternal *now*. It is a kind of life that might be endless but is actually beyond or outside of time altogether. It is what T.S. Eliot was writing about when he talked of "the intersection of the timeless with time." It's the kind of fullness of living we get hints of in rare moments here when God, or the life force, or however we care to express it makes us feel "in time, yet out of time," at one with the universe, ourselves and others. It may be at the birth of a child or when we are in love, in deep meditation or when we experience nature in some profound way, or perhaps when we thrill to music, art or some other vision of great beauty.

Eternal life supremely means sharing in the life of God. Once again, as with the Kingdom of God, eternal life is not something pushed off into the future or an excuse for turning one's back on this earth, on this time-oriented existence, this reality of living. Rather, the life of the age to come is something one embarks upon here and now. Awareness of what we really are—the offspring of God—and of where we are ultimately going to be—in the realm where God will be known face to face—means a radically new quality of life at this very moment, a sense of being wholly present or alive as never before. We may not always feel like it or always hold firmly to this belief from an intellectual standpoint. We will not be spared the normal vicissitudes of earthly life. We live this life here upon the "cross" of matter. But John's Jesus assures the readers that eternal life remains a reality all the same. It is, he says, God's will that everyone who puts their trust in him "may have eternal life." It is thus a present possession as well as a future hope.

I believe Carl Jung sums up best what is intended by all of this when he writes in his memoirs, "The decisive question for man is: is he related to something infinite or not? That is the telling question of his life. Only if we know that the thing that truly matters is the infinite can we avoid fixing our interests upon futilities, and upon all kinds of goals which are not of real importance . . . If we understand and feel that here in this life *we already have a link* with the infinite, desires and attitudes change. In the final analysis, we count for something only because of the essential we embody, and if we do not embody that, life is wasted [italics mine]."9

The story of the raising of Lazarus in John's Gospel, chapter 11, is not historical. I say this not to be controversial, nor because of some dogmatic, liberal assumption that miracles are by definition impossible or unbelievable. The story seems improbable to me because such a stupendous event, especially if, as John insists, it was the last straw that precipitated the final decision of the authorities to have Jesus done away with, is hardly likely to have escaped the earliest Gospel tradition. Yet none of the other Gospels include it, nor is it anywhere mentioned by Paul in his letters. In *The Pagan Christ* I show the origins or prototype of the Lazarus story (El Asar was Osiris, the resurrected Egyptian sun god). The evangelist here "borrows" the earlier version. But the passage is spiritually important for Christians. This is particularly so since it leads up to the Gospel saying of the Christ, attributed to him because his own resurrection is seen as already well in the past at the time of writing, that he himself is "the resurrection and the life." This saying, so integral a part of the Anglican (Episcopal) and other churches' funeral services, says in full, "I am the resurrection and the life. Whosoever believes in me [meaning, in the message I bring], even if he dies, yet shall he live. And everyone who believes in me shall not die unto the age to come." The meaning is clear. To trust in the living God whom the Jesus Story reveals means that one may die physically but he or she will never perish, but be "raised up" in a new, fully spiritual body. It is a loud echo of Egyptian religion.

Many Mansions

There is one other passage in John's Gospel that merits some mention. It contains the saying of Jesus that in the house of the Father there are many "mansions." Jesus says he is going to prepare a place for his followers that they may be with him always. The Greek word at this point for "mansions" is transliterated into English as *monai*. This means, quite literally, stopping places, way stations or resting spots where one may refresh oneself on a journey before travelling on again. The Judaism of that period believed in various compartments or dwelling places in the life to come. But it is important to notice that in this saying the sense is not that of any static, permanent rest—for many people, suggestive of endless ennui—but of centres of recreation and renewal as the resurrected person progresses ever onwards towards greater freedom, knowledge and enlightenment. The Bible's view of eternal life is definitely not about instant perfection of some kind but about growth and adventure beyond any earthbound expectations.

The Gospels and the Resurrection of Jesus

Scholars almost universally agree that the earliest Gospel, Mark's, was probably written in Rome some time shortly after 70 CE. It is clear that many of the sayings and "events" of the Jesus Story recorded in Mark and the other three Gospels circulated for generations in an oral form. It is quite possible that there was a collection of some sayings and parables written in Aramaic at an earlier point, and there is every possibility that what is called "The Passion Narrative"—the story of the Betrayal and Crucifixion—may also have been written down at an earlier date. Certainly it was in its outlines and themes already an "old, old story" in the Greco-Roman Egyptian world. But the literary form known as a Gospel, which collated, edited and structured this diverse oral and written tradition, came into existence well after Paul's testimony in his first letter to the early Christians at Corinth.

I have discussed the Gospel accounts of the Resurrection elsewhere, and for those with a more conservative bent, other theologians, such as Hans Küng in his book *On Being a Christian*, have treated the topic with such thoroughness that it is unnecessary to cover the same ground in detail here.[10] Nevertheless, the matter is so central to our subject and so crucial for an understanding of the grounds for Christian belief in life after death that certain key elements must be examined here at least briefly.

Mark's Gospel

The ordinary reader, particularly if he or she has read only the King James Version of the Bible, is probably unaware that the most ancient and authentic Greek manuscripts of Mark's Gospel end abruptly at chapter 16 verse 8. What appears after that, verses 9 to 19, is called the "Longer Ending of Mark" and is obviously an attempt by a later hand to fill in an embarrassing gap. The reader can check this out personally by reading Mark 16 in the King James Version and then in any of the more modern translations such as the Revised Standard Version or the New English Bible. The much more ancient Greek texts upon which our modern, scholarly translations are based were simply not available to the scholars who created the King James Version. Here is how Mark ends according to the best available Greek text today:

"And when the Sabbath was over, Mary Magdalene and Mary the mother of James and Salome brought spices to come and anoint him. And very early in the morning, just after sunrise, on the first day of the week, they came to the tomb. And they said among themselves, 'Who will roll away the stone for us from the door of the tomb?' And looking ahead, they saw that the stone had been rolled away: for it was extremely large. Then, entering into the tomb, they saw a young man seated on the right side, clad in a white garment; and they were quite amazed. But he said to them, 'Don't be frightened; you seek for Jesus of Nazareth who was crucified. He has been raised up; he is not here; look, this is the place where they laid him. But go your way; tell the disciples and Peter that he is going before you into Galilee. You will see him there even as he told you.' And, they came out and fled from the tomb; for they were seized by trembling and were beside themselves. And they said nothing to anyone, for they were afraid."

Several things stand out sharply. As in all the Gospels, the women are first to the tomb and the first to recognize that something quite unexpected, something immensely portentous, has occurred. (John, however, unlike the others, says that Mary Magdalene came to the tomb alone that first morning.) Luke and John have two angels at the tomb, Mark has a "young man," and Matthew says there was one angel. Mark's young man tells the women that Jesus will appear to the disciples in Galilee, a statement Matthew echoes. However, if you look at the account in Luke you will find that in it there are no recorded appearances of the Risen Christ in Galilee at all. Matthew describes but one (in a passage which is obviously a fictional creation of the early Church) and in John the only such appearance is in an appendix added to the Gospel later.[11]

We begin to get a feel for some of the various contradictions and discrepancies that mark the four accounts of Jesus's Resurrection when you lay them side by side. While such differences may seem to rule out any attempt by critics to argue that the Gospel writers colluded or conspired to cook their stories and make them match, thus adding to their general surface credibility (after all, witnesses to any happening rarely agree in all details), nevertheless, it is obvious that we can never begin to have the sort of precision about the first Easter that many Christians somehow blindly assume.

What is really startling is the way in which Mark's account ends with the sheer terror of the women and their failure to tell anyone. It is, of course, possible that the original papyrus or vellum manuscript was torn off or spoiled in some way, and that Mark did go on to the kind of happier conclusion later supplied for him in the Longer Ending, but we don't know that for certain. The other point that should be made here is that although Mark and the others record that the tomb was empty, they nowhere attempt to describe the Resurrection itself. Scholars know this, but many church members seem unaware that none of the Gospels describe the actual "event" of Jesus being raised from the dead. This restraint on their part is not necessarily a virtue. They are trying to deal with what was the realm of myth, not history.

Clearly, whatever happened was not an event like any other. If, as Christians believe, God raised Jesus Christ from the dead, what happened was never described because it was, in principle, something that lay quite beyond our normal senses or abilities to comprehend. It was quite literally indescribable—a *miraculum*. Perhaps this is the real message behind the stark terror of the women in Mark's primitive narrative. He gives us no appearances, nothing save the journalistic description of the women themselves as they struggle to cope with the shock of thinking the unthinkable. My own view, of course, is that the real nub of the difficulty with the Resurrection stories is that they are "true myth" dressed up as fact. Their inner truth is wholly in the realm of spirit or mysticism.

The Appearances in Matthew, Luke and John

None of the Gospels describes the appearance of the Risen Jesus to Peter alone (Luke merely mentions it in passing), although this is given as fundamental to Paul's account of the appearances in I Corinthians. Similarly, Paul obviously knew nothing of the tradition about the tomb being empty since he never speaks of it; indeed, it does not seem to have formed any part of the earliest preaching. Nevertheless, Paul does agree with the Gospels in that, for him, as for Matthew, Luke and John, the stories of the appearances of the resurrected Master form the bedrock of the Christian message. Yet, there is absolutely no way to reconcile all the various appearance stories, in spite of what fundamentalists and others may claim. The present Archbishop of Canterbury, Rowan Williams, a noted Biblical scholar in his own right, in writing about the Resurrection says the "only early testimony" is Paul's list in I Corinthians 15 and there are "difficulties with this list." Apart from its failure already cited, to match the Gospel appearances, it gives no indication of time, place or circumstances. Moreover, as Professor G.A. Wells points out in his important book *Can We Trust the New Testament*, Williams admits that what the Gospels contribute is "a monumentally confused jumble of incompatible stories."[12] Wells, who has written seven books contending that there never was a historical Jesus, notes that Williams even goes so far as to state that the "Easter texts" are "imaginative approaches"—that is, fictional narratives—to show the inner meaning of the assertions that Jesus who was put to death is "alive with God and with his followers." The archbishop goes on to call John 21, with its account of Jesus's appearance to the disciples who have gone back to their old jobs as fishermen, a "Galilean fantasy." The chapter is undoubtedly a mythical add-on to the original account.

In Matthew, the appearances are attended by both fear and doubt on the part of the disciples, but they are able to approach

Jesus, grasp his feet and pay reverence.[13] Obviously, he is supposed to be recognizable. He speaks to them and bids them characteristically not to be afraid. In Luke we have the unique story of the two disciples who are walking back to the village of Emmaeus, just outside Jerusalem, when they meet a stranger. Later, invited in to eat with them, the stranger says a blessing over the bread and distributes it to them. At this point, "their eyes were opened and they knew him." Jesus then suddenly vanishes from their sight. This passage is plainly not historical either. If it were a historical event, it would undoubtedly have been part of the earliest tradition and so known to Paul and to the other evangelists. It seems more likely that it is a theological construct. That is, here we have the Risen Lord making himself known in the breaking of bread—at the eucharist. In other words, it is part of the author's belief that if you want to know the Risen Christ you can do so at the celebration of the Lord's Supper or Holy Communion. Jesus is present there and opens the eyes of those with the faith to "see" him.

Luke's version of the appearance to all the disciples cites their fear that they are seeing a disembodied ghost or spirit. What follows are definitely attempts to combat such an idea. Jesus is made to tell them to look at his pierced hands and feet and then invites them to touch and handle him: "A spirit doesn't have flesh and bones as you see me to have." He then eats a piece of fish. We are reminded here of the appearance to the disciples in John's Gospel when Jesus invites Thomas to allay his doubts by thrusting his finger into the holes in his hands and feet and by thrusting his hand into his wounded side. I agree with those scholars, such as Professor F.W. Beare and others, who find the references to eating and to being touched decidedly crude and at variance with Paul's earlier contention that Christ's Resurrection body was of a more subtle or spiritual nature. And it is interesting in this connection to note that John, who does write of both the suggestion to Thomas of touching and of the Risen Jesus eating, also has the apparently contradictory story in which Mary Magdalene in the garden is forbidden to touch her Master "because I am not yet ascended."

What is influencing these narratives, no doubt, is the criticism by some early opponents of sheer literalism that Jesus was not a historic person raised up from the dead in some bodily way but that all that was seen was a ghostly wraith or pale spirit, much in the fashion of a near-death experience. The ancient world held a wide variety of beliefs in the survival of some kind of spirit or soul after death. What was difficult about Pharisaic Judaism and Christianity was the belief that there would be a resurrection of the total person—not just the soul but a transformed bodily reality as well. The seeming contradictions in the appearance accounts may well be the result of trying to bear witness to these two truths: one, that resurrection is a spiritual event, and two, that it is also a bodily event—the physical body is there but radically changed. Thus, the Risen Christ is apparently able to be in more than one place at once: he can pass through closed doors, he can appear or vanish at will. He is at times instantly recognizable; at others, even someone as close to him as Mary Magdalene has difficulty knowing who it is. In other words, in his risen body Christ can somehow control how and by whom he is perceived.

A Final Word

Sometimes preachers and others talk as though after the Resurrection anyone in the vicinity could have observed the Risen Master walking about or talking to his various followers. This was obviously not so. All the Resurrection appearances were to disciples, to his own circle of friends, with the exception of Paul, and we have already seen how he alone "saw" Christ on that occasion. The word used in the Greek is the same as that used in the various mystery religions to denote seeing a vision. There was something mystical, paranormal and beyond our everyday experience about "seeing" the resurrected entity known as Jesus of Nazareth. Everything about all of these appearance stories—despite almost insuperable contradictions and problems—resonates with the conviction that something quite new and different is being encountered. Jesus as the Christ had, it was believed, entered into a new and higher plane of being. And, having done so, he had become the exemplar or forerunner of a destiny intended for all humankind.

I can but add here that the fresh understanding and insight gained during the research and writing of *The Pagan Christ* has only served to add to my conviction that the New Testament rings with truth on the entire theme of "eternal life." It is a truth, however, not dependent upon a crudely literal, historicized reading of the texts, but one rooted in a spiritual vision. Expressed through myth—that which never was (historically) but which always is—and through allegory, the universal story of our true, inner nature and our ultimate destiny sounds forth in all its glory. It gives us what the distinguished Canadian literary critic Northrop Frye, relying upon his mentor William Blake, called "Double Vision"—a glimpse of another higher world interpenetrating and illuming the panorama of here and now. This is not the kind of certainty of a science lab but it is a certainty nonetheless.

8

HELL, PURGATORY, AND END TIMES

I HAVE DELIBERATELY not devoted a chapter to the concept of heaven because the subject matter involved has already been covered by my discussion of eternal life and will be touched on again in the conclusion. Nevertheless, it is important to state here that the popular notion of heaven has been almost as great a stumbling block to belief in a life beyond the grave as the concept of a burning hell. The imagery and other descriptive embroidery is so crassly materialistic and the accompanying world view so naive that the average thinking person can easily conclude the whole subject is one for children or for lovers of pure fantasy.

Some of the most familiar and best-loved hymns in our churches abound in descriptions of heaven that are frankly embarrassing to the modern mind. It is clear enough for the most part that the author's intention is not literal but symbolic. However, the cumulative effect of generations of believers singing these uncritically, coupled with the almost total absence of alternative explanations, has meant that in popular thought heaven is perceived to be boring and banal. Nobody today is interested in some form of existence whose highlights consist of a steady diet of milk and honey—

"Jerusalem the golden, with milk and honey blest"—pavements of gold, playing harps to accompany angelic choirs, or lying prostrate before the throne of God "to gaze and gaze on Thee." It is often stated by conservative theologians and preachers that the greatest coup of the devil has been to persuade people he doesn't exist. But it is a far greater devilish success to have so many people thinking that the final goal and consummation of all human striving is either incredible or boring!

Emanuel Swedenborg (1688–1772) was one of the most learned men of his time. In the year 1744 he began an open communion with the spiritual world that continued uninterrupted for the rest of his life. In his landmark book, *Heaven and Hell: From Things Heard and Seen*, he said that heaven is a place and state of infinite variety, entrance into which is denied to no one who desires it. Only a person's own dedication to evil could possibly exclude him or her. Certainly he saw it as no static existence, but a dimension of ongoing growth and development. Whatever one makes of his claims to have had regular dialogue with persons who had died, his many books, all published in Latin, bear the marks of a sane and balanced mind. The Swedenborgian Church of North America continues today to teach his views on the reality of a spiritual world.

Hell

There are few ideas in the entire history of religion that have caused more misery, cruelty, or misunderstanding than the concept of a fiery hell. There is no place where insistence upon a crude literalism has done more lasting damage to the human psyche. It is not just a question of the terror suffered by sensitive individuals down the ages because of fear of everlasting torment, either for themselves or for their loved ones. This is bad enough in itself. But the idea of a place of fiery, eternal punishment awaiting the damned has crucially warped our western understanding of God.

Since it is a fundamental spiritual law that the worshipper becomes like the object of his or her worship, the worship of a deity assumed capable—for whatever reasons—of eternally tormenting billions of people has led to disastrous results. The inquisitors, in torturing and burning the "enemies of God," were simply emulating their Master! It is no accident today that the most vigorous supporters of an ever-increasing nuclear arsenal, including the Strategic Defence Initiative (known popularly for some years as "Star Wars") are right-wing fundamentalists and their ilk in both Canada and the United States. Support for the war in Iraq and for President G.W. Bush's policy of pre-emptive violence to fight terrorism also came most strongly from Bible-believing, born-again Christians. If you believe in a God who has prepared a literal hell for his enemies, it is an easy jump to argue for strategies that may include the incineration of most of humankind.

One of the earliest memories of my boyhood is of preachers at a little gospel hall we attended ranting and raving until the perspiration rolled down their faces and the hairs at the nape of my neck stood on end. Their endless theme was the horror of hell and the need to escape its awesome clutches by being "saved." They were following a time-hallowed formula of holding sinners over the flames in order to persuade them to "get right with the Lord." One of their most common tactics was to point at various members of the congregation and ask, "What if you should die tonight? What if a car should strike you dead on your way home from here or a heart attack call you before your Maker? If you haven't been born again, my friend, prepare to spend a godless eternity in the fires of hell." This was strong stuff and it was no wonder that when the altar call came, every youngster in the place and most of the adults answered it—regularly.

This kind of preaching still goes on. Not just on television, where electronic evangelists flail away, but in countless churches everywhere. If you ask these preachers of the Gospel why they proclaim hellfire and eternal damnation, they have a single, simple answer, "Because it's in the Book." Since indeed it is not only "in the Book" but deeply embedded in the art and literature of our entire culture, no study of life after death can avoid it. One has only to read Dante or Milton, or visit the Sistine Chapel at the Vatican, to comprehend the visceral grip that the popular idea of hell holds on our western imagination. Where did it come from? Did the Jesus of the Gospels believe in it and preach it? And what is its validity for us today?

Old Testament Beliefs

The earliest descriptions of life after death in the Old Testament are somewhat vague and partake of concepts widely held by all the Semitic peoples of the ancient Near East. The oldest of all is expressed in such descriptions of death as "being gathered to one's fathers." This phrase, found in Babylonian records as well as in the Hebrew Scriptures, is evidence that people then believed that at death the family circle was joined. Indeed, there was widespread worship of ancestors in that culture and the dead could be invoked for guidance. This art, called necromancy, is as we have seen frowned upon in the Old Testament, but several passages make it plain that it was part of the popular cult in early times. The classic example, of course, is a distraught King Saul disguising himself and going to the Witch of Endor to "bring up" the prophet Samuel from the dead to give him counsel. When Samuel appears, he asks Saul, "Why hast thou disquieted me, to bring me up?"[1]

The dead could not only be invoked, they were viewed as needing food and other necessities. The placing of food on graves or even with corpses was widespread all over the ancient world. There is an inscription of the Assyrian king Ashurbanipal (who died in 626 BCE) in which he says, "The rules for making offerings to the dead and libations to the ghosts of the kings my ancestors . . . I reintroduced. I did well unto god and man, to dead and living."[2] There is no attempt to reason out exactly where or how these ancestors lived, but they were alive and still powerful.

There is, however, another strand of thought that overlaps the ancestor cult and has elements common to all early Semitic mythology. It was particularly strong in Babylonian religion, and the forced exile of the Jews into Babylonian territory in about 590 BCE confirmed its hold upon early Judaism. This has to do with She'ol, the underworld place of departed spirits. The earliest mention of She'ol comes from the eighth century BCE and references abound in the Old Testament. For example, when Joseph's brothers sell him into slavery and lie to his father, Jacob, that he was killed by wild beasts (showing him the torn and bloody coat of many colours as proof), Jacob mourns and cries, "I will go down into the grave unto my son mourning."[3] The word here translated as "grave" is the Hebrew word "*She'ol*," and the old man speaks of "going down."

The derivations of the word "*She'ol*" are still debated by scholars, but the prevailing opinion is that it comes from a root word meaning "to be hollow." It is variously described as a hollow place under the earth or as a walled, subterranean city where there is neither hope nor joy of any kind. The dead feed on dust and murky waters in a shadowy existence that is but the palest reflection of anything that could be called life. The best way to describe this is the summary in the *Oxford Dictionary of the Christian Church*: "The notion reflects an undeveloped and shadowy belief in the future life which was gradually superseded by the more defined beliefs of later Judaism."[4]

In She'ol there is no thought of punishment or reward. Unfortunately, the translators of the Authorized Version sometimes render the word as "hell," as in "Thou wilt not leave my soul in hell . . ."[5]

This falsely creates the impression that the Jews believed in a fiery place of punishment from the beginning. In fact, as we shall see, it was a very late development indeed.

While the She'ol belief implies a kind of future life, it was at best an unsatisfying, ill-defined doctrine. The shades in She'ol had no sense of God's presence: "For the grave [She'ol] cannot praise thee, death cannot celebrate thee: they that go down into the pit cannot hope for thy truth."[6] The Psalmist, in fact, is continually making the point that God should keep him alive, "for in death there is no remembrance of thee: in the grave [She'ol] who shall give thee thanks?"[7] The dead are those whom God "rememberest no more: and they are cut off from thy hand."[8]

The idea of hell as a place of fiery punishment for the wicked appears for the first time in Jewish writings in the second century BCE. To understand it properly one must comprehend the various pressures and influences at work. The conquests of Alexander the Great (who died in 323 BCE) had spread the Greek language and culture over the whole of the ancient world. The Jews themselves were under Greek rule from the time of Alexander to the middle of the second century BCE. Some scholars, most notably F.W. Beare, argue that the popular concept of hell owes its origins to this source. He points out that it was no less an authority than Plato himself who first gave full-scale promotion to the idea of a hell of torment for evildoers in the life to come. "Hell was a Greek invention," he says.[9] But I agree with those who feel Beare overstates the case. In addition to Greek ideas, Jewish thought was influenced by other, more congenial concepts from ancient Persia. In the religion of Zoroaster, the conflict between good and evil, light and darkness, was to culminate in the resurrection of the dead, a fiery judgment and then the creation of a new world where there would be no more crying or pain. It is easy to see how these ideas appealed to Jewish theologians of the time when you think about the specific problems of justice and oppression they were trying to solve.

It became impossible, as belief in the personal, caring nature of God developed, to continue to accept the She'ol view of life after death. Here and there, in hints and guesses at first, we find expressions of a growing conviction that to be true to himself God's concern for his people must transcend death. In the midst of his terrible sufferings, Job at first is afraid he will go down into She'ol and be no more remembered. The injustice of this, however, and his intense faith in God's mercy and faithfulness gradually bring Job to a daring leap of faith. He utters those words that have come down the centuries as part of the burial service of the Anglican Church, and which I have myself in the past so often read at funerals: "For I know that my redeemer liveth, and that he shall stand at the latter day upon the earth: And though after my skin, worms destroy this body, yet in my flesh shall I see God."[10]

Professors W.O.E. Oesterley and T.H. Robinson, in their classic work *Hebrew Religion*, have commented on this text: "There is no general or formulated doctrine of the resurrection of the dead here. Yet, there is the conviction that, for Job at least, death is not the end . . . There is no thought of eternal life, no suggestion of heaven, but there is an assurance which will inevitably lead to these doctrines."[11] Similarly unformulated glimpses of the way this doctrine was beginning to emerge can be found in several places in the intimate, devotional prayers of the Psalms as well as in one of the most moving passages in the Old Testament, Isaiah 53. In describing the martyrdom of the suffering servant of God, the author clearly implies that God will vindicate him and raise him to complete the work he gave him to do.

However, in addition to wrestling with the issue of God's justice and mercy vis-à-vis the individual, there was the even more profound dilemma of God's dealings with the nation as a whole. The long-held belief in the political reality that God would one day smite Israel's enemies and restore the throne of David had to undergo a radical change in the face of inescapable, hard facts. As one foreign conqueror succeeded another in grinding the Jewish nation under its heel, there was widespread disillusionment and despair. How could God really be not only Israel's God but Lord of all the empires of the earth when he permitted his people to suffer such ignominy and repeated defeat?

The answer to this appeared in what is known as apocalyptic literature. The word "apocalypse" comes from Greek and means a revelation of secrets, in this case particularly, secrets concerning the future. These writers solve the problem of God's justice by postulating a day of divine intervention when all his promises to Israel would be fulfilled. Jewish apocalyptic literature, written from about 200 BCE to 100 CE, includes the Old Testament Book of Daniel and such writings as the Book of Enoch, the Book of Jubilees, the Testaments of the Twelve Patriarchs, the Secrets of Enoch and the Assumption of Moses. The classic Christian apocalypse is, of course, the Revelation of St. John the Divine, although there are passages of apocalyptic writing in the Gospels, most notably Mark, chapter 13, and elsewhere in the New Testament. A sentence from II Peter 3 verse 10 is typical of the genre: "But the day of the Lord will come as a thief in the night; in which the heavens shall pass away with a great noise, and the elements shall melt with fervent heat, the earth also and the works that are therein shall be burned up."

In the Sibylline Oracles, a collection of Jewish and Christian writings from 140 BCE to 70 CE, we read: "Then fire shall come upon the whole world . . . the whole world shall hear a rumbling and a mighty roar. And He [God] shall burn the whole earth."[12]

Christian apocalyptic literature borrowed heavily from Jewish writings and cannot be understood apart from them; Jewish apocalyptic writings, in turn, owed much to Persian sources. For example, the judgment of Israel's enemies becomes the final judgment of all people, the conflagration and burning become cosmological in scope, the establishment of God's Kingdom becomes the creation of a new world. This is behind the statement in Revelation: "Behold I saw a new heaven and a new earth: for the first heaven and the first earth were passed away."[13] There is no consistent teaching about a fiery hell in any of this apocalyptic material, just as no overall schema is adhered to. The writings share common elements and imagery, but the details differ considerably. Sometimes resurrection is followed by judgment and punishment by fire; sometimes resurrection comes at the last and affects only the good. In some writings there is the idea of an intermediate state after death and before resurrection in which the good go to paradise, the evil to a place of torment. Then comes eventual final judgment leading to either lasting bliss or never-ending pain.

The two Old Testament passages that give undisputed evidence of the growing Jewish belief in the resurrection of the body both come from this kind of thinking and can be dated with a degree of certainty to the second century BCE. The first is from Isaiah 26 verse 19 and reads: "The dead men shall live, together with my dead body they shall arise. Awake and sing, ye that dwell in dust [that is, in She'ol]: for thy dew is as the dew of herbs, and the earth shall cast out the dead." The second is from the apocalyptic work Daniel. In chapter 12 verse 2 we read: "And many of them that sleep in the dust of the earth shall awake, some to everlasting life, and some to shame and everlasting contempt." It would be wrong, however, to take any of this language too literally. As we have noted before, religious language is necessarily picture or image language, the attempt to utter the unutterable. That this punishment was not actually seen as never-ending can be understood from a third-century CE rabbinical treatise that says: "After twelve months their souls become extinct . . . and they turn to ashes."[14]

Some readers will want to learn more about apocalyptic literature while others may feel this is already more than they needed to know. But it must be said in the plainest terms that this is the context for the references to hell in the New Testament. You cannot appreciate isolated sayings attributed to Christ in the Gospels without at least a nodding acquaintance with this complex of religious ideas.

The Gospels

We should expect then what indeed we find in the four Gospels, that the texts reveal much of the imagery and metaphors involved in apocalyptic thinking. We find a belief in a bodily resurrection, a final judgment and the imminent coming, by divine intervention, of the last days. But a closer examination of the Gospels throws some startling light upon beliefs regarding hell and "eternal" punishment.

The idea of a fiery hell of punishment occurs only once in the earliest Gospel, Mark, once in Luke and not at all in John's Gospel or the Johannine Epistles. Matthew, written about 80 CE, some twenty years after Mark, is the chief source of sayings attributed to Jesus on this theme. Professor Beare suggests, "For Matthew, it seems to have had a morbid fascination."[15] The sole reference to hell in Mark deserves a closer look. It comes closely after the striking, and much-neglected, saying of Jesus that he who is not actively engaged against us (the disciples and their cause) is "on our side." Here is the passage as it is rendered by me from the currently approved Greek text:

"And whosoever shall offend [cause to stumble] one of these little ones that believe in me, it is better for him that a millstone were hanged about his neck, and he were cast into the sea.

"And if thy hand offend thee, cut it off: it is better for thee to enter into life maimed, than having two hands to go into Gehenna, into the fire that never shall be quenched. And if thy foot offend thee, cut it off: it is better to enter lame into life, than having two feet to be cast into Gehenna. And if thine eye offend thee, pluck it out: it is better for thee to enter into the Kingdom of God with one eye, than having two eyes to be cast into Gehenna, where the worm does not die and the fire is not put out."[16]

It is unfortunate that the translators of the King James Version used the word "hell" here (and even "hellfire" for verse 47) because that is not what the Greek original plainly says. The word actually used, and repeated, by Mark is "Gehenna." Gehenna is the transliteration into Greek of the Hebrew *Gehinnom* or Valley of Hinnom (sometimes called the Valley of Ben Hinnom) and refers to a deep gully immediately southwest of the old City of Jerusalem. It was considered accursed by the Jews because it had been used for human sacrifices to the god Moloch by the Canaanites in the pre-conquest days.[17] By the first century CE it had long been used as the city's garbage dump, a place of burning and decay and therefore a vivid symbol of desolation, destruction and loss.

Once you realize this, it becomes abundantly clear that the story is using contemporary imagery as a striking way of highlighting the fact that important issues are at stake. Sacrifices must be made by those who would be disciples, but they are worth it because the alternative is to endure a haunting sense of loss. In trying to avoid the discipline of discipleship one risks desolation, or being cast on the refuse heap. There is absolutely no warrant here for the later, terrifying doctrines of the Church about hell. The proof, if more is needed, that Mark is speaking symbolically here can be had by asking oneself whether Jesus is really calling on people to go ahead and mutilate themselves by literally cutting off arms and hands or gouging out their eyes! The one reference to Gehenna in Luke (also translated as "hell" in the King James Version) is similarly metaphorical.[18] The only other case where the word "Gehenna" appears in the New Testament is in the Epistle of James, where it is used in a purely figurative sense that has nothing whatever to do with eternal punishment. The King James Version says:

"And the tongue is a fire . . . and it is set on fire of hell [Gehenna]."[19]

Matthew, who as we have seen is darkly obsessed by the themes of judgment and "furnaces of fire," has his own reasons for piling on images of terrible punishments to come. Modern scholarship has shown how the particular situation in the life of the early Church that this Gospel was written to address made strident polemic against the Pharisees and the synagogue inevitable. The author, facing bitter rivalry between the vigorous Judaism of his time and the emerging Christian community, often heightens elements in the older tradition to the point where they no longer represent the earlier teachings at all. Thus, as many scholars have noted, even where Matthew puts sayings about fiery torments in Jesus's mouth we can see they do not fit the context and, in some cases, war against it. Frank Beare, in his classic commentary on this Gospel, queries "whether this imagery of a hell of fire was used by any historical Jesus at all. Apart from Matthew, it finds almost no echo in the Synoptic tradition."[20] When you add to this the silence of the Johannine literature on the topic and the fact that Paul never mentions it, the case for a Christly sanction of such a concept weakens to the point where it is no longer sustainable. (Paul speaks instead of the consequences of unbelief as "death" or "destruction" or "annihilation." See Romans 6:21, 23; Philippians 3:19.)

The Apocalypse

Apart from Matthew, the main source of subsequent thinking and teaching by the Church about a fiery hell of everlasting torment is the Book of the Apocalypse, better known as Revelation. Before citing examples from the text itself, a brief introduction is necessary.

The Book of Revelation is not just positioned as the last book in the New Testament, it was the last book to be included in the canon of authoritative New Testament writings. Most lay Church members, never mind outsiders, are unaware that this book was long regarded as questionable by the early Church, and its place was hotly debated for several centuries. It was particularly rejected by the Church in the eastern part of the empire and it was omitted from the Armenian and Syriac versions of the New Testament in their original form.

Although it claims apostolic authorship and was originally thought to be the work of St. John the Apostle, it was (and still is) evident to anyone who reads Greek that its barbarous style has nothing in common with the other works ascribed to John. Moreover, the author nowhere witnesses to a historical Jesus and refers to the twelve Apostles in a very reverential and removed manner, which is incompatible with one who belonged to such a group himself. He says he was in exile on the bleak, volcanic-rock island of Patmos, just off the coast of Asia Minor (modern Turkey) "for the word of God." That, and the obvious context of his visions, received "in the Spirit," has led scholars to believe he was a Christian who had been banished during the reign of the emperor Domitian. The date of the work, accordingly, may not have been earlier than that reign—81 to 96 CE.

While many contemporary fundamentalist Christians and sectarians now have a field day explaining the book as a blueprint for present and future world events—including the much-heralded Day of Armageddon—the imagery and references all make perfect sense *in the context of that time*. In an hour of persecution, when it was feared that the hated Emperor Nero had literally come back to life as Domitian, the author uses the apocalyptic mode to name the "beast" or Antichrist under a symbolic or coded message. The near-psychedelic nature of the visions and imagery suggests that they may have been caused by prolonged fasting and sensory deprivation. According to the tradition, the author lived in a cave and was forced to work in a marble quarry. This comment is by no means meant to imply, however, that divine inspiration was not also involved—as I hope to make plain later. Tourists visiting Patmos today are shown both the cave and the ancient quarry as the chief highlights of an otherwise desolate spot.

In exile, on a bleak, volcanic outcropping that itself suggested the end of the world, and in despair over the apparent triumph of evil in the form of Roman oppression and cruelty—Domitian had assumed the mantle of a despot and demanded that public worship be given him as *Dominus et Deus*, Lord and God—the author sees world cataclysm and a supernatural victory as the only just solution. Not unnaturally, his indignation and his desire to see the fate of the wicked expresses itself in images of fire without end.

The classic passages occur near the end of the book. In chapter 19, we read that the false prophet and the beast are taken and thrown into a lake of fire burning with "brimstone" (sulphur). The following chapter describes how the devil is also thrown into the lake of fire, where all three "shall be tormented day and night for ever and ever." The most horrendous passage comes in chapter 21 verse 8: "But the fearful, and unbelieving, and the abominable, and murderers, and whoremongers, and sorcerers, and idolaters, and all liars, shall have their part in the lake which burneth with fire and brimstone: which is the second death."

The article on hell in *The Oxford Dictionary of the Christian Church* rightly comments: "From such texts as these, often understood overliterally, the popular idea of hell was derived." From what has already been said above, it should by now be obvious that these verses are definitely not to be taken literally. What's more, they have little in common with the overall teaching given by the Gospels or the compassionate nature of God as revealed by them.

Subsequent Developments

One thing stands out in our survey of the roots of the doctrine of hell: there is no overall, consistent paradigm or metaphysical system worked out in the Bible. The ancient Hebrew mind was not given to philosophical or metaphysical abstractions; it thought in concrete images. As Oesterley and Robinson point out, "The forms most characteristic of the Hebrew genius are the lyric and the short prophetic oracle, instinct with life, throbbing with emotion, but rarely the product of deep and conscious reflection. Among such a people we must not look for any elaborate or deeply conceived metaphysic."[21] Thus, it is a mistake to try to impose a tight structure or pattern and say, This is what the Bible teaches about hell. The other contributing factor to this (to me) less than satisfactory imprecision is the way in which the Bible itself was formed. When you have a collection of some sixty-six writings or "books" written in different places by widely differing people at different epochs as much as several centuries apart, you must expect to find a development or process rather than a precise doctrine formulated neatly for all time.

This accounts for the way in which various groups and denominations in the history of the Church have been able to seize upon different strands in the tradition and thus develop a whole range of sometimes conflicting views. In his book *Early Christian Doctrines*, J.N.D. Kelly remarks that there was "great uncertainty, not to say confusion" over the details of the fate of the soul after death in all the writings of the early Fathers.[22] People like Origen, Gregory of Nyssa and Gregory Nazianus took a "soft" view of the meaning of hell, while others, including the great preacher John Chrysostom (347–407 CE) took a harsh, literal view. However, by the mid-fifth century "the stern doctrine that sinners will have no second chance after this life and that the fire which will devour them will never be extinguished was everywhere paramount."[23] Those who are familiar with the way other doctrines, for example, the teaching about the divinity of Jesus, developed during this same period, will realize that what later came to be believed by all or nearly all was not necessarily always an accurate reflection of the original meaning of the Biblical texts.

There is no consistent teaching about the fate of the "wicked" or the unrepentant in either the Old or the New Testaments. Nor,

172 THE WITNESS OF RELIGION

considering the figurative language used to describe hell, is there justification for the traditional, popular view of a literal place of eternal, fiery punishment for the "damned." No Jesus of history ever taught such a doctrine, and it desecrates the name of a loving God to preach and teach that he did. This conclusion will not please those Christians who hate to be disturbed by the facts, but it seems to me inescapable on the basis of the evidence.

In the Gospels, Jesus is frequently portrayed as using the argument that if we as earthly parents long to give good gifts to our own children how much more must "your heavenly Father" desire to give good gifts to those that ask.[24] If I, as a father, would never torment and punish a child for an hour, let alone a day, how blasphemous it is to suggest that a loving God would punish his "children" for eternity! This is not a God to be worshipped but one to be shunned and abhorred as a sadistic monster.

Yet if, as I have argued earlier, religious language is often metaphorical, what is the reality to which the metaphor or imagery of hell points? It is clear throughout the Bible that the holiness and justice of God, counterbalanced by his mercy and grace, always stand in judgment upon human thoughts, motives and actions. Given this, it makes sense that at the end of life there would be some kind of judgment passed upon us. As we have seen, even the most optimistic view of the contemporary near-death experience holds that there is a moment of review, or a kind of "tribunal," where the dying person sees the full meaning and direction of his or her life.

I believe, as we shall see more fully later, the evidence indicates that this judgment is a kind of self-judgment induced by finding oneself in the presence of God or of the Light. To see for the first time, perhaps, the full implications of what we have done and the way we have at times fallen short of our true humanity will be a kind of suffering or hell. To the extent that they were really a part of the teaching of the historical Jesus, this is what the stern imagery of his warnings was pointing to. Thankfully, this fleeting, though deeply humbling experience is not the whole story. It is the beginning of the road to growth into fuller life and maturity.

Since writing the above, I have come across a passage in Origen (185–254 CE), the brilliant Alexandrian Bible scholar, in which he roundly criticizes those who foolishly read the Scripture passages about life after death in a crudely literal fashion. Each sinner, he says, kindles his own fire and his or her vices "form its fuel." Professor Kelly comments: "In other words, the real punishment of the wicked consists in their own interior anguish." Moreover, Origen goes on to state emphatically that all such punishment must have an end. In his view, all things will ultimately be restored. In the end, all humanity and even the devil, he says, will return to wholeness—not by coercion but through persuasion and instruction. At the last, they will recognize their own true good and be reconciled with God. Origen thus preserves human free will on the one hand and God's merciful goodness, as well as justice, on the other.[25] His "universalism," that is, that all will ultimately be "saved," is a belief I also hold to be true.

What About Purgatory?

The failure to realize that all language about God is in the end metaphorical—a phenomenon most obvious in the traditional teachings about a fiery hell—crops up again when we examine the notion of Purgatory. Purgatory, from the Latin verb *purgare*, to cleanse or purify either physically or spiritually, is traditionally believed to be the place or state of temporary punishment "where those who have died in the grace of God [Christians] are expiating their venial faults and such pains as are still due to forgiven mortal sins," before being admitted to the Vision of God. The early Christian Fathers were faced with a problem. It was fairly easy to say that obviously holy people who died in the arms of mother Church were immediately ushered into the presence of God and granted the beatific vision after death. And the fate of those who were notorious sinners or pagans was quite clear also; they went to hell. But, what about the great throng of those who had been nurtured in the Church and its sacraments but had then fallen away? What about others who were practising Christians but, as St. Augustine said, were too much entangled with the things of earth to be fit to see God or enter His Presence? Using the same religious symbols and ideas (largely derived from Persian sources) that had shaped the doctrine of hell, the concept of a time of spiritual cleansing before the full beatific vision seemed to make good sense.

The main scriptural source was a passage in the Apocrypha (late Jewish writings that were part of the Greek version of the Old Testament but were not part of the Hebrew Bible itself). In 2 Maccabées 12 verses 39 to 45 we read how Judas Maccabaeus is said to have "made propitiation for them that had died that they might be released from their sin." There is nothing whatever about Purgatory, however, in the New Testament. Some scholars down the centuries have taken the saying of Jesus about the sin against the Holy Ghost being the one thing that can't be forgiven "either in this world or the next" as implying the possibility of expiation for *other* sins after death.[26] But this is not the obvious meaning. To suggest that a person's sins could be forgiven beyond the grave is not the same thing as insisting that there is a temporal place or state of suffering where such sin must be consumed or "paid for." In any case, the Gospel writer was not making a doctrinal statement about life after death in the verse cited. To say that an offence against the Holy Spirit is beyond forgiveness here or hereafter is simply a characteristic way of stressing how serious this sin is.

One other similarly figurative passage, this time from Paul, has been used to support the belief in Purgatory.[27] Paul is talking about a time when every deed or "work" will be tried by a kind of fire. Some works will be abiding; others will not stand the test. The person will suffer loss, he says, but "he himself shall be saved; yet so as by fire." If you take this phrase in the context of the whole metaphor that Paul is using here—that of a master builder who lays a foundation and then has others build various edifices upon it—you quickly see that nothing is further from his mind than setting down a basis for a doctrine of Purgatory, or indeed making any definitive statement about a future life.

Nevertheless, it is clear that the early theologians of both the Eastern and Western Churches used a belief in Purgatory to justify prayers for the dead and to answer the question of how visibly imperfect people could be made ready to behold perfection. St. Clement of Alexandria says that those who repent on their deathbed but have no time to do works of penance will be sanctified in the next world by "purifying fire." This thought was developed further by Origen and others, such as St. Cyril of Jerusalem and the famed preacher St. John Chrysostom. In the West, St. Ambrose taught that the souls of the departed await the end of time in different dwelling places, their fate varying with their deeds. St. Augustine, the greatest mind of all in the early Church—though capable of horrifying statements on such subjects as women or slavery—clearly taught that purifying suffering and pains are an absolute certainty in the life to come. This teaching was taken over later by St. Thomas Aquinas (*c.*1225–74) and other scholastics. These medieval teachers of theology and philosophy held that whatever its beneficial power, the least pain in Purgatory is "greater than the worst on earth."[28] The pain, however, is relieved, according to Thomas, by the certainty of salvation, which brings the souls of the faithful departed a great peace.

Aquinas and his contemporaries taught that those in purgatorial pain may be helped by the prayers of the faithful, and especially by masses said on their behalf. Aquinas based this belief on his firm commitment to the idea of the Communion of Saints, that is, the belief that the Church militant here on earth and the Church of the

faithful departed enjoy a spiritual unity. The practical result, however, was to extend the control of the Church beyond the grave to
the souls of the dead. The abuse of this power through, among
other things, the sale of indulgences (forgiveness of sins) and many
other distortions led to the protest of Martin Luther and the begin-
nings of the Protestant Reformation in Europe.

The sixteenth-century reformers, basing their doctrines on
Scripture alone, rejected the doctrine of Purgatory and taught that
souls are freed from sin by faith in Christ and, if saved, go directly
into God's presence. The Thirty-nine Articles of Religion set
out in the Book of Common Prayer by the Anglican scholars of
the Reformation state this view quite bluntly. Article XXII reads:
"The Romish doctrine concerning Purgatory, Pardons, Worshipping and Adoration as well as of Images as of relics and also Invo-
cation of Saints, is a fond thing vainly invented, and grounded upon
no warranty of Scripture, but rather, repugnant to the Word of
God."

While I find myself in agreement with the Reformation theologians on the absence of any firm scriptural foundation for the
Roman Catholic and Eastern Orthodox insistence upon Purgatory
as a place or state of refining punishment, I believe from my studies
that in throwing out the idea completely, Protestantism and Angli-
canism lost the truth to which the imagery of Purgatory really points.
What is missed, I am convinced, is the deeply intuitive sense that
whatever the life after death may be, it is not one of instant perfection. The doctrine is an imperfect and even crude attempt to witness to a belief that life beyond the grave involves growth into an
ever-greater spiritual maturity. Hans Küng seems to me close to the
mark when he argues that there is really no need, nor justification,
for a special place, event or time frame for this. What is intellectually required is a belief that our encounter with God after death will
be "profoundly humiliating, painful and therefore purifying."[29]
Küng sees Purgatory as a symbolic way of speaking of "encounter

with God in the sense that it judges and purifies, but also liberates and enlightens, heals and completes man."

In summing up, then: the purgatorial concept of fire and pain must be understood, as so much in the Bible, as an allegory. The reality is a matter of spiritual and mental awareness of one's shortcomings in the Presence of God. To be aware of this and to be in that Presence is to find gradual wholeness and holiness. The fire is the symbol of the pain that any such growth in consciousness requires. While it is comforting, as well as natural, to pray for the deceased, their well-being depends not upon our efforts—or expenses—but upon the all-encompassing mercy of God.

Limbo

Finally, a word about a much-misunderstood concept, limbo. Latin theology, with its love of systematizing and categorizing everything no matter how slim the evidence, postulated that in addition to heaven, hell and purgatory there must be another "place" for those who don't otherwise fit the scheme. Thus they spoke of a region on the borders of hell known as "the hem of Hell" or limbo. Here again there were held to be two divisions, the *limbus patrum*, in which the Old Testament saints were thought to stay until Christ's Second Coming and the redemption of the world, and the *limbus infantium*, the eternal place and state of infants who died unbaptized, and so unregenerate, but innocent of actual sins. Such infants were said to be excluded from the beatific vision of God, but, at least in the opinion of St. Thomas Aquinas, they enjoy a fully natural happiness.

Earlier, St. Augustine, perhaps led on by his polemics against the Pelagians, taught firmly that, since all who die unbaptized are still tainted by original sin, these infants necessarily must suffer some degree of "positive punishment."[30] Needless to say, there is absolutely no warrant for such a strangely sadistic view in any of the Scriptures. It is repugnant to common sense and our own moral judgment. In fact, it is the sort of nonsense which, if true, would render us more moral and compassionate than God. Sadly, the teaching regarding limbo has caused enormous suffering down past centuries among the uneducated and illiterate masses. It is one aspect of the Church's teaching about life after death that ought to be repudiated officially as unworthy of credence, now or ever. Significantly, *USA Today* (April 20, 2007) carried a prominent news story on this theme. It said Pope Benedict XVI has now reversed centuries of Catholic teaching about limbo by publicly approving a report about it from the Vatican's International Theological Committee. In essence, it said there are "serious grounds to hope" that children who die unbaptized can go to heaven. One can only comment that this kind of thinking is long, long overdue.

End Times

We return now to some problems touched on briefly in our discussion of the concept of a fiery hell—those posed by the very last book in the New Testament. Without question, the Book of Revelation, as interpreted by self-professed experts on "prophecy," has spawned more confused, speculative nonsense than any other book in the Bible. Because of a total unwillingness to acknowledge the peculiar, culture-specific nature of this work, combined with a stubborn determination to force literal meanings upon highly symbolic terminology, fundamentalists of various warring schools have twisted the text to fit patterns never intended by its author. The amazingly popular, doomsday-style books of the American Hal Lindsey and the multi-million-dollar industry of books and films of the Left Behind series are a part of this.

Scholars—and indeed anyone willing to use their reason and do even the most basic reading and research, particularly those who take the time to read Revelation—recognize that the book makes no claims to prophecies about events in the late-twentieth century. All the elaborate attempts to see the European Common Market, China, Russia and its satellites or Islam cited as major players in a drama leading up to a nuclear Armageddon are simply a deluded, paranoid exploitation of our contemporary fears. The point is that we know the kind of book this is and the kind of social and religious conditions that gave rise to the literary genre to which it so clearly belongs. It is a Christian version of the style of writing known as "apocalyptic," popular in Judaism in the two centuries before and in the period immediately after the birth of Christianity. As we have seen, it is the product of persecution and of despair of ever seeing God's justice done to his people *in this present life*. Thus it predicts an immediate, dramatic, divine intervention by God, the punishment of the wicked (oppressors) and the inauguration of eternal blessings for the righteous. It is a theology of despair.

Apocalyptic writing makes abundant use of colourful imagery and quite unashamedly sets events *that have already happened* in the future to throw new light upon their inner meaning. This was part of the coding, familiar to contemporary readers at earlier times but open to misunderstanding today by the naive or those with a preconceived fixation about the "inerrancy" of anything that appears in the Bible. What's more, apocalyptic books were regularly ascribed to prestigious personages from the past in order to ensure their being read and taken as fully authoritative.

For example, the Book of Daniel in the Old Testament was not written by Daniel. We know from its style and other similarities with second-century Jewish apocalyptic writings, plus the fact that it is written in Greek, not Hebrew like the rest of the Old Testament, that it came into being centuries after Daniel. Similarly, while the Book of Revelation may have been written by a man named John—one of the commonest male names of the period—it was certainly not written by the apostle John. Nor was it written by the

John to whom the Gospel and epistles are ascribed in the New Testament. There is absolutely no way anyone who knows Greek could suppose that all these works were penned by the same hand.

I suggest to those still reluctant to follow where the argument has taken us so far that they take a look at the ending of Revelation. As he sums up, the author once again follows a convention of his day—one that applied not just to apocalyptic writings but to all sorts of other documents as well. In Revelation 22 verse 19, he issues a stern warning that if anybody tampers with his book and cuts out parts of it God will damn him or her by cutting them out of "the book of life." I have heard evangelical preachers use this text to reinforce their own very subjective interpretations of this and other Biblical books. They utterly ignore the fact that this kind of warning was written into pagan documents from all over the ancient Near East at that time. There were no copyright laws, no guarantees that once a book left the author's hands it wouldn't be altered to suit the tastes of whoever acquired it. Consequently, you sent your work out complete with a curse on anyone who would dare to change it!

One of the clearest examples of this from antiquity is the paragraph added to the Greek translation of the Old Testament—commonly called the Septuagint, because there were allegedly seventy-two translators—in the third century BCE. The Epistle of Aristeas tells us that when the work was finished "the whole company . . . bade them to pronounce a curse in accordance with their custom upon anyone who should make alteration either by adding or changing or omitting anything."

I refer the reader to any scholarly, modern commentary on Revelation for a detailed exegesis or interpretation of its contents. It is important to stress that the language is that of myth and symbol. It conveys a meaning, certainly, but not that of the literal or surface rendering. Some of the concepts are quite conventional to apocalyptic writing in general, and quite out of step with what is taught elsewhere in the New Testament. For example, all the material about a first resurrection and a second resurrection is borrowed straight from the Jewish apocalyptic tradition and is without any corroboration or backing from the rest of the New Testament.

This is also true of the passages—fruitful of endless disputations between various kinds of fundamentalists today—that deal with a millennium or thousand-year reign of Christ on this earth, a belief known as millenarianism. I doubt very much whether any other single idea has ever caused so much division and acrimony among Christians as this one. Yet it was never put in the mouth of Jesus or Paul, it appears in only one book out of twenty-six in the New Testament and was clearly borrowed by the author from stock teaching in non-Christian sources. Millenarianism is thus an alien concept to the mainline teaching of Christianity about a future life. As the *Oxford Dictionary of the Christian Church* says: "Though Millenarianism has never been formally rejected by orthodox Christianity, it may be doubted whether there is adequate justification for it either in Scripture or in Christian tradition."[31]

Nevertheless, in spite of all that has been said so far, or, rather, in light of it, the Book of Revelation contains much that is sublime in relation to our understanding of Christian beliefs about the afterlife. If we realize that the author, in describing the world to come, is doing the best he can within the limits of human vocabulary, and that it is a fallacy to confuse metaphors and images with the realities being described, there are some very inspiring words here indeed. For example, who could fail to be moved by "And I saw a new heaven and a new earth. For the first heaven and the first earth were gone and there was no more sea. And I saw the holy city, the New Jerusalem, coming down from God out of heaven, prepared like a bride for her husband. And I heard a great voice coming from out of the throne saying, Behold the dwelling of God is with humanity and he will tabernacle among them, and they shall be his people and God himself will be with them. And He shall wipe away every tear from their eyes, and there shall be no more death, neither grief nor crying nor pain any longer . . . And He that sat upon the throne said: Behold I am making all things new."[32]

Equally haunting are the words that begin the final chapter of the book: "And He showed me a river of the water of life as shining as crystal proceeding forth out of the throne of God and of the lamb. In the midst of the plain and on either side of the river there was the tree of life, which bore twelve kinds of fruit . . . and the leaves of the tree were for the healing of the nations. And there shall be no more curse." Only the foolish would take this literally: There is no "throne" with a river flowing out of it. But the promises here of eternal life and of healing so powerfully expressed under the imagery of the tree of life and the flowing, crystal waters resonate with mystical truth. The throne is the author's only way of communicating his conviction that God reigns, and that because of this, life and wholeness are the ultimate destiny of humankind.

Elsewhere in this book, the author describes the New Jerusalem, his favourite metaphor for the life beyond, in the familiar terms of streets of gold and walls of amethysts, sapphires and other precious jewels. He, too, is responsible for the traditional hymnbook imagery of harp-playing crowds in white robes and endless, angelic choirs. Down the centuries, unfortunately, such caricatures of eternal bliss have become so familiar through religious art and language that they still are the first associative ideas to spring to most people's minds when the words "heaven" or "afterlife" are mentioned. If it is too late to convince contemporary men and women that none of that was ever meant to be taken literally—that the author of Revelation simply used the most precious things he knew to describe the indescribable—then it would be better to scrap the imagery altogether and begin again. That is the topic for a later chapter.

9

OTHER WORLD FAITHS

Zoroastrianism

ZOROASTRIANISM is one of the world's oldest living religious traditions. Although many Zoroastrians were reticent in recent years about identifying themselves in countries where they had at one time faced a great deal of persecution, recent publications of many major encyclopedias and world almanacs estimate their population worldwide to be between 2 and 3.5 million. Zoroastrians profess a faith that is estimated to be 3,500 years old and one that has had a profound influence upon Judaism, Christianity and Islam. Much of Hebrew thought concerning the Day of Judgment, angels, the afterlife and the nature of God as Light stems from this ancient source. Scholars believe Zoroastrian concepts lie behind some of the theology of the Essenes who produced the Dead Sea Scrolls (for example, the idea of a final battle between the Sons of Light and the Sons of Darkness). Similar thinking crops up again in New Testament references to the divine light, notably in the opening verses of John's Gospel. My own research leads me to the conviction that many other New Testament themes exhibit Zoroastrian parallels as well: a virgin-born Messiah, the coming of the Magi in Matthew's nativity story, the three days Jesus is said to have spent in the tomb, angels and demons, the importance attached to the figure seven, a flaming hell, a final battle between God and Satan and the belief in a restored or new earth at the end of time.

Zoroaster, or Zarathustra as he is also known, lived in ancient Persia. His precise dates are a matter of considerable learned debate, with some experts opting for a relatively recent sixth century BCE date and others for one as early as 1500 BCE The majority of scholars, however, seem to be leaning today towards some time between 1200 and 1500 BCE. We know he lived at a time when many gods and goddesses were the objects of popular devotion. Personal ethics or conduct were largely irrelevant to these cults; priests alone were thought worthy of entering Paradise.

Married, with a family, Zoroaster at the age of thirty had a series of revelatory experiences that changed his life. It was revealed to him that there was but one God over all, the Lord of Light, Ahura Mazda. He immediately began to preach against the polytheism of his neighbours and to warn that, at death, there would be a day of judgment when Ahura Mazda would weigh the deeds done in a lifetime. Like all the other prophets to come after him, he was met with rejection and persecution. It took him ten years to make his first convert, a cousin. But eventually, his beliefs not only took hold of the population at large, they became the official creed of the Persian Empire. The Magi (the Wise Men of Matthew who came from the East) belonged to a priestly tribe that acted not only as royal chaplains but as missionaries for their religion throughout the realm. By the Christian era, Zoroastrianism was widespread throughout much of the ancient Near East.

Cardinal Beliefs

Ahura Mazda, the Creator of all things, demanded a deeply personal, ethical response from every human being. We are all part of a cosmic battle that goes on continually between Ahriman (Satan) the evil spirit, and the forces of Light. The Light, which is the ultimate symbol for the deity, will one day prevail, but meanwhile Ahriman does his best to tempt and mislead us. There is a strong emphasis upon personal responsibility and integrity, because of which Zoroastrians, or Parsis (pronounced Parsees) as they are called in India, have always enjoyed a high reputation for industry and honesty wherever they have spread. They have been enormously successful in business and the various professions, and it is worth noting that the first three Indians ever elected to the British Parliament were Parsis.

Their temples, today as in antiquity, are beautiful in their chaste simplicity. The focal ornament at the front is a font-like bronze or copper stand where the flame, "symbolizing Him Who Himself is that Eternal Light," always burns. One or two pictures of Zoroaster, who is respected but not worshipped, may hang on the walls. Little lamps, fed by vegetable oil—not candles, which might contain animal fats—sit on trays in front of the fire and may be lit as a form of prayer. In North America, the temples are open to anyone who observes the simple rules of removing his or her shoes and covering the head with a shawl (for women) or a round, Persian-style cap. Zoroastrians have a profound reverence for all of creation, especially for the basic elements of air, earth, water and fire.

Death and the Tower of Silence

It is in Zoroastrian beliefs concerning death and the life to come that some striking features of this faith confront us. I knew about them, of course, from past study, but in order to see them afresh and to obtain them from a living source rather than written documents, I spent a morning at a Zoroastrian temple in Toronto. There are Zoroastrian communities today in India and Pakistan, as well as smaller ones in East Africa, London, Toronto, Montreal, Vancouver, Winnipeg, New York, Washington, San Francisco and Los

Angeles. The centre for the Zoroastrian Society of Ontario (1,000 members) stands on a secluded, wooded corner in Toronto, overlooking a branch of the Don River. It is only metres away from one of the busiest intersections in the north end of this sprawling metropolis, and yet it has about it the feeling of a rural sanctuary. The elected president of the society was Sam Vesuna, an accountant with a multinational company. He met me, showed me the grounds and the temple, and then spent considerable time explaining what Zoroastrians believe about death and the hereafter.

Undoubtedly the most unusual aspect of the entire discussion was the description of what is known as "the Tower of Silence." Today there are only a few of them still in use, in Karachi, Pakistan, and in various parts of India. These circular structures are placed on the highest point of ground in the area and consist of high walls around three gratings, one for men, one for women, and another for children, where the corpses of the deceased are exposed. The sun beats down, the vultures and crows consume the flesh (one source said this takes an average time of about thirty minutes), and the rains wash the remains. The ground beneath the gratings slopes to a central drain where everything is filtered and subsequent rainwater is then filtered four more times before being allowed to dissipate into the earth. When the elements have bleached the bones clean, they are gathered and buried reverently. The idea behind all of this is to avoid any possible contamination of the earth with the corruption of decay.

Vesuna explained that Zoroastrians in Iran use normal burial for their dead and in Bangalore, India, where there is a Tower of Silence, the community is divided between those who use it and those who bury their deceased. Here in North America, some inter the body in a burial plot and many practise cremation, later scattering the ashes on a special plot of ground. Smiling, he said his mother tells him she is happy to be living in Canada and to know she will not be exposed in the ancient manner. But, speaking with obvious depth of feeling, he said he wished there were a Tower of Silence here. "Personally, I believe that from an environmental point of view it is the ideal and correct way to dispose of the material body. And besides, our sacred books, particularly the Gathas [seventeen songs of Zarathustra], ask us to preserve all the elements of creation."

Because death is regarded as a temporary victory of evil over good, it is a time when there is a risk of evil spirits being present, but a number of rituals limit or prevent their influence. The soul of the departed is believed to hover close to the physical body for three days after death. At dawn on the fourth day the soul begins to travel and goes to the bridge of judgment known as the Chinvat Bridge. The soul or consciousness, before crossing the bridge, meets face to face with the representation of his own conduct, a guide called his *daena*. If his good deeds in earthly life outweighed his bad, his guide appears in the form of a beautiful maiden who leads him across to "the best existence" or heaven. Where the bad has exceeded the good, the spirit guide takes the form of a "very ugly maiden" and leads the soul to "the worst existence" or hell. There is a third, neutral place called Hamistagan, which is the temporary abode of those whose good and bad deeds balanced out. Here there is neither much happiness nor much pain.

Each of these "places" has several subdivisions depending upon the soul's "vibrations." The thinking here, Vesuna said, was that the holier a soul is, the greater the frequency of its vibrations and consequently the better its place in the "astral world." However, and this is where Christianity might have done well to have followed more closely, according to Zoroaster, this is not the last of the story. For some to remain in hell would mean a kind of defeat for Light or Ahura Mazda. Consequently, one day there will come a collective, final resurrection in which all are redeemed to spend eternity with

God. The good ultimately will prevail, and the earth and the heavens will be made new.

Vesuna told me that Zoroastrians believe in prayers for the dead as well as prayers asking the dead for their assistance. The Zoroastrians have a calendar with twelve months of thirty days each. The remaining five days are called the Days of the Gathas and constitute the major holy season. At this time, Vesuna explained, they thoroughly cleanse the sanctuary, recite the sacred Gathas and remember all the departed. Among the things prayed for are the various attributes of Ahura Mazda himself, such as "good mind," the power of self-control, perfection and, ultimately, immortality.

"It's a very moving time for all of us," he said. "I like to dwell on the various good things about deceased relatives, friends and others of my acquaintance. I have a deeply personal feeling that they are going to assist me as I try to live a better life."

The first time I ever met a Zoroastrian was in Rudyard Kipling's *Just So Stories*. In his story of how the rhinoceros got his wrinkly skin, Kipling has a character whom he calls the Parsee Man. When the Parsee teaches the rhinoceros a lesson for stealing his cakes by putting crumbs inside his skin while it hung out to dry in the sun, the Parsee chants: "Them as takes cakes that the Parsee Man bakes, makes dreadful mistakes!"[1] But, I have met many Zoroastrians now in real life as contrasted with fiction and they are without exception very find, hard-working people of high integrity.

Hinduism

Because the two cardinal tenets of Hinduism—the law of karma and the principle of the cycle of reincarnation—are by now so well known in the West as to be almost commonplace, it is not necessary to set out here a detailed description of this ancient world religion.

Nevertheless, some background information is essential to our understanding of Hinduism's approach to an afterlife.

What has to be realized first of all is that Hinduism is a faith that is in many ways very different from most of those we examine here. Hinduism has no one founder or prophet, and there is really no such thing as a Hindu creed; it is more like a massive spiritual and cultural movement holding within itself many complex and diverse schools of thought and rituals. Its origins lie deeply obscured by the mists of thousands of years—just as the Himalayan peaks that inspire its loftier moments are so often hidden by clouds.

The very word "Hindu" is itself the creation of Islamic invaders who referred to those living beyond the Indus River as "Hindus" in about 1200 CE. Radhakrishnan, a former president of India, is once said to have remarked that Hinduism is "more a culture than a creed." Certainly one cannot comprehend the "feel" and the essence of Hinduism without appreciating its deep-rooted relationship with the land of India itself—its mountains and life-giving rivers, its incredibly rich river valleys and broad plains, its demonstration of nature's nurturing kindness and of nature's fury, its cycles of teeming life and of unrelenting decay. For Hinduism, every rock and pebble, every aspect of the natural world, is filled with the energy of life and is part of the Divine. This is described by theologians as pantheism—everything is part of God—or as monism, all things are ultimately one.

Hindus practise yoga and meditation. The whole point of yoga, which means "yoke," is harmony with the one source of all being. Meditation has this same focus—inner attunement and union with ultimate reality or God. Brahman, the pure, absolute being or one God behind all and through all and in all, is defined (as in Christian mysticism) chiefly by negatives. In other words, Brahman is beyond any possible human descriptions. He is "the God beyond the word God." The many deities in the Hindu pantheon are all in varying degrees manifestations of aspects of Brahman. Another way of putting it is to say that they symbolize or express the broad range of energies active in nature and the cosmos.

Thus, while to westerners Hinduism seems like polytheism (and by inference, therefore, primitive and inferior), Hindus see themselves as truly monotheistic or better still as henotheistic ("hen" in Greek means "one"). There is but one Brahman, but there is a multiplicity of ways of approaching him. This accounts for the fact that the gods worshipped in one village in India may be quite different from those worshipped in the next, and also for the great tolerance shown by Hinduism for other faiths. Since there are many avatars or incarnations of the Divine in Hindu thought, the orthodox Christian view of Jesus or the saviours in other faiths make perfect sense to a Hindu.

What is important for our study is the belief that the *atman* or soul of each individual is a part or seed of Brahman. The divinity of the self must be perceived in order to see through the illusion of change and decay all around and ultimately achieve the peace of *moksha* (eternal release). This truth runs throughout the Hindu scriptures, but nowhere is it more eloquently described than in "the bible of Hinduism," the Bhagavad Gita. In this ancient, epic poem, "The Song of God" as it is often called, the core teaching is that our life on earth has one single end and purpose: to identify with our inner, eternal self and so attain the knowledge that we are one with the divine ground of the cosmos, God. For those familiar with John's Gospel, there are startling parallels. For example, Krishna, the incarnation of God, says to his friend Arjuna:

"For I am Brahman
Within this body,
Life Immortal
That shall not perish:
I am the Truth
And the joy forever."[2]

Again, speaking of the life to come, Krishna tells Arjuna: "'At the hour of death, when a man leaves his body, he must depart with his consciousness absorbed in me. Then he will be united with me . . . Therefore you must remember me at all times, and do your duty. If your mind and heart are set upon me constantly, you will come to me. Never doubt this. Practise meditation and do not let your mind be distracted. In this way, you will finally come to the Lord, who is the light-giver, the highest of the high.'"

Krishna here is the form in which the impersonal, absolute God, Brahman, becomes the personal, tenderly loving friend of humankind. Though there are marked differences, anyone familiar with the cycle of stories in the Hindu scriptures about Krishna cannot help but see other features that remind us of Gospel themes. Krishna has a miraculous birth and later has a narrow escape from those who would do him harm. Just as Moses had to be hidden from Pharaoh and Jesus from King Herod, so Krishna has to flee from his evil cousin Kamsa.

When it comes to reincarnation and the immortality of the soul, however, the Gospel parallels end. There are no words of Jesus to match Krishna's about the *atman*:

"Know this *atman*
Unborn, undying,
Never ceasing,
Never beginning,
Deathless, birthless,
Unchanging forever.
How can it die
The death of the body?"

And the same is true of Krishna's description of the rebirthing process:

"Worn-out garments
Are shed by the body:
Worn-out bodies
Are shed by the dweller
Within the body.
New bodies are donned
By the dweller, like garments."[3]

Since Hinduism is as much a culture as it is a religion, to be born a Hindu and to be a practising believer are not necessarily the same thing. (A situation not unknown in "Christian" societies either!) Trying to set a figure for the number of Hindus worldwide is made even more difficult by the fact that there is no centralized form of ecclesial organization. No membership rolls are kept and so no precise figures are available. Various informed sources I have consulted put the total somewhere around 1.3 million globally. There are roughly 200,000 Hindus in Canada and many beautiful temples.

The Afterlife: Rebirth or Liberation?

"The yogi's highest recompense is to become so firmly united with God after death that he need never again return to the status of migrating, mortal man. Several times in his life Mahatma Gandhi expressed the hope not to be born anew."[4]

Gokula Ranjana came from New York City, and in 1969, having graduated from a Boston college in occupational therapy, was working as a therapist in a New England Baptist hospital. At the same time, however, he was living a kind of bohemian, "hippyish" lifestyle and was deeply aware that there was a spiritual vacuum in his life. He met with some Hare Krishna youth one day and, intrigued, decided like many other young people in the late 1960s to "give it a try." By 1971, he was ready to become a full member himself and when I first interviewed him, at forty-one, he was an enthusiastic member of the Toronto Hare Krishna Temple.

Ranjana was an articulate spokesperson for a Krishna-centred form of Hinduism that has an ancestry going back centuries beyond the birth of Christ. In an interview, he explained the classical Hindu understanding of life after death:

"At the moment of death, the spirit-soul [*atman*] leaves the gross, natural body made up of the four elements of earth, air, fire and water. There is also a subtle body made up of mind, intelligence and the false ego. Depending upon the kind of life the person has led and what he or she is thinking of at the time of death, the spirit either takes this subtle body and enters another material body to be reborn or, discarding it, is liberated from the cycle of rebirth. This liberation is called *moksha*. The cycle of rebirth is *samsara*."

Ranjana was asked whether or not *moksha* or liberation was the result of one's own personal efforts (works) or a result of the gift of God (grace). The question, much debated in Christian circles, is solved, he said, by a combination of both. "Everything is of the grace of God or Brahman," he said. "But everything also depends upon how we as individuals use our free will to respond to this grace."

It is worth pointing out here that in Hindu thought this works-grace dilemma is illustrated by two theories. One, called the "kitten" approach, takes as its metaphor the way a mother cat carries her kitten in her mouth. The kitten is entirely passive, symbolizing the view that God's grace is the supreme element in salvation. The other theory, called the "monkey" approach, uses the way a mother monkey carries her young to make the point. The baby monkey is carried by the mother but plays his part by hanging on for dear life! The mother is ultimately responsible for the baby's life and safety, but not without some effort on his part as well. Most Hindu traditions take this latter view.

Ranjana went on to speak of the nature of *moksha*: "There are really two views of the liberation experience as well. The impersonalist view is that we are all God and there is no personal God. At the time of liberation from *samsara*, we are simply absorbed into the all and this itself is bliss. This union, however, is only for a time and then the process of rebirth will begin again. The predominant approach, though, is the personalist one. According to this, when one finally achieves liberation from *samsara*, the eternal person, with his or her spiritual body (a seed of which is always carried in the soul), goes into the spirit sky or 'heaven' to be with God forever. The individuality of the person always remains, but he or she is united in love with God and never returns to the cycle of rebirth again."

At this point, in spite of the differences, what he had to say was very close indeed to the Christian understanding of death and the life to come as I have defined it. Ranjana stressed that, in spite of the many gods and demigods of Hinduism, "there is but one God," but he can expand or make himself known in a thousand different ways. "After all, he is God!"

A Hindu Prayer
From the unreal lead me to the real!
From the darkness lead me to the light!
From death lead me to immortality!
    – From the Briha-Aranyaka Upanishad[5]

Buddhism

In contrast to what was believed by the scholars of the nineteenth century, there now seems little doubt in most circles that there may well have in fact been a historical person known as Siddhartha Gautama, later to become "the Buddha" or "enlightened one." However, because no "life" of the Buddha was written until several centuries after his death, the mixture of fact and legend is such that it is extremely difficult to reconstruct his biography. Suffice it to say that he was born in or about the year 563 BCE at Lumbini, on India's border with Nepal. Legend has it that his mother, Maya, gave birth to him miraculously. She had taken a vow of chastity but one day she dreamed that a white elephant had entered her womb. She died seven days after giving birth to Siddhartha Gautama and so, in a sense, like the Virgin Mary, can be said to have remained a perpetual virgin. (There are in fact many other startling parallels with the Jesus Story.) The young man grew up as a prince in great wealth and splendour and was protected from all outside influences by his watchful father, a rajah, and by his sister. Eventually, still inexperienced in the outside world, he married Yashodara and had a son by her, Rahula.

Even as a boy, he had shown an unusually keen intelligence with a remarkable thirst for knowledge. Anxious to know more about the world beyond the palace, he set out one day for a drive with his charioteer, Channa. The story tells how he took three journeys in all and each time saw something that caused him great questioning and disquiet. The first sight was that of a frail old man. The second was of an invalid, his body wracked with pain. The third was of a funeral cortège with its weeping mourners. When he asked Channa what these things meant, he was told that age, disease and death are the common lot of all men. Pondering all of this and becoming increasingly dissatisfied with the luxury and unreality of his courtly existence, the young man came to the conclusion that the cycle of birth and rebirth was the source of all human misery. He determined to discover some way out of this morass of suffering and to teach it to others. On a fourth trip away from the palace grounds, he came across a holy man who was a beggar. The monk seemed the happiest man he had ever met, and he decided that that was to become the way of life for him.

Thus, according to the tradition, at the age of twenty-nine Sid-dhartha Gautama bade farewell to his sleeping wife and child and set out on his personal journey alone. He travelled to famous gurus for a while and then, for a time, tried a life of even more extreme asceticism, almost ruining his health completely. Finally, he adopted a quieter, more meditative, trusting approach to his search.

One night, during the May full moon, having been deep in med-itation for some hours under the Bo tree, enlightenment came. In a flash of illumination, he saw for the first time the origins of evil, the cause of all suffering and the way by which it could be overcome. His first temptation was to enter into Nirvana, to be, as it were, a Buddha only unto himself. But he resisted this in the deep convic-tion that he was being called to preach the deliverance or way of sal-vation he had found to the rest of humankind.

The Buddha's first sermon was preached at Benares during the July full moon, and he won as his converts five ascetics who had previously spurned his company. Immediately, they were ordained by him and sent out to teach "the Dharma" (the Way) to their fel-low Indians. Ignoring the Hindu caste system, Gautama Buddha took his disciples from every walk of life. As soon as there were sixty of them, he sent these out as missionaries as well. At first he didn't permit women to be disciples because they epitomized the cycle of rebirth and the craving for life; but before too long, he admitted them as well. He died at eighty years of age at a place called Kushinagara.

The Teaching

Although later developments moderated his teaching on this point, Buddha himself denied the existence of the gods of Hinduism and of other religions. Pure Buddhism can be described as a form of atheism. He took over the belief in karma and the cycle of rebirth from Hinduism, but with a significant difference. He did not accept the idea of an individual *atman*, or soul, which one day will be re-united with Brahman, or God. He believed that good deeds bring a good rebirth and evil deeds the reverse—that, he said, was the moral order of the cosmos and hence inescapable. But the basic components of the world are always coming together and dissolving to combine in new ways. It is an illusion, he believed, to hold that the individual is an independent or permanent unit. We are just a flowing together of constituent aspects which come to form a new person after death. There is no "self" to remain constant through these rebirths. Yet paradoxically, to us at any rate, though there is no immortal soul, karma links the consecutive lives together.

Buddha's need to deny the reality of the soul or self becomes apparent as soon as one examines his thought further. Here are the "Four Noble Truths," which were revealed to him at his enlightenment:

- Suffering is universal, no human is free from it from birth to death;
- The cause of suffering is desire or craving and these lead to rebirth and more suffering;
- Deliverance from suffering is man's only salvation. This means escape from the enslavement of desire;
- This can only be attained by following the Eightfold Path of right belief, right attitude or aspiration, right speech, right action, the right occupation or means of living, right effort, right memory or mindfulness and right meditation or composure.

What this boils down to is an overwhelming concern with the moral principles of right living rather than with religious rites or ceremonies. The spread of Buddhism happened amazingly quickly. Its reverence for all life, its emphasis upon non-violence and its high moral demands soon made it a way of life for most of Asia and beyond.

There are, as with other religions, two main branches in Buddhism today, the Theravadins, who are the stricter, more conservative group, and the much larger Mahasanghikas, the liberal movement. The Theravadins, more widely known as Hinayana Buddhists, reject prayers to Buddha, images, rituals and any form of divine help in the moral quest. The others, known today as Mahayana Buddhists, hold that salvation is not just for monks and sages but for all humankind. It's a broad, very humane religion with many concessions to the needs of popular piety. It comes close to Christianity with its belief in saviours and in its Paradise of the West, the land of Sukhavati, where the blessed live in ecstasy after death. Sukhavati was originally thought to be a stage on the way to Nirvana but it is now increasingly seen as an end in itself. In this form of Buddhism, worshipping a particular Buddha or enlightened one can be a way of holiness for those too weak to follow all the disciplines of stricter Buddhism.

Nobody knows how many Buddhists there are in China today or in Russia and its former Soviet satellite countries. That, together with the fact that Buddhists are not organized in the way many other religions are, means that it is very difficult to say with precision how many there are worldwide. There are only some 5 million in India, but, when you take into consideration Japan, Myanmar, Tibet, Sri Lanka, Korea, Campuchea and other parts of Southeast Asia, as well as emigration and the growing number of converts to Buddhism in the West, the total, according to some authorities, could be as high as 500 million.

"Life After Life" in Buddhism

Samu Su Nim is a Zen Buddhist master and when I first talked with him, he was spiritual head of a Zen Buddhist temple on Vaughan Road in Toronto. In an interview, he explained that Zen Buddhism, which originated in China and was further developed in Japan, doesn't make "a big thing" out of life after death. He said: "We prefer to speak of life after life, or of the emergence of a new birth rather than of death itself." He noted that classical Buddhism believes there are four stages or periods that are repeated until the spirit escapes the wheel of rebirth and enters Nirvana. These are conception, one's earthly lifetime, death, and the intermediate stage known as "the Bardo."

Upon death, the spirit wanders to find its "proper place" for forty-nine days. In the cases of individuals who have had some very strong "attachment" to worldly ambitions, cravings and desires— even some strong emotional tie such as a deep resentment—this period can last up to one hundred days. But, at some point during this Bardo state, the decision is made and a new conception or rebirth takes place. Very holy people, sages, monks and others, would normally be expected to escape rebirth at this point and go to Nirvana, Samu Su Nim said. But very often they are reborn because they have taken an oath to put off Nirvana for a specified series of cycles so that they can return to help others. The technical name for such a person is a Bodhisattva. He or she becomes more than just a teacher; he or she is a kind of saviour figure who assists others to attain enlightenment.

I asked the Zen master about what it is that survives from life to life. Since Buddhism asserts that the primary source of pain and suffering is illusion and that the chief illusion is the identity of the ego itself, it cannot be the self of the ego that carries on from life to life. He replied that this is precisely why Buddhists prefer to speak of rebirth rather than of reincarnation; the latter term suggests the ongoing experience of the same soul. Buddhists do not believe it is the same individual who survives but rather "the karmic forces" organized around him or her.

Nirvana, which means quite literally extinction—as in the blowing out of a candle—is a difficult concept for westerners to comprehend. In fact, Samu Su Nim himself admitted that Zen Buddhists, who like to work with paradoxical riddles known as *koans*, find the concept of Nirvana to have a *koan*-like or riddling nature. It is spoken of as extinction and as nothingness, and yet it is also described as ultimate peace and bliss. You can get the idea that it means total obliteration, but this would be to misunderstand. What is extinguished, he said, is all delusion, all defilement, all attachment to illusions of any kind. "Whatever is left is good and pure and enters into peace and happiness." When I asked him if this means some kind of absorption into the All or into the Source of all things, the master said he likes to think of it as entrance into a "universal identity" or into Buddhahood itself. As Hans Küng remarks, this is not as far from the Christian concept of heaven or paradise as a superficial glance might suggest. There is the promise of a kind of personal bliss which is entered into by trust in the teachings and power shown in and by the Buddha.[6]

The Tibetan Book of the Dead

Before leaving Buddhism, a few words must be said about this, one of the most remarkable treatises ever written. Its full title is *The Tibetan Book of the Dead, The Great Liberation Through Hearing in the Bardo*, the intermediate state before rebirth. Probably the best modern translation of this singular work is by Chogyam Trungpa Rinpoche, with an introduction by Francesca Fremantle.[7] Chogyam Trungpa first received the tradition contained in the book at the age of eight and was instructed in its teachings by special tutors steeped in Tibetan Buddhist lore. He was given intensive training in dealing with dying people and, while still a child, began visiting the dead and dying. He tells us in the preface:

"Such continual contact with the process of death, particularly watching one's close friends and relatives, is considered extremely important for students of this tradition, so that the notion of impermanence becomes a living experience rather than a philosophical view."[8] The texts to be read in the presence of the dying or recently dead are a means of guiding the deceased through the various levels of post-death consciousness so that, if possible, rebirth can be prevented. There are instructions on how to avoid the "mouth of the womb" and being reborn in some animal, bird or human form.

What is quite remarkable is that there are some extraordinary parallels between the kind of experiences described here and those attributed to the near-death experience by contemporary researchers. Most notable of all is the sense of luminosity. The text explains how at the moment after death the deceased will see his loved ones gathered around and will not be certain whether or not he or she is dead or what has happened. The sense of being without one's ego brings a kind of "shakiness." But this is quickly followed by a state of luminosity where one sees images of light and then "dazzling light." To understand the book fully would take a longer explanation of Buddhist psychology than we have need of for our central theme. But it is important to be aware that, whereas we in the West think of sin as always associated with guilt and punishment, Buddhism looks beyond sin and suffering to their root cause. This, as we have seen above, consists of a false belief in the self and the illusory world it projects. Instead of seeing the real world, the self creates a false universe of its own. As Fremantle notes, the purpose of *The Tibetan Book of the Dead* is to help the person to recognize his or her projections and to be liberated from the ego in the light of reality. The various stages the book says the deceased spirit passes through are spoken of in terms of different deities. These are not really gods in the usual sense but a way of speaking symbolically about the energies and emotions that make up our conscious lives.

Thus, to quote Fremantle again, while the book was written ostensibly for the dead, "it is in fact about life . . . It is often emphasized that the purpose of reading the Bardo Thotrol [Book of the Dead] to a dead person is to remind him of what he has practised during his life. This Book of the Dead can show us how to live."[9]

Having been once a parish priest myself and, as stated before, having been present with many dying persons at the end, I have been deeply impressed by the wisdom and depth of understanding shown by Chogyam Trungpa in his commentary on these texts, even though much of their content seems foreign to my own background. This is supremely true when he speaks about the need for honesty and for the communication of a deep sense of solidarity with the dying. "Fully being there is very important when a person dies," he instructs. "Just relating with nowness is extremely powerful, because at this point there is uncertainty between the body and the mind [of the dying]. The body and the brain are deteriorating but you are relating with that situation, providing some solid ground."[10] If those attending the dying person are very stable, he says, those entering the Bardo state will relate to that. "In other words, present a very sane and solid situation to the person who is going to die. Just relate with him or her, just open to each other simultaneously, and develop the meeting of two minds." Unfortunately, with so many of us dying in hospitals, heavily drugged and often full of tubes, this kind of "good death" is in the West today the exception rather than the norm.

Judaism

The Jewish religion, the most ancient of the world's three great Abrahamic faiths, is parent to both Christianity and Islam. The current Jewish Year Book puts the number of Jews at just over 14 million, with about 6.5 million of these living in North America and 3.5 million in Israel.

Unlike some other faiths, most notably Christianity, Judaism has no formal creeds to which one is required to give assent. The heart of the religion is found in the Shema (from the Hebrew word for "hear"), which is the name given to three passages of the Hebrew

Bible that are recited twice daily by every deeply pious Jew. The Shema begins: "Hear, O Israel, the Lord our God, the Lord is one, and you shall love the Lord your God with all your heart, and with all your soul, and with all your might. And these words which I command you shall be upon your heart." Love of the one God is expressed by obedience to His law, the Torah, or the first five books of the Bible.

The real distinctions to be made between the major branches of Judaism today are not primarily a matter of theology so much as of practice. The extent to which adherence to the ritual, dietary and other laws is maintained depends upon the attitude taken to the Torah, the "Books of Moses." Thus, while the Orthodox take the view that the words of the Torah are divine and totally authoritative, and hence are very strict about adherence to all 613 commandments laid down there—on everything from personal hygiene to diet—more liberal Reform Jews take a much more relaxed position. Conservative Judaism stresses the importance of the tradition but tries to balance this with the kind of accommodations felt to be necessary in the modern world. Accordingly, although the Orthodox, who see themselves as the only "Torah-true" Jews, might deny it, it is very difficult to make the statement "Judaism believes or teaches this or that" about specific aspects of religious life. Among devout Jews of every major branch, Orthodox, Conservative or Reform, there is widespread agreement or acceptance of the reality of an afterlife, but it ranges all the way from "a strong sense of hope" on the part of many Reform Jews to a literal belief in the physical resurrection of the body by most of the Orthodox. It would take several books to do justice to a theme as large as this where Judaism is concerned. Here I can just sketch the main outlines, and I have chosen once again to let representatives of Judaism do the talking rather than impose my interpretations on them.

We will begin with two Reform rabbis who are both internationally known and who have been friends of mine for some time.

The late Rabbi Jordan Pearlson was the leader of the large congregation at Temple Sinai, in the north end of Toronto, and Rabbi Dow Marmur was the senior rabbi at Holy Blossom Temple, Toronto, one of the oldest and most prestigious centres of Jewish worship in Canada. Asked for his personal beliefs about the afterlife, Pearlson admitted to having been fairly skeptical when he first came out of college: "I felt then about theology the way (though I was still single) that I felt about doing marriage counselling. Since I was unencumbered by experience, I knew all the answers! But the longer I sit in the rabbi's chair and listen to my people, the more I become convinced that there are whole realms of life which can't be expressed mechanically or mathematically. I have found that the essence of spiritual maturity is the refusal to slam doors."

Noting that one distinguishing feature worth stressing about Judaism is that there never has been a concept of damnation or of eternal punishment, Pearlson said that in Reform Judaism there is a full range of options—all the way from a belief in reincarnation or the transmigration of souls to physical resurrection. He pointed out that there is unanimity among believing Jews (as testified to in prayers of memorial said for the deceased) about the concept that all souls rise to a higher level after a year in a kind of purgatorial state (She'ol). In other words, there is a period of spiritual cleansing which takes place. "An Orthodox boy will say prayers for his dead father for eleven months rather than the entire twelve to avoid the impression that he had not accumulated enough merit for at least one month."

Pearlson said that the idea of a physical resurrection has been unacceptable to the majority of liberal, western Jews, but that the belief that there is "something which does continue beyond physical death" is an important part of the Reform tradition: "In our memorial prayers we ask that God take notice of this particular soul." The rabbi noted that the idea of an afterlife is implicit rather than explicit in the Hebrew Bible. It became an important doctrine during the two centuries immediately preceding the beginning of the Common Era (the time since Christ's birth), when the old conviction that the righteous would be vindicated in this life was virtually impossible to hold in the face of repeated oppression of the Jews by foreign powers. It was the development of this teaching by the Pharisees (as opposed to the Sadducees) that ensured that life after death would remain a key tenet of Judaism for more than two thousand years.

Rabbi Dow Marmur told me he likes to express his personal approach to the matter of life beyond death in terms of hope rather than as a creedal proposition. "We don't know for certain what happens, but we have a lively hope. It is this hope that permeates our memorial prayers and our entire understanding of death." Marmur was critical of Reform Jews, particularly rabbis, who simply dismiss or skirt the issue of life after death and leave others to "fill in the gaps themselves." He said: "This is unacceptable to me. The rabbis and Rabbinic Judaism are heirs to the Pharisees and they were the party that believed in a future life."

Marmur agreed with Pearlson about the difficulties Liberal Jews have with a literal understanding of the resurrection of the body and made this interesting comment: "The ancients knew as well as we do what happens to the body when one dies. But because they believed in the unity of the body and soul—seeing man as a psychosomatic entity—they used the concept of a physical resurrection as a metaphor to express their belief that this unity continues after death." (I found, however, in talking to Orthodox and ultra-Orthodox or Hasidic rabbis, that most, though not all of them, take the language about physical resurrection literally.) In Marmur's view, the beliefs of both Orthodox and mystical forms of Judaism about the afterlife stem from the human "thirst for certainty, where hope is not enough."

Rabbi Barry Levy, professor of Jewish Studies at McGill University, Montreal, belongs to the Orthodox tradition. He too stressed the broad spectrum of beliefs held by Jews about the afterlife, no matter which branch they belong to. He himself is "not sure" about the matter of a literal, physical resurrection. At the same time, he feels some sympathy with those Jews who quote a saying from an ancient rabbinical source in support of their literalist belief: "If God can put a soul into the body of a baby which doesn't yet exist, why can't he put a body which once did exist back together with its soul?" Levy also said he does not personally believe in repeated reincarnations, just the possibility that our soul or inner essence will be reunited with a body in the life to come. However, he pointed out that the Talmud and other Jewish sources do testify to an ancient belief in reincarnation among Jews and said that, while it is not preached as an article of faith, it is a position still widely held by many traditional, Orthodox believers today.

Jewish Mysticism

Many ordinary Jews with whom I spoke in my research were totally unaware that there has also been a strong mystical tradition within Judaism from earliest times that holds quite firmly to a belief in reincarnation as part of its overall understanding of life after death. The Kabbalah (also spelled Cabbalah), a Jewish mystical tradition that developed in Spain in the thirteenth century but has roots going back to at least the second century CE, uses a kind of esoteric approach to the Hebrew Bible, including direct, mystical insights, allegory, various ciphers and at times even astrology. The aim is to get at the "secret" meanings behind the surface texts. The most important Kabbalistic work is the Zohar, attributed to a second-century writer but actually written much later and edited into its final form by Rabbi Moses de Leon in Spain in the Middle Ages. It has been called the Talmud of Jewish mysticism and was a major influence upon Israel ben Eliezar known as the Baal Shem Tov (1700–60) who founded the Hasidic movement. Hasidism began in

Poland under the Baal Shem Tov and has been from its inception a popular type of religious expression, combining passionate devotion to God—expressed in ecstatic prayer, singing and dancing—and a strict commitment to the Law in every aspect of life. These ultra-Orthodox Jews are characterized by their old-world style of dress, with black coats and curled earlocks, and their enthusiastic approach to worship. They have many different sects around the world but the best-known in North America are the Lubavitchers.

I spoke with Rabbi Dr. Ronnie Fine, who was at Chabad House, a synagogue in Montreal, and was a chaplain at McGill University. Fine is a Lubavitcher and totally convinced that reincarnation is an essential part of Judaism. He pointed out that the Talmud, which is "accepted by every observant Jew," has many stories and references to reincarnation. The purpose of reincarnation, Fine said, is to enable every soul to fulfill its purpose. "Every soul has a purpose and if it doesn't fulfil it in one life then it comes back again until it accomplishes it. A person could come back and live sixty or seventy years just to do a favour to one person—if that was their purpose and it hadn't yet been done." Cranston and Williams, in *Reincarnation: A New Horizon in Science, Religion, and Society*, devote a whole chapter to the Hasidim and include the following Hasidic prayer: "Master of the Universe! I hereby forgive anyone who has angered or vexed me, or sinned against me . . . in this incarnation or in any other." Those who wish to pursue the subject further should read *For the Sake of Heaven*, by Martin Buber, one of the greatest Jewish thinkers and literary figures of the twentieth century. The story concerns two Jewish mystics who were gifted with the ability to gauge from the lines in the foreheads and hands of those who came to them, as well as from their general auras, the paths their souls had taken in their previous incarnations and wanderings from life to life.

In our interview, Rabbi Fine went on to describe the position held by the Orthodox in general on the afterlife. After death, he explained, the soul goes through a period of cleansing and then goes to be with God. Once the Messiah comes, with the kindling of the "spark of God" in all who are alive at that time and the ensuing peace that will grow from that, the stage is set for the final resurrection. At that time, the soul will be reunited with the physical body and people will then be ready to live in a wholly renewed earth forever. The peace and wholeness of the original Eden will have been restored.

In summary, it can be said fairly that contemporary Judaism affords its members a very broad range of options regarding life after death and, since it is an area where absolute knowledge is not possible, most rabbis I interviewed are quite content with that. The uniting factor behind this spectrum of choices is, as already noted, the strong belief that the soul or whatever we choose to call the real person lives beyond the grave and ultimately returns to its Creator.[11]

Islam

Few North Americans are aware that there are now far more Muslims—over 3.5 million—in the United States than there are Episcopalians (Anglicans). This means that Islam is now a major American religion. The same situation prevails in Canada, where some 750,000 Muslims exceed many of the old "mainline" denominations such as Presbyterians, by a very large margin. While Muslims do not need a mosque in order to worship Allah, there are now well over 125 mosques in the United States and one in at least every city in Canada, with several in Toronto and Vancouver. Worldwide, there are about 1.5 billion Muslims—and 2.3 billion Christians, making Islam the second-largest religion in the world next to Christianity. In spite of this, and in spite of the fact that Islam is a religion of peace and conciliation, as its holy book, the Qur'an, makes quite clear, there is a widespread tendency in the West to equate "Muslim" with "terrorist." The violent actions of a few fanatics in the Middle

East combined with such events as shattering suicide bombings in the Middle East and the world-traumatizing devastation of 9/11 in the United States have tarnished the image of the entire religion. The view that all Muslims are extremists or terrorists has as much validity as the claim that all Catholics are thugs because of the bombings and shootings by the IRA, or that all Protestants are bigots and killers because of the outrages of a few Ulster Loyalists.

Space and the focus of our inquiry do not permit me to even skim the surface of the story of Islamic development or to begin to give details of the complexities of Muslim theology and laws. It would take a full volume just to describe the enormous contributions to art, architecture and general learning that Islam has made down the centuries.[12] But, in order to set the teachings of Islam on the afterlife in their proper context, some introductory remarks must be made about the origin and leading tenets of the faith.

Since the cardinal affirmation of any true Muslim is: "There is no God but God [Allah] and Muhammad is his prophet," the place to begin is with the Prophet himself. But, it will help make things easier to look first at the etymology of the words "Islam" and "Muslim." In Arabic, the root *slm* means "to be in peace, to be an integral whole." From this comes Islam, "to surrender to God's laws and be an integrated whole." A Muslim, accordingly, is a person who surrenders to the rule and sway of God. Muslims believe that Islam is God's eternal religion. It was the religion of the Old Testament patriarchs and not just of Muhammad and his followers. Its central teachings about the one true God are those brought by every prophet of the past, including Jesus, or Issa ben Yussuf as he is called in Arabic. Muhammad, however, is regarded as the last and greatest of God's Messengers, "the Seal of the Prophets."

Muhammad was born in Mecca, in what is now Saudi Arabia, in or about the year 570 CE. Early in life he lost both parents and knew great poverty and hardship. At age twenty-five, however, having led several successful trade caravans for the wealthy widow

Khadija, he married her and took his place among the privileged elite of the city. Mecca was already a prosperous and renowned centre of both commerce and religious cults. Its strategic position made it a meeting place for the caravans trading between the Middle East and Asia, and its ancient shrine of the Ka'ba, which houses the sacred black stone (actually an ancient meteorite), had been a focus of pilgrimages from earliest times. Polytheism and immorality were rampant. Muhammad, who was troubled by the religious and political divisions of the various competing tribes and disillusioned with the wealth and lifestyle of the privileged class, began to spend more and more of his time in solitude in the desert. About 610 CE, while meditating in a cave on Hira Mountain, overlooking Mecca, he received the first of what were to be many revelations from the angel Gabriel. These messages, written down and collected together, eventually formed the Qur'an.

You have to read the Qur'an yourself (preferably in Arabic!) to get its full sweep and beauty, but its central theme can be briefly stated: That Allah is One God; his attributes are unbounded might and unlimited mercy. As creator and judge of every individual and nation, he will one day call all to account before his judgment throne. The greatest error is to assign divinity to any god or person other than Allah. Thus, while Jesus is highly respected as one of the greatest of the Messengers of God and his mother, Mary, is accorded the greatest of respect, the Qur'an explicitly condemns the view that Jesus is part of the Godhead.

In the Qur'an, there are provisions for every aspect of personal and community life. Thus, for the Muslim, there is no breach between religion and, say, politics. The faith is meant to be a total way of life. There are five basics of faith: belief in God, in angels, in revealed books, in God's Messengers and in the judgment of the Last Day. Corresponding to these are the five rules of practice: bearing public witness at least once in a lifetime that there is no god but God and that Muhammad is his prophet; praying towards

Mecca five times daily; paying *zakat* (charitable offerings); fasting during the month of Ramadan, the ninth month of the Islamic lunar year; and making the pilgrimage to Mecca at least once, provided one can afford to do so without harming close family members.

As with Buddhism and Christianity, there are two major denominations, the Sunni (90 percent) and the Shi'a, who make up the rest. The split began as a dispute over who could properly succeed Muhammad as ruler over the Muslim community. The Sunnis believed that nobody could succeed the Prophet and so were content to choose a caliph or guardian of the prophetic legacy. He had to come from Muhammad's tribe but not necessarily from his clan or house. The Shi'as, on the other hand, insisted that after Muhammad, the rule had to pass to 'Ali (his cousin, adopted son and eventual son-in-law), and then from him to 'Ali's descendants. In the course of time, however, many theological and other differences emerged, none of which need detain us here.

The Afterlife

In regard to basic teachings about life after death, there are no major differences between the two main groupings. The key theme is that God has promised to reward those who do good and to punish those who do evil on the Last Day. In Islam, the moral significance of every earthly deed, thought and word is taken to the highest intensity. The life to come, *Al-Aakhira*, is totally shaped by one's present life. The hereafter begins with the general resurrection of humanity and is followed immediately by "a moment when every human will be shaken as he is confronted with his intentions and his deeds, good and bad, and even by his failure to do good in this life."[13] By this means, the dilemma of why bad things happen to good people, while often the wicked seem to flourish, is ultimately resolved. Because of the nature of God's mercy and justice, the injustices of this present life will be compensated for.

The Qur'an more than once addresses the doubts and hesitations of those who find the idea of a physical resurrection impossible to believe: "O mankind! If you are in doubt concerning the Resurrection, [remember that] verily We have created you out of dust, then out of a drop of sperm, then out of a germ-cell, then out of an embryonic clump complete and yet incomplete, so that we might make your origin clear unto you . . . And [if you still doubt] you can see the earth dry and lifeless—and suddenly when we send down waters on it, it stirs and swells and puts forth every kind of lovely plant! All this happens because God alone is the Ultimate Truth, and because He alone brings the dead to life . . . and will indeed resurrect all who are in the graves."[14]

The judgment itself is expressed—as in many religions and myths—in terms of a weighing or balance of the good and evil to see which has predominated: "And We will set up a just balance on the Day of Resurrection, so no soul shall be dealt with unjustly in the least, and though there be the weight of a grain of mustard seed, We will bring it forth, and sufficient are We to take account."[15]

On reading through the Qur'an in its entirety, the non-Muslim will be struck by the vividly detailed descriptions both of heaven and of hell. They occur with almost startling frequency and there is no indication that they are meant to be taken as purely symbolic or metaphorical. For example, on hell: "Verily, We have prepared for the wrongdoers a fire whose flaming canopy shall enclose them. And if they cry for help, they will be helped with water like molten lead which will burn their faces. How dreadful the drink, and how evil is the Fire as a resting place!"[16] Heaven or paradise, on the other hand, is described like this: "And He [Allah] will reward them for their steadfastness, with a Garden and a raiment of silk; reclining therein upon couches, they will find there neither excessive heat nor excessive cold. And its shades will be closed over them, and its clustered fruits will be brought within easy reach . . . And there will wait upon them youths who will not age."[17]

Interestingly, there will be different degrees or stations within both paradise and hell, and the Qur'an speaks as well of a kind of intermediary place between them where those who didn't incline either to good or to evil will go. "These are the indifferent ones. They will be placed in a station between Heaven and Hell, longing to go to Paradise and fearing to be put among the evil-doers."[18] In spite of the apparent starkness of this picture, there are some ameliorating factors. Those who are believers in God but whose balance of evil deeds outweigh their good deeds will only experience hell for a period of time. According to the Qur'an, God can and will forgive those who repent during this time—excepting the sin of *shirk*, which means the associating of others with his Godhead or glory. What is more, in one of the *hadith*, or traditions of the Prophet not in the Qur'an, he is reported to have said that even hell may not be a permanent place. "Surely a day will come over Hell when it will be like a field of corn that has dried up after flourishing for a while. Surely a day will come over Hell when there shall not be a single human being in it."[19] In the end, God's mercy triumphs over his justice and all shall be saved. As the Qur'an says, Allah is always "the Mighty, the Great Forgiver."

Reincarnation in Islam?

Under the heading "Religious Schools of Islam," the authors of *Reincarnation: A New Horizon in Science, Religion, and Society* attempt to show that reincarnation has always been a significant part of Muslim teachings about life after death.[20] They cite a number of authorities and texts, but this is certainly one of the weakest links in their overall argumentation. For example, they quote a couple of passages from the Qur'an which, in their view, support the case for Muslim belief in this doctrine. However, the meaning of the verses is quite plain and fits entirely within the framework we have already examined above. They are quite similar, and so it will be sufficient to quote one only: "Allah hath caused you to grow from the earth, and afterwards He maketh you return thereto, and He will bring you forth again."[21] This obviously means that Allah created us, is with us as we die, and will one day raise us up in the general Resurrection. To foist reincarnation upon such wording is to play fast and loose with the text.

It is true that there have been and are all kinds of different small sects and schools within Islam, as is true in the other great world religions. There is also little doubt that some of these tiny mystical minorities have believed in a form of reincarnation. But it has never been a mainstream element in the way it has, for example, within Judaism. The overwhelming majority of Muslims and their leaders have always been stoutly opposed to reincarnational theories on the basis of "one lifetime, one chance to be responsible before God."

Baha'i

"You shall, most certainly, return to God, and shall be
called to account for your doings in the presence of Him
Who shall gather together the entire creation."

– Baha'u'llah

The Baha'i faith is a religion that, although it draws heavily from all religions and honours all, nevertheless sees itself as a new revelation addressed by God to the entire world. Today, the Baha'is have national centres in over 145 countries and claim (though Muslims would strongly dispute this) to be the second most widely distributed faith in the world after Christianity (organized in 235 countries or territories). There are an estimated 6.5 million Baha'is, with the majority of them concentrated in India (2.5 million) and other parts of Asia, Iran (where they have suffered constant and continuing persecution) and Africa. The figure for Canada is about 22,000 and for the United States some 140,000.

The religion of the Baha'is grew out of the teachings of two prophets or visionaries who lived in Persia (Iran) in the nineteenth century. The first was Mirza Ali Muhammed, who called himself "the Bab," which means "gateway." The Bab (1820–50) saw himself as the latest in the long list of prophets going back all the way to Adam. Somewhat like John the Baptist, he predicted the coming of one who would be an earthly manifestation of God. He gathered a few followers but was executed in his thirtieth year for an alleged attempt to overthrow the Shah. His remains are entombed at the Baha'is' strikingly beautiful world administrative centre in Haifa, Israel. I have visited this shrine on several occasions and am always impressed by its panoramic view of the busy harbour below, and the sense of peace that emanates from its lofty interior and from the gorgeous gardens surrounded by soaring cypress trees.

The real founder and inspiration for this new religion, however, was Mirza Husain Ali (1817–92) who took the name Baha'u'llah, meaning "the glory of God." In 1863 he declared himself to be the manifestation promised by the Bab, "Sent to redeem the world at the end of the age and to interpret God's will for a new era." He sent out notices to proclaim this fact to numerous kings and other heads of state in the Near East with the result that he was promptly persecuted, imprisoned and finally exiled to a series of cities from Constantinople to Acre in Palestine. Baha'u'llah wrote over one hundred volumes and, while his followers were few during his lifetime, this literary legacy, filled with spiritual truths of a very lofty calibre, became the foundation of a rapidly expanding movement.

Teachings

Baha'u'llah saw himself as the fulfillment of the predictions in all faiths of a coming Messiah or Holy One to renew the world. His mission was, he believed, to teach "the true religion of God," fill the world with justice, and save it from moral chaos and despair. He taught that truth is one, but traditions are many. All religions come from the same source and reflect the progressive revelation of divine wisdom to humankind. Religion and science are perfect partners and their resources must be brought into absolute harmony in building a better world. Sex discrimination must be abolished and all racial prejudice uprooted. Universal peace must be established. Universal and compulsory education must be provided for all. Extremes of poverty and wealth are to be eliminated through laws and the working of the individual's own conscience. There must be a universal language adopted and taught throughout the world, a single currency and, eventually, one world government to regulate international affairs. The aim of the Baha'i religion is an inner transformation of man and society so that the world will move from the edge of ruin to harmony and lasting peace.

The whole of the Baha'i faith is marked by a moral seriousness and a commitment to the perfection of the social order that have made the Baha'is an effective and powerful presence wherever they have gone. The story of their persecution as a matter of public policy by various leaders in Iran, from the last Shah to the Ayatollah Khomeini and his successors, is one of the more tragic tales of the tragedy-torn twentieth century.

Life After Death

The best source for a concise account of Baha'i teachings on death and immortality is a paperback put out by the Baha'i Publishing Trust called *Unto Him Shall We Return*.[22] It contains selections from the writings of Baha'u'llah, the writings of the Bab, and from those of Baha'u'llah's eldest son, his official interpreter. Some of the meditations and insights are among the most comforting and inspirational I have read anywhere, particularly those dealing with the death of a child. The doctrine of reincarnation is regarded as an absurd "superstition," and there are warnings against mediums and trances as ways to commune with the dead. But, once again, rather than simply quoting from this or other books, I want to let a believing Baha'i explain her faith about ultimate reality.

Nancy Ackerman is the director of public affairs for the Canadian Baha'i National Centre, located in Thornhill, Ontario. In a lengthy interview, Ms. Ackerman said that as a Baha'i she believes deeply in the immortality of the soul, that "mysterious part of us which is the essential self, the capacity for conscious thought and moral striving." Baha'u'llah, she said, called the soul "a sign of God." It reflects God's light and then returns to him. Death "comes as a messenger of joy" to the believer. When a loved one dies, he or she is not lost but has stepped from one world to another. They live in everlasting companionship "immersed in an ocean of light." Quoting from the sacred writings, she said that it's as if a gardener were to uproot a flower or shrub not to destroy it but to transplant it from a narrow place into a wider room in which to grow.

From a human viewpoint death seems to be a rude end, but from the eternal aspect it is an enlargement of life and growth. She told me: "Our purpose here is to acquire the full spiritual capacities of which we are capable. We will strive and continue to make spiritual progress in the next life based upon the progress we've already made here. The qualities we attain to here are eternal, and we continue to mature and grow there until we attain the full presence of God." Heaven will be a purely spiritual existence but we will recognize and know one another, she believes. At death, the physical body disintegrates but nothing is annihilated. The various components live on in other forms. Death, then, is really a transformation or change of form. The body returns to the elements it was made up of; the soul returns to its Maker.

Ackerman said she and her fellow members see the life after death as "the world of vision where all concealed realities will be disclosed. We will know the truth. We will also discover those who influenced our lives unknown to us as well as those whom we knew." We will all one day be called to account for our lives; we will know we did right or wrong. But all of this will be seen in the light of the grace and mercy of God who alone knows the secrets of our hearts. There will be no physical hell, she said, but souls will be remote or close to God depending upon how they are judged. "That will be heaven or hell enough."

The Baha'is believe in praying for the dead and also that the dead can intercede on behalf of the living. She said: "When a person dies, loved ones here can assist the soul's progress [already helped by the grace of God] by special prayers and intercessions. Souls can also be assisted by good works or other acts of charity done here in their name." Finally, she noted that "everyone, believers and non-believers alike, enters the next realm in the spiritual condition they have attained to on earth. The tests we failed to pass here will have to be passed in the world to come!" Interestingly, Baha'u'llah believed that dreams of dead loved ones and of another world to come are evidence of a life beyond: "God, the exalted, hath placed these signs in men, to the end that philosophers may not deny the mysteries of the life beyond nor belittle that which hath been promised them."[23]

Native Spirituality

"Religious personalities from the European culture have been especially limited in their ability to see the profoundly religious and spiritual qualities of the [North American] Indian traditions," according to cultural philosopher Father Thomas Berry.[24]

This is not the place to deal with the full implications of Thomas Berry's indictment of the failure of Christians and others to take the American Indian's spirituality seriously. This sad story is part of the worldwide crucifixion of aboriginal peoples over the past five hundred years. In many parts of the world, most notably in the Amazon River hinterland, this process of cultural, religious and even physical elimination is still going on. Yet today, a remarkable resurrection of the religious traditions of indigenous peoples has taken place. What is more, it is coming precisely at a time when our devastation of the planet demands the insights into a new mode of relating to the earth that Native spirituality has to offer. As Berry has said, "Awareness of a numinous presence throughout the entire cosmic order establishes among these peoples one of the most integral forms of spirituality known to us."[25] So far from being "primitive" in some pejorative sense, study of the original religion of the American Indian, for so long repressed and ignored by non-Indian society, shows that it contains some of the highest forms of spiritual teaching ever conceived. Indeed, its discernment of the importance of what is now called "the feminine principle" in nature, in human consciousness, and in the being of the Creator Spirit, coupled with its insistence on the sacredness of the natural world, reveals that it has possessed from time immemorial truths that are presently considered avant-garde in Christian theology!

Years ago, while at university, I spent three summers in one of the most remote Indian reserves—Big Trout Lake, Ontario—in northern Canada working among the Swampy Cree. Since that time, and most recently as a journalist, I have had many close contacts with Native people, going with them on the caribou hunt on the eastern shores of James Bay, visiting them on the traplines and researching numerous stories, from the impact of pollution on their ancient way of life to epidemics of teenage suicide in some Native communities, or the tragically high infant mortality rate. This does not make me an expert on Native life, but it has given me a deep appreciation both for Indian suffering and for the enormous contribution these people have to bring to contemporary crises affecting us all. As Berry puts it, "The fate of the continent, the fate of the

Indian, and our own fate are finally identical. None can be saved except in and through the others."[26]

Amerindian Religion

The most recent scholarly studies of so-called "primal religion" and the religious belief systems of native peoples around the world have revealed that the old view of a linear, evolutionary development of religion from simple superstition to the great, classical world religions is no longer valid. The myths, rituals and beliefs of indigenous peoples are exceedingly complex and often show a theological sophistication—for example, in the insistence upon the concept of a Supreme Being—that surpasses that of many "more developed" cultures. They uniformly give witness to a rich view of the cosmos and of the relationship among humans, nature and the supernatural dimension of existence.

Because of the extraordinary size and diversity of the North American continent and the cultural differences that have developed over the centuries, it would be foolhardy to suppose that the space available here is adequate to do justice to the full complexity of this subject. The religion of the Indians of the Great Plains is different from that of the Indians of the northwest coast or those of California and the intermountain region of the Southwest. The Cree of the subarctic muskeg differ greatly from the Indians of the Maritimes or the Southeast. Yet many traits or elements of Amerindian religion are shared not just by the Indians of North America but by aboriginal peoples the world over. Two distinctive characteristics of the North American scene are the marked dependency of the North American Indian's religion on visions and dreams of the spirit world and the extremely intricate and time-consuming ceremonialism of most tribes.

All Amerindians hold a belief in a spirit realm or dimension that permeates the whole of creation. This world of spirits, gods, wonders and numinous powers has a deep and abiding connection with the natural world. Certain natural features—rocky outcroppings, cliffs, waterfalls, lakes, forests and islands—are regarded as sacred because at or around them the spirit presences can be felt in special intensity.

All Amerindians believe there is a Supreme Being—sometimes symbolized by a collectivity of divine beings—who most typically is a sky god, the ultimate maker of heaven and earth, called by some the Gitchi Manitou. The view of some scholars of a generation ago who argued that Amerindian belief in a Supreme Being postdated the arrival of the Christian missionaries has now been completely refuted. This belief, though not identical to Christian monotheism, was already there when the Christian Europeans first came ashore.

All Amerindians believe in a culture hero, the one who acts as a sort of intermediary between God and humanity in imparting various aspects of the culture itself—language, the arts, hunting skills and so on. At times, this figure is known as the trickster who acts as a quasi-opponent of the Creator and causes divine intentions to go awry. At times, the trickster is there to explain the problem of evil, to help explain the quirkiness of fate. At others, his or her role (the trickster can take either male or female form) is to lampoon human frailties or to objectify human passions and longings. Often he or she is symbolized by a zoomorphic form—the hare, the raven, the coyote—depending on the tribe and its geographical range.

The shaman or medicine man (in some tribes these could also be women) is the most powerful person in the community. Aided by special spirit-helpers, he or she has a measure of influence or control over the impact of the spirits upon the natural world. Shamans act as intermediaries between the tribe and the forces of the supernatural. Thus, the shaman is above all, a healer, a diviner of the future, an enabler who can change the weather, influence the crops, strengthen the hunter for the chase or the warrior for the fight. He or she can even communicate with other shamans across vast distances when special need arises. It is the shaman who wards off the evil spirits or the ghosts of enemies.

All Amerindians hold elaborate rituals marked by a single overall aim—to maintain a balance or harmony between the individual, the tribe, nature and the supernatural. The main tools of these rituals are prayers and the imitative acting out of supernatural events through dances, masks, chants and drum music. The sun dance is undoubtedly the classic instance of this approach. At death, the traditional place of the departed is the southwest. There the deceased live very much as they did on earth and so food and weapons—even a horse in some tribes—were left at the grave or cremation site for use on the journey.

The vision quest marks the rite of passage at puberty for boys, and in some tribes for girls also. Through solitary fasting and meditation the initiate is given a dream or vision of the kind of future he or she is meant to follow. Sometimes this comes in the symbolism of a conversation with a particular animal or bird; sometimes the seekers are given the name of a specific spirit-helper or of a particular amulet to guide them into adult life. The practice of going on a vision quest is being widely revived among young Native people in the United States and Canada today. What's more, it is being emulated by many non-Natives who see in Native spirituality an openness to mystical experience that seems lacking in their own lives.

An Indian Elder Speaks

Rather than tell the story of Indian views on life beyond death myself, based upon the reading and research I have done for this book, I spent several hours interviewing an elder of the Ojibway Nation who was an internationally respected spokesperson for Native religion. I first met him when he appeared as a guest on *Harpur's Heaven and Hell*, a weekly, hour-long interview program that I hosted on the VisionTV network across Canada. His baptismal name is Art Solomon. His Ojibway name, which means "fast-moving cloud," is Kesheankwut. Solomon was born many years ago in the tiny, picturesque village of Killarney, on the northwest shore of Georgian Bay, Ontario. He was raised in a Jesuit-run Indian residential school at Spanish, Ontario, but left it before reaching grade nine. Yet, while his formal education was meagre, his learning and leadership in Native spirituality won him honorary degrees from Queen's University, Kingston, and Laurentian University, Sudbury. He lectured frequently on university campuses and, under the auspices of the World Council of Churches, he represented Native peoples at religious conferences in Nairobi, Melbourne, the Island of Mauritius and at the Vancouver World Council of Churches (WCC) Assembly back in 1983.

Solomon was a quiet-spoken man, but when addressing issues such as the injustice of the penal system towards Native people— he worked for twelve years in one of Canada's best-known federal penitentiaries—or the way missionaries and government schools combined to suppress and destroy Indian language and culture, his words were powerful and disturbingly blunt. At the same time, he was a poet and storyteller. His creative work mixed a deep compassion with a righteous outrage. A book about him, filled with his poems and prayers, is called *Songs for the People—Teachings on the Natural Way*.[27] Solomon renounced his Christian upbringing about twenty years ago and, while he eventually came to appreciate the deep unities between the two faiths, he saw himself as totally committed to the traditional Indian belief system. His wife, Edna, remained a practising Roman Catholic and two of his daughters (they had ten children) became nuns.

Solomon's description of Native beliefs concerning the afterlife has to be seen in the context of Indian spirituality as a whole. Briefly, he said that his people see the continuum of life and the universe as a sacred, delicately balanced harmony and whole. The idea of anyone owning any part of the natural environment, the land, the lakes and rivers, was anathema to him: "It all belongs to the Great Spirit; so it is like blasphemy to say that any individual or group owns any of it. It's a common heritage and we are here simply as caretakers." The aim of life is to live with deep appreciation of the natural world, struggling heroically against life's challenges and always seeking the help and guidance of the spirit world. All of the various rituals and ceremonies—burning offerings of sweetgrass or tobacco in prayer, passing the pipe of peace, the vision quest, enduring the rigours of the sweatlodge or offering the cosmic renewal symbolism of the sun dance—emphasize this close communion among humankind, nature and God. When Solomon talked about the way in which the Thunder People or spirit-helpers make themselves known, and when he described the way in which the very elements are alive with God, you could well think this is a form of pantheism, the belief that everything is divine. Yet Native spirituality is monotheism of the highest kind. The Great Spirit, whom Solomon movingly calls "Grandfather-Grandmother of all creation," is one Lord over all.

Dr. Ed Newberry, who founded the Department of Native Studies at Laurentian University and who knew Solomon better than any other non-Indian, told me that in many ways the kind of religion articulated by Solomon and other Native leaders resembles most the Process Theology of Christian thinkers like professor John Cobb at the University of California.[28] "There is the kind of witness to the relationship between the human and the natural world in Native religion that the rest of us so sorely need just now," Newberry said.

What struck me most in all Solomon had to say was the deep awareness he had of living in two worlds simultaneously. The spiritual sphere is so penetrated by the natural and the natural so imbued and surrounded by the spiritual that life and death, and life beyond death, all seemed to flow as part of a seamless unity. He described death as "just as completely natural as birth, part of the life process," and he went on to say he found it surprising and distasteful to hear anyone saying they feared or couldn't face death. "Only those who have no idea of how to live don't know how to die," he argued. "We are spiritual beings and our journey here on earth is very short. It only makes sense that death is the gateway to our return to the spiritual world that gave us birth."

After death, he said, each one of us has to give an account of how we have used the gifts entrusted to us in the course of life. There is no concept of hell or enduring punishment, but he said his people believe there will be an experience of remorse or shame for misdeeds or failure to obey the spirit guides. Traditionally, it is believed that at death the spirit entity or soul travels southwest and goes down with the setting sun. He smiled when asked about the "Happy Hunting Ground" idea of heaven and said it was, in his view, simply a way of trying to put in human words a reality that is by nature indescribable. In conclusion, Solomon gave several examples of the dead returning as spirit-people to warn someone of impending trouble or to bring them a challenge to some heroic task or mission in life.[29]

I'd like to conclude here with a lovely Ojibway prayer which gives one an authentic feel for Indian spirituality:

Grandfather,
Look at our brokenness.
We know that in all creation
Only the human family
Has strayed from the Sacred Way.
We know that we are the ones
Who are divided
And we are the ones

Who must come back together
To walk in the Sacred Way.
Grandfather,
Sacred One,
Teach us love, compassion, and honour
That we may heal the earth
And heal each other.[30]

Three Christian Sects

In introducing how three Christian sects look at life after death, I want to make it clear that I am not using the word "sect" in a pejorative sense. *The Concise Oxford Dictionary* defines a sect as a "body of persons agreed upon religious doctrines usually different from those of an established or orthodox Church from which they have separated." The three groups described here fit that description. The first two, Seventh-day Adventists and Jehovah's Witnesses, arose from similar historical roots and have much in common, in spite of their marked differences. The third, Christian Science, though also "born in the U.S.A.," stands rather more by itself.

The Seventh-day Adventists

Adventists as a religious movement within Christianity are universally characterized by their emphasis on the expectation of an imminent return of Christ to inaugurate the consummation of the present world order. In other words, they expect the Second Advent or coming of Jesus Christ at any moment. Their origins can be traced to the early part of the nineteenth century when extraordinary religious ferment swept through much of the northern United States. As a denomination, they date from about 1831 and the teaching of a man called William Miller in Dresden, New York. Having spent many years studying the Bible, particularly Old Testament prophe-cies thought to predict the end of the world, Miller became con-vinced that the Second Coming would take place in 1843–44. His movement attracted numerous converts from the more staid, tradi-tional churches, and a newspaper, *The Midnight Cry*, became the chief vehicle for spreading the Adventist message. Many tent meetings and conferences were held throughout the Northeast as crowds thronged in to get instructions on the impending millennium.

Very soon, however, particularly after the 1844 date came and went without a sign of the promised Advent, the movement split into a number of factions. Miller kept saying the end was immi-nent, but others disagreed. It became impossible to get unanimity on alternative dates; every factional leader had his or her own views. And there were other, theological differences as well, for example, over whether or not the soul itself is immortal. The original church, called the Evangelical Adventists, maintained a more or less ortho-dox Christian position regarding the nature of the afterlife and gradually lost out to more adventurous-minded sects. Today, the chief Adventist denominations are the Second Advent Christians and the Seventh-day Adventists. Since the latter are the largest and by far the best-known, they afford the obvious example of Adven-tist-type thinking for the purposes of our study.

As their name reveals, the Seventh-day Adventists have decided, on the basis of Bible study, that the Jewish Sabbath, from sundown on Friday to sundown on Saturday, is the proper day for rest and worship. Their beliefs are characterized by a staunchly Protestant theology with a firm conviction that the final, infallible authority in matters of faith is the Bible. Adult baptism, by full immersion in water, is the norm. Independent research has frequently con-firmed that their well-known disciplines of abstinence from alco-hol, tobacco, tea, coffee and meat have resulted in health statistics significantly better than those of the general population in North America and other developed countries. There are some 54,000

Seventh-day Adventists in Canada, about 800,500 in the United States, and the global figure stands at about 13 million.

The Afterlife

The director of public affairs, religious liberty and communications for the Ontario Conference of Seventh-Day Adventists told me in an interview about life after death that at death a person goes into a sleep. "The soul, by which we simply mean the life essence or energy, returns to God [is absorbed back into God] and the body, of course, returns to the dust. Things remain that way until Christ's visible return to earth. Then, those who are in Christ [faithful believers] are resurrected in a perfect body and, together with the living who are in Christ, they are caught up to reign in the heavens with Christ for a thousand years. [This is the promised millennium.] Those who died without Christ remain in the grave. At the end of the millennium, Christ again returns to earth with all the saints or faithful ones. Those remaining in the grave are resurrected, and Satan is loosed for a final battle between the forces of good and evil. Satan will be defeated, together with the wicked who fought on his side, and the earth will be consumed by fire and destruction. At that point, God will create a new heaven and a new earth, according to the prophecies, with a new Jerusalem as its capital. The saints will inhabit this renewed earth forever."

I asked about final judgment and the spokesperson said: "You are judged at the moment of dying. All who have loved God and lived in conformity with Christ's teaching will one day be saved."

He said that in the Adventists' view, you don't necessarily have to be an Adventist or even a Christian to inherit eternal life. It's a gift to all who love and obey God with their whole heart. There is no such thing as a fiery, eternal hell in their beliefs. Those who are finally rejected are "extinguished completely."

What will the life to come be like? "It will be all that your heart ever desired, a renewed earth, renewed relationships—Paradise."[31]

Jehovah's Witnesses

Most people know little about Jehovah's Witnesses except that they refuse blood transfusions, are sometimes difficult to get rid of when they come knocking on the door and can be seen standing resolutely, if somewhat forlornly, on street corners at odd hours of the day or night holding up a tract or magazine. As one parishioner said to me at the church door some years ago: "I don't know what they believe but I sure admire their zeal."

The religious organization known today as Jehovah's Witnesses (The Watchtower Bible and Tract Society) numbers roughly 6.5 million members in well over two hundred countries. There are about one million of them in the United States, and their struggles for religious freedom not only there but in Canada, Great Britain and many African nations have been instrumental in securing the rights of all other religious groups as well. They have been persecuted frequently in their 130-year history, particularly in fascist or newly independent states, because of their refusal to salute the flag, vote or take part in any of the other rituals of loyalty traditionally thought to belong to citizenship.

While not totally pacifist, because they would fight for Christ in the final battle, Armageddon, they refuse to take up arms on behalf of the civil authorities. Their well-known stand against blood transfusions, based upon a literal reading of both Old and New Testament passages that forbid the eating of blood (see Genesis 9:4, Leviticus 7:26, Psalm 16, I Chronicles 11:17–19, and Acts 15:29) has been another key area of controversy. Although not much has been said or published about the fact, Jehovah's Witnesses were among the first victims of Hitler's infamous concentration camps.

The movement, like many other adventist groups, originated in the United States in the nineteenth century. A draper's son, Charles Taze Russell (1852–1916), left traditional Christianity because he could not reconcile the teaching about a loving God with the concept of a fiery, eternal punishment in hell for obdurate sinners. He drifted as an agnostic for a time before coming under the influence of the same kind of thinking that had led to the founding of Mormonism, the Seventh-day Adventists and other millenarian denominations.

Russell gathered a group around him in Pennsylvania in the 1870s to study the Bible prophecies about the Second Coming of Christ. They called themselves the International Bible Students and in 1879 began publication of *The Watchtower* magazine, which has a circulation today of over 26 million copies in dozens of languages around the world. Publishing this, plus another magazine called *Awake!*, as well as numerous books and pamphlets, remains the key activity and service of the organization wherever it has spread.

Basic Beliefs

Russell and his successors believed that Christ would return soon to lead the forces of Jehovah (from *Yahweh*, the name for God from the Hebrew acronym for the name of God, YHVH) against Satan and his minions in the Battle of Armageddon. This would mark the end of the world order we have known and begin the millennium, or one-thousand-year reign of Christ on earth. At the end of the millennium, Satan will be let loose for a brief time for one more trial of the faith of believers, and then the total perfection of paradise will be instituted and last forever. As early as 1872, Russell believed that Christ would return secretly in 1874 and that the end battle would come in 1914. His convictions were set down in a small book, *The Object and Manner of Our Lord's Return*, which was widely circulated.

Russell's successor, "Judge" J.F. Rutherford (1869–1941), revised and developed his ideas, particularly stressing the concept of allegiance to Jehovah's theocratic Kingdom and opposition to all existing institutions, from traditional, organized religion to the apparatus of the state. Rutherford believed that the secret coming of Christ occurred in 1914 and that Armageddon could break out at any moment. It was he who first coined and promulgated the familiar Jehovah's Witness slogan: "Millions now living will never die."

The movement has been plagued from time to time by mass defections when various dates set for the return of Christ or Armageddon have passed without incident (1975 was once held as the certain date of the end until that too passed by quite harmlessly). In Jehovah's Witness teaching, Jesus was not God nor part of a Holy Trinity. He was the perfect man, created by God for the redemption of the world. By his death he has atoned for sin and by being raised up in a spiritual resurrection he has opened the way to immortality for all who obey Jehovah. There is no distinctive caste of clergy in the Jehovah's Witnesses and the services in their Kingdom Halls are not so much concerned with worship as with instruction in the Bible, understood quite literally.

The Afterlife

I met with several members of the movement for some time in order to learn first-hand what the Witnesses believe about life after death.

"The first thing we believe is that death is real," they said. "When you're dead, you're really dead. We don't believe in the immortality of the soul because it's not in the Bible."

They went on to explain that "we don't have souls, according to the Bible. We *are* souls. The soul is you, the essential person." In their view, the dead know nothing and are held as a memory in the mind of God. At death, the entire organism disintegrates and is returned to the dust. The life force or energy returns to God. But there are two classes of people, two resurrections and two kinds of eternal bliss. Taking a verse from Revelation, the two men said Jehovah's Witnesses believe that there are 144,000 of "Jehovah's anointed," including the apostles and martyrs of the earliest Christian era, who will be resurrected to a spiritual life with Jehovah in heaven; of these, some 10,000 are still living. Since they believe that Christ has already secretly returned (in 1914), those of the

144,000 who have died since then have gone immediately to be with their God. This, they said, is the "first resurrection." The general resurrection of all others who have died before Armageddon begins—some time very soon—will take place gradually over the millennium. During this period, the earth will progressively be cleansed and returned to the paradisal state of the first Garden of Eden. Those faithful who live through Armageddon will remain and will be able to procreate until the proper population level is reached, according to Jehovah's plan. Any who have resolutely and stubbornly resisted Jehovah's call to obedience will simply be annihilated. There is no such thing as hell or everlasting punishment. As the dead are resurrected, they will be given a "second chance" to align themselves with the divine will.

After the brief, final fling of Satan at the close of the thousand years, those who have proved worthy will go on to live forever on this by now perfected planet, this earthly paradise, where sin, suffering and sorrow will be no more. As the Bible says, "The lion will lie down with the lamb" and all of nature will be restored. Those sinners who have steadfastly refused salvation will simply be annihilated. Jehovah's Witnesses, since Jehovah is a "God of organization and order," will run the entire show under Christ's command. They were in solid agreement that "paradise is not a democracy!" Of death itself, they had this to say in summation: "Death is simply like falling asleep. So, whether you are a believer or not, there's really nothing to fear either way."[32]

Christian Science

"The Physical healing of Christian Science results now, as in Jesus' time, from the operation of divine Principle, before which sin and disease lose their reality in human consciousness and disappear as naturally and as necessarily as darkness gives place to light and sin to reformation. Now, as then, these mighty works are not supernatural, but supremely natural."[33]

These words from Mrs. Mary Baker Eddy, in the preface to her now-famous book, *Science and Health*, sum up the essential teaching of this movement. Born in New Hampshire in 1821 into a family with a strong Calvinist background, she suffered from various ailments throughout most of her childhood and early adult years. She then experienced what she believed to be a complete healing through an encounter with a well-known mesmerist or hypnotist, P.P. Quimby. As a result, she became greatly impressed with the power of the mind to heal both itself and the body. Detractors later tried to accuse Eddy of plagiarizing Quimby but in *Science and Health* she repudiated his major thesis. (The chapter was called "Animal Magnetism Unmasked.") In a brief biographical sketch in her book *Retrospection and Introspection*, she tells us that as early as 1862 she had begun to write down and share with friends the results of her private study of the Bible, her "sole teacher." By the time Quimby died in 1866 she had discovered the "system" of thinking she named Christian Science.

Jesus Christ, she taught, was the first true Scientist. His mighty healings were wrought by following the natural laws of divine Principle rather than by some miraculous, external power. Suffering and death, according to Mrs. Eddy, are the effects of false belief in the reality of matter. For her, only the world of the Spirit is real. Thus, for the restoration of health, the proper course is not medical treatment but correcting one's thoughts. The patient must yield his or her illusions about the reality of sickness and matter and replace them with knowledge of the Truth.

In the glossary used in *Science and Health*, death is described as "An illusion, the lie of life in matter; the unreal and untrue . . . Any material evidence of death is false, for it contradicts the spiritual facts of being." Elsewhere in the book she again calls death an illusion, "for to the real man and the real universe there is no death process." In other words, then, death, according to Christian Science, is wholly unreal, an "error of thinking."

This radical approach to faith healing has been shunned by the main body of Christian churches as extreme and at variance with more orthodox Christian views on matter, sin, suffering and death. It has even been satirized in an old limerick:

> There was a faith-healer from Deal,
> Who said, Although pain isn't real,
> When I sit on a pin and it punctures my skin,
> I dislike what I fancy I feel.

Mary Baker Eddy herself claimed thousands of cases of well-authenticated healings, and personal testimonies of healings still make up an important part of every Christian Science worship service today in more than two thousand churches in at least fifty-seven countries around the globe.

The chief reason for the initial impact of Christian Science was that for a long time the traditional churches had simply ignored Bible passages on spiritual healing and the obviously deep connection between the mind and wholeness. In spite of its early success, however, the movement only really began to flourish after the founder's third marriage, to Mr. Eddy, an experienced businessman. In 1879 the First Church of Christ Scientist was opened in Boston, and, in 1881, the Metaphysical College was founded in that same city. During its first seven years, Mrs. Eddy personally taught some four thousand eager students.

Since the death of the founder in 1910, the organization has been run by a rotating board of directors. Their leading asset, the *Christian Science Monitor*, is one of the world's most well-informed and responsible newspapers. There are some 1,700 Christian Science churches in the United States and 45 in Canada. Church spokespersons told me that the church has a policy, originally set by Mrs. Eddy, of not publishing actual membership statistics. The reason she gave for this ban apparently was her fear, during the first, rapid growth of the movement, that people would get caught up by the allure of numbers. She reportedly wanted sincerity of purpose and the experience of valid healings rather than a mass of nominal members.

A First-hand View

J. Don Fulton, a man I had known and respected for many years in my work as a journalist, was the chief spokesperson for Christian Science in central Canada. His official position in the church was head of the Christian Science Committee on Publications for Ontario. I wrote to him and said how important it was for the purposes of this book to hear from an "insider." Then I listed a few key questions on how he and his fellow members view death. He kindly gave me a written reply and here, as briefly as possible without changing any of his exact meaning, is what he had to say:

"The question of death is an important one. Obviously it affects the way life is lived—not just the future life, but our present life . . . Christian Scientists are human enough to be saddened when anyone dies, especially those we love, but Christian enough also to believe in life everlasting."

Fulton pointed out that his movement believes that death is neither "just lying in the grave" nor some kind of "instant propulsion to glory." In other words, there is a "working through and a progression" after death.

He wrote: "I believe that until human life is fully redeemed, we will find ourselves after death with the same challenges, the same limited mortal sense of existence we had before death . . . Death is not a solution to challenges; it is not a friend. Paul characterized death as an enemy, the last enemy to be overcome. Death does not resolve things. What does resolve them is regeneration of our thought and heart. It is not the experience of death itself, but our reaching out to God that helps us to realize, know, and live more fully in accord with God. Willingness to learn and obey is the basis of our progress, and through God's grace I believe we will be helped onward."

Fulton said he was convinced that those who die without knowing God are given a "second chance." The Bible affirms God is love, and that this love is impartial and universal. Ultimately, nothing can ever separate any of us from this divine concern. God is life and He made man in His own image and likeness. "Therefore man can no more die than God can die. But this has to be spiritually discerned and proven step-by-step—or demonstrated in daily life, as a Christian Scientist might say."

Fulton said he is very much looking forward to heaven, but added: "I do not believe that heaven is a place so much as a state of consciousness, an awareness of God's presence comforting and guiding each of us, here and now. It's an awareness of the harmony, wholeness, and holiness that are ours as His beloved children. As Jesus taught, only when a false sense of self has been abandoned does one's life truly come rushing back, a divine gift of God. That new life, to me, includes an increasing sense of heaven, or God's presence, at hand."34

10

PERSONAL REFLECTIONS AND CONCLUSIONS

IT WAS A BRIGHT, sunny day in south Florida, January 28, 1990. The unprecedented hot, dry spell that had been going on since Christmas, causing a severe drought, persisted. The waters of the Atlantic Ocean sparkled brightly and in the sky above several large buzzards wheeled in lazy circles above the royal palms. I was reminded of vultures in the desert and told my wife in jest that I hoped it wasn't an omen. The fact was, we were about to attend a lengthy seminar on death and dying at the Unity of the Palm Beaches Church in West Palm Beach. The birds were directly over the spot!

We were there to hear Dr. Raymond Moody, who was the chair of Consciousness Studies at the University of Nevada, and at that time was the pioneer explorer of the near-death experience, report on his twenty-five years of experience in the field. Moody, a round-faced, spectacled man in his late fifties at that time, was formerly a professor of psychology at West Georgia College, Carrollton, Georgia, and a psychiatrist with a large, active practice. His best-selling, watershed book, *Life After Life*, has gone through well over forty printings. The title of his two-hour seminar was "The Light Beyond."

What struck me most about his presentation, apart from the fact that it was an opportunity to hear and talk with him first-hand, was the way he began it. Moody explained that in the past twenty-five years he had personally heard the NDE stories of some 2,500 patients. Describing himself as "a lapsed Presbyterian" whose father, a surgeon, was a hard-headed skeptic about matters of faith, he said he himself had always believed that being dead meant the end of all consciousness—finis, oblivion. His personal "conversion" came when he could no longer ignore or explain away the evidence his patients were bringing him. Moody made it plain that in the near-death experience we are not dealing with scientific proof of life after death but with "the relationship between two different levels of reality." In other words, the evidence for life after death deals with a reality that science is not yet equipped to weigh, measure or validate in a laboratory. He said: "The fact that it is not scientific proof doesn't worry me in the slightest. I want to tell you I have absolutely no doubt now that there is a transformation of consciousness at the point of death and we do go on." Describing the expanding research that had gone on intensely since the publication of *Life After Life*, and the fact that during his recent visit to nine European countries he discovered that doctors there are reporting exactly the same experiences he has documented, Moody summed up: "My own conviction today is that these patients have indeed had an experience of another life beyond."

What is important is that when this former skeptic was repeatedly faced by the unanimous testimony of those who had come close to death and returned, he found the evidence such that he was persuaded to change his mind. If this were the case with just one doctor, it would be interesting but hardly convincing. The truth is, however, that this is a phenomenon I have observed over and over again in the years since in my own research. It is truly remarkable how many atheists and agnostics have felt compelled to soften or change their stance on this issue when faced themselves with a near-death experience, or when they objectively examine those of others. What holds true of the NDE seems also to apply in regard to the wider picture. As Colin Wilson, the author of *Afterlife* and himself a case in point, concluded: "In almost every single case where a sceptic has persisted in studying the facts, he has ended up more or less convinced of the reality of life after death."[1]

My own conviction, following much thought and in light of what I consider to be the continuously mounting evidence and also the vast range of the arguments for and against, can be put in far stronger terms. I am today fully persuaded and assured that life after death is very much like birth. It is the traumatic but essential passage into a new phase of life. There is life after death. It is not for some holy huddle or a select few, but for all. And it will so far surpass anything we have ever dreamed of as to make all present attempts to describe it, religious or otherwise, seem tawdry and utterly inept. What's more, it's my deep conviction that such a belief is completely congruent with the utmost respect for both intellect and science. Indeed, I am now convinced it would be flying in the face of intelligence and rationality to believe otherwise. I will give the grounds for what I call this "reasonable faith" in a life beyond and try to flesh out what I believe this life will be like in a moment.

First, though, there will be those who, knowing my background as an Anglican minister and a former professor of the New Testament, will say that I came to this question not as a skeptic but as one within the tradition of faith—in other words, that I was already committed to my conclusion before beginning to study the matter. Naturally, you have to begin from where you are and nobody is a tabula rasa completely without biases. But it is a serious error to suppose that where one comes from inevitably dictates where one will arrive.

When I began my study of the putative historic Jesus for my books *For Christ's Sake*, and later *The Pagan Christ*, I had no idea the argument and evidence would lead me where it did. Those who knew my evangelical upbringing have been greatly surprised at my conclusions. Indeed, the ongoing furor over *The Pagan Christ* might never have occurred had I not tackled Christology with a completely open mind. I have adopted the same approach in tackling the question of death and I have no doubt that some of my conclusions will not sit well with orthodox believers in many camps. No one can prove his or her attempt at objectivity, it has to be recognized as present or lacking from the work itself. But it would be a great mistake for anyone to think that because a person has belonged to a particular religion or grouping that this is an unquestioned commitment or one arrived at easily and without intellectual effort. My book *Born Again* describes my journey.

I am extremely grateful to past teachers at Oxford who taught me the nature of evidence, especially my philosophy tutor, Richard Robinson, who constantly forced me to rethink all the faith presuppositions of my youth. He was, into his nineties, an atheist and with a mind like a steel trap. I owe him a lot. I am also indebted to the great philosopher Gilbert Ryle, whose lectures on logical positivism—the view that only sense-data can give rise to true knowledge—were a must for every classics student during my Oxford days. His position denied the very possibility of knowledge about life after death. Ryle was wrong, but he forced me to confront one of the most formidable arguments I was to encounter.

Why the Sudden "Boom" of Interest?

One of the central themes of my writing for years has been that there is a vast spiritual hunger in western society just at a time when the influence and membership of traditional religious bodies are in decline. Organized religion has always addressed the existential issues of the meaning, value, purpose and ultimate fate of human life, but for many years now its answers are not being heard or no longer make sense to the greater part of the population. This problem arises partly from a communication gap of gargantuan proportions; partly, it seems to me, it stems from a certain embarrassment at a past, undue emphasis upon spiritual things to the neglect of the body, social action and this world altogether. The present attempt to prove Karl Marx was wrong when he described religion as the "opium of the people," the search for justice and the "preferential option" for the poor as opposed to a religion of "pie in the sky when you die by and by"—all this is praiseworthy and long overdue. But instead of dealing with both sides of "what God hath joined together," the rush to social justice has left out the matter of personal, spiritual concerns almost completely.

I was not a great admirer of the pronouncements of the present Pope Benedict XVI while he was Cardinal Josef Ratzinger, head of the Vatican's Congregation for the Doctrine of the Faith (the modern successor to the notorious Inquisition). However, I found myself in total agreement with Ratzinger when he was quoted in the *Catholic New Times* of Toronto in the nineties saying that there is a great lack of teaching about "last things" in the Church of today. "Belief in eternal life has hardly any role to play in preaching. . . . The Kingdom of God has been almost completely substituted by the utopia of a better future world . . . which becomes the true reference point of morality," he said. This lack, in my view, still exists today and accounts in some measure for the growth of the more conservative and fundamentalist groups, as well as various sects and cults.

But the real impact of the lack of teaching in this area can be seen in the popularity and omnipresence in the media of New Age thinking and practices. There is the same abhorrence of a vacuum in the spiritual realm that there is in the world of physics. In the discussion of life after death, the spiritual gurus who fill the vacuum today are Browne, Edward, Van Praagh and others, not the Pope or the Archbishop of Canterbury. To be perfectly blunt, there is an incredible lack of intelligible teaching and thinking about ultimate matters in our seminaries, churches and synagogues. The old formulae are either tediously boring or nonsensical. What I believe we are seeing in the contemporary secular and in the non-traditional spiritual awakening regarding life after death is the voice of the collective unconscious. It is saying, if the traditional symbols, language and thinking about so central an issue are so utterly inadequate, then new ones must emerge. Since there is such a thing as life after death, this is too essential a concern to be left to outdated concepts or worse, to total neglect.

Dr. Marie-Louise von Franz spoke of the "symbol impoverishment" of traditional Christian thinking about death and eternity.[2] It is this poverty that the modern NDE and other similar phenomena may be meant to enrich. The time for traditional faiths to awaken to the challenge is long overdue.

Wish Fulfillment?

As mentioned in a previous chapter, the most common criticism levelled against anyone who believes in a life beyond death is that it is simply wish-projection. It was the argument proposed adamantly by Lord Bertrand Russell, and you can hear it in almost every discussion of the subject. One of the respondents to a research questionnaire I sent out gave a typical version: "There is no life after death. Religious theories that maintain that the soul or spirit lives on or joins a universal spirit stem from fear of death. It is natural to have that fear but foolish to let it sustain illusion. What happens to the flame when the candle burns down? It is the same with consciousness . . . We humans have invented immortality because we do not want to die." But, as in the case of Sigmund Freud's thesis that belief in God is an illusion fostered by wish-projection, this argument cuts both ways. It is equally possible that an adamant refusal to believe either in God or in immortality is itself an instance of wish fulfillment. Plenty of people with an absent or violently abusive father have abundant subconscious reasons for denying the existence of a deity characterized as a heavenly Father. Indeed,

Freud's own atheism may well have had its roots in his acknowledged inner conflicts over his own father.

Similarly, those who cannot abide the thought of being answerable to any other being than themselves, those who wish to live completely self-centred, selfish lives, or those who know they have committed unspeakable crimes against their fellow humans all have cause to hope that death brings oblivion and that the grave is the end. There is more than one kind of fear where death is concerned. Historically, one can point to many bright people who sincerely wished that life after death were an illusion. Colin Wilson offers an interesting observation from the autobiography of the Cambridge philosopher C.D. Broad: "So far as I can tell, I have no desire to survive the death of my present body, and I should be considerably relieved if I could feel much surer than I do that no kind of survival is possible."[3] Broad told Wilson in an interview that he'd been so lucky and successful in this life that he wouldn't want to have to take a chance in another world. "I'd rather just come to an end."

The truth is that the more I contemplate the matter the more I am convinced that just the very opposite of the wish-projection theory is true. I now believe that the near-universal, extremely ancient human belief in personal survival after death is the result of the kind of experiences of contact with another world or reality we have already examined in this book. The so-called primitive belief of all aboriginal peoples in such survival, for example, flows not from wish fulfillment but from the hard evidence of their own experience that death is not the final word. They live in contact with the "ancestors" on a daily basis.

Anthropologists and others have often noted the fact that many native peoples, living much closer to nature and with their minds uncluttered by modern media babble, are in a much more intimate relationship with "other worlds." Their experience of the phenomena described in the first two chapters of this book, plus other paranormal forms of awareness which we as sophisticated moderns may well have lost, have convinced these people down the ages. Not the other way around. This, I believe, is the true source also for the amazing congruence of thought about life after death in the world's great religions.

Escapism or Commitment to Life?

This leads directly to another key question. Why be concerned at all with this problem when there are so many burning issues to be faced right now in this world—poverty, global wars and hunger, the AIDS crisis, the environmental deterioration of the planet and much more? Isn't concern about ultimate survival a form of escapist narcissism? Obviously, I don't think so or I wouldn't have engaged in researching and writing this book in the first place. It is important, however, to answer this line of reasoning. Of course we must admit that undue concern about one's personal survival can indeed be a form of escape from tough realities close at hand. And it is all too true that at times in history religion has been exploited to keep the masses so preoccupied with rewards or punishments in the next world that they had little time or thought for the cause of their miseries in this one. But, as the old Latin proverb says, *abusus non tollit usum*, the wrong use of something in no way makes its proper use illegitimate or wrongheaded.

Escapism goes in two directions. Individuals or groups can use undue preoccupation or busyness with this world's needs and problems as an escape from facing all spiritual questions completely. Many people refuse to think or talk about a hereafter because it reminds them very sharply of their own mortality. It may seem paradoxical, but they blot out the entire subject as part of their attempt to repress or deny the fact that in life we are all caught in what the iconoclastic British psychiatrist R.D. Laing once described as "a sexually transmitted disease with a 100 per cent mortality rate." Nobody is getting out of here alive, yet in spite of a lot of progress in recent years, death is still a taboo subject in western society. At an international conference I attended a few years ago in London, Ontario, of more than five hundred people who deal daily with the dying and bereaved, Dr. Sandra Bertman, then professor of humanities at the University of Massachusetts School of Medicine, observed: "We're generally uncomfortable with death and dying because it brings us face-to-face with our own mortality." Bertman went on to say that people are most afraid, not so much of death itself, but of the dying process. "They especially fear a raw and agonizing death—the indignity of deterioration, dependence, and unlimited, hopeless pain," she said.[4] People rightly fear the thought of dying alone, in hospital, wired to a tangle of machines.

Far from being escapist, the consideration of and commitment to a belief in a life beyond death lends an enhanced intensity to living in the here and now. It means that the whole of one's life is lived *sub specie aeternitatis*—in light of the eternal. As the chairman of philosophy at Emory University in Atlanta, Thomas Flynn, told the conference: "We focus on death, not out of morbidity but to appreciate what life really is." In 1979 I accompanied Mother Teresa in her mission of mercy to the poorest of the poor in Calcutta.[5] However, in my travels as a journalist, I have visited with many lesser-known but equally committed heroes of other denominations and faiths in remote corners of the world. All of these were eloquent witnesses to a faith that is firmly rooted in this world and its agony, and yet which draws its inspiration and hope from the conviction that there is a fuller life to come.

One thinks of the late Archbishop Oscar Romero in El Salvador or heroes for justice such as Archbishop Desmond Tutu in South Africa. The point is clear. A firm understanding of and a belief in a destiny beyond the joys and griefs of this life infuse one's earthly life with a sense of depth and meaning and purpose that energizes the whole of one's being. Responsible, zestful engagement with practical, down-to-earth opportunities and problems results from the realization that what is done has lasting or ultimate consequence. It has a larger context or meaning than the surface one.

This is not a matter of seeking future rewards or of fearing future punishments, as some skeptics might argue. Rather, it's an awareness of being fully alive and in touch with a Source beyond oneself. Carl Jung, in *Memories, Dreams, Reflections*, talks about the great importance of everyone, especially as he or she grows older, having a faith or "myth" about death. He cites the way in which this can conjure up helpful, enriching pictures of life "in the land of the dead," and how these in turn lead to more intense living at the end of life: "The man who despairs marches towards nothingness, the one who has placed his faith in the archetype follows the tracks of life *and lives right into his death*. Both, to be sure, remain in uncertainty, but the one lives against his instincts, the other with them [italics mine]."[6]

The Reality of Death

Some words of Chief Seattle are often quoted: "There is no death, only a change of worlds." This is an eloquent and epigrammatic way of affirming belief in a hereafter. We know what is meant. But, taken literally, it contradicts experience and harsh reality. I cannot accept the sometimes sentimental, sometimes overly ethereal explanations of those who sermonize at funerals or who erect elaborate philosophies on the theme that death is unreal or simply an illusion. I believe in the immortality of the soul but the transition we call death is a reality, like birth, which we all must experience. The earliest church Fathers, like Clement of Alexandria and Origen, believed this. So did Plato, and his later great expositor, Plotinus. But, when I see books with such titles as *You Cannot Die* (on reincarnation, by the late Ian Currie) or stories in the press with similar headings, I read them with more than a little suspicion.

Few people in our culture come into natural contact with death. It has been so sanitized, professionalized and removed from daily life that its very naturalness as part of the human cycle is remote from all but a tiny minority. However, when you have been an active priest for seventeen years as I have, with more than eight years in a large parish setting, you constantly come face to face with death and bereavement. Someone who has never presided at the funeral and the graveside of a dead child, a beloved spouse, an esteemed friend or a devoted parent cannot know fully what it is like. You know, as the casket is lowered into the grave and you turn to try to offer comfort to those closest to the deceased, that death is very real indeed. Yes, it can come as a friend when one has suffered long or when one is old and "full of years." But even then it has a finality and marks a separation that is tragic and real for those who remain.

Death, no matter how firmly committed one may be to the conviction that it is the gateway to a new stage of being, is an end of something very important. We have a deep, inner sense that it is an intruder or, as the New Testament firmly declares, an enemy. It is not the last word, but it is a word that has to be heard by each of us. It is the gateway to life beyond but it is a narrow one—with all the pain as well as all the joy of birth. It is the one supreme act that no one else can undertake for us. To minimize it or to attempt to gloss it over with pretentious terms is to trivialize and mask its significance in the total drama of what it means to be a human being.

Weighing the Evidence

I have said that the evidence to believe that death is ultimately transcended by new life is compelling. This evidence does not, however, provide by itself total, irrefutable proof. There is an act of faith or trust involved here, just as there always is with belief in God as well. But it cannot be stated too strongly that this is supremely not an act of what is commonly called "blind faith." It is faith firmly supported by and based upon a process of sound, rational thought.

The great philosopher of religion, William James, said that the evidence for life after death is "abundant" but it always leaves room for doubt.[7] This principle, of course, holds true for most of the areas of life that really matter. We do not have hard-and-fast scientific proof for our ultimate values of goodness, beauty, justice, love, fidelity or the sanctity of life either. As I have written elsewhere, "All of us, scientists, agnostics, believers, or unbelievers alike hold values and truths which no scientific experiment could ever verify."[8] What matters most to me in reaching the decision I have regarding life after death is the amount and the quality of the evidence on its side. If one is to have a "reasonable faith," as opposed to "blind trust," one ought to have some very sound reasons, and none by itself would be sufficient. Cumulatively, though, they make a body of argument which I, at any rate, find thoroughly convincing.

The Principle of Catholicity

By catholicity, of course, I mean universality. It has always been a criterion for orthodox Catholic doctrine that it be what has always and in all places been believed by everyone. Belief in life after death extends far beyond any Church dogma in meeting this test. It is one of the most fundamental, most universal of all human convictions, whether we consider the earliest cultures of our ancestors or take public opinion polls of North Americans in the early twenty-first century. It is expressed and understood in a myriad of different ways, but the essential intuition is identical. Critics will say, of course, that truth is not a matter of opinion polls or weight of numbers. If the majority of people, for example, were convinced that the earth is flat, that wouldn't make it so. But that's too facile. There is overwhelming evidence on the other side that this quaint belief, however popular we hypothetically agree it could be, is dead wrong. Such is not the case with life after death.

I doubt if one could find a single scientist, philosopher, intellectual, or even high school student for that matter who would come forward to espouse the flat-earth view. But with life after death we're not just talking about billions of people down the ages from every race and continent, we're talking about some of the most brilliant minds of all time, many of them scientists or doctors, as well as the great mystics or the founders of various religions. For only one example, Sir Bernard Lovell, one of Great Britain's most distinguished astronomers, was a committed believer and could be found on Sundays serving as a lay reader in his parish church. In addition, Francis Collins, who headed the Human Genome project, is a man of deep faith. In summary, then, when a belief is as ancient and as widespread as this, it might be unscientific to take it as proof of anything, but it would be even more unscientific to disregard it or to try to slough it off with clever but hollow quips.

Science

I do not know if science will ever "prove" life after death because, by definition, it concerns a dimension or level of reality with which science may never be able to deal. The idea that only science can give us true knowledge stems not from science but from its bastard offspring, scientism, and is itself incapable of scientific proof. What weighs heavily with me, however, is not just the number of scientists today who themselves believe in an afterlife, but the way the new physics, new consciousness studies and the findings of neurosurgeons in regard to brain/mind functioning have opened a path for belief through difficulties once thought insurmountable.

We have seen how the majority of modern physicists have moved to the view that the whole of the material universe is a cosmic dance of energy. Indeed, physicists such as David Bohm and others speculate that the universe is essentially an indivisible whole, with each part a holograph of the other. The material, visible world is but the unfolded or "explicate order," which is the surface or outer layer, so to speak, of an invisible, implicate order of being.[9] Consciousness or mind would belong to this underlying, psychic order of being and would be the cause of matter rather than emerging from it as was previously thought. Questions of time, "before" and "after" take on wholly new meanings.

It is significant to me that so great an authority on the human psyche as Marie-Louise von Franz has concluded from her study of the dreams of the dying that the symbolic statements about another realm beyond this natural world have "relevance to the fact that modern physics has also begun to speak about universes 'with which we cannot communicate.' We stand at a great turning point in modern science, which points towards the healing discovery that we are everywhere surrounded by rationally impenetrable mysteries."[10]

At the same time, brain specialists such as Sir John Eccles, or more recently, the neuroscientist Candace Pert, have postulated that the human psyche exists independent from the physical brain.[11] This was the belief of William James, Wilder Penfield, Sir James Jeans and even of the man who was a scientist, skeptic and materialist for most of his life, Thomas Huxley. In his *Essays on Some Controverted Subjects*, published in 1892, Huxley said that there is more to the universe than just matter and energy: "There is a third thing . . . consciousness, which I cannot see to be matter or force, or any conceivable modification of either." He went on to say that a student who admits the existence of immaterial phenomena in the form of consciousness must also admit the possibility of "an eternal series of such phenomena."

An article in *Science Digest* as far back as July 1982 referred to Sir James Jeans's book *The Mysterious Universe*. Even in the early thirties Jeans foresaw that scientific knowledge was headed towards belief in "a non-mechanical reality; the universe begins to look more like a great thought than a great machine. Mind no longer appears as an accidental intruder into the realm of matter; we are beginning to suspect that we ought to hail it as the creator and or governor of . . . matter."[12] Then, from Albert Einstein himself: "Everyone who is seriously involved in the pursuit of science becomes convinced that a Spirit is manifest in the Laws of the Universe—a Spirit vastly superior to that of man, and one in the face of which we, with our modest powers, must feel humble."[13]

Should anyone still doubt the significance of the kind of thrust I'm describing here towards a belief in life after death, I suggest he or she read Guy Murchie's latest book, *The Seven Mysteries of Life*.[14] Murchie, who was eighty-three at the time of writing, with a science degree from Harvard and a lifetime of observation and philosophizing about the universe, argued strongly for transcendence as we engage in "the inexorable drift from our present earthly finitude toward some sort of an infinitude far beyond." In his preface, Murchie said "the seventh mystery of life, the greatest of all" is divinity or whatever one chooses to call "the unknowable essence that leading thinkers have long believed somehow exists behind the creation and maintenance of all body, mind and spirit." This kind of growing consensus from those who take science seriously can no longer be ignored.

The NDE Revisited

I do not agree with Hans Küng's view in his book *Eternal Life?* that one cannot be a believing Christian and a believer in reincarnation. Some notable Christians of the past, as we have already seen, have believed in it. However, I respectfully must say I still do not find the evidence produced to be wholly persuasive. Reincarnation does not solve the problem it first came into being to deal with, that of suffering and injustice, and the more I read and hear of alleged past lives the more convinced I am that these are the induced products of the imagination, repressed memories and what Jung calls the collective unconscious of the participants in these hypnotic regressions.

The case with the near-death experience seems to me to be quite different. I have no doubt that the roughly 10 million North Americans who have experienced an NDE have experienced the threshold of another mode of being. At the seminar in Florida with which I introduced these reflections and conclusions, one had to be impressed with the vividness of the details described and with the results in the lives of those who had these experiences. Dr. Bruce Greyson, a psychiatrist at the University of Connecticut where much of the leading research on NDEs is being done today, said on a *Man Alive* program on CBC TV (April 3, 1990) that he has been amazed at the way in which personalities have been changed by the NDE. Whereas psychiatrists might work for months or even years to effect very small modifications in someone's behaviour and outlook, "the NDE seems to achieve so much more almost overnight." Insufficient attention has been given to this otherwise inexplicable dimension of the NDE in my considered opinion. None of the debunkers has ever adequately dealt with this undeniable phenomenon.

Moody says that his patients reported that, so far from being a kind of dreamlike reality, what they experienced had such a compelling clarity and power that it made this life seem like a dream in comparison. "They became quite convinced that our consciousness here is quite limited," he said. "In the realm where they went, to think something was to communicate it. To see something was to feel you had it under a microscope and could vision its very being." Moody's patients, corroborated in the following years by thousands of others, said they had no sense of space or time during the NDE. "They are aware of having a body," he said. "But it's like a cloud of light." The biggest difficulty of all, Moody reports, is that the NDE is so ineffable, so unlike anything previously experienced, that the experiencer can scarcely find words to come close to it. "They do the best they can but they keep telling you that they can't really describe it." That's a little like the problem the author of Revelation had some two thousand years ago.

It is my opinion that while these people have not been dead, they have obviously been very close to death, and so what they have to say must be listened to. Their experience, tying in as it does with similar experiences down the ages and in every culture, must be taken seriously. It is evidence that something quite extraordinary begins to happen at death. It also suggests very strongly that the glimpses and hints of an afterlife in the great religious literature of the world may well be based not upon flights of fancy but upon a kind of knowledge we are only now beginning to understand.

The uniform witness of those who have NDEs, whether they are atheists, agnostics, lapsed religionists or devoted believers, is that to enter the dying process is to be led towards an incredible light. This is why Moody has entitled his latest book *The Light Beyond*. But the near-universal testimony of mystics and prophets from the beginning has also been that the ultimate source of all being, God, is Light. Well over two thousand years ago, the prophet wrote: "Arise, shine: for thy light is come . . . The sun shall be no more thy light by day; neither for brightness shall the moon give light unto thee: but the Lord shall be unto thee an everlasting light, and thy God thy glory."[15]

There are those who claim too much for the NDE and feel they now have the elusive proof that many have sought for immortality. They don't have any such proof. But, again, I would argue that it is foolish and unscientific to go to the other extreme and pretend that all of this has no relevance. No natural explanation has been found that can sweep this phenomenon away. In its absence, there is little alternative but to accept some kind of transcendental explanation in its stead. The NDE is only a plank in the platform of evidence, but it's an important one, in my view.

Religion

We have already looked at the testimony of Christianity, Judaism, Islam and other religions regarding death and a life to come. I resist the temptation to cite the relevant passages from the scriptures of the world's great faiths to illustrate my point. The majority of dedicated believers in these various folds may feel it is grounds enough for certainty that their sacred books affirm life after death. But as a critic of fundamentalism of any kind, whether it be religious, political or economic, I cannot follow that route myself. It is not enough to say "It's in the book" and demand assent. As I have said elsewhere, one of the most serious mistakes of ultra-conservative Protestantism is that it has rejected the idea of an infallible Pope only to create the idol of an infallible "paper Pope"—the Bible. Other religionists too are guilty of this type of bibliolatry concerning the Qur'an, the Bhagavad Gita or whatever. On the other hand, it does not follow from this that one loftily dismisses the wisdom and insights of the world's inspired scriptures. Quite the opposite. Standing as I still do within the Christian tradition, I take the witness of the Old and New Testaments with total seriousness. I have studied them for years and find new spiritual light and truth breaks out from them continuously. I believe God speaks powerfully through them to our human condition.

Thus, when the Bible and other sacred books describe unseen realities beyond this present order, I find it the intelligent thing to do to listen carefully. If I wanted to learn about any other area of life, from fly-fishing to gourmet cooking, I would listen to the experts. I would read the most experienced writers in the field. I would pay particular attention to the "superstars." It makes sense, then, to do no less when it comes to the most central issue anyone can face: Is there a life to come and what is it like?

I am only too aware of the shadow side of religion and I am far from blind to its failures and shortcomings. But still, for me, as for countless millions of others, the really great, inspired geniuses of history are those who pioneered and taught in the spiritual arena, who addressed the ultimate questions of God, origins, meaning, ethics or conduct, and the final purpose and destiny of all things. Their voices, their willingness to die for their vision of an eternal truth, and its resonance within my own innermost being, the sense that their testimony confirms what I have already unconsciously known to be so—all these constitute essential evidence indeed.

The Resurrection of Jesus, of course, is of utmost importance for me. In researching and writing *The Pagan Christ* I came to see it not as a historical "event" but as the central motif in a mythical drama almost as old as humanity. To say it was mythology, however, is a far cry from saying it was a fairy tale or a lie. As I explained fully in that book, myths contain more and deeper truths than history. They convey the inner meaning of history itself. The reality witnessed to by the patently symbolic Gospel narratives never changes. Their testimony is that we all, as bearers of the "Christ" or spark of divinity within, shall conquer death and rise in glory to newness of life. The first Easter was not about the resuscitation of a corpse. It was a total transformation into an entirely new mode of being, a sign and seal of the New Age to come. I believe the New Testament witness that, as the Christ of Easter was raised, so too shall we all— and all humanity.

The reader must form his or her own conclusions. I can only say this: there are very few areas of life where absolute certainty is possible. One of the more tragic seductions of religion, as well as other spheres of thought, is the promise of total certainty. What we have to do in most cases—indeed as they do in any court of law—is weigh up the available evidence and make our decision. When it comes to life after death, I can say with humility that I am now convinced the overwhelming weight of evidence falls on its side.

God, Faith and Life After Death

In the course of my research, I received a very thoughtful letter from a skeptic in which he chastised me for giving any thought to "evidence" whatever. His point was that, since belief in God and belief in a life to come are really matters of faith, it is a sign of weakness or of unbelief to look for concrete signs or reasons. I believe he has a restricted view of faith, and that any leap of faith must be based upon a right-brain as well as a left-brain approach. Theology, for example, is *fides rationem quaerens*, faith seeking a rational basis and mode of expression. Our belief in God is certainly not an irrational act; its final step of trust is better described, perhaps, as non-rational instead. It is an act of commitment like marriage or friendship. But, at the same time, my critic had a point. When all is said and done, my belief in life after death is ultimately rooted in the nature and grace of God.

Although I have radically revised many of my understandings of my own faith, Christianity, over the years, I am more convinced and sure of the reality whom we call God today than ever before. It is because of the kind of God revealed by the teachings of Judaism, Christianity and Islam in particular—"the People of the Book"— that I am persuaded of the truth of spiritual planes beneath, through and beyond this world of space, sense and time. It is for this reason that I believe God has a destiny for each of us that transcends the grave. We will live in a dimension of being where all of life's promises will be fulfilled, not because of our inner merit or innate immortality, but because of God's faithfulness and love. Because God is God, the forces of evil, disease, decay and death do not have the last word. When one stands by the grave of anyone, be they dearly beloved or total stranger, it is this faith that is the source of all comfort and hope. You believe it with your intellect; in your heart you know it to be true.

What Will It Be Like?

In "The Love Song of J. Alfred Prufrock," poet T.S. Eliot depicts Prufrock at a tea party in a room where women "come and go / Talking of Michelangelo."[16] Upset by the idle chatter and tormented by existential doubts about the meaning of life, he wonders what would happen if he were to try to squeeze the universe into a ball, "to roll it toward some overwhelming question." To say, in fact, "'I am Lazarus come from the dead, / Come back to tell you all.'" He imagines what he would feel like, if, having done this, someone "settling a pillow by her head," should say: "'That is not what I meant at all. That is not it, at all.'"

This is more than a mere indictment of the triviality of much of what passes for social conversation; it recognizes the overwhelming importance for humanity of the issues we have been discussing. If there is a God, and if there is a destiny beyond the grave, the questions of what kind of God and what kind of destiny become absolutely crucial. Unfortunately, there is no Lazarus come back from the grave to tell us all.

I know that throughout the centuries there have been individuals who have claimed to have gone farther than our modern NDErs and to have actually been given the privilege of touring heavenly realms. Those who are familiar with the voluminous writings of Emanuel Swedenborg will know that this brilliant scientist-turned-theologian claimed to have had direct contact with angels and the spiritual world. In his longest, eight-volume treatise, the *Arcana Coelestia* (*Heavenly Mysteries*) from 1756, Swedenborg gives detailed descriptions of the world to come. Without wishing to offend his current followers, however, I have to say that I have found his and other, similar visionary expositions interesting but unconvincing. They are a testimony more to the inner, imaginative life of those concerned than to an objective reality.

Leaving the visionary approach on one side, then, what can be said with any degree of certitude? One thing is for sure, life after death will be utterly different from what we, from our limited stance, have supposed. As T.S. Eliot has reminded us, words sometimes crack and strain under the burden we impose on them. If there is one thing all those who have ever tried to describe otherworldly realities agree upon it is that ordinary language cannot express the glory. We see as yet, to quote Paul, "through a glass darkly; but then, one day, face to face."

Judgment

After leaving a tunnel of light, those who have had a near-death experience say that they are drawn to a Being of Light and that in this Presence they have a review of everything they have ever said or done. Some patients of Dr. Moody described this as a kind of "memory theatre." They saw their lives from a third-party perspective and were able to feel how their actions had been injurious or helpful to others. "There is some regret," he said, "but it is not a harsh experience." Reading both modern and ancient accounts of the NDE, you have to be impressed by the constancy of this theme of an evaluation or judgment process of some kind. In religions and mythologies of every type the symbolism of weighing scales, of judgment thrones, of difficult bridges to cross or of narrow gates witness to the near-universality of this belief. It lies behind the use of such antithetical images as heaven and hell, damnation and bliss.

Several things combine to convince me there will be a reality corresponding to these descriptions or metaphors—my own inner, moral sense, my belief in justice and my understanding of God's nature. In the words of the Anglican prayer, we have all done and said things "we ought not to have done" and we have left undone the "things we ought to have done" during a lifetime. There is both justice and wisdom in seeing the real meaning and implications for ourselves and others of all we have been. Part of our being human consists of our awareness of responsibility to our Creator, the ground of our being. The judgment or evaluation process is a necessary corollary of that. I think it would be a serious mistake to downplay or attempt to gloss over this aspect of a future life. While I have already made it abundantly clear that I cannot find any rational grounds for a belief in a literal hell, Purgatory, or any other form of temporal or eternal punishment, we will realize just what we have been and done, and this could bring more than mere regret. It could be a terrible experience indeed, and will surely be so for the murderous tyrants and torturers of this age. But it will be in the presence of the Light that not only reveals and brings judgment but brings love, mercy and forgiveness as well. That, I believe, is why the researches of Moody and the others have shown that the millions who have had an NDE testify to the incredible sense of love and of healing that surrounds them, even at the moment of deepest remorse.

Healing and Growth

The word "salvation" is an old-fashioned one and greatly misunderstood as well. It comes from the Latin words *salvus* and *salvatio*, meaning wholeness. In fact, it comes close to the essential meaning of our word "holy," which also refers to a wholeness of mind, body and spirit. In any case, all the sacred literature of the major religions and mythologies speak of the life after death as a restoration to wholeness. It is salvation. It is tempting here, because of their great emotional power and haunting beauty, to quote an entire anthology of such passages, but space does not permit it. These words speak of the crooked being made straight, the blind to see and the deaf to hear. All imperfections of mind or body will be done away forever. Let me just cite one such vision: "And God shall wipe away all tears from their eyes; and there shall be no more death, neither sorrow, nor crying, neither shall there be any more pain . . ."[17]

What is fascinating in this respect is that when you examine the experiences of the millions who have now had an NDE you find these people—many of them agnostics, atheists or lapsed believers—saying that when they are greeted by deceased loved ones they appear whole and in the very prime of life. According to Moody and a host of other researchers, the "dead" are said to seem to be as they were (or would have been) at about age thirty rather than the age at which they died. But it will not be solely a matter of physical and mental healing. As St. Augustine said, "We shall know, and we shall grow." Life after death, as we have hinted already, will not be a static, boring contemplation of eternity. Our spiritual journey has only just begun in this life.

There is much to discover ahead, much maturing to do, many new challenges to understand and overcome. In *Harpur's Heaven and Hell*, I suggested that it may well be that God will allow us to become co-creators of entirely new, unimaginable worlds and universes yet to come. Consider the possibility of having one's deepest questions answered—how this world was made, why God thought our free will worth the risk of all the terrible suffering we have inflicted upon each other and the planet, what the inner meaning of our own lives really was. As a writer, I know how often the vision in my mind and what I can actually find words to express differ when the work is done. Imagine the joy of a Mozart, a Beethoven or a Glenn Gould on hearing and being able to express for the first time the music behind the music they were able to write or play! Think of the scientists or the philosophers who once wandered along the shore of the ocean of knowledge now able to plunge right in. As Paul says, "I shall know even as also I am known."

To know like this is to grow beyond the shadow to the reality of what we are meant to become. We will not all start at the same place, and no doubt we shall assist one another as the grace of God assists us all. There is a lovely passage in a book by Jungian analyst Marion Woodman called *The Pregnant Virgin* in which she is talking about the way in which the various stages in our earthly lives can resemble the caterpillar's metamorphosis into a butterfly. She notes that we can look back at our own lives and see this process at work. Then she adds: "As we mature, we are astonished at the accuracy with which fate uses one situation to develop the attributes necessary for another. From the soul's standpoint, it is possible that life as we know it now is a uterus in which the subtle body is preparing itself for the world in which it will be born when our physical body dies. Many of us, at one time or another, have felt a propensity for wings."[18]

Space and Time

We have already had reason to comment on the way in which language, designed to deal with this world and its experiences, fails us badly when we try to express feelings and thoughts about other dimensions and levels of reality. This becomes very evident when you examine the semantics involved when we talk specifically about death and a transcendent life to come. We realize that such a life will be one that is somehow freed from the shackles of time and space. Yet, because these are the spectacles through which we look at things, we repeatedly use time and space metaphors or imagery. Thus, for example, we speak of life *after* death, a time-based formula, or of life *beyond* death, which reveals a spatial bias. Indeed, much of what seems like crudity or incredulity in our language about heaven—"above the bright, blue sky" as the children's hymn puts it—stems from this kind of linguistic inadequacy. It is not easy to escape from this trap, but we must at least be aware of the problem and make some attempt to surmount it. Not to do so is to put an unnecessary obstacle in the way of those who are struggling for understanding in this area yet are put off by most descriptions of it.

When I was an undergraduate at Oriel College, Oxford, I belonged to a group called The Socratic Club. The president at the time was the well-known writer and Christian apologist C.S. Lewis. Lewis, an articulate agnostic who then found faith, was a don at Magdalene College and later became professor of English literature at Cambridge. I well remember one evening when he was talking about coming to grips with the notion of an existence or state of being free of space or time. He used the example of a novel and its author. Within the pages of the book, the story unfolds and the characters develop in an orderly fashion. They live inside a certain pattern of both time and space. But to the author (or the reader) standing outside the confines of the drama, these limitations need not apply. We accept them tentatively as we read, but there is a sense in which everything in the book is here and now for us. We can open it at any part of the story we wish to. We can see it all happening in a flash. Neither the late Professor Lewis nor I would have argued that there are not faults with this illustration, but it does help a little. At death, it is as though we have stepped out of the book. The old restrictions will be replaced by a new kind of freedom.

Significantly, one of the points Dr. Moody said has impressed him in the NDE accounts of his own patients and those of other researchers is the way in which those who have the experience testify to this phenomenon. He told us at the Florida seminar: "While our language is either temporal or spatial when talking about this subject, the NDErs uniformly report that there is no awareness of space or time in the experience they have had. Nevertheless, they are aware of having a body which they describe as being 'like a cloud of light.'" All of this brings us back to what was said earlier about eternal life. This, we saw, describes not an endless or infinite time stretching menacingly and forever before us but rather a totally different quality of life lived in an everlasting *now*.

If this interpretation is correct, as I am convinced it is, it is of enormous help because it surmounts what I consider to be one of the greatest difficulties in the Christian teaching about what happens at and after death. Unable to escape from the snare of time-space thinking, the Christian view (as well as that of other religions) is that there is a considerable waiting period between the decay of the physical body and the general resurrection for the life to come. While the soul or spirit struggles in Purgatory or waits, disembodied, in some other place, the body is not resurrected or somehow reproduced until the end of the world. We are never told how this is supposed to occur.

Dr. Marie-Louise von Franz rightly calls this a "gap" in Christian thinking that is both striking and serious in its consequences for belief. But if to die is to escape immediately from the whole time-space web of being, then the entire concept of waiting periods or intervals between death and final resurrection falls to the ground. The resurrection is at the moment of death. As Paul rightly says, "To be absent from the body, is to be present with the Lord." The miracle of the resurrection of the body—be it the emergence of an astral or subtle body or some other form—occurs immediately.

This is not the place to elaborate upon the ramifications of this approach for some of the more bizarre timetables for the afterlife erected by religions both ancient and modern. But it is the chief reason why I find such predictions so totally wanting. In conclusion, I find it encouraging that several important contemporary theologians, Karl Rahner and Ladislaus Boros in particular, also espoused this approach. They, too, argue that the resurrection and final judgment take place immediately after death. Linear or historical time stops at death and the new life in its fullness begins. They see the resurrection no longer as "a recreation of the old body" but rather as a prolonged existence of the person in a spiritual body.[19]

Who Goes to Heaven?

Asking the question Who will go to heaven? is not my preferred way of posing this concern. Nevertheless, I have phrased it so because it is a quickly recognizable formula. The traditional teaching of most religions, particularly Judaism, Christianity and Islam, has been that some will and many will not "inherit eternal life." Indeed, talking with some groups or watching television preachers, one gets the impression that the next life will be a very restricted one indeed. They and their followers will be in and the rest of us will be out! I'm reminded of the familiar but not terribly sound (theologically speaking) hymn that declares: "When we all get to heaven, what a day of rejoicing that will be." Of course, when it says "all" it doesn't really mean all. It means all those who think as we do, all those who belong to our particular little group.

My wife and I shared an unsettling experience a few years ago at an Anglican church. The preacher said quite bluntly in his sermon that only those who have been "washed in the blood of Jesus" will go to heaven. When I told him at the door of the church that it seemed he had a very narrow view of heaven he simply nodded and agreed that he had indeed. It was evident he liked it that way. In this view, only a small minority of fundamentalist Christians will end up in heaven, never mind the vast majority of other Christians, the Muslims, the Jews, the Hindus and all the others of different faiths or of none.

But it's not just extreme Protestants who take this route. I remember once *The New York Times* carried a front-page story on the threat by the then assistant Roman Catholic bishop of New York, Austin Vaughan, that the state's governor, Mario Cuomo, "is in danger of going to hell" for being pro-choice on abortion. Vaughan said: "I think for a believing, educated Catholic to take the position he's taken, he takes a very serious risk of going straight to hell."[20] There have been similar pronouncements much more recently in the debate in Canada and elsewhere over same-sex marriage. Frankly, I find such a rigid, short-sighted pronouncement almost incredible. I would have thought the days of preachers spending the first half of their sermon making people feel guilty and afraid, dangling them over a fiery hell, and then the second half telling them the Church just happens to have a remedy for their remorse and terror, were over and long past. Unfortunately, that's not so, and a great deal of unnecessary grief and harm results.

You can, it is true, read the Bible in such a way as to make it appear that life in a world to come is only for the chosen few. But you can interpret the Bible to make it teach almost anything you want. The truth is that, while I do not belong to the "It's in the Book" school, there are many passages that make it clear that it is God's will and intention to reconcile the entire cosmos, including every human who has ever lived, to Himself/Herself. There will ultimately be "one fold, one shepherd." My own deep conviction is that none of us deserves or earns eternal life no matter who we are or what we have done or not done. It is not a reward for good works; it is a sheer gift of love. Therefore it makes both sense and justice to recognize that the grace of God by which we are given it is there for all humanity. If we truly believe in an all-loving, gracious Source of all things, the kind of accepting presence imaged by the father in the parable of the prodigal son, then it seems to me to be utterly incongruous to hold that anyone will be ultimately "lost." We are all God's offspring or children, as New Testament Christianity—and most other religions—makes clear.

If none of us would ever want to see our own children separated from us forever, how much more will this be the case with "Our Father in Heaven"? God wills to bring all his children home. All will be "saved," to use an old-time Gospel expression, not by compulsion or abrogation of their free will but by the attraction and transforming power of the Divine Love. Personally, I fail to see how heaven or eternal life would be bliss of any kind unless one were assured that all will be sharers in it. At this ultimate family occasion there will finally be no empty chairs, no missing faces.

Will There Be Animals in Heaven?

While some may regard the question of whether or not there will be animals in a life beyond death as quite frivolous, there are many for whom it is of very great importance. I once wrote a feature on this issue and it provoked an astonishing amount of mail, much more than on many other topics one might have thought to have been of greater urgency.

It seems to me there are two reasons why there are those who believe in some form of life after death yet treat this matter as irrelevant or foolish. One is what is now called "speciesism"—the arrogant supposition that human beings are all that matter in the sight of God or the universe. We are only now beginning to realize that the ecological crisis is in no small measure attributable to precisely this kind of misguided hubris. On the other hand, if we see ourselves not as lords and exploiters of creation but as very much an integrated part of the whole fabric of life, it is natural to wonder whether the future will contain all of those creatures who shared this mortal coil with us and, in so many cases, brought us such great joy.

The second reason is the way many religious people, particularly Christians, think about the soul. Animals, they argue, don't have souls, therefore they don't figure into God's ultimate salvation. This reasoning is based upon a serious error. It assumes that humans "have" something called a soul. But this is not what the Bible teaches. In the Genesis myth, it says: "And the Lord God formed man of the dust of the ground, and breathed into his nostrils the breath of life; and man became a living soul." Notice it doesn't say that God *gave* humankind a soul. It says plainly that Adam (which simply means human being) *became* a living soul. People don't have souls in the same way they have arms or noses. We *are* souls. We are living centres of energy, thought and personality. We bear the *imago Dei* or the inner Christ in our freedom to choose and in our power of self-reflection. Animals, birds and fish may not be "made in the image of God" but they are God's creatures whom He/She saw to be "very good" at the Creation. In my view, to the extent that they have consciousness at all, they are souls too. They share in the great Oversoul of the universe.

Incidentally, I have very great sympathy with those animal lovers who feel instinctively that "heaven wouldn't be heaven without them." A friend of mine who is an avid birdwatcher looks forward, she says, to one day seeing those birds she has never seen before—especially those species that have already vanished from the earth!

Rigidly orthodox religious people who bridle at any of this need to be reminded of some aspects of Scripture that have been much neglected. Nearly all the passages in Jewish and Christian Scriptures, particularly those that deal with "the age to come," speak of the restoration or re-creation of nature itself. There will be a "new heaven and a new earth," the Scriptures say. The lion will lie down with the lamb and there will be no more killing—but he will remain a "liony" lion all the same, not an emasculated cat.

Epilogue

Hans Küng has written: "Eternal life is seen at its deepest level as a matter of trust." He quickly goes on to add, however, that such a trust must be rooted in reality. It must be "an absolutely reasonable trust."[21] That is precisely what we have been concerned with throughout this book: a rational foundation for such a trust. But it would be wrong to leave the reader feeling that this has been a merely academic discussion calling simply for assent or dissent. Something much more profound is at stake. It is, I believe, significant that those in our time who report that they have come back from the brink of death with an experience of a transcendent "beyond" do not just say they have lost their fear of death. With virtually total unanimity, they say they have come back with an intensified commitment to life. Their new certainty that death is a gateway or entrance into glorious, unseen dimensions of being has filled them with a greatly enhanced sense of purpose and meaning here and now. Old anxieties and problems that once seemed intractable, even overwhelming, are seen in a new perspective. There is an inner assurance that God or the Cosmic Spirit is in ultimate control.

Thankfully, we don't all have to have a close brush with death to come to this kind of spiritual experience. To conclude that there is life after death is to recognize that there is an Author or Creator of that life. The act of trust by which we commit ourselves to the one involves a commitment of ourselves to the other. In the end, it is because of that numinous Presence that brought us into being and that sustains the cosmos that we believe in a life after death. To trust that there is a life after death is to trust God. It is to trust that the ultimate energy at the foundations of the universe is love. With that kind of commitment, we can face both life and death with fearlessness and hope. Trust, hope and love are the most powerful, most revolutionary forces the world has ever known. They are needed today more than at any previous moment in history.

Finally, to those of you who have read this book in grief seeking solace and understanding in the face of the death of someone dearly loved, let me just say this. All sorts of questions and mysteries surround you right now. Nobody can answer them all. But I assure you that I am as convinced of this as I am of anything in this world: a day is coming when all separations will be over. We will one day be reunited (in the words of the old hymn) with those "whom we have loved long since and lost a while." We will return to the source of our being, not as rivers return to the ocean and are swallowed by it, but as recognizable individuals. As Eliot says, we will find that our end is our beginning. We will "arrive where we started / And know the place for the first time."[22] The deepest longings of all our hearts will be satisfied. Meanwhile, we can safely entrust ourselves, our loved ones and all the human community to the grace and mercy of God. In one of the most magnificent, most comforting pieces of writing ever penned, Paul says: "For I am persuaded that neither death, nor life, nor angels, nor principalities, nor powers, nor things present, nor things to come, nor height, nor depth, nor any other thing in all creation, shall ever be able to separate us the love of God in Christ Jesus our Lord."[23] That's not a narrow, one-faith vision. It is an insight into the heart of reality for the whole human race.

Notes

INTRODUCTION

1. *Toronto Star*, 11 May 1987, p. C3.
2. *Toronto Star*, 21 Oct 1987, p. A27.
3. A.E. Wallis Budge, *The Book of the Dead—The Papyrus of Ani* (New York: Dover Publications, 1967), pp. xlviii-lv.

1: STRANGE ENCOUNTERS

1. Andrew Greeley, "Mysticism Goes Mainstream," *American Health Magazine* (January/February 1987), pp. 47ff.
2. Reported by Tom Harpur, *Toronto Star*, 2 April 1983.
3. Terry Clifford, "Shirley MacLaine's Spiritual Dance," *American Health Magazine* (January/February 1987), p. 50.
4. Cited by Colin Wilson, *Afterlife* (London: Grafton Books, 1987).
5. Tom Harpur, *Toronto Star*, 5 July 1987.
6. For further information on the mystical boom in North America, I recommend all the relevant articles in the 1987 issue of *American Health Magazine* already referred to above. For further polling regarding American attitudes to life after death, see George Gallup Jr., *Adventures in Immortality* (New York: McGraw-Hill, 1982).

2: THE NEAR-DEATH EXPERIENCE

1. Raymond Moody, *Life After Life* (Georgia: Mockingbird Books, 1975).
2. *Philadelphia Enquirer*, December 1988, and the *IANDS Newsletter*, passim. (See bibliography for IANDS address under *Journal of Near-Death Studies*.)

3. Carol Zaleski, *Otherworld Journeys: Accounts of Near-Death Experience in Medieval and Modern Times* (New York: Oxford University Press, 1987).

4. Raymond Moody, *The Light Beyond* (New York: Bantam Books, 1988), p. 2.

5. *Canadian Medical Association Journal*, 104 (May 1971), pp. 889–90.

6. Aniela Jaffe, ed., in Carl Jung, *Memories, Dreams, Reflections* (New York, 1965).

7. For further documentation of the NDE and related experiences, I recommend Dr. Michael Sabom, *Recollections of Death: A Medical Investigation* (New York: Harper & Row, 1982), also Dr. Kenneth Ring, *Life at Death: A Scientific Investigation of the Near-Death Experience*, and *Heading Toward Omega: In Search of the Meaning of the NDE*.

8. Maurice Rawlings, *Beyond Death's Door* (Nashville: Thomas Nelson, 1978).

9. Margot Grey, *Return From Death: An Exploration of the Near-Death Experience* (London: Arkana, 1985).

10. Ibid. p. 41.

11. Karlis Osis, review of *Return From Death*, by Margot Grey, *Journal of Near-Death Studies*, 7, no. 3 (Spring 1989), pp. 183ff.

12. Grey, *Return From Death*, p. 72.

13. Zaleski, *Otherworld Journeys*, p. 7.

14. Ibid. p. 161.

15. Ibid. p. 167.

16. Moody, *The Light Beyond*, pp. 181ff.

17. Zaleski, *Otherworld Journeys*, p. 175.

18. Deepak Chopra, *How to Know God* (New York: Three Rivers Press, 2000), p. 219.

19. Carl Jung, quoted by Moody, *The Light Beyond*, p. 198.

20. Judith Miller, review of *The Light Beyond*, by Raymond Moody, *NDE Journal of Near-Death Studies*, Spring 1989, pp. 191ff.

3: THE SPIRIT MEDIUMS

1. A full account of the actual conversation between Pike, Fletcher and Spraggett can be found in Martin Ebon, ed., *True Experiences in Communicating With the Dead* (New York: Signet Books, 1968).

2. Ibid. p. 18.

3. Colin Wilson, *Afterlife* (London: Grafton Books, 1987), pp. 100–102.

4. Ibid. pp. 92–96.

5. Henry Gordon, *Channeling into the New Age* (Buffalo: Prometheus Books, 1988), p. 100.

6. Shirley MacLaine, *Out on a Limb* (New York: Bantam, 1984).

7. Gary E. Schwartz and Linda Russek, *The Afterlife Experiments: Breakthrough Scientific Evidence of Life After Death* (New York: Atria Books, 2002), p. 275.

8. *The Afterlife Experiments*, p. 268.

9. In the two-hour television special *Mediums: We See Dead People* on the Arts and Entertainment Channel on Saturday, November 11, 2006, Dr. Gary Schwartz was interviewed at length and gave a detailed update on his findings with regard to mediumship in general. He repeated the claims made in his earlier book and came across as a very credible witness.

4: REINCARNATION

1. www.religioustolerance.org. Accessed Summer 2005.

2. Ibid.

3. Ibid.

4. Hans Küng, *Eternal Life?* (New York: Image Books, 1985).

5. Sylvia Cranston and Carey Williams, *Reincarnation: A New Horizon in Science, Religion, and Society* (New York: Julian Press, 1984).

6. Ibid. pp. 106–7.

7. Geddes MacGregor, *Reincarnation in Christianity* (Wheaton, Illinois: Quest Books, 1978), p. 118.

8. Mark Albrecht, *Reincarnation: A Christian Critique of a New Age Doctrine* (Downers Grove, Illinois: InterVarsity Press, 1982), p. 65.

9. Ernest Hilgard, *San Francisco Examiner*, 17 March 1977, p. 24.

10. Albrecht, *Reincarnation*, p. 69.

11. Colin Wilson, *Afterlife* (London: Grafton Books, 1987), pp. 21ff.

12. Dr. Ian Stevenson, *Xenoglossy* (Charlottesville, Va: University Press of Virginia, 1974), and *Unlearned Language* (Charlottesville, Va.: University Press of Virginia, 1984).

13. Sri Sri Somasundara, quoted in Albrecht, *Reincarnation: A Christian Critique*, p. 129.

14. Chopra, *How to Know God*, p. 245.

15. Shirley MacLaine, *Out on a Limb* (New York: Bantam, 1983), pp. 234–35.

16. For more on this see pp. 273ff.

17. Job 14:14.

18. Geddes MacGregor, *Reincarnation in Christianity* (Wheaton, Ill.: Quest Books, 1978).

19. Sylvia Cranston and Carey Williams, *Reincarnation: A New Horizon in Science, Religion, and Society* (New York: Julian Press, 1984), p. 201.

20. John 10:15.

21. John 8:12ff.

22. John 9:1ff.

23. Cranston and Williams, *Reincarnation: A New Horizon*, p. 209.

24. Matt. 16:13–14.

25. Northrop Frye, *The Great Code* (Toronto: Harcourt Brace Jovanovich, 1983).

26. Geddes MacGregor, quoted in Cranston and Williams, *Reincarnation: A New Horizon*, p. 210.

27. Ibid. p. 209.

28. Joel L. Whitton and Joe Fisher, *Life Between Life* (New York: Doubleday, 1986).

29. Teilhard de Chardin, Jesuit scientists, 1881–1955, *The Phenomenon of Man* (published posthumously, 1956).

5: DREAMS OF DEATH AND DYING

1. Fraser Boa, *The Way of the Dream* (Caledon East, Ont.: Windrose Films Ltd., 1988), p. xii.

2. Dr. Marie-Louise von Franz, *On Dreams and Death: A Jungian Interpretation* (Boston: Shambhala Press, 1986).

3. Ibid. p. viii.

4. Ibid. p. ix.

5. Ibid.

6. Ibid. p. xvi.

7. John 12:24.

8. von Franz, *On Dreams and Death*, p. 64.

9. Ibid. p. 64.

10. Ibid. p. 89.

11. Ibid. p. 156.

6: NEW LIGHT FROM SCIENCE

1. Dr. Wilder Penfield, *Second Thoughts* (Toronto: McClelland & Stewart, 1970).

2. Bertrand Russell, *Why I Am Not a Christian* (London: Unwin Paperbacks, 1957), p. 45.

3. Thomas Henry Huxley, quoted in Robert M. Augros and George N. Stanciu, eds., *The New Story of Science* (Chicago: Gateway Editions, 1984), pp. 9–10.

4. Russell, *Why I Am Not a Christian*, p. 107.

5. Augros and Stanciu, *The New Story of Science*, p. 6.

6. Dr. Marie-Louise von Franz, *On Dreams and Death* (Boston: Shambhala Press, 1986), p. 152.

7. Augros and Stanciu, *The New Story of Science*, p. 6.

8. Sir Charles Sherrington, quoted in *The New Story of Science*, pp. 11–12.

9. Sir John Eccles, *Facing Reality* (Berlin and New York: Springer-Verlag, 1970), p. 162.

10. Adolf Portmann, *New Pathways in Biology* (New York: Harper & Row, 1964). Quoted by Augros and Stanciu, *The New Story of Science*, p. 27.

11. Dr. Wilder Penfield, *The Mystery of the Mind: A Critical Study of Consciousness and the Human Brain* (Princeton: Princeton University Press, 1975).

12. Augros and Stanciu, *The New Story of Science*, p. 34.

13. Penfield, *The Mystery of the Mind*, p. 80.

14. Ibid. p. 12.

15. Sir John Eccles, *Facing Reality*, p. 174. See also Augros and Stanciu, *The New Story of Science*, p. 35.

16. Carl Jung, *Letters*, vol. 2, p. 45, quoted in von Franz, *On Dreams and Death*, p. 144.

17. von Franz, *On Dreams and Death*, pp. 144–45.

18. For a review of Dr. Frank J. Tipler's 1996 book, *The Physics of Immortality, Modern Cosmology, God and the Resurrection of the Dead* by Danny Rich, Ph.D., a Christian writer, see www.doesgodexist.org/janfeb96/physicsofimmortality.html.

7: CHRISTIANITY

1. Gal. 1:15–16.
2. II Cor. 12:2–4.
3. I Cor. 2:9.
4. I Cor. 13:12.
5. II Cor. 4:16ff.
6. II Cor. 5:1–10.
7. Phil. 3:20–21.
8. II Cor. 5:8.
9. Carl Jung, *Memories, Dreams, Reflections* (New York: Pantheon Books, 1961), p. 325.
10. For a fuller treatment, see Tom Harpur, *For Christ's Sake* (Toronto: Oxford University Press, 1986).
11. Matt. 28:16ff; John 21:15ff.
12. G.A. Wells, *Can We Trust the New Testament?* (Peru, Ill.: Open Court Publishing, 2004), p. 192.
13. Matt. 28:9.

8: HELL, PURGATORY, AND END TIMES

1. I Sam. 28:8–15.
2. W.O.E. Oesterley and Theodore H. Robinson, *The Hebrew Religion— Its Origin and Development* (London: Society for the Propagation of Christian Knowledge, 1930), p. 322.
3. Gen. 37:35.
4. *The Oxford Dictionary of the Christian Church*, F.L. Cross, ed. (London: Oxford University Press, 1958) pp. 1250–51.
5. Psalm 16:10.
6. Psalm 38:18.
7. Psalm 6:5.
8. Psalm 88:5.
9. F.W. Beare, *The Gospel According to Matthew* (San Francisco: Harper & Row, 1981), p. 148, and see the other references there.
10. Job 19:25–6.
11. Oesterley and Robinson, *The Hebrew Religion*, p. 314.

12. Ibid. p. 348.

13. Rev. 21:1.

14. Beare, *The Gospel According to Matthew*, pp. 148–50.

15. Ibid.

16. Mark 9:42ff.

17. Jer. 32:35; II Kings 23:10.

18. Luke 12:5.

19. James 3:6.

20. Beare, *The Gospel According to Matthew*, p. 149.

21. Oesterley and Robinson, *The Hebrew Religion*, pp. 333ff.

22. J.N.D. Kelly, *Early Christian Doctrines* (San Francisco: Harper & Row, 1960), p. 482.

23. Ibid. p. 484.

24. Luke 11:11–13, and other Gospel parallels.

25. De Principiis, 2, II, 2. Quoted in Kelly, *Early Christian Doctrines*, pp. 473–74.

26. Matt. 12:31.

27. I Cor. 3:11–15.

28. F.L. Cross, ed., *Oxford Dictionary of the Christian Church* (London: Oxford University Press, 1958), p. 1125.

29. Hans Küng, *Eternal Life?* (New York: Image Books, 1985), p. 139.

30. *Oxford Dictionary of the Christian Church*, p. 810.

31. Ibid. p. 901.

32. Rev. 21:1ff.

9: OTHER WORLD FAITHS

Zoroastrianism

1. For further reading, see: "The Cosmic Battle: Zoroastrianism" in Eerdman's *Handbook to the World's Religions* (Grand Rapids, Mich.: William B. Eerdman's Publishing, 1982), pp. 80ff.

Hindu

2. *Bhagavad Gita*, Swami Prabhavananda and Christopher Isherwood, trans. (New York and Scarborough, Ont.: New American Library, Mentor Books, 1944), p. 29.

3. Ibid. p. 37.

4. Louis Fischer, *Ghandi: His Life and Message for the World* (New York: New American Library, Mentor Books, 1954), p. 19.

5. For further reading, see: Eerdman's *Handbook to the World's Religions.*

Buddhism

6. Hans Küng, *Eternal Life?* (New York: Image Books, 1985), pp. 57–58.

7. *The Tibetan Book of the Dead*, Francesca Fremantle and Chogyam Trungpa Rinpoche, translators (Boston: Shambhala, 1975).

8. Ibid. p. xii.

9. Ibid. p. xx.

10. Ibid. p. 29.

Judaism

11. For further reading, see "Afterlife" in *The Encyclopedia Judaica*, vol. 2 (Jerusalem and New York: Macmillan, 1971), pp. 335–39.

Islam

12. For further reading, see the articles on Islam in *The Encyclopedia of Religion*, vol. 7, Mircea Eliade, ed. (New York: Macmillan, 1987).

13. Abdul Wahid, *Islam: The Natural Way* (London: Mels Publishing, 1989), p. 164.

14. The Qur'an, 22:5–7. The Statesman Commercial Press, Calcutta, 4th ed., 1977.

15. Ibid. 21:47.

16. Ibid. 18:30.

17. Ibid. 29:13–20.

18. Wahid, *Islam: The Natural Way*, p. 170.

19. Ibid. p. 169.

20. Sylvia Cranston and Carey Williams, *Reincarnation: A New Horizon in Science, Religion, and Society* (New York: Julian Press, 1984), pp. 175–77.

21 The Qur'an, 71:17–18.

Baha'i

22. Hushidar Motlagh, *Unto Him Shall We Return* (Wilmette, Ill.: Baha'i Publishing Trust, 1985).

23 Ibid. p. 17.

Native Spirituality

24. Father Thomas Berry, *The Dream of the Earth* (San Francisco: Sierra Club Books, 1988), p. 182.

25. Ibid. p. 184.

26. Ibid. p. 193.

27. Michael Posluns, ed., *Songs for the People—Teachings on the Natural Way* (Toronto: NC Press, 1989), p. 287.

28. John Cobb and Charles Birch, *The Liberation of Life* (New York: Cambridge University Press, 1985).

29. For further reading, see Jordan Paper, *Offering Smoke* (Vancouver: Rain Coast Books, 1989). Also, *Handbook on the North American Indian*, in 20 volumes, William C. Sturtevant, ed. (Washington: The Smithsonian Institute, 1978–). And Jamake Highwater, *The Primal Mind* (New York: Harper & Row, 1981).

30. George Appleton, ed., *The Oxford Book of Prayer* (London: Oxford University Press, 1985), p. 351.

Seventh-day Adventists

31. For further reading, see any good encyclopedia of religion. Also, The Ministerial Association, General Conference of Seventh-day Adventists, *Seventh-Day Adventists Believe. . . .* (Hagerstown, Md.: Review & Herald Publishing Assoc., 1988).

Jehovah's Witnesses

32. For further reading, see *United in Worship of the Only True God* (New York: Watchtower Bible and Tract Society, 1983). Also, Alan Rogerson, *Millions Now Living Will Never Die* (New York: Constable Publishing, 1969).

Christian Science

33. For further reading, see *Science and Health, with Key to the Scriptures* (Boston: First Church of Christ, Scientist, 1971).

34. For more information, see Gill, Gillian, *Mary Baker Eddy*, Perseus Books, 1998.

10: PERSONAL REFLECTIONS AND CONCLUSIONS

1. Colin Wilson, *Afterlife* (London: Grafton Books, 1987), p. 144.

2. Dr. Marie-Louise von Franz, *On Dreams and Death: A Jungian Interpretation* (Boston: Shambhala Press, 1986), p. xi.

3. C.D. Broad, from *The Philosophy of C.D. Broad*, quoted in Wilson, *Afterlife*, p. 266.

4. Dr. Sandra Bertman, *Toronto Star*, 25 May 1989.

5. See my account in *Harpur's Heaven and Hell* (Toronto: Oxford University Press, 1984), pp. 175ff.

6. Carl Jung, quoted in von Franz, *On Dreams and Death*, p. x.

7. William James, quoted in Wilson, *Afterlife*, p. 183.

8. Tom Harpur, "Reasonable Faith," *Toronto Star*, 11 Feb. 1990.

9. Von Franz, *On Dreams and Death*, pp. 152ff.

10. Ibid. p. 157.

11. Sir John Eccles, *The Human Psyche* (Berlin and New York: Springer-Verlag, 1980).

12. *Science Digest*, July 1982; Sir James Jeans, *The Mysterious Universe* (New York: Macmillan, 1931).

13. Albert Einstein, *The Human Side*. H. Dukas and B. Hoffman, eds. (Princeton: Princeton University Press, 1979).

14. Guy Murchie, *The Seven Mysteries of Life* (Boston: Houghton Mifflin Co., 1989).

15. Isa. 60:1, 19.

16. T.S. Eliot, "The Love Song of J. Alfred Prufrock," in T.S. Eliot, *Selected Poems* (London: Faber & Faber, paperback ed., 1961), pp. 11ff.

17. Rev. 21:4.

18. Marion Woodman, *The Pregnant Virgin* (Toronto: Inner City Books, 1985), p. 73.

19. von Franz, *On Dreams and Death*, p. xi.

20. *The New York Times*, 22 Jan. 1990.

21. Hans Küng, *Eternal Life?* (New York: Image Books, 1985), p. 78.

22. T.S. Eliot, "Little Gidding," from *The Four Quartets* (London: Faber & Faber, paperback ed., 1959), pp. 49ff.

23. Rom. 8:38–9.

Selected Bibliography

Albrecht, Mark. *Reincarnation: A Christian Critique of a New Age Doctrine.* Downers Grove, Ill.: Inter Varsity Press, 1982.

Aries, Phillippe. *The Hour of Our Death.* Trans. by Helen Weaver. New York: Random House, 1981.

Augros, Robert M. and Stanciu, George N. *The New Story of Science.* Lake Bluff, Ill.: Gateway Editions, 1984.

Barrett, William, Sir. *Death-bed Visions: The Psychical Experiences of the Dying.* New York: Aquarian Press, 1988 (originally published in 1926).

Beauregard, Dr. Mario. *The Spiritual Brain.* New York: HarperCollins, 2007.

Bohm, David. *Wholeness and the Implicate Order.* London & New York: Routledge and Kegan Paul, 2002.

Boris, Ladislaus. *The Mystery of Death.* New York: Crossroad, 1973.

Budge, A.E. Wallis. *The Book of the Dead—The Papyrus of Ani.* New York: Dover Publications, 1967.

Callanan, Maggie, and Kelley, Patricia. *Final Gifts: Understanding the Special Awareness, Needs and Communications of the Dying.* New York: Bantam Books, 1992.

Campbell, Joseph. *The Power of Myth.* New York: Doubleday, 1988.

Campbell, Joseph, with Boa, Fraser. *This Business of the Gods.* Caledon East, Ont.: Windrose Films Ltd., 1989.

Capra, Frithjof. *The Tao of Physics.* Boulder, Col.: Shambhala, 1976.

Chopra, Deepak. *How to Know God.* New York: Three Rivers Press, 2000.

———. *Life After Death—The Burden of Proof.* New York: Harmony Books, 2006.

Cranston, Sylvia, and Williams, Carey. *Reincarnation, A New Horizon in Science, Religion, and Society.* New York: Julian Press, 1984.

de Chardin, Teilhard, Jesuit scientist, 1881-1955. *The Phenomenon of Man*. Published posthumously in 1956.

Dossey, Larry. *Recovering the Soul: A Scientific and Spiritual Search*. New York: Bantam Books, 1989.

Dumont, R.G., and Foss, D.C. *The American Way of Death: Acceptance or Denial*. Cambridge, Mass.: Schenkman, 1972.

Eccles, John C. *Facing Reality: Philosophical Adventures by a Brain Scientist*. Berlin and New York: Springer-Verlag, 1970.

———. *The Human Mystery*. New York: Springer-Verlag, 1979.

———. *The Human Psyche*. Berlin and New York: Springer-Verlag, 1980.

Eerdmans' Handbook to the World's Religions. Grand Rapids, Mich.: William B. Eerdman's Publishing, 1982.

Einstein, Albert. *The Human Side*. H. Dukas and B. Hoffman, eds. Princeton: Princeton University Press, 1979.

Encyclopedia Judaica, vol. 2, "Afterlife," pp. 335–39. Jerusalem and New York: Macmillan, 1971.

Encyclopedia of Religion, Mircea Eliade, ed. New York: Macmillan, 1987.

Fenwick, Peter, and Fenwick, Elizabeth. *The Truth in the Light: An Investigation of Over 300 Near-Death Experiences*. New York: Berkley Publishing Group, 1997.

Fox, Mark. *Religion, Spirituality and the Near-Death Experience*. London & New York: Routledge, 2003.

Gallup, George, Jr., with Proctor, William. *Adventures in Immortality*. New York: McGraw-Hill, 1982.

Gordon, Henry. *Channeling Into the New Age*. Buffalo: Prometheus Books, 1988.

Grey, Margot. *Return From Death*. London: Arkana, 1985.

Greyson, Bruce. "Near-Death Experiences and Attempted Suicide." IANDS, *Anabiosis*, 11 (1981), pp. 10–16.

Greyson, Bruce, and Flynn, C.P., eds. *The Near-Death Experience: Problems, Prospect, Perspectives*. Springfield, Ill.: Charles C. Thomas, 1984.

Guggenheim, Bill, and Guggenheim, Judy. *Hello From Heaven*. New York: Bantam Books, 1995.

Hanson, Paul. *The Dawn of Apocalyptic*. New York: Fortress Press, 1979.

Harpur, Tom. *Harpur's Heaven and Hell*. Toronto: Oxford University Press, 1984.

———. *For Christ's Sake*. Toronto: Oxford University Press, 1984.

———. *Always On Sunday*. Toronto: Oxford University Press, 1988.

Heinberg, Richard. *Memories and Visions of Paradise*. Los Angeles: Jeremy P. Tarcher, Inc., 1989.

Hunt, Valerie. *Infinite Mind*. Malibu, Calif.: Malibu Publishing, 1996.

Huxley, Thomas. *Essays on Some Controverted Subjects*. New York: 1892.

Ingber, D. "Visions of an Afterlife." *Science Digest*, Jan./Feb. 1981.

James, William. *The Will to Believe and Human Immortality*. New York: Dover Press, 1956.

Jeans, Sir James. *The Mysterious Universe*. New York: Macmillan, 1931.

Journal of Near-Death Studies (formerly *Anabiosis*). The International Association for Near-Death Studies (IANDS), P.O. Box 7767, Philadelphia, PA 19101.

Jung, Carl G. *Memories, Dreams, Reflections*. New York: Random House, 1961.

Kason, Yvonne, and Degler, Teri. *A Farther Shore: How Near-Death and other Extraordinary Experiences Can Change Ordinary Lives*. New York: Harper-Collins, 1994.

Kelly, J.N.D. *Early Christian Doctrines*. San Francisco: Harper & Row, 1960.

Kubler-Ross, Elizabeth. *On Death and Dying*. New York: Macmillan, 1969.

———. *Living with Death and Dying*. New York: Macmillan, 1981.

Küng, Hans. *Eternal Life?* New York: Image Books, 1985.

LaGrand, Louis E. *After Death Communication: Final Farewells*. St. Paul: Llewellyn Publications, 1997.

MacGregor, Geddes. *Reincarnation as a Christian Hope*. London: Macmillan, 1982.

Mead, G.R.S. *The Doctrine of the Subtle Body in Western Tradition*. London: Stuart and Watkins, 1967.

Moody, Raymond A., Jr. *Life After Life*. Georgia: Mockingbird Books, 1975. New York: Bantam, 1976.

———. *Reflections on Life After Life*. London: Corgi Books, 1977.

———. *The Light Beyond*. New York: Bantam, 1988.

Motlagh, Hushidar. *Unto Him Shall We Return*. Wilmette, Ill.: Baha'i Publishing Trust, 1931.

Osis, Karlis, and Erlendur, Haraldsson. *At the Hour of Death*. New York: Avon, 1980.

Oxford Dictionary of the Christian Church. F.L. Cross, ed. London: Oxford University Press, 1958.

Paterson, R.W.K. *Philosophy and the Belief in a Life after Death*. Library of Religion and Philosophy series. New York: St. Martin's Press, 1995.

Peake, Anthony. *Is There Life After Death?* New Jersey: Chartwell Books Inc., 2006.

Penfield, Wilder. *Second Thoughts*. Toronto: McClelland & Stewart, 1970.

———. *The Mystery of the Mind*. Princeton: Princeton University Press, 1975.

Pert, Candace. *Molecules of Emotion*. New York: Scribner, 1999.

Rawlings, M. *Beyond Death's Door*. Nashville: Thomas Nelson, 1978.

Ring, Kenneth. *Life at Death: A Scientific Investigation of the Near-Death Experience*. New York: Coward, McMann & Geoghegan, 1980.

———. *Heading Toward Omega: In Search of the Meaning of the N.D.E.* New York: William Morrow, 1984.

Ring, K. and Cooper, S. "Near-Death and Out-of-Body Experience in the Blind: A Study of Apparent Eyeless Vision." *Journal of Near-Death Studies*, 1997, 16:101–47.

Ring, K. and Valarino, S. *Mindsight: Near-Death and Out-of-Body Experiences in the Blind*. William James Center for Consciousness Studies, 1999.

Russell, Bertrand. *Why I Am Not a Christian*. New York: Simon & Schuster, 1957.

Sabom, Michael B. *Recollections of Death: A Medical Investigation*. New York: Harper & Row, 1982.

Sagan, Carl. *Broca's Brain*. New York: Ballentine Books, 1993.

Schwartz, Gary E. with Wm. L. Simon. *The Afterlife Experiments*. New York: Atria Books, 2003.

Sheldrake, Rupert, and Fox, Michael. *Natural Grace*. New York: Doubleday, 1996.

Short, Robert. *Something to Believe In*. San Francisco: Harper & Row, 1980.

Shroder, Tom. *Old Souls: The Scientific Evidence for Past Lives*. New York: Simon & Schuster, 1999.

Siegel, Ronald K. "Hallucinations." *Scientific American* 237 (October 1977), pp. 132–40.

———. "The Psychology of Life After Death." *American Psychologist* 35 (1980), pp. 911–31.

Spalding, John Howard. *Kingdom of Heaven as seen by Swedenborg*. New York: E.P. Dutton & Co., 1916.

Steiger, Brad. *Real Ghosts, Restless Spirits, and Haunted Places*. Detroit: Visible Ink Press, 2003.

Stevenson, Ian. *Children Who Remember Previous Lives: A Question of Reincarnation*. Revised ed. Jefferson, N.C.: McFarland & Company, 2001.

———. *Twenty Cases Suggestive of Reincarnation in the Mystery of the Mind: A Study of the Physiology of Consciousness*. Princeton: Princeton University Press, 1975.

The Tibetan Book of the Dead. Francesca Fremantle and Chogyam Trungpa Rinpoche, trans. Boston: Shambhala, 1975.

Vincent, Ken. *Visions of God from the Near-Death Experience*. Burdett, New York: Larson Publications, 1994.

Von Franz, Marie-Louise. *On Dreams and Death*. Boston: Shambhala, 1986.

Weatherhead, Leslie. *The Christian Agnostic*. Nashville: Abbington-Cokesbury Press, 1959.

Wilson, Colin. *Afterlife*. London: Grafton Books, 1987.

Zaleski, Carol. *Otherworld Journeys*. New York: Oxford University Press, 1987.

Zukav, Gary. *The Seat of the Soul*. New York: Simon & Schuster, 1989.

Index

THE AUTHOR Robert Cole is Professor of Modern British and European History at Utah State University in America and a Fellow of the Royal Historical Society, and has lectured at British colleges and universities. He has travelled extensively in Europe, and especially in France. His writings include *A Traveller's History of Paris*, *Britain and the War of Words in Neutral Europe, 1939–1945*, *A.J.P. Taylor: The Traitor Within the Gates*, a number of articles on propaganda and historiography, and several scripts for radio.

SERIES EDITOR Professor Denis Judd is a graduate of Oxford and is a Fellow of the Royal Historical Society. He is Professor Emeritus in History at the London Metropolitan University and currently a Professor in History at New York University in London. He has published over 25 books including the biographies of Joseph Chamberlain, Prince Philip, George V, George VI, Lord Reading and Alison Uttley and the bestselling *Empire*. He has reviewed and written extensively in the national press and in journals and is an advisor and regular contributor to the BBC *History* Magazine.

Other Titles in the Series

A Traveller's History of France

ROBERT COLE

Series Editor DENIS JUDD

Line Drawings ALISON HEPBURN

Armchair Traveller
at the bookHaus

Ninth Edition published in 2011 by

The Armchair Traveller at the bookHaus
The bookHaus, 70 Cadogan Place, London SW1X 9AH
www.thearmchairtraveller.com

ISBN 978-1-907973-04-8

Cover: Getty Images

A CIP catalogue record for this book is available from the British Library.

Typeset by DP Photosetting, Glamorgan, Wales.

Printed and bound in Great Britain by
CPI Mackays, Chatham ME5 8TD

Visit our website at *www.thearmchairtraveller.com*

À Catherine Taylor,
n'oubliez jamais ces merveilleux moments
aujourd'hui disparus

Contents

Preface

Few nations have affected the modern world as profoundly as France. For many centuries she was the colossus of Europe, dominating her neighbours and pursuing a policy of territorial aggrandizement at their expense. Heavily populated, richly endowed, fertile, prosperous and centralised, France was the fulcrum of the continental balance of power. With the Age of Discovery, French commercial and maritime enterprise made a global impact from Canada to India, from the Far East to Louisiana and the Caribbean. By the end of the nineteenth century, the French Empire stood second only to that of Britain, and had incorporated much of North and tropical Africa, Indo-China and many Pacific islands.

But France was not merely a great military and imperial power. French philosophers, French writers and painters, French architects, scientists and engineers inspired and challenged their contemporaries. Two hundred years ago the French Revolution shook the established European order to its core and liberated forces that have yet to be subdued. Even today, with her Empire gone and her frontiers fixed, France is a dominant founder-member of the EEC and enjoys a world-wide cultural influence. Above all, French style is pervasive, and seductive, from the great fashion houses to the dining table, from the boudoir to the international film and motor shows.

In this comprehensive, scholarly and lucid book, Professor Cole explains how the French nation emerged from pre-history to take its place as a world-shaping force. In the process he unravels many myths and puts the inevitable prejudices of France's neighbours in their proper perspective.

Hundreds of thousands of travellers visit France each year. The glories of the French countryside, the essential harmony of much of French architecture, the wealth of historical remains and associations, the enormous variety of experience that France offers, act as a perennial and irresistible attraction. For these visitors, this lively and useful guide provides the essential clues to any understanding of France's past, and present, in entertaining and sometimes surprising detail.

Denis Judd
London, 1988

CHAPTER ONE

The Land, People and Culture of Early France

FRANCE, like other European nations, is a phenomenon born out of conscious striving rather than from the natural affinity of its parts. Conflict has characterized France throughout its history. The historical landscape sets province against province, province against crown, authority against individuality, Christianity against paganism, church against state, papacy against crown, town against country, the country against the centre, and France against its neighbours. It has been wryly observed that all Frenchmen love France, but decry all other Frenchmen for demeaning her. There is the central theme of French history: the French created France almost in spite of themselves.

Geography

If French history is complex and diverse, so too is the geographical landscape over which it unfolded. Even the great plain stretching from beyond the Rhine River to Brittany and south to the Pyrénées is cut by deep river valleys, high plateaus, and the low hills of the Armorican Massif. It covers roughly three-quarters of the country in a triangle. The Atlantic and English Channel coasts form two sides, and a line of westward-facing hilly escarpments from Toulouse in the south to Verdun in the north-east form the third. The other quarter consists of hills and mountains.

The Alps and Pyrénées, with the Mediterranean coastline between them, define France's southern and south-eastern frontiers; and the Vosges, Massif Central, and Ardennes are rugged hills which break the landscape also in the east and south. Geographical detail varies greatly from one region to the next: the sheer walls of the Pyrénées, the soaring peaks of the Alps with Mont Blanc over 4000 metres, bizarre volcanic cones in the Puy-de-Dôme of the Massif Central, park-like expanses in the Loire Valley, wooded hills in the Paris Basin, flat plains to the east of La Rochelle, granite cliffs on the Breton coast, marshlands in Burgundy, and treeless plateaus in Champagne, to mention only some of what catches the eye.

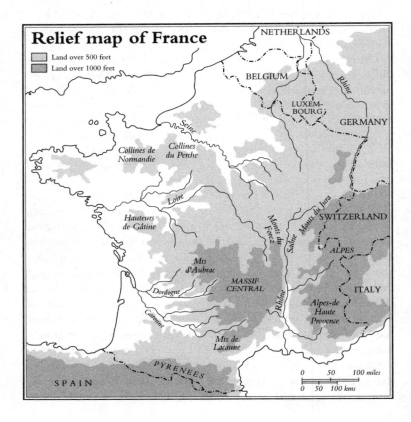

Relief map of France

Land over 500 feet
Land over 1000 feet

NETHERLANDS

BELGIUM

LUXEM-
BOURG

GERMANY

Rhine

Seine

*Collines de
Normandie*

*Collines
du Perche*

Loire

*Hauteurs
de Gâtine*

*Monts du
Forez*

Saône

Monts du Jura

SWITZERLAND

ALPES

*Mts
d'Aubrac*

MASSIF
CENTRAL

Dordogne

Rhône

ITALY

*Alpes-de
Haute
Provence*

Garonne

*Mts de
Lacaune*

PYRÉNÉES

SPAIN

| 0 | 50 | 100 miles |
| 0 | 50 | 100 kms |

CLIMATE

All of the country escapes extremes of heat and cold, save the highest Alpine peaks; but a damper, cooler climate prevails across the north and north-east, while dry, hot, Mediterranean conditions characterize the south and south-west. Wine is produced nearly everywhere, but the principal areas are in the warm Mediterranean or semi-Mediterranean areas: the Loire Valley south and south-east to the Languedoc region, and along the Rhône River between Lyon and Arles. Mediterranean France also is subject to the legendary *Mistral* and *Sirocco* winds. The *Mistral* is a cold, winter wind originating in the central plateau, which blows down the Rhône Valley. The *Sirocco*, either moist and warm or dry and hot, blows out of North Africa. Both are said to produce unusual, even bizarre, behaviour among people living in the areas affected.

Climate and geography influenced the course of French history, but did not dictate it. A mild climate and vast, rich agricultural plains, plateaus and river basins made France attractive to settlement and then to acquisitorial competition from Neolithic times to the present.

RIVERS

Long river systems (the Loire is over 1000 kilometres long) provided direction and invitation for migration, trade, invasion, and conquest – and still more acquisitorial competition. France, on the extreme western edge of the European continent, lies at the end of a great plain extending unbroken north and east to western Siberia. It has been a highway for the movement of peoples and cultures for thousands of years. Only the Rhine separates France from this plain to the east, and the Rhine has proved no barrier at all. Meanwhile, four great river systems quarter France, three of them in the great plain area. They served as conduits for the settlements and movement of peoples. To some extent the history of France can be written in terms of how the Saône-Rhône, the Garonne, the Loire, and the Paris Basin (Seine) evolved from areas of primitive habitation into centres of warring duchies, counties and kingdoms. Only the Rhône drains into the Mediterranean. The others follow the gentle slope of the western and northern plains to the Atlantic. Over the centuries, this Atlantic orientation has prevailed, for these are the richest watersheds. The economic and political centre, when there was a centre, lay northward, and eventually the Paris Basin emerged as the hub around which the wheel of the French nation revolved.

Paleolithic

The presence of Paleolithic or old stone age remains in the Dordogne Valley indicates clearly that 25,000 years ago and more there were thriving communities, however rudimentary, in what became France. These people moreover were capable of making sophisticated art as well as assorted simple flint tools. Cave paintings abound in the Dordogne east of Bordeaux, most famously in La Grotte de Lascaux at Montignac, although the 300 cave paintings discovered in December 1994 at Vallon-Pont-d'Arc in the Ardèche are said to eclipse even the Lascaux art. Fleeing reindeer and charging bison are rendered in rich and vivid colour and in such motional fluidity as to be nearly photographic in their realism. The human form by comparison is rendered only symbolically. It is absent from the paintings, and appears only in crude statuettes of females with huge breasts, stomachs and buttocks, suggesting their function as fertility goddesses.

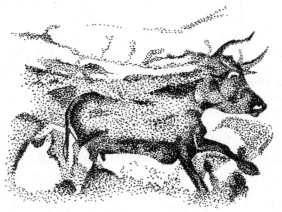

A cave painting at Lascaux

Neolithic

In the Neolithic or new stone age 12,000 years ago, human habitation reveals far more. Pottery and architecture join other remains to provide a fuller picture of the peoples then in residence. Agricultural villages were established in the Paris Basin by 4600 BC. Similar settlements from the same era appeared in the Rhône Valley and along the Aude in Languedoc.

Neolithic life flourished in all four river systems, and appears to have been both solidly established and increasingly sophisticated culturally, politically and economically. Indeed, the Neolithic period faded gradually into the earliest metal period, the Bronze Age, and it is clear that Neolithic and metal cultures sometimes existed side by side. But before they disappeared, the Neolithic peoples established settlements, developed rudimentary social organization, fought one another, and laid the foundations of organized, or at least ritualized, religion or mythology. Decoration and burial practice indicate the latter, while pottery, kitchen-middens (refuse heaps) and architectural leavings illuminate the former. The remains are plentiful in all categories, at Cysla-Commune and Berry-au-Bac in the Paris Basin, Il Corrège in Languedoc, La Grotte des Fées in the Haute-Rhône, Villeneuve-Tolosane and Saint-Michel-du-Touch in the Garonne Valley, Saint-Rémy-la-Varenne in the Loire region, and Carnac in Brittany, among other sites. Menhirs (standing stones), cromlechs (circles of menhirs), and dolmens (flat stones atop menhirs), formed into burial and ceremonial megalithic structures, indicate communities capable technically and socially of considerable achievement. Moreover, between 4600 and 1000 BC Neolithic and early metal cultures in the four major river systems evolved social hierarchies, simple political structures probably organized around the figure of a petty chieftain, colonization practices and far-reaching trade networks which may have connected the Atlantic and Mediterranean well before the appearance of Celtic peoples during the 1st millennium. Thus appeared the first features of a social and political landscape in France more than 60 centuries ago.

Only a handful of remnants survive from this epoch to identify actual peoples: the Ligurians gave their name to the Genoese Riviera, Liguria, and are recalled also in a few Provençal place names. The Iberians left only the name of the south-western tip of the European peninsula. The theory that the Basques, with their peculiar and untraceable language and distinctive physical appearance, are present-day remainders of the Iberians, remains only a theory.

Celtic Gaul

The Romans so named the region of modern France which was populated after 1000 BC by a metal-age people from northern and central Europe, known generically as Celts. Their identity is not precise, since 'Celtic' connotes variously race, language and tribe, and the Greeks and Romans used Celts interchangeably with Gauls to denote the people of the region. Julius Caesar, who described Gaul as being in three parts, recognized only one of the three as truly Celtic. Even so, in Roman eyes the Gauls were Celts; and whether they were called Belgae, Cimbri, Alemanni, Boii, Marcommani, Arverni, or some other name, they were much the same. Only the Aquitanians (Iberians) were descriptively different, and the Belgae were *said* to be different, but probably were not. Perhaps the Romans' practical turn of mind led to lumping the peoples of Gaul together into this Celtic category for convenience.

More is known about the Celts, or Gauls, than any other western European people from this epoch. If Neolithic dwellers left megaliths and pots, Celts left weapons, armour, tools, ornaments, traces of language and other evidence of a lively, wide-ranging cultural, political and economic life. Gold and other precious metals were widely used, though for decoration as much as for money. Caesar, Germanicus, and other Roman travellers identified them as tall, blond or red-haired Nordic types, organized into a complex social-political system. More recently, archaeologist Daphne Nash described this system as warrior-agrarian, in which peasant labour was the most important source of social wealth and was appropriated by the nobility through contractual and military relationships; in short, a structure similar to later feudalism.

The Greek geographer, Strabo, from his vantage point at Massilia, the Greek colony which would become Marseille, depicted a trading network encompassing the four river systems, the English Channel, and western and southern England. It began with the Celts and was co-opted by early Greek and Roman traders. The first-century cross-channel wine trade was a thriving concern, indicating that 'our claret, chianti or vino tinto, is very much old wine in new bottles'.

CELTIC DOMINATION

The Celts moved into Gaul as part of a general European migration spread over a thousand and more years, the result of population pressures, warfare and territorial acquisitiveness. They also crossed the English Channel to Britain as early as the tenth century. Over the next half-millennium Celts imposed their domination throughout Gaul, and became a great nuisance to Republican Rome, which they sacked and burnt in 390 BC despite, as historian Albert Guérard put it, 'the watchful and patriotic geese of the Capital', whose excited honking at the Celts' stealthy approach went unnoticed. For four centuries the Celts mastered Gaul, challenged Roman hegemony in northern Italy, and built up a culture, though hardly a civilization, which spread from Cornwall to the Alps.

CELTIC RELIGION

They practised a form of organized religion which held forests, streams and mountains to be the sacred places of naturalistic spirits. A priestly order, the Druids, famous equally in Gaul and Britain, was the fount of Celtic religious expression. The Druids practised human sacrifice and worshipped mistletoe as the sacred symbol of life and a panacea. The Druids also fulfilled a judicial function in the sense of providing arbitration in disputes between nobles.

None of the features of Celtic Gaul prepared its ruling peoples to compete with the Romans, however. The Celts never were a united force, only a marauding one. They fought among themselves as frequently as against others. Celtic Gaul was never more than a geographical expression and bequeathed little of substance to the French – neither language, faith, institutions, nor customs – save for a long-standing trade in wine moving westward and eastward out of Bordeaux.

Roman Gaul

The Romans first entered Gaul in the second century BC for defensive reasons, and stayed for trade and conquest. The first Roman soldiers in Gaul were mercenaries defending Nice and Antibes in 153 BC for Marseille, Rome's Greek ally. These soldiers and their descendants remained for six hundred years. Marseille lay just east of the Rhône estuary and the Romans simply followed others in using the river systems as conduits. By 121 BC Roman control extended up the Rhône Valley to Vienne, and up the Garonne Valley to Toulouse. Military and trading posts soon turned into cities in the Roman style such as Aix, Arles and Nîmes, and Roman engineering was applied to communications (a road system which spread from Aix to Boulogne eventually) and the water supply (Pont-du-Gard, a three-tiered aqueduct near Nîmes).

Actually, while the Roman presence began in response to Celtic or Ligurian marauders around Nice and Antibes, it was motivated in a

The Roman amphitheatre at Nîmes

larger context by the general movement of peoples out of Germany into southern Gaul and northern Italy. In the early first century, the Roman general, Marius, annihilated the Teutons in Provence and the Po Valley. This saved Rome, but it remained for Julius Caesar, beginning in 59 BC, to check this barbarian pressure and roll these Germanic peoples back to the Rhine.

JULIUS CAESAR

Caesar came to Gaul by invitation of the Celts as an ally against the Germans. But in his words, he came, saw and conquered Gaul. Caesar acted as ally, liberator and arbitrator between warring tribes and factions, and then as exploiter when he used his arbitrator's role to expand Roman power. In the process he did not flinch from the massacre, mutilation, and enslaving of the Celts. Such behaviour created a backlash, and in 52 BC Vercingetorix, an Arvernian chief, led a 'popular' uprising against Caesar. A bitter struggle followed with great battles at Bourges, Clermont, and Mont Auxois on the Côte d'Or. His back to the wall, Vercingetorix finally surrendered. The young chief was imprisoned, dragged behind Caesar's chariot in a triumphal procession in Rome, and then executed. Thereafter the Romanization of Gaul proceeded swiftly and surely.

THE ROMANIZATION OF GAUL

The people of Gaul actually welcomed Roman civilization, and in the end embraced it. With Rome came sound government, high technology, profitable trade, and in time, Roman citizenship. More cities developed on the Roman model, beyond the early examples at Arles and Aix: Narbonne, Lyon, Paris, Trèves, Toulouse, Bordeaux and many others. Latin replaced Celtic everywhere: classical Latin among educated and aristocratic Celts, and the slang Latin of soldiers, traders and slaves, blended with Celtic, among the rest. It was not French, but it was moving in that direction. Education flourished in the great schools of Autun, Reims, Toulouse and Bordeaux. Professors were well paid and men such as Eumenius of Autun and Ausonius of Bordeaux were among the great personages of the epoch. Rome gave the Celts internal peace and security, a frontier corresponding roughly to modern France, and a model administrative centre in the capital, Lyon. It is no surprise that the Celts took to Romanization, and held on to it for five centuries.

THE DECLINE OF ROME

But it couldn't last forever. Rome itself was falling apart in the fourth century AD and barbaric pressure increased. The Roman military machine was still up to confronting it (Stilicho's victories at Pollenzo and Verona in 402–3, and Aetius' at Châlons in 451, for example), but the political will was fading. Jaded and jealous emperors had a proclivity for murdering their best generals – such was the fate of Stilicho and Aetius. Chaos then was not far off. First Gaul, then Italy itself, was threatened, invaded and overrun by barbarians. In 410 Alaric the Goth sacked Rome; it was Genseric the Vandal's turn in 455; and Attila the Hun came close. Driving all before him, the 'Scourge of God' invaded Gaul in 451, but was checked in a great battle on the Champs Catalauniques, near Châlons, the last great Roman victory in Gaul. The next year Attila entered Italy, but died before reaching Rome.

Barbarian Gaul

Once more Gaul was a region of warring factions, division and barbarian settlements: Visigoths in Aquitaine, Burgundians in the valley of the Saône-Rhône, Alemans in Alsace, a self-styled Roman king tenuously ruling north of the Loire, and Franks between the Rhine and the Somme. One of their chiefs, Merovech of the Salian (Salt Sea) Franks, had fought with Aetius against the Huns at Châlons. Of the great Roman past, Christianity, a vulgarized Latin – yearly more vulgarized by the infusion of barbarian dialects – a network of cities and roads, and many southern aristocrats styling themselves *patricii*, remained. No doubt the stability of the Roman influence was missed, but as the pope advised, 'go with the power'. And they did, while in Arles, Avignon and other Roman cities, Roman literary and philosophical tradition lived on.

Christian Gaul

It would be wrong to depict the fifth-century barbarians as quite the rough and ready marauders of earlier times – except for the Huns, of course. For one thing, many of them were Christian. Christianity came early in the Roman era, brought by Greek and Jewish converts. It was the third step in Gaul's known religious history after Druidism and a Greco-Roman pantheon into which many Celtic deities were assimilated. Christianity would be the last step, for it was monotheistic, radical, and uncompromisingly bigoted against paganism. Early Christians were hardy and welcomed martyrdom. In Gaul, the early martyrs added impetus to a faith grounded in humility, salvation and an apocalyptic world view. Persecution of the Lyon church in 177 by Marcus Aurelius provided some famous martyrs, while the beheading of the aged Bishop Denis of Paris on Montmartre (Martyr's Hill) in 262 provided both a martyr and a miraculous legend. Denis supposedly picked up his severed head, washed it, and walked 6000 paces to the north before expiring. Later, the Abbey Church of Saint-Denis was built on the site, and its patron, Dagobert I, was the first of many kings to be buried there.

THE RISE OF THE CHURCH

In 312 Constantine the Great embraced Christianity and made it the Roman state religion. Thereafter the Christian Church was virtually unassailable within the empire. Indeed, Christians insisted upon an end to paganism. Martin, bishop of Tours, waged a holy war against paganism in the late fourth century. He founded monasteries and destroyed pagan monuments. Most of urban Gaul and certainly the aristocracy were Christianized by the end of his life. It took much longer for Christianity to settle in fully with the peasants, who kept alive pagan traditions for centuries. Mistletoe, for example, has had a very long religious history, and shows no sign of fading in our own time. Meanwhile, the Church, in alliance with the state and the landed aristocracy, took over, flourished, and by the end of the fifth century played a great role in governmental as well as spiritual life for all of the people of Gaul. Church property was largely untaxed, each Gallo-

Roman city was a bishopric (64 in all), and there were 17 seats for archbishops or metropolitans. Many offences were adjudicated by Church leaders, rather than by civil authorities. Often, too, they organized local defence against barbarian invaders, like Bishop Lupus at Trèves and Bishop Aignan at Orléans.

The critical moment for Christian Gaul occurred when the Church adopted Clovis the Frank as the 'sword of the true faith', at the end of the fifth century. This action gave the Church a formidable secular support in place of a Roman empire now gone from Gaul, save for Aquitainian or Burgundian kings who fancied themselves Roman in outlook. It also gave the Franks sanction above rival barbarians. 'Clovis fought, the bishops conquered,' was the way it worked, and out of this union of Frankish power and Roman Church eventually evolved the foundation of France itself.

Paris

At the centre of the Seine Valley, long before Caesar, a tribe of river people lived on and around several islands in the Seine, the largest of which was just 1000 by 300 metres. It eventually became the Ile de la Cité, the heart of Paris. Of this city Michel de Montaigne wrote in the sixteenth century: 'I am French only through this great city, great above all things and incomparable in its variety, the glory of France and one of the most noble ornaments of the world.'

Paris wasn't quite Montaigne's vision in 53 BC when Julius Caesar established the Assembly of Gaul at Lutetia Parisiorum, the village closest to territories then in rebellion. A few days later he left, and the Parisii (boat people), the local Celtic tribe, joined in the uprising led by Vercingetorix. The Romans returned and the Parisii were subdued, fittingly, in a battle waged on the present site of the Champs-de-Mars and the École Militaire. The Romans established a permanent garrison on the Ile de la Cité and the life of Paris – called Lutetia until the fourth century – began.

THE ROMAN TOWN

River trade passed through Paris in increasing volume under Roman jurisdiction. The village prospered and a votive column to Jupiter was raised in thanksgiving exactly where Notre-Dame Cathedral now stands. Roman soldiers garrisoned on the Ile took the boat of the river people as their central symbol, and Paris was on the way to becoming integral to the life of Gaul under Rome. Soon the island in the river was too small for the community developing on it, and Paris expanded onto the Left Bank. Meanwhile Gaul was pacified and Romanized, and the village became a town and a crossroads to France. Now roads pushed outward in all directions – to Melun, Meaux, Soissons, Pontoise, Rouen, Dreux and Chartres, and Paris became a hub at the centre of a communication system. The main road remained Caesar's road to Orléans, which was so heavily travelled that a relief road was built to parallel it. This road, the *via inferior*, or *via infer*, survives in the name Avenue Renfert-Rocher.

Within the expanding town a bath appeared where the Musée de Cluny now stands, an amphitheatre on the site of Arènes de Lutèce, and a theatre near Place de l'Odéon. That this was a Gallo-Roman town is remembered in the name of the Latin Quarter on the Left Bank.

Roman Paris was only two centuries old when Christianity arrived in the person of Denis, bishop of Paris, who challenged the interdict against Christianity imposed by the official Roman religion. His tomb became a holy place, and contributed enormously to the later importance of Paris. When Dagobert chose the Abbey of Saint-Denis as his burial place, the abbey became 'the royal necropolis'.

If the Emperor Constantine made Christianity prosper by making it the state religion, he could not improve the Parisian economy. By the early fourth century the barbarians were again on the move, and Paris suffered a decline along with every other northern Gallo-Roman city. Paris might have gone into eclipse had not Julian the Apostate arrived in 351 to drive out the encroaching barbarians. This restorer of pagan religion came as a military commander and administrator to secure the frontier, but left, in 360, at the insistence of the legionaries, to take the imperial throne by force if necessary. During this time, Paris was the seat of government. Never again would it be an inconsequential village on the River Seine.

Neither Julian nor his successors in Rome or Constantinople could keep the barbarians from the door, and one after another various

Teutonic tribes passed through the Paris Basin. They fought each other as well as the empire, confusion reigned, and Paris faced continual threat. Aetius made it the seat of his administration as a strategic centre from which to campaign against the Alemans, Burgundians, and Huns. The Huns, indeed, were the greatest threat.

GENEVIÈVE

The Huns inspired the second great Paris miracle after Saint Denis. Attila was on the march into Gaul in 451. The Roman government withdrew first to Orléans, then Tours, and finally to Bordeaux, where they made cause with the Visigoths of Aquitania against this common enemy. The Parisians prepared to flee – until a girl of 15, a zealous *religieuse* burning with Christian fervour, promised them that if they would pray to God and remain in the city, Attila would not come. The girl was Geneviève. As it happened Attila did not appear. The people rejoiced, and in its good time the Church canonized her. Geneviève became the patron saint of Paris. She was still alive 40 years later when Clovis, grandson of Merovech, king of the Salian Franks who fought with Aetius against Attila, 'cast an acquisitive eye on Paris from his temporary capital at Reims'. This time she did not keep the invader at bay, and a new era opened for Paris and for Gaul.

CHAPTER TWO

From Clovis to Hugh Capet
500–1000 AD

It is only after Frankish domination began in Gaul that the foundations of France were truly laid. These foundations had as much to do with diversity as with unity. Frankish Gaul was a collection of ethnic, political and philosophical communities, linked in many ways but self-consciously distinct from one another. This period, when the Franks' Gallic lands, called Francia, were held together only by a loose central authority which reigned rather than ruled, has been termed the Dark Ages. It is not altogether an accurate description. There was a life of the mind in France even before Rabelais.

Gallic Community

Community evolved on many levels in the five centuries of Frankish rule: Goths, Basques, and Gascons in Aquitania from the Loire to the Pyrénées; Burgundians, Alemans, Alans and Romans in Burgundy and Provence; and Bretons and then Normans (Scandinavians) in the north and west. All retained a measure of tribal identity, and sometimes political power, distinct from the Franks and often in opposition to them and to each other. The cultural outlook of south and east retained a Roman character up to the sixth century, and in Provence well into the tenth. Roman landowners continued to dominate Aquitania and Provence as aristocracy and church leaders, and referred to themselves as *patricii* (patricians). Law codes reflected Roman and local custom, as in Aquitania north of the Garonne where the Franks recognized the Code of Euric, a fifth-century Romanized Goth and king of Aquitania. Only the Salic Law in the north, a compilation of Frankish codes, or

15

Cologne

AIX-LA-CHAPELLE
(Aachen)

Rouen · Soissons
PARIS · Châlons

· Auxerre
Dijon·
Tours   Autun ·
· Poitiers

· Saintes

LYON
Vienne   Milan

Bordeaux

Nîmes
Arles Aix-en-Provence
Narbonne   Marseille

ROME

· Important towns & cities

Archbishoprics

–·–·– Boundary of Roman Gaul (approx.)

Greatest extent of Frankish
Empire under Charlemagne

**Roman Gaul and Early
Medieval France**

| 0 | 50 | 100 | 200 miles |
| 0 | 50 | 100 | 200 kms |

rather several compilations, was distinctly and solely Germanic as opposed to Gallo-Roman.

THE STRENGTH OF ROMAN INFLUENCE

Towns retained their Roman character in varying degrees and the countryside, never as Romanized as the towns, reverted quickly to tribal conventions. In the towns, where the basic elements of civilization were carried forward, Rome remained the standard, especially in the south and east. Toulouse, Narbonne, Arles, Aix, Marseille, Lyon and Clermont retained their Roman character for at least another two hundred years. Provençal cities actually *were* Roman for the same period. In Provence the Roman Empire held out the longest against barbarian incursions. Even today Arles, for example, holds bull fights, an entertainment introduced by the Romans, in a second-century Roman amphitheatre.

Throughout Gaul towns were often governed by a bishop or archbishop, frequently elected by the populace rather than appointed by the papacy or the local lord as would become the case in later centuries. These churchmen functioned in a similar manner to that established by the Romans for their provincial administrators. Indeed, bishops and archbishops often were Rome's administrators in the latter days of the empire. Towns built walls when barbarians came, behind which urban dwellers and nearby residents sheltered in wartime. The walls remained to offer similar protection from quarrelling local dignitaries in the Frankish period and after. Walled towns also made for a very effective separation of town officials from territorial aristocracy later on. In time, as effective Roman power broke down and local dialects overtook Latin, towns dropped their Latin names and took over old tribal designations: Lutetia became Paris, after the Parisii, and Augusta Trèves, after the Trevarii.

RELIGIOUS SCHISMS

The apparent religious unity of Gaul, where Aquitanians, Burgundians and even Franks were or were becoming Christianized, was frail. The papal writ ran much deeper in theory than in practice, and the Church itself was split for a significant period at the beginning of Frankish rule, between the Arian heresy which argued that in the Trinity the Son is not equal with the Father, and the Trinitarian orthodoxy which said that they were equal. Burgundian and Aquitanian Christians often were Arians. Clovis, king of the invading Franks, embraced Trinitarianism and thus gained Church backing for his enterprises in conquering Gaul. Also, Jews were quartered in every important town and Islam thrust into Aquitania after the seventh century. Among the common country people pre-Christian and pagan traditions continued to exist side by side with Christian orthodoxy, or in place of it. Bishops despaired. Peasants were 'lustful, drunken, and irreligious', and only in the eighth century was anything done systematically to ensure baptism and some knowledge of Christianity among them. It is certainly the case that the French *paysan* (peasant) derives from the Latin *paganus* (countryman), which is the root of the Christian word 'pagan' (worshipper of false gods).

LANGUAGE DIFFERENCES

Language likewise resisted unity for centuries. By the eighth century, out of a combination of vulgarized Latin, German, and, even earlier, local dialects, there had evolved two distinct variations of what would become French. Romance, or *Langue d'Oïl* (*yes* = *oïl* or *oui*) was the language of the north. In the south, from Provence to the Atlantic coast and north to the Loire, *Langue d'Oc* (yes = *oc*) prevailed, save in Gascony and the Basque regions of the Pyrénées, where a variant of *Langue d'Oc* existed along with the Basque *Euskara*. The latter is not an Indo-European tongue at all. Meanwhile, settlers from southern England established Celtic as the language of Brittany, and a Scandinavian vernacular for a short time competed with *Langue d'Oïl* in Normandy, though the Vikings adapted to the local tongue within a generation. Latin remained the language of the educated, of church and school and of law and administration. In the end, for political and economic reasons, *Langue d'Oïl* prevailed. But many centuries passed first and *Langue d'Oc* remained the language of civility for this Frankish epoch and beyond. As Gallus, a Belgae, put it: 'When I remember that I am a Gaul and am going to hold forth in front of Aquitanians, I am afraid that my rather rustic speech may offend your over-civilized ears.' Of course, he may have spoken tongue-in-cheek.

Clovis

Despite diversity, power in Gaul centred in the north and east for the second time after the Franks came in the late fifth century. However much power might be dispersed at various times thereafter, it settled in the Seine Valley from which the Franks first imposed their rule in Gaul, and from which France eventually evolved.

The warlike Frankish king, Clovis (482–511), started in 486 by defeating the Gallo-Roman King Syagrius at Soissons. In 493 he made a far more important conquest by marrying the Burgundian Clotilda, the only Catholic princess in Gaul. On that occasion he 'bowed his proud head' and accepted baptism in the Roman Church. Thereafter he and his Frankish successors became the strong right arm of the Church. Frankish king and Roman Church made a powerful combination. After his baptism, Clovis could do no wrong. According to Bishop Gregory of Tours, miracles followed him everywhere. A dove from heaven brought the vial of holy chrism with which he was anointed; a white doe showed him a ford for his army across the River Vienne; and a mysterious white light illuminated Poitiers Cathedral and guided his army towards their victory over Alaric II of Aquitania. This was all Church propaganda, of course, meant to strengthen the link with Frankish power, and to make that power appear sacred so that linkage with the mundane would not blot the ecclesiastical escutcheon.

Clovis was appointed a Roman consul by Anastasius, the emperor in Constantinople, presided over a council in Orléans which confirmed the clergy in their privilege, and for all of this was made 'invincible by God'. At least Gregory thought so. 'Thus day by day God brought low his enemies before him, so that they submitted to him and increased his kingdom, because he walked before Him with an upright heart, and did that which was pleasing in His sight.' This too was propaganda. Clovis warred against his neighbours and murdered his relatives, lest they become rivals for the throne. He then complained that he had no one to turn to in case of need. If any kinsmen did remain, none stepped forward to claim this dangerous honour. Piously, Clovis built a church for each murdered relation. Historians recognize his significance, but find Clovis 'a detestable character' all the same.

THE MEROVINGIAN DYNASTY

Clovis was the first Merovingian. Over the next century the dynasty brought most of Gaul under its sway. This was not a unitary kingdom however, but rather a family enterprise containing four 'natural and more permanent divisions': Austrasia in the east (Metz), Neustria in the north-west (Paris), Burgundy to the south-east (Lyon), and the semi-independent duchy of Aquitania north of the Garonne (Poitiers). The monarchs of these regions, like the later Roman emperors, neither ruled nor governed so much as they reigned – they led armies, presided over ceremonial, rewarded their followers, and left government to servants such as the mayors of the palace. Of these more will be said presently. Clovis and his successors left behind a dreary trail of murders and atrocities to rival the worst excesses of the legendary court at Byzantium.

THE NOBILITY

An aristocracy at once powerful and undisciplined contributed greatly to Merovingian blood-letting. Gregory of Tours' description of Guntram Boso of Austrasia during the reign of Chilperic depicts a typical member of this aristocracy: 'an unprincipled man, eager in his avarice, covetous beyond measure of the property of others, giving his word to all, keeping his promise to none'.

Brunhild

The treatment of Brunhild, widow of King Sigebert of Austrasia, by the Austrasian royal dukes is a better instance. Brunhild was accomplished by any standard. Brought up in the Roman manner, she spoke classical Latin and had an uncommon grasp of general ideas and political concepts. Her qualities of decision, command and perseverance were equally superior. Brunhild was friendly to the Church and attempted to curb aristocratic lawlessness and restore the declining dignity of the kingly office. That was her undoing. None of Brunhild's accomplishments or aspirations impressed these aristocrats, and she had to fight them at every turn, usually with their own weapons. Her husband, King Sigebert, and sister were murdered by the Neustrian branch of the Merovingians, so she instigated the murder of the Neustrian ruler, Chilperic. She then purged many of the Austrasian aristocrats from involvement in royal affairs, and tried to play kingmaker. At that the magnates rebelled, led by Clothar II, son of King Sigebert's murderer, and took Brunhild prisoner. She was tortured, led through the ranks of the soldiers on a camel, and tied by her hair, one arm and one leg to the tail of an unbroken horse, which cut her to pieces with its hooves as it ran.

At the time of her death Brunhild was a white-haired grandmother and beloved by her less exalted subjects, who took a dim view of these proceedings. It was in Brunhild's era, wrote Gregory, that the common people grew apart from the aristocracy and chafed at their arrogance and venality, on occasion even attacking unpopular nobles.

Dagobert I

This Merovingian was perhaps the last effective ruler of the line. Through the instrument of the Edict of Paris in 613 – 'a mixture of pious wishes for law and order' – and the taxation policies of his predecessors which were single-mindedly implemented by Eligius, bishop of Noyon, Dagobert (628–637) attempted to restore the Frankish kingdom after the civil strife which had dominated Brunhild's career.

Eligius was only one of many bishops employed by Dagobert in civil administration, from Rouen to Metz and Paris to Bordeaux. As the Edict gave him the right to appoint bishops, it may be that the use of such 'loyalists' as royal agents was Dagobert's way of holding the kingdom together in the face of self-aggrandizing aristocrats. Eligius was the most important bishop under this king. He attracted a general attitude of loathing among the populace for his taxation policies, and upon the death of Dagobert retired hastily to Noyon with a Paris mob speeding him on his way.

Dagobert's restoration project succeeded only briefly. When he died in 637 the kingdom again split between royal sons, and the Merovingian dynasty began its descent into the succession of *rois fainéants*, or 'do-nothing' kings, in the eighth century. These Merovingians were remote from their subjects, and given over to debauchery, gluttony and internecine plotting. Merovingian princes in these years often ended up in monasteries, and not always by choice. By the end of the eighth century effective government throughout Frankish Gaul was in the hands of the mayors of the palace.

MAYORS OF THE PALACE

For several generations the Merovingians employed managers of the royal estates called mayors of the palace: *major domus*. These were royal officials and presumably aristocrats as well. Their power waxed in lieu of effective kings, and with a victory in battle over Berchar the Neustrian mayor at Tertry in 687, one Pepin of Heristal established both the supremacy of Austrasia in the Frankish lands and of his own house in Austrasia. Anarchy reigned for a generation afterward, until his bastard son, Charles Martel (the Hammer), routed all serious opposition to this wealthy Moselle Valley family, and a new power was established. With Charles Martel began the Carolingian line which was to include his grandson Charlemagne, the greatest of all Frankish kings.

Charles Martel

Austrasia and Neustria were torn by internal clashes. Meanwhile, Aquitania, Burgundy, Gascony, Provence and Moslem Septimania (the coast between the Rhône and the Pyrénées) fiercely resisted submitting to Frankish rule. This gave Charles his opportunity. The Hammer smashed the Arabs near Tours in 732 and the Burgundians in a campaign in 734, after which he rewarded his followers with confiscated lands. A significant gesture: such awards were technically reserved for kings to make. He campaigned in Aquitania in 735, in Burgundy again in 736, in Provence and Septimania in 737, and against the Saxons in 738. Charles soon won a great reputation and became the centre of power in the Frankish lands. He never proclaimed himself king, but he was virtually king and in documents of the time was often designated *rex*. Further, when King Thierry IV died in 737, 'Charles did not even bother to look around the monasteries for another one'. The Hammer's son, Pepin known as the Short, had no qualms about being king and in 751 had himself crowned Pepin I.

Martel and his grandson Charlemagne were heroes in their own time, but were castigated by later descriptions. Einhard's biography of Charlemagne is virtually hagiography, but Church writers in the ninth century treated both him and Charles Martel as sinners doomed beyond redemption. In the 850s Hincmar of Reims wrote down the 'vision of Eucherius', wherein this eighth-century bishop of Orléans, once exiled by Charles Martel, had been led into Hell by an angel. There he saw Martel burning. Eucherius told his story to Boniface of Mainz and Fulrad of Saint-Denis, who ordered Martel's tomb opened. A snake slithered out and the walls were blackened as if by fire. (The fact that Eucherius had actually died *before* Charles Martel was not mentioned.) Similarly, a story circulated at the same time that Charlemagne was a denizen of Hell, where for all eternity he had to suffer his genitals being torn at by a wild animal in punishment for his debauchery on earth. What inspired these revisions? Simply that they *were* sinners, guilty of the greatest sin that the Church could conceive: they confiscated Church lands and distributed them among their secular followers.

Pepin I

The debunking of the great Carolingians occurred in the ninth century, at a time when tension between Church and crown was rising over the issue of pre-eminence. The seeds of the issue were planted in Gaul in the reign of Pepin I (751--768), Martel's son and premier Carolingian king.

The Church always resented royal interference in clerical affairs, but needed secular power for its security in tempestuous times. Both Pepin I and Charlemagne made good relations with the papacy central to their policy. In 751 Childeric III, the last Merovingian, was deposed by Pepin and sent, naturally, to a monastery. At Soissons, 'by election of all the Franks, the consecration of the bishops and the submission of the great', Pepin became king. (Not too much should be made of the similarity of language between this declaration and preambulary sections of the Magna Carta in England four-and-a-half centuries later, attractive though the parallel might appear.) Pope Zacarius sanctioned this usurpation by observing that 'it is better to call king the man who has the power rather than the man who is deprived of it'.

This papal declaration, which got Pepin over some sticky moments with subjects who regarded him as overly self-aggrandizing, warmed Pepin's heart. In 754 he offered the new pope, Stephen II, on the run from Byzantines and Lombards, sanctuary in the Abbey of Saint-Denis. There on 28 July in the same year, either in gratitude or as a ploy to bind the Frankish king to the papal cause, Stephen anointed and crowned Pepin in the basilica. The act had monumental significance. Never before had a Frankish ruler been anointed or crowned in this sacerdotal manner. Thereafter kingship in Gaul was sacred; it was bestowed as a divine right. To oppose the king was to commit sacrilege, a principle of great value to any monarch. In the end it even helped overcome the greatest burden faced by kings of France, the resistance of great magnates to the centralization of authority.

Pepin was happy to become the 'sword of God', the strong right arm of the Church. So was Charlemagne. Henceforth the clergy were treated in Gaul as a privileged class – which did not, however, prevent Charlemagne from expropriating ecclesiastical property, an action which was taken in part to forward ecclesiastical reforms and break the power of truculent aristocrats. The clergy saw it otherwise. Actually, had the anointed king been both temporal and spiritual head of the Church in one, there would have been no problem. However there were both king and pope. This meant that power had to be tested, and more than one king was excommunicated and pope imprisoned in the centuries ahead. But for the time being the arrangement between pope and king was a happy one, and the events of 28 July gave Pepin I the blessings of the Church for his wars against the Aquitanians and Burgundians, who still resisted Frankish rule. In 768 Pepin died with these territorial questions unresolved. But the linkage with Rome was firmly established, and with it the principle of sacerdotal monarchy.

Charlemagne

As was Frankish custom, Pepin's kingdom was divided upon his death between his two sons, Carloman and Charles. Carloman died three years later and Charles, soon to be known as Charlemagne, a man of strength, resolve and boundless ambition, seized the whole of the kingdom for himself. Charlemagne (768–814) was proof that the power of medieval kings lay in their character and personality. Institutional rule was for the future. This, the greatest of Carolingian rulers, was physically powerful and energetic, a great warrior, dominating, colourful, accessible and jovial. He maintained his capital at Aachen (Aix-la-Chapelle), an old Roman spa where the whole court and often the palace guards as well would frolic together in the baths.

Charlemagne was also cruel and unyielding. He Christianized Saxony at the point of a sword, beheaded four-and-a-half thousand men at Verdun, and dispersed a third of the Saxon population to Franconia and

The Palatine chapel at Aachen, consecrated in 805

Alemannia. And he was judicious. Charlemagne rewarded loyal supporters. He treated the Aquitanians and Burgundians with respect – he dressed his young son in Aquitanian garb before naming him king of Aquitania – and there were few rebellions against him from these quarters. He brought the sons of the aristocracy to court for their education, ruled according to law (more or less), patronised scholars and made Aachen the cultural centre of Europe. Scholars such as Alcuin of York and Einhard went to Aachen. A great cathedral and a school were built there. In a time that is often termed the Carolingian Renaissance, Aachen surpassed every city in Europe including Rome.

As a ruler, Charlemagne appeared to think that a mix of personal magnetism, generosity and tyranny, overlaid by an appeal to vanity, was the way to get results. Within limits he was right. By his death in 814, after a rule of 47 years, the Carolingian Empire incorporated central and western Europe, save for Spain, Britain and part of Italy. That it was an 'Empire' referred again to the Carolingian alliance with the papacy. On Christmas Day, 800, Pope Leo III crowned and anointed Charlemagne in Rome as 'most pious, Augustus, crowned of God, great and pacific Emperor of the Romans'. The act became significant only later, and more for Germany than for France.

One achievement escaped Charlemagne, and it makes an interesting commentary on the Franks as a people. They entered Gaul four hundred years earlier, took over and ruled a country both Romanized and relatively sophisticated, wherein lay many centres of literacy if not of learning, embraced many customs and some of the language of the Roman Empire – but remained, in the eyes of Aquitanians and many others, barbarians. Perhaps Charlemagne gives a clue to this. Great emperor, *patricius* and Protector of the Roman Republic, patron of scholars and instigator of great buildings, ecclesiastical and otherwise, Charlemagne never learned to read or write. According to Einhard he tried, 'taking the opportunity of moments of leisure to practise tracing letters; but he had begun too late and the result was poor'.

SYSTEM OF GOVERNMENT

Being illiterate did not prevent Charlemagne from creating a kingdom with a structure more advanced than that of his predecessors, although similar to it. The kingdom lasted only his lifetime, for there was little of the modern state about it. Charlemagne's rule was strictly personal. The fundamental unit was the county, governed in the king's name by a count and appointed by him. Most counts were drawn from the local aristocracy, whether Frank or other. Charlemagne oversaw their work personally, and frequently called them away to consult, serve in war, or simply to interrupt any rebellious thoughts they might be entertaining. He instituted the office of viscount to deputize when the count was away, and made certain that these officers had ample reason not to take the count's side against kingly authority. Counties on the extreme edges of the kingdom were grouped into 'marches' and overseen by a military prefect, later called a 'marquess', in German 'margraf', and in French 'marquis'. Austria and Brandenburg Prussia began as Carolingian marches. Charlemagne also employed special emissaries, the *missi dominici*, invested with considerable powers to root out corruption, injustice or disobedience among his subjects throughout the empire.

One part of kingly rule was to keep subjects from rebelling. Under Charlemagne the *missi* as well as his own watchful eye were deployed for this purpose. So too was the process of securing loyalty by establishing personal bonds between king and subject through the oath of fealty and the institution of vassalage. This process began well before Charlemagne, but certainly he expanded on it. From the process derived the horribly complicated and unwieldy, but ultimately inescapable, concept of feudalism.

FEUDALISM

'Better not even to use the term', wrote historian Edward James, who preferred simply to describe what happened between ruler and subject on the matter of the personal king-subject relationship. A vassal – a count, let us say – placed his hands between his lord's, swore an oath of loyalty (fealty, to be faithful), and 'commended' himself to the lord. Often the oath was sworn over holy relics, giving it the quality of sanctification so that violation put the swearer at risk of eternal damnation. It cut both ways, of course. Charlemagne laid down that if a lord mistreated his vassal – tried to kill him, reduce him to slavery or seduce his wife, for instance – the fealty owed to the lord was forfeit.

The language of the feudal relationship evolved over time until meaning changed. Vassal originally meant slave; by Charlemagne's day it meant only one subordinated by fealty to his lord. By the ninth century everyone from the top of society to the bottom was part of the system. Ordinary people were easier to control within the system than were aristocrats. To ensure aristocratic loyalty beyond the oath, it became customary to award fiefs, which term was a specific of the more general term benefice. The vagueness of this term is a major reason why feudalism is such a variable concept. One historian has found 41 different shades of meaning for benefice. In time, granting fiefs naturally worked to undermine the system by creating 'over-mighty subjects'.

HEREDITY

Meanwhile, as feudalism evolved, the element of heredity appeared and became part of it. Charlemagne allowed his counts to pass their counties to their heirs, since revenue from these lands supported the counts. Soon all titles were regarded as hereditary. Whatever specific meaning they once or still had – duke, a great leader, marquis, guardian of a march, count, administrator of a district, or viscount, deputy for a count – they began to take on a quality of territoriality that went well beyond simply administrative or military responsibilities. This advance was a privilege not taken lightly or surrendered easily. In one famous instance in 877 when Louis the Stammerer thought to revoke many benefices, as he had the legal right to do, and redistribute them among personal followers, the whole aristocracy rose in rebellion against him and the plan was abandoned.

This point should not be misunderstood. The *power* of these rising 'territorial' aristocrats still derived from their role as agents of the crown. The identification of power with landedness would come later. The same was true of obligation and landedness: it was only in the north of France and in Belgium at the time that the bulk of the peasantry were tied to the land through legal obligation, the condition which evolved into serfdom. In much of the rest of the countryside there were many free peasants, particularly in Languedoc, living on their own allodial land; even when they merely were tenants of a lord, they discharged their obligations through payment of rent rather than through service.

Charlemagne's Heirs

Briefly upon Charlemagne's death, the centre held. Charlemagne, just before dying, crowned his son Louis. Louis, who tortured his nephew to death and then felt remorse and did public penance, was called 'the Pious'; he declared that the empire would continue undivided. His sons objected, fearing the loss of their inheritance, and the aristocracy protested, fearing the loss of privilege. Over the next half-century compromises were made and, in the best Frankish tradition, the empire was divided after all. In 817, 843 and 855 the Frankish lands were parcelled out. The kingdom of West Francia emerged as part of the subdivision. These divisions constituted the regional framework within which the aristocrats would build their own small empires. The Carolingians survived until the end of the tenth century, each generation becoming less able to hold on to the once proud family tradition. West Francia was France; however its Carolingian kings held it in name only. Francia resembled by AD 1000 a patchwork quilt in which the royal domains (the territorial lands personally possessed by the king) were smaller than those of the dukes of Normandy, Burgundy, Aquitaine and Gascony, smaller even than those of the counts of Brittany, Flanders, Provence and Toulouse. There were no mayors of the palace in these late days, but there were powerful aristocrats, landed now and able to oppose their king. One such was Robert, count of Anjou and lay-abbot of Marmoutier near Tours, known as the Strong.

Robert the Strong

In 856 Robert the Strong was deprived of some of his power when Charles II the Bald made his son Louis the Stammerer king of western Neustria (Brittany and Normandy). Robert rebelled. He was made marquis of the Breton marches in exchange for abandoning the rebellion, an indication perhaps that local power was fully in the ascendant against the centre. In 865 he was given power also in Burgundy, and Charles, frustrated by the Stammerer's incompetence as military leader against marauding Vikings, made him give up this role to Robert. Robert was killed in 866 in battle against the Vikings, but

left behind two young sons under the protection of Hugh the Abbot.
They grew up to be, each in turn, counts of Paris and kings of West
Francia. The Robertian line, as it was called, was established. It led
straight to Hugh Capet.

Odo of Paris

Paris, already important for economic reasons and as a crossroads, was
now to become the power base of the kings of France. Robert's eldest
son, Odo, was appointed count of Paris by the emperor, Charles III the
Fat. There Odo made his name with his defence of Paris against a
Viking attack in 886. The Vikings were unable to force a surrender,
thus greatly enhancing Odo's reputation both as warrior and organizer.
Then Charles, who was both emperor and king of West Francia, lost all
respect among the Parisians for his weak-kneed intervention when he
appeared with a vast army before Paris after long delays and, rather than
fall upon the Vikings, allowed them to negotiate a safe passage for
themselves up the Seine and into Burgundy. There they subjected the
region 'to the worst winter it had ever known'. After that Charles was a
broken reed. When he died in 888, the bishops, counts and other
magnates refused to have another German prince in West Francia, and
elected Odo king. It was a large kingdom, but royal power was strictly
limited by powerful local magnates perfectly capable, oaths of fealty
notwithstanding, of throwing in their lot with other 'kings': Rudolph
in Upper Burgundy, Louis and Guy in Provence and Burgundy
respectively, and Rannulf in Aquitania. Even so, the Robertians were
strong and from this moment dominated from their centre in Paris.

It was a confused domination however, and a limited one. The
country was afflicted by usurpations, rival claimants to the throne,
rebellious aristocrats, invading Vikings, weak kings and powerful
kingmakers. Odo was followed in 898 by a restored Carolingian,
Charles III the Simple (king of West Francia, but never emperor), who
was not so much confused, as this sobriquet might suggest, as
straightforward and honest. Better had he been duplicitous, as were
those around him. He was deposed in 922 by Robert I, the second son
of Robert the Strong, who was killed the following year by supporters

of the deposed Charles. However, Ralph of Burgundy took Charles prisoner and seized the throne for himself, leaving Charles to rot in prison where he died six years later. Ralph died in 936 and was followed by Louis IV, called the Foreigner because he returned from exile in England to be king. Louis too was a Carolingian, urged upon the magnates by Hugh the Great, a Robertian playing kingmaker. Then came Lothaire, and another Carolingian, Louis V, who had no sobriquet but might well have been named 'the Last'. He was killed in a hunting accident after a reign of only one year. Hugh Capet, son of Hugh the Great and grandson of Robert the Strong, followed him to the throne of West Francia. The Robertians were triumphant and with them Paris, future hub of France. It was, however, a hub of which Gaul yet was only casually aware, and concerned about not at all.

Hugh Capet

So-called because he favoured a short cape called a *cappa*, Hugh Capet (987–996) ascended a throne nominally over all of western and southern Gaul, but practically only over the north. He was nominated for the throne most eloquently by Archbishop Adalbero of Reims. His brother, Henry of Burgundy, and his brother-in-law, Richard of Normandy, were his chief supporters. The great southern princes such as William Ironarm, count of Poitou and duke of the Aquitanians, had no objection to him so long as he did not interfere in their affairs. Hugh was, so far as can be determined, the first king of 'France'. He actually controlled (as distinct from reigned over) a territory 200 kilometres long by less than 100 kilometres wide.

Hugh was a famous warrior, as were all of the Robertians, and a powerful Francian duke as well as count of Paris. His capital was Paris in so far as it was anywhere. There was a palace, where now stands the Palais de Justice on the Ile de la Cité. In reality the capital was wherever the king was, and Hugh moved regularly among Étampes, Poissy, Senlis and Orléans. He was crowned, probably, at Noyon, once the seat of Eligius, Dagobert's hated tax collector, by Archbishop Adalbero of Reims. Succeeding Capetians were crowned at Reims. Hugh's hold on France was tenuous owing to the fragmentation of actual power at the end of the tenth century. But he had several moral advantages. He was a sacerdotal figure, the legacy of Pope Stephen anointing Pepin; and, as king, he had most of the great magnates bound to him by oaths of fealty. While this was no guarantee against disloyalty, it at least provided the king with recourse of a legal and moral nature when subjects did rebel. Hugh Capet was shrewd. He understood his limitations, and reigned rather than ruled outside his personal domain, the Ile de France. He interfered in local affairs only when asked. France now was governed by castle-holding magnates who might be intimidated by a strong king, but could in turn intimidate a weak one. It still was much a matter of personality.

Normandy

In 793 Viking longships landed on Holy Island off the coast of Northumbria and sacked the famous Lindisfarne monastery. 'May God preserve us from the fury of the Northmen,' intoned many a monkish prayer thereafter. By contrast, the monastery of Mont-St-Michel, also on an island, on the coast of lower Normandy, was too well-fortified to be successfully attacked. Over the next century and more, the Vikings continued to assault Britain, and travelling up the Seine, Loire and Rhône, conduits for invaders and conquerors since Neolithic times, plagued Gaul almost beyond endurance.

They first appeared among the Franks in the 840s, striking swiftly, brutally and successfully. The Vikings were a pagan culture in search of movable wealth, usually precious metals (although in the cartoon strip Viking Hagar the Horrible often brings wife Helga dresses from chic Paris designers), which meant they preyed on churches and towns. Both were very vulnerable.

The Vikings' great advantage in Gaul was the political confusion of the ninth century when magnates, emperors and kings quarrelled constantly among themselves and could not mount any sustained, unified campaign against these northern marauders. Robert the Strong, for example, was killed in 866 fighting the Vikings but that was chance. He spent a great deal more time at war with Charles the Bald and Louis the Stammerer, his overlord and neighbour. It was understandable, then, that Charles the Simple decided to deal with the Vikings by making them respectable. In 911 he bought off the Viking chief Rollo, known as the Ganger, by appointing him count of Rouen with a substantial grant of land to support the honour. Rollo then left Charles alone, although he and his followers, at least through the reign of Rollo's successor, William Longsword, continued to regard Brittany as fair game. Actually, attacks on Brittany were often retaliation for Breton attacks on Normandy and elsewhere, and therefore part of Rollo's obligation as a count. Meanwhile, the bishop of Coutances fled in panic from his Norman See, despite Rollo's promise in the agreement of St-Clair-sur-Epte not to raid the Church. The bishop of Rouen remained in place to oversee the Christianizing of these pagans and apparently was not molested by them.

Rollo proved to be a competent administrator. So too were his successors, becoming over the next decades Christianized, pacified and, to some degree, Frankified. For himself, Rollo, who became Christian as part of the bargain, left nothing to chance and on his death bed ordered both benefactions to Christian churches and human sacrifices. But his death signalled the passing of the 'old guard' so to speak, and his successors married Franks – for instance, Richard I married the daughter of Hugh the Great, thus becoming Hugh Capet's brother-in-law – and the Normans learned to speak the local dialect. Some of them in time entered monasteries or joined the clergy, and in due course became as French as anyone else in West Francia. The duchy of Normandy, as it soon became, grew strong and rich, a duchy to be reckoned with. It was to contribute to the fragmentation of Gaul at the end of the tenth century as it became yet another powerful feudal territory quarrelling with its neighbours and maintaining a great degree of autonomy. The feudal relationship was complex enough, given the weakness of those who held the Ile de France. It was to be complicated a hundredfold when one of the great Norman dukes, William II, bastard son of Duke Robert I, went off to become king of England in 1066.

CHAPTER THREE

Capetian France
987–1328

Political power was fragmented in the France of the Capets until reconsolidation began in the thirteenth century. Territorial princes and lesser nobles had real power, and it was greater the further they were from the Ile de France. There was no clearly defined feudal hierarchy to subdue this regionality. Even in the north, ties of vassalage and fief were little more than treaties to be broken at will, whether between king and noble, or noble and noble. It varied in degree, but generally a kind of aristocratic anarchy reigned involving princes, nobles, castellans (keepers of castles) and knights.

Territorial Princes

Each major feudatory of France (Brittany, Normandy, Aquitaine, Champagne, Toulouse, Gascony and Anjou, among others) was ruled by a duke or count acting with sufficient independence and power to be regarded as virtually a kingly equal. Fulk Nerra of Anjou, Odo II of Blois, William II of Normandy and William X of Aquitaine, for example: dominating personalities, able rulers, renowned warriors. They were vassals of the king, and lesser lords and knights were their vassals. But this was often a formality, enforceable in the last resort only by the deployment of armed strength. Meanwhile these princes ruled virtually without hindrance, imitated the ceremonial, language and practice of royalty, and often made war against the king as well as against each other. The only difference was that the royal title, conferred by crowning and anointing, gave the kingly office a sacred and special feudal dimension beyond mere territorial titles.

In some regions hierarchical feudal relationships were firmly fixed: in Normandy, Flanders and Aquitaine, for example. Regarding these regions the Ile de France often sustained itself only by making alliance with one set of princes against another.

However, while the princes were often virtually independent of the king, none among them ever disputed the existence of the royal office. Odo II of Blois often said – with tongue in cheek, no doubt – that he did not wish to be king, but the king's master. By the middle of the eleventh century the Francian (French) monarchy had arrived to stay, and the main currents of French history thereafter swirled around it.

Royal Power

Crowning and anointing made kings 'clean different' from their subjects, as England's Charles I was later to put it. Even so, they had first to be chosen by an assembly of nobles, knights and clerics from the royal principality, and then consecrated and blessed by the bishops (who had transferred the sacerdotal tradition and their political loyalty from the Carolingians to the Capetians), anointed with holy chrism, invested with sword, ring, sceptre and rod (also by the bishops), and crowned and enthroned. The king was then recognized as lawgiver, the keeper of God's peace, and overlord of the whole of France, to whom all territorial magnates and lesser lords owed service and counsel as vassals.

The theory was greater than the fact. Capetian power was limited to the Ile de France, that collection of secular and ecclesiastical lands and rights which the kings ruled directly, and any other areas which they could dominate. Within the Ile de France they controlled a primitive government machinery which any vassal could call upon for assistance. This government was usually limited to issuing royal charters. They also held a number of castles and towns, including *villeneuves*, or 'new towns', chartered for commercial or strategic purposes. But even in the royal principality many ancient and powerful hereditary castellan families defied these kings: of these Montlhéry, Montmorency and Montfort were among the most troublesome. On his deathbed, Philip I told his son never to let the tower of Montlhéry out of his keeping, 'Frankly, that tower has made me old before my time.'

Political power, royal or princely, depended upon the personal strength or weakness of rulers, on the extent of feudal pluralism (wherein a vassal commended himself to two or more lords), and on the knightly class which emerged in the tenth century. Knights – mounted war machines supported first as household retainers and then as holders of fiefs and benefices in return for service – were, by 1000, the core of royal and noble armies. Sometimes they were little better than roving mercenaries, and their presence was the 'yeast of anarchy and a threat of disorder for society' – the essence of feudalism, in the historian J.F. Larignier's view.

By 1100 many knights were castellans, but still exhibited the anarchic and savage behaviour of the mercenary. Thomas de Marle of Laon was credited with warring against his father, cutting the throat of his relative, the archdeacon Gautier of Laon, giving sanctuary to the murderers of the bishop of Laon, and confiscating ecclesiastical property. He was excommunicated in 1114, and Louis VI outlawed him. The kings sat at the top and the knights at the bottom of a very loosely constructed feudal pyramid.

The First Capets

Hugh behaved as a territorial prince and did little more than survive. His successors into the twelfth century were not more promising: they fell foul of the Church for engaging in sexual *mésalliances*, they warred endlessly with their vassals, and they expanded the interests of the monarchy only slightly, if at all. Robert II, the Pious (996–1031), was the first French king credited with curing scrofula by touching. Henry I (1031–1060) married Anne of Kiev, whose father's court rivalled Constantinople in brilliance. Henry by comparison was a bumpkin, never sure 'he would not have his pocket picked if he ventured more than three leagues from his palace'. Philip (1060–1108) was 'indolent, fat, and unfit for war', as was his son, Louis VI (1108–1137). Louis also fathered at least seven illegitimate children, and was noteworthy mainly because Suger, abbot of Saint-Denis, was his principal administrative servant. Not a brilliant beginning for the Capets. At least Henry was credited with having 'put royal power back on the map', if not of actually expanding it. By his day the prestige of the monarchy was such that when Henry summoned vassals to his aid, they usually came.

Normandy and England

In 1066 William II, duke of Normandy, invaded England, overthrew King Harold in a battle near Hastings, and became king himself. The pictorial record of this event, a large, sewn cloth wrongly called a tapestry, hangs in Bayeux in Normandy. Could William, now a king in his own right, continue to swear fealty as duke of Normandy to King Philip, his feudal overlord? That very real problem was soon joined to a much greater one: could Philip maintain his throne in the face of William's enlarged prestige and power?

Philip did much better than some accounts might suggest. He fought successful holding actions against William and his allies, and after William's death encouraged divisive jealousy between William's sons,

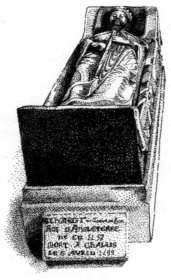

The tomb of Richard Coeur de Lion at the Abbey of Fontevrault

William Rufus, king of England, and Robert Curthose, duke of Normandy. Philip continued to fish in these troubled waters when Henry I succeeded William Rufus, but died with nothing resolved. Louis VI simply took up where his father left off: he fought with Henry over Gisors in Normandy, encouraged rebellion among Norman nobles, and even appealed to Pope Calixtus II for aid. It was only the beginning. Anglo-French wars dragged on for the next three centuries.

Crown and Clergy

The Church was not the problem for the Capets that Normandy was, but it was a problem all the same. French bishops in the north – at Reims, Sens, Laon, Orléans and elsewhere – made alliances with the throne and expected royal support for their privileges in return. When they did not get it, they were disloyal; as they also were rich and powerful, their disloyalty was both annoying and dangerous. French kings did not care for these uncertain arrangements.

CLUNY

The Cluniac reforms showed a way out. The Benedictine abbey of Cluny in Burgundy, founded in 909 by Bruno of Baume and chartered by Duke William of Aquitaine, led a wide-ranging monastic reform in the eleventh century. It called for the free election of abbots, a direct link with papal authority, guarantees for monastic property (Cluniac monks embraced personal poverty but the Order lived in richly decorated and ornate houses), elaborate liturgical ceremony and prayer, and strict discipline. Cluny soon had two thousand dependent houses, the right to reform others where discipline was slack (such as the abbey of Saint-Denis), and independence from the bishops. The bishops did not care for that, but both popes and kings did, for they were plagued equally by 'over-mighty' episcopal subjects.

There were drawbacks. The Cluniac movement could be used against powerful bishops and archbishops, and often was, by both popes and kings. But the Cluniacs meant what they said and such saintly, and powerful, abbots as Hugh of Cluny brooked no pragmatic nonsense from crown or tiara (as the papal crown was named) on the matter of the 'new morality'. Robert the Pious was a great enthusiast for the Cluniacs; Henry I chafed under them and Louis VI, with his brood of royal bastards, found them annoying. Philip I preferred them to independent and uncooperative bishops, but only just. His sins were as numerous – and of the same sort – as those of his son.

PAPAL REFORM

Worse was to come. In the eleventh century the papacy too was bitten by the reforming bug, and set out to recover prestige and moral authority eroded by weak popes and a corrupt clergy. Leo IX and Gregory VII led the way. They condemned simony (the buying and selling of church offices) and lay investment (clergy receiving symbols of office from lay lords), and asserted papal supremacy over temporal rulers.

French kings, among the worst offenders against ecclesiastical privilege, tried to take it all in their stride. When accused of simony, Henry I ignored the charge and took over more religious houses. Philip I, condemned and excommunicated for his 'marital excesses and self-indulgent way of life', turned without a qualm to bishops Walter of Meaux and John of Orléans, whom he had created, for support against the papacy. They gave it. It was Philip's view that the Church existed to be exploited, and that bishops ought to serve the crown in this as in other areas. The role of the bishops has always been ambiguous in the history of Christian monarchy.

THE CRUSADES

Clearly a crisis was brewing when popes, bishops, princes and kings all claimed powerful rights and were unprepared to compromise. (Henry of Germany kneeling penitently in the snow at Canossa was a political chess move against Pope Gregory, not an admission of defeat.) The laity had physical power, but the Church held the ultimate trump: moral authority. It also controlled the main channels of propaganda, the pulpits. In 1095 at Clermont, Pope Urban II called for a crusade to liberate Palestine from the Saracens (Moslems). This crusade was eloquently preached across Europe by the papal legate, Bishop Adhémar of Le Puy. The idea caught on, and over the next few decades men and women from every class and condition in Europe participated in holy expeditions *outremer* (overseas), urged on by the likes of Adhémar and Bernard, the firebrand abbot of Clairvaux.

It was a masterful stroke. Could King Philip disapprove as Peter the Hermit emptied his realm of starving peasants, various fanatics, beggars and adventurers for the 'Peoples' Crusade'? Could any prince object to enhanced moral stature gained by 'taking the Cross'? Could the papacy fail to gain from diverting secular energies away from the brewing church-state crisis? Did not nobles who remained at home profit from the departure of their rivals for Palestine? And were not aristocrats with few acres and many sons pleased that the pope now sanctioned abroad the practice of looting, which had been discouraged in Europe by the 'peace and truce of God' movement after the Council of Limoges in 994? The crusades, wrote the historian Elizabeth Hallam, 'canalised the piety, pugnacity and greed of the western nobles and earned much prestige for their lay and ecclesiastical leaders'.

The French above all: by 1099 Bohemond of Hauteville, Godfrey of Bouillon, Hugh of Vermandois, Raymond IV of Toulouse, Robert Curthose of Normandy, and Robert II of Flanders had established four Latin states in Palestine. The crusades degenerated thereafter into war between Christian princes.

Suger of Saint-Denis

Suger, abbot of Saint-Denis, was the invaluable right-hand man of Louis VII (1137–1180), the first French monarch to take the Cross. Perhaps Louis, who left for his crusade in 1146, went as penance for having burnt a church at Vitry with 1500 people inside in about 1143. Neither he nor France profited from his venture abroad, nor from much else that he did. The best part of his reign was the service given him by Suger, whom he 'inherited' from Louis VI.

Leaving Suger in charge, Louis went off to Palestine with his wife and an army. The crusade was a débâcle, and Louis spent his time making pilgrimages to shrines – commendable, probably, but of little military value. At home, his brother Robert of Dreux, who had fallen out with Louis in Palestine, plotted with dissident nobles in Paris to seize the throne. In 1149 Suger called them to an assembly at Soissons and in eloquent phrases (including threats of excommunication) talked them out of it. He wrote to Louis urging him in strong language to come home. The king was alarmed and, disgruntled with events in Palestine, came at once. Suger died soon after, exhausted from his efforts on behalf of Louis's throne. He was a great churchman, and a greater administrator; a most loyal ecclesiastical subject. Best of all, he was patron of the new basilica for the abbey church, which introduced that highly decorative, pointed-arched and rose-windowed church-style that is called Gothic, and which replaced the simpler but no less elegant Romanesque style. Saint-Denis was the model for the cathedrals of Chartres, Amiens, Reims, Notre-Dame, and many others.

Twelfth-century Gothic carving at Cunault Church

Eleanor and Louis

Louis VII's failure on his crusade was of small account compared to his failures at home. Duke William X of Aquitaine bequeathed his duchy to his daughter, Eleanor, and both of them to Louis VI. In 1137 Louis married Eleanor to his son, who as Louis VII and ruler of Aquitaine ascended the French throne as a *puissant prince* (as the troubadour literature of Eleanor's duchy termed it), at least on paper. He relished this view of himself.

Louis intervened in the affairs of Anjou, Normandy and Champagne, and worked hard, behind Eleanor's urging, to expand the interests of Aquitaine. He was not remarkably successful, losing, in the end, more than he gained. Above all, he was no match for the strong-willed, vigorous, vivid and brilliant Eleanor, who always put Aquitaine ahead of France. She produced only daughters for Louis, which disgruntled him. Their relationship deteriorated steadily, and when he insisted that she accompany him on crusade, Eleanor had had enough. In Antioch she 'fell into the arms' of her youthful uncle, Raymond of Aquitaine, with whom she was accused of 'lewd and improper' behaviour. When she returned to Paris she was pregnant, probably by Raymond.

In 1151 Louis also had had enough, and procured a papal annulment of the marriage. Eleanor went happily, taking Aquitaine with her. A year later she made a brilliant match with Henry Plantagenet, son of Geoffrey 'the Bel' of Anjou, who was soon to be King Henry II of England. They married in 1152. For him Eleanor bore four sons, each of whom proved to be, in some degree, a disaster. By contrast her daughter by Louis VII, Marie of France, did well. She married Henry of Champagne and wrote Arthurian romances on a par with Chrétien de Troyes.

The Angevin Empire

Eleanor's marriage was a blow to Louis VII. In 1154 Henry mounted the English throne as master of England, Normandy and Aquitaine; a quarter of a century of vigorous warfare later, and he had created the vast Angevin Empire: Scotland, Ireland, Wales and England; Normandy, Anjou, Aquitaine, Brittany, Gascony, and Béarn (the Pyrénées). The French crown barely hung onto the royal principality.

Actually, Henry acknowledged the feudatory status of his French holdings. When he set off to attack Toulouse in 1159, Louis backed Count Raymond V and occupied the city. Henry was not prepared to lay siege to his suzerain and withdrew. Thus the feudal system perhaps worked better than is supposed; or, more likely, Henry thought that to attack the king from whom he held Normandy and other French lands might give ideas to his own vassals in England, a surly and contentious lot at the best of times.

Louis had other ways of resisting which also met with some success.

When Thomas à Becket, archbishop of Canterbury, fell out with Henry and fled to Louis for protection, the French monarch gave it, thereby strengthening his ties with the Church. When Becket was murdered and blame fell on Henry, Louis's reputation expanded greatly as the godly king who had protected the martyr. Finally, Eleanor set her four sons against their father when they grew up, still in the interest of Aquitaine, discord which Louis did everything in his power to encourage. By 1175 he was still confronted with overwhelming Angevin power in France, but had managed to contain it. In 1179 he crowned his successor, Philip *dieudonné* (gift of God), his son by his second marriage to Adela of Champagne. Things were about to change dramatically in royal France.

Philip Augustus

Philip II, Augustus (1180–1223), was intelligent, prudent, cunning and successful. He reversed the Angevin trend and expanded royal power into Picardy, Normandy, Anjou, Maine, and Languedoc. He married Isabella, daughter of Baldwin V of Hainault, which gave him Artois, access to other properties and young Louis, his heir. When Isabella died he married Ingeborg of Denmark, whom he disliked immediately they were wed. He set her aside in favour of Agnes of Méran. Like many Capetians, Philip Augustus found it difficult to work out the dynamics of successful marital relations.

In 1182 an alliance with the ageing Henry II, arranged at Gisors on the Seine, Henry's favourite Norman château, gave Philip support in his wars with Flanders and Champagne. In the later 1180s he and Henry fell out over Brittany, and Philip, like Louis before him, played off the Plantagenet sons against their father. Eleanor was also involved. Philip made alliances with her and with Richard Coeur-de-Lion, the future King Richard I of England. When Henry died in 1189, all of his sons, his wife and Philip were plotting against him.

Philip made war against the Plantagenets over the Angevin Empire until little of it was left. King John of England was known appropriately as Lackland for all the French territory he lost, notably after his disastrous defeat at Philip's hands at Bouvines in 1214. Philip used every

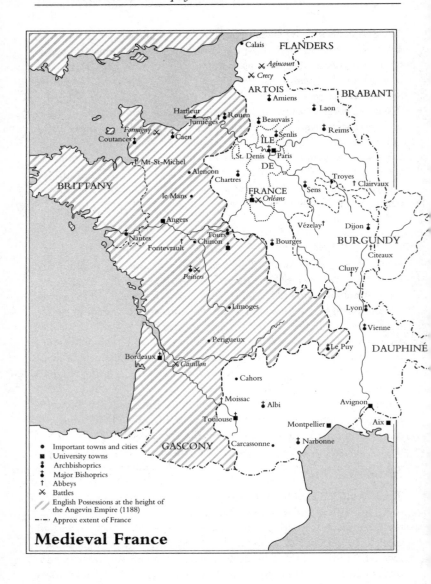

Calais

FLANDERS

✗ *Agincourt*

✗ *Crecy*

ARTOIS

☦ Amiens

BRABANT

☦ Laon

Harfleur • Rouen

Jumièges

Beauvais •

• Senlis

☦ Reims

Formigny ✗

Coutances ☦ • Caen

ILE

St. Denis • Paris

DE

Troyes

☦ • Clairvaux

Mt-St-Michel

• Alençon

Chartres

FRANCE

Orléans ✗

Sens

Vézelay ✝

Dijon

BRITTANY

le Mans •

• Angers

Bourges

BURGUNDY

Nantes • Tours

Fontevrault ✝ • Chinon

Citeaux

Cluny ✝

✗ Poitiers

• Limoges

Lyon

• Perigueux

Vienne

Bordeaux ■ ✗ *Castillon*

Le Puy

DAUPHINÉ

• Cahors

• Moissac

☦ • Albi

Avignon ■

Toulouse ■

Montpellier ■

Aix ■

GASCONY

Carcassonne •

Narbonne

- • Important towns and cities
- ■ University towns
- ☦ Archbishoprics
- ☦ Major Bishoprics
- ✝ Abbeys
- ✗ Battles
- ⁄⁄ English Possessions at the height of the Angevin Empire (1188)
- —·—· Approx extent of France

Medieval France

channel open to him to advance the interests of the crown against the Angevins, and against his own recalcitrant vassals, including paying lip service to, and participating briefly in, the crusades in order to gain favour with the papacy and divert the attention of his rivals. His efforts did not go unopposed.

Many territorial princes continued to behave as independently as their personal power allowed, and in the 'liberated' Angevin lands they often showed their gratitude to the monarch of France by backing the English. This was true especially in the south-west where the Bordeaux wine trade with England was very old and very lucrative.

Philip backed the Church against the Albigensian heresy (centred in the episcopal city of Albi, it was anti-Rome and anti-clerical) in Toulouse and Languedoc, acted as lawgiver and patron of church-building, and advanced Paris as the commercial centre of France. In Paris, he built hospitals, rebuilt many churches, including Saint-Geneviève, caused the work on Notre-Dame cathedral, begun by Bishop Maurice de Sully in Louis VII's reign, to go forward, oversaw the first cobbling of Paris streets (it was said that he tired of having to wade in mud every time he left the palace), and created a form of a metropolitan police force. In 1200 he codified the study of medicine, and civil and canon law. When Philip died in 1223 royal lands were three times as extensive as in his father's day, and Plantagenet holdings had shrunk merely to Gascony and Béarn.

Philip's son, Louis VIII, reigned only until 1226. Thus between Philip Augustus, arguably France's greatest monarch, and his grandson Louis IX, arguably its most pious, almost nothing intervened save a spectacularly bloody campaign against the Albigensians.

Social Change

The growth of the Capetian centre was in the context of economic, social and urban change, which may indeed have encouraged it. During the eleventh and twelfth centuries much forest land was cleared for the plough and colonized at the landlords' urging. Long-distance trade increased, inspired by the rising demand for luxury goods. Local markets multiplied and money became a more common medium of exchange.

Serfs declined in numbers as a group, and rents and dues often replaced labour service for peasants. Urban communities grew in importance and independence, with many now able to negotiate successfully for charters granting them privileges separate from the surrounding countryside: Orléans, La Chapelle, Aude, Étampes, and Souvigny offer examples of the general nature of this development. Extravagant lifestyles for the nobility created an ever-increasing burden of debt, an affliction also of many religious communities. In consequence many territorial lords became patrons of trade and commerce. The counts of Flanders and Champagne, and Philip Augustus himself adopted deliberate economic policies. It may have been the result of changing climatic conditions which favoured agriculture in the rich lands of Picardy and the Ile de France, and of the invention of the horse-drawn iron plough.

ABÉLARD AND THE UNIVERSITY OF PARIS

At the dawn of the twelfth century, Peter Abélard, a Breton, arrived in Paris and challenged and surpassed the teaching supremacy of Guillaume of Champeaux at the cathedral school. The young philosopher was brilliant, poetical and musical, and attractive. He set up his rival school in the cloister of Sainte-Geneviève. Students came to him in droves, leaving Guillaume high and dry. One of these was Héloïse, niece of Canon Filbert of Notre-Dame and Guillaume's patron.

The attraction for her was not wholly intellectual. Soon Héloïse was pregnant. Abélard took her away to Brittany where they were secretly married, and she bore a son. Canon Filbert was not pleased. He hired some ruffians and a barber to abduct Abélard and perform such rough justice on him that he was forced into a life of chastity. Abélard became a monk and persuaded Héloïse to enter the convent at Argenteuil. There she wrote her famous letters which prove that the flame burning within her was anything but spiritual. Abélard took up teaching again, and began writing the books which prove him to have been among the greatest minds of that or any other age.

As a thinker, Abélard was always at the centre of controversy. His early work was condemned and burnt at Soissons because of its personalized theology. This did not deter him, and thereafter he produced some of the great writing of the Middle Ages, including the famous rationalist treatise *Sic et Non*. Abélard claimed that he was now 'the only philosopher on earth and saw no rival whom I need fear'. False humility was never a problem for him. The last great confrontation for the ageing philosopher was against Bernard of Clairvaux at a council at Sens in 1140. Bernard, fearing he was intellectually no match for Abélard, refused to debate and merely read off 17 prepared propositions condemning Abélard's work. The monk stormed from the session and retired to a Cluniac priory at Châlons where he ended his days.

Intellectual life in France 'took off' after Abélard. When the University of Paris was founded, chartered, and officially recognized by Pope Innocent III and Philip Augustus a generation later, Abélard's school at Sainte-Geneviève was the embryo. True to his character, the university began life amid controversy: brawls and rifts between students and the *prévôts* (police officials) and citizens of Paris were customary. These have continued to be part of university life, on and off, ever since.

THE CHURCH

In the early thirteenth century the Capetians took control in the endless task of sorting out church-state relations. Louis VI granted and chartered religious houses, and aided popes against emperors. But he reformed monastic houses on his own, used ecclesiastical office to enrich his family, and insisted upon his regalian (royal) right to supervise episcopal and abbotical elections. Louis VII acted similarly, although perhaps less dramatically, and despite his great reputation for piety never relaxed his control over royal churches. Often he used his pious reputation for gain, as in his aid to Thomas à Becket: it was 'piety with valuable political consequences'.

Philip Augustus paid well-publicized deference to Church and clerical rights; but in practice he did not allow any extension of papal power in France. He allowed free clerical elections, but let it be known he expected his candidates to be elected. The Church and churchmen complained, fulminated, cajoled, excommunicated, pleaded, threatened, plotted and manipulated on behalf of their privileges. But by the end of Louis VIII's short reign the crown controlled most of the French Church, and more importantly, the French Church gave its loyalty to the king before the pope.

Saint-Louis

Louis IX (1226–1270), the only French king to be canonized, continued strongly in the established warring traditions of the house of Capet: he fought England (under Henry III), his own territorial vassals, the Saracens and the Albigensian heretics. He also built churches (most famously the Sainte-Chapelle on the Ile de la Cité in Paris), was pious (just), supported the papacy (so long as it did not encroach upon his domain), dressed simply and, so far as a king could be, was humble. Louis died while on a crusade. For these things and for providing what his chronicler Joinville called good government, he was canonized.

His canonization simply shows up the importance of propaganda even at that early date. Louis's exploits were substantively no greater, if as great, as those of his grandfather, Philip Augustus; but they were of the sort to impress the Church. The Church was grateful for them; hence Saint-Louis. However, the only truly distinctive thing about his reign was the remarkable women it brought to light.

Blanche of Castile

Louis came to the throne as a minor with his mother, Blanche of Castile, as regent. Henry III of England, various French territorial magnates and members of Louis's own family tried to forward their interests at his expense: even, as in the case of the counts of Boulogne and Brittany, to dethrone him. Blanche held France for Louis, 'a remarkable achievement for a foreigner and a woman in a land where politics were dominated by men', with the aid of loyal castellan families. Among those, ironically, were the Montmorency and Montfort, who had made life so difficult for Philip I and Louis VI. Blanche played a key role in consolidating royal power.

Margaret of Provence

Louis married Margaret in 1234. Blanche hated her from the start, for fear that she would dominate the royal household. For a time Blanche held her at bay, but after 1244 Margaret's influence with the king grew while Blanche's influence waned. Louis took his wife on a crusade in 1248. The campaign was a disaster, and Louis himself was taken prisoner and had to pay a huge ransom. Meanwhile, Margaret held the Egyptian seaport of Damietta for him, and gave birth to their son, John Tristan, at the same time. She was the sister of Henry III's wife, Eleanor, and probably influenced Louis to side with Henry against the Provisions of Oxford, imposed upon the English king by his barons in 1263 to reaffirm the Magna Carta. Margaret survived Louis by 25 years. In that time she was no less spirited on her own behalf, wresting concessions from Charles of Anjou, her brother-in-law, regarding her Provençal inheritance, and furthering the interests of her son, Philip III. In the end Margaret received Beaufort, Baugé and Anjou itself, which she administered effectively until her death.

The thirteenth century produced a striking collection of women in France, beginning with Eleanor of Aquitaine, who lived well into it, and including Blanche, Eleanor's granddaughter, and Margaret. There also were Alice of Cyprus, who fought an unsuccessful war for the possession of Champagne, and Isabella of La Marche, widow of King John, who organized resistance to the French king in Poitou in league with her husband, Hugh. She was consigned to the abbey of Fontevrault for her trouble. In centuries to come there would be others. It remains a mystery why the assumption grew up that women could not manage affairs with as much cunning and strength of will and intellect as could men; or why French women received the vote only in 1945.

The Last Capetians

Fifty-eight years remained to the Capets after Saint-Louis. Between 1270 and 1328 five kings reigned: Philip III (1270–1285), Philip IV, the Fair (1285–1314), Louis X (1314–1316), Philip V (1316–1322) and Charles IV (1322–1328). Only Philip III and Philip IV lasted longer than a half-dozen years, but all saw advances in the prestige and power of royal France. By 1328 more of the country than ever before was under the royal house, directly or through lands attached to members of the family. The royal administration, judicial court (*Parlement* of Paris), and style of the monarchy was increasingly urbane and sophisticated; the Church was humbled; and the economy waxed strong. Even so, there were clouds on the horizon as well as bright sun at the zenith of the royal day.

THE ALBIGENSIAN CRUSADE

During the thirteenth century, the Capets appeared to profit from nearly every venture, so long as it was in France proper. Between 1209 and 1330 the crown made war in Toulouse and Languedoc against the Albigensian heretics, who were backed by the counts of Toulouse and other southern nobles. This heresy was inconsistent in its beliefs except that it opposed the corruption of Rome and antedated the Protestant reformers. Successive French kings campaigned against the Albigensians with the blessings of the Church, seizing, burning and slaughtering: in one day in 1245 royal officers and members of the Inquisition burnt 200 heretics at Montségur. When the smoke cleared the traditional independence of these principalities was broken along with the heresy, and they were brought under royal control.

THE TEMPLARS

Another crusade of a different but equally profitable nature was Philip IV's suppressing of the Templars, one of the holy orders of knights created during the crusades. Rich and powerful, they were a particularly tempting target for a king both pressed for cash and anxious to rid himself of any form of opposition from ecclesiastical sources. First the Templars had to be discredited. This was managed by Guillaume of Nogaret, Philip's principal hatchet-man and a skilful propagandist.

In 1307 Templars were arrested throughout France and made to confess under torture to the most diabolical practices, including witchcraft and Satanism. Pope Clement V condemned all of this and did not believe what he was being told about the Templars. Nogaret then produced public confessions by the Grand Master, Jacques de Molay, and other leaders. Finally after more than 70 Templars confessed before the pope on his visit to Poitiers, Clement compromised and the suppression was carried through to its bitter conclusion.

Templar property was transferred to the Hospitallers, another knightly order, who were compelled to pay Philip huge sums for it.

The rank and file were pensioned off to religious houses, but de Molay and other leaders were condemned and burnt. The chronicler Villani concluded: '[The king] ... made secret arrangements with the pope and caused him to promise to destroy the Templars, laying to their charge many articles of heresy; but it is said that this was more in the hope of extracting money from them ...' There was nothing new in all of this: even the pious Saint-Louis extracted money from the Church in the name of crusading causes. Philip merely surpassed others in the brutality of his extractions.

AVIGNON

Clement V was elected pope through Nogaret's intervention, and even though he eventually gave in over the Templars, Philip had him seized and removed to Avignon in Provence, virtually a prisoner of the French monarch. (Provence then belonged to the counts of Anjou, feudal vassals of the king.) There the papacy remained until 1377, freer under Clement's successors but still surrounded by French cardinals.

THE PRINCES

With the Church humbled and Toulouse and Languedoc gained for the crown, the appearance of royal supremacy achieved by 1328 is compelling. Princely power, however, was only constrained; it was not broken. Indeed it was gathering itself even as royal supremacy was acknowledged. Europe marvelled at Philip IV's authority; but it was a power maintained at great strain and cost, and could easily be disrupted by any significant wrench in society or in the body politic. Professor J. Le Patourel suggested that in the thirteenth century the great territorialities were compromised; in the fourteenth they began reconsolidating their power; and in the fifteenth they again dominated the crown. In Brittany, by 1297, the count was a duke and peer of France, with his own *parlement* and financial institutions. In the 1340s the Breton dukes, with English backing, claimed that Brittany was a kingdom. In the 1390s they claimed it was not part of France at all. This was an extreme case, but it suggests that the Hundred Years War in the fourteenth century was a civil war as well as a struggle with England.

SOCIAL CRISES

Over the centuries, strong economic differences emerged from region to region, usually reflecting geography and climate. For example, the Ile de France and Picardy were agriculturally advanced and prosperous, while less lucrative subsistence farming and stock-raising characterized Languedoc and the Massif Central. The former comprised rich, well-watered soil; the latter were dry and rocky. Montaillou, a village in Foix in the Pyrénées, and a Cathar (Albigensian) stronghold, is well documented in the records of the Inquisition. It is a good example of the poorer sort of place: landless peasants working as shepherds; landed peasants raising poor crops on poor soil; and the difference between them of personal wealth much less than would have been the case in Blois or the Vexin. The *châtelain* had very little more land than the Clergues, a comparatively rich peasant family. The Clergues dominated village life. One of them was a womanizing priest, which, added to Montaillou's heresies, probably explains why the villagers resented the Roman Church more than they did the local nobility.

Montaillou represented marginal living at all social levels, and its inhabitants might be thought easy prey in hard times: to extremist causes, to *jacqueries* (peasant uprisings) and to exploiting landlords. They were, but no more so than their more affluent counterparts in the north. Landlords always tried to expand their seigneurial rights in hard times in order to make ends meet, no matter where they were, and famines and crop failures devastated social tranquillity and stability equally wherever they occurred.

Consider the example of the north in the opening decades of the fourteenth century. Economic and social crises loomed in the Ile de France. Long years of warfare had brought royal expansion and apparent prosperity; they had also drained economic resources and weakened the social fabric. Then weather patterns abruptly changed and bad harvests followed: food shortages in Paris in 1305; grain scarce everywhere in 1309; bad harvests in the Ile de France in 1314; and freezing rain and flood-ravaged coastal areas throughout the summer of 1315, destroying crops on a wide scale. The psychological impact was horrendous. The price of wheat reached unprecedented levels, and starvation, disease, crime and even cannibalism followed. A chronicler in 1317 described a prayer procession to Saint-Denis in which poor people were barefoot and wholly or nearly naked. In 1320 a great band of poor men and fanatics roamed the land massacring Jews. In 1321 a similar massacre of lepers took place. The more economic conditions deteriorated, the more Philip's administrators manipulated the currency: they raised living costs, diminished the value of fixed incomes, created hardships for everyone, and sought to solve financial problems through such expedients as suppressing the Templars. No wonder the reign of Saint-Louis began to look like a Golden Age. The situation only worsened when the Hundred Years War began in 1339.

ORIGINS OF THE WAR

In 1328 Charles IV died leaving only a daughter. The throne passed to Philip VI of Valois (1328–1350), a grandson of Philip III. However the succession was clouded. The last Capets produced many daughters but few sons, and it was an erroneous presumption that the ancient *Lex Salica* of the founding Franks denied that royal inheritance could pass through the female line. This actually was an excuse to deny the claims to royal lands put forward by these daughters or their sons – or to the throne, a claim made by Isabella of England, daughter of Philip IV and mother-regent to the boy-king Edward III. When Edward grew up he did homage as lord of Gascony to Philip VI. Then in 1337 Philip seized Gascony, and Edward asserted his claim to the whole of France as Philip IV's grandson. He backed his claim with force, and in 1339 the Hundred Years War began. It reduced the crown to destitution, but raised the territorial princes to new heights. France again fell prey to the tensions and antagonisms of its disparate parts. It was to take a woman to sort it out.

CHAPTER FOUR

The Lily and the Lion
1328–1515

The Hundred Years War

The Hundred Years War effectively ended the French Middle Ages. The reign of Louis XI which followed it represented a bridge to the Renaissance.

'Hundred Years War' is a term less descriptive than symbolic; that is, it was a war and it lasted a very long time. But since the major feature was the struggle between France and England – the Lily and the Lion – for control of French lands, it could be argued that the war began in 1066 and only ended when England gave up Calais in 1558. Even the conventional dates, 1337–1453, are well beyond one hundred years. Nevertheless, the term provides a convenient handle for the war which started because Edward III, king of England, duke of Gascony and Philip IV's grandson, argued that his claim to the French throne was superior to that of Philip VI of Valois.

Philip, enthroned in 1328, naturally did not share Edward's views. In 1336 Edward, as duke, renounced his homage to Philip, who proceeded to seize Gascony and the war was on. It was in part a civil war: Edward was more French than English, and his Gascon barons gladly followed him against their French compatriots. Admittedly, they also expected that a king in distant England would be less interfering than one closer to home.

The war brought clearly into focus several long-standing issues: the perpetual struggle between the centralizing Paris monarchy and the independent-minded territorial princes; the question of who should control the crown, quite apart from the person wearing it; the conflict between the great lords for control of the economic resources upon which the royal government could call; and the security of the wine trade between Bordeaux, the principal Gascon city and port, and England. Ultimately, the war devastated wide areas of France and precipitated drastic alterations in internal social and economic relationships.

Edward tried to raise an anti-French coalition in the Low Countries, supported by the counts of Hainault and Brabant and wealthy merchant Jacob van Artevelde, who led an urban workers' revolt which drove out pro-French Louis of Nevers. But the revolt petered out, and with it the coalition. After 1339 the war settled into its 'heroic' phase: thirty years of the great, if often brutal, generalship of Edward III and his son, the Black Prince, and periodic *chevauchées*, 'scorched earth' campaigns in which English armies ravaged the countryside destroying and killing at random. There were also great battles which pitted French chivalry against English bowmen, to the former's discomfiture.

The English were singularly successful in the heroic period. In 1340 they destroyed most of the French fleet off Sluys, near the Scheldt River mouth in Flanders. It was the beginning of a very uncomfortable time for the French monarch, whose court, claimed King John of Bohemia, offered 'the most *chivalric* sojourn in the world'. Prophetic words: it was the chivalric mentality of French arms, the undisciplined, arrogant, glory-seeking individualism of the mounted knights, which brought defeat after defeat over the next 70-odd years.

After Sluys Philip was forced to levy additional taxes: the *gabelle*, a salt tax, which was extended to the whole nation in 1341, followed by a hearth tax in 1342. The *paysans* and townspeople regarded these taxes as extortionate and soon rebelled against them.

CRÉCY

The opening *chevauchée* occurred in 1345 in Poitou, the first of many over the coming years. It was followed in 1346 by the campaign which culminated in the battle of Crécy, in Artois. After capturing Caen, King Edward's idea was to withdraw from Flanders before the ponderous French feudal army could be mobilized. He feinted towards Paris, then looked for an undestroyed bridge across the Somme. There were few left, and he was delayed several days. The French caught him at Crécy.

Badly outnumbered, the English fought a defensive, almost a guerilla, action. The infantry shot arrows from their longbows from behind hedges and fences at the French knights, who charged in reckless disorder. Edward's style of warfare was not chivalric, but it was effective. The French cavalry, wrote the chronicler Froissart, tried to push ahead of each other 'from mere pride and jealousy'. It was impossible to call a retreat even when it was clear the knights were being slaughtered to no purpose. Philip was lucky to escape from the débâcle. Edward too was lucky to leave Crécy unscathed, for he had been caught in a position where the skilful use of French cavalry could have turned English victory into a devastating defeat. But he came away whole, and pushed on to Calais where six townsmen (their sacrifice immortalized in sculpture by Auguste Rodin) surrendered their lives so that Edward might spare the city. Why they had to die is not clear.

Back in Paris Philip summoned the Estates, the representatives of Church and nobility who advised him. There were recriminations. The Estates complained that Philip had humiliated French chivalry by losing the battle; Philip argued that the Estates were niggardly in providing him with adequate supplies.

The Black Death

'[In] men and women alike there appeared ... certain swellings, either on the groin or under the arm-pits, whereof some waxed of the bigness of a common apple, others like unto an egg ... and these the vulgar named plague-boils.' Then came black and red blotches on arms and thighs, until the body was covered, 'a very certain token of coming death ...' Thus Giovanni Boccaccio described the bubonic plague introduced into Europe probably from China, which reached France and England in 1348. An estimated third of the French population was wiped out with dramatic consequences: manpower shortages drove up labour costs; rural productivity and town manufacturing declined; the import market dried up, creating economic dislocations elsewhere in Europe; and the nobility, often facing bankruptcy, forced royal government to impose edicts freezing labour and rent obligations owed by peasants and labourers, so that aristocratic privilege would not be curtailed. The immediate consequence of these edicts was the *jacqueries*, the peasant uprisings of 1358 and 1381. But the clock could not be turned back, as these edicts with their strong hint of revitalized serfdom and even slavery attempted to do. Labour acquired a new value and the relationship between the landed classes and the peasantry was altered forever. Feudalism was doomed by the Black Death. The devastation of subsequent *chevauchées* and the outmoded military styles of French chivalry would finish it off.

The Dauphin

In 1349 France acquired control of Dauphiné, remote, rugged and backward, east of the Rhône and above Provence. Nominally Dauphiné was part of the Holy Roman Empire, that loose confederation of Germanic and some Italian regions (the legacy of Charlemagne's 'special relationship' with Rome), which came permanently under the rule of the House of Habsburg in the fourteenth century and was the basis of their power through the eighteenth. Henceforth Dauphiné was an *apanage* for the royal heir, who would be known thereafter as the dauphin. Coincidental circumstance made successive dauphins supremely important in coming years.

The Black Death only briefly curtailed the war. The first dauphin replaced Philip in 1350, with the war in full swing. This was John II, the Good (1350–1364). He was not especially good, either as military leader or as king. Blunt, honest, even kindhearted on occasion, this king was also stubborn, narrow-minded and inflexible. John was unlucky as well: he had to concern himself from the start with Charles of Navarre, a cruel, thoroughly evil man who murdered Charles of Castille, the Constable of France, and made deals with the English. At Poitiers in 1356 John not only lost an important battle, but was taken captive into the bargain. The responsibility for France and for containing Charles of Navarre then fell on the none-too-sturdy shoulders of John's son, the dauphin Charles.

While John enjoyed a comfortable captivity (his captors treated him like royalty), Charles faced uprisings in Paris. Étienne Marcel, a rich merchant, and Robert Le Coq, bishop of Laon, channelled popular discontent over the evils and deprivations attending the war, and made the dauphin their virtual prisoner. He was forced to watch as two of his friends and counsellors were murdered. The Paris riots spread beyond the city and turned into the *jacquerie* of 1358. But the dauphin escaped from Paris and made his peace with Charles of Navarre. The dauphin and Navarre were enemies, but anarchy and riot among the common people threatened them both. They could always continue their quarrel later.

In 1360 the dauphin agreed to the Treaty of Bretigny with England, by which France had to pay three million gold *eçus* ransom for John, and the English were confirmed in possession of the Calais area and Aquitaine. John reigned for four more years, creating confusion and difficulty before he died.

Charles V

The dauphin became Charles V, the Wise (1364–1380). He actually was wise, or at the very least prudent. Charles found men of ability to serve him – the abbot Fécamp, Hugh Abricot, *prévôt* of Paris, and Bertrand du Guesclin, a Breton mercenary who understood the changing rules of warfare. Despite the annoyance it caused both his chivalric nobles and the English, Charles refused to fight more than minor engagements. In exasperation Edward III called him 'that lawyer', and it was not meant as a compliment. Perhaps Charles, not a strong, robust military figure on the lines of his father, simply followed his natural inclinations.

It was the correct policy. By 1374 France regained most of what had been lost, and even penetrated Gascony, where the usually pro-English nobility were rebelling against the Black Prince's efforts at streamlining the administration. Efficiency, they found, interfered with their privileges. The Gascons did not now resist the French king with their former enthusiasm.

Unfortunately for France, Charles's successor was a minor. In turbulent times almost nothing could be more destabilizing, and the accession of Charles VI, the Fool (1380–1422), brought out the royal uncles to take charge of him and to use this excuse of a royal minority to enhance their power as territorial lords. In 1388 Charles's brother, the duke of Orléans, goaded him into taking a stand, something the timid and none-too-bright king had remained reluctant to do even as an adult. But now he acted, dismissing the uncles and gathering around him able counsellors – called the Marmosets – some of whom had served his father.

Civil War

Sadly, Charles VI became deranged following an attempt on his life in 1392. The uncles returned, expelled the Marmosets and busied themselves exploiting crown resources for their own interests. Soon the duke of Burgundy was involved, and a civil war broke out. Burgundy encompassed part of the lands once comprising Lotharingia, a sub-division of the Frankish empire after Charlemagne, and had always been autonomous even though its dukes were vassals of the French king. Their autonomy made the dukes a natural rallying point whenever control of France was being contested. One side followed Burgundy's lead; the other, the so-called Armagnacs, adhered to the duke of Orléans and crown interests. It was a desperate time: the king was mad and his son, the future Charles VII, was unequipped to act decisively. Moreover the uncles had married Charles VI to Isabella of Bavaria, a woman of strong sexual appetites, who put it about that the dauphin was not the king's son.

Again a common enemy came to the rescue. In 1381 there had been another *jacquerie*, just after Charles was enthroned; in 1413 Simon Caboche, a butcher, led an uprising. These events were separated by three decades, but nonetheless reminded both sides that more was at stake than merely who controlled the poor, sick king or his irresolute son. The Caboche rising united the warring noble factions – just in time to confront a resurgent English army.

AGINCOURT

After 1377, with both King Edward and the Black Prince dead, the English were hampered by domestic quarrels and weak leadership. The war petered out until the accession of Henry V in the early fifteenth century. Strong, ambitious, anxious to reassert Plantagenet claims in France, he resumed the war. In 1415 Henry campaigned in Artois, took Harfleur, and then at Agincourt faced a far superior force of French cavalry. Once again English archery prevailed. By 1415 armour was a complete metal cocoon; on horseback a knight, encased in seventy pounds of metal plating, was impregnable. If, on the other hand, the horse was shot from under him and he fell to the ground, the knight was helpless and easily dispatched by mallet-wielding infantry. At Agincourt the English longbow drove the last nail into the coffin of French feudalism. However, Agincourt was to be England's last major victory in the Hundred Years War.

THE TREATY OF TROYES

In 1420 Charles VI was forced to accept the Treaty of Troyes: the dauphin was disinherited in favour of Henry V; France was divided for purposes of administration between England (Aquitaine and a much enlarged Normandy including Anjou and parts of Brittany) and an Anglo-Burgundian alliance; and Henry would marry Catherine, Charles's only daughter, and upon Charles's death would become king of France. The dauphin was stuck in Bourges, maintained only by remnants of the Armagnac faction and seemingly a lost cause.

Joan of Arc

Henry and Catherine married and produced a son. Eight months later both Charles VI and Henry V were dead. The dauphin claimed the throne; so did the English on behalf of the Plantagenet heir. They held Paris and the baby Henry VI of England was duly enthroned. But with a child of such tender age as their king, the English lords immediately fell out over who should actually govern. Preoccupied with this internal struggle they left the dauphin unmolested in Bourges, where he seemed content to wait until doomsday. But, in fact, he delayed only six years, until Joan of Arc entered the picture and forced him into action.

Joan, the Maid of Orléans, was the stuff of which legends are made. Only she was no legend. This daughter of Jacques d'Arc, a well-off peasant from Domrémy on the Meuse, was 'a young woman of robust flesh and healthy blood, full of courage and tenderness, of common sense and racy humour'. Instructed by what she believed were the voices of the saints Michael, Margaret and Catherine, she set out in 1428 to save France. The moment was opportune. In October the English besieged Orléans. The dauphin Charles by then had sold his last jewels, had to have sleeves patched into his old doublet, could not get credit from a cordwainer for new shoes, and had only four crowns in his purse. He needed a miracle. What he got was Joan: much the same thing.

At first no one listened to Joan. But in this age, people believed in miracles. Finally Durand Laxart, her cousin by marriage, took Joan to the Sire de Baudricourt. Joan was compelling and convinced the Sire to take her to Chinon, to the dauphin. Joan persuaded the dauphin that she was directed by her 'voices' to throw the English out of France. He put her in charge – spiritually at any rate – of any army to raise the siege of Orléans. It was a curious but effective force including among its captains: Gilles de Rais (the legendary Bluebeard); La Hire, a good soldier and author of this unique soldier's prayer: 'God, I pray You that You will today do for La Hire what You would wish La Hire to do for You, if La Hire were God and You were a man-at-arms'; and Dunois, bastard son of the duke of Orléans, an exceptional soldier and Joan's devoted companion-in-arms. The army believed in her, took Orléans, and marched on Reims with Charles in tow where he was crowned in the cathedral. Joan's mission was complete; the rest was up to the king. She continued with the army, however, and in an attack on Compiègne in 1430 she was wounded and then captured by the Burgundians.

They sold her to the English who hated her (she was called a whore by her English guards who threatened to rape her on several occasions), and who gave her to the Church for trial as a heretic. It was a show trial, of course, carried on at Rouen in Normandy, deep in English territory. The earl of Warwick masterminded it and Pierre Couchon, bishop of Beauvais, prosecuted. Joan was convicted, condemned, and on 30 May, 1431, burnt at Rouen. Charles did nothing to save her. Historian Martin Scott observed: 'Alive she would have been an embarrassment;

Agnes Sorel, the favourite of Charles VII

as a martyr she formed a telling witness to the brutality of the English.' Her final achievement, it seems, was to become a propaganda weapon.

By 1432 Charles VII (1422–1461) sat firmly on a throne made available to him by Joan of Arc. But he was not out of the woods. Burgundy still sided with England, and he had yet to live down his reputation as the do-nothing 'King of Bourges'. To aid him, Charles had merchant-banker Jacques Coeur of Bourges, the richest man in France, forward-looking military planners who understood the uses of gunpowder, and an Estates which understood the need for a regular army supported by regular taxes. Not for nothing was Charles VII called 'the Well-Served'.

It was to take another generation, but by 1453 English power in France was broken once and for all. Joan of Arc created the momentum which made it possible. Her presence generated the popular enthusiasm which goaded Charles to action in 1429, to a reconciliation with the duke of Burgundy in 1435, and to the victories at Formigny in 1450 and Castillon in 1453, after which English civil and military administration was withdrawn entirely from Normandy. The war was then over.

The Impact of the Hundred Years War

The Black Death, *chevauchées, jacqueries:* together they left an indelible mark, a scar of vivid hue, on the face of fifteenth-century France. A late fourteenth-century priest of Cahors recorded that he had seen nothing in his lifetime but war, and that in his diocese '... neither cock nor hen is crowing', instead 'wolves and beasts of the forest' furrowed the fields. The Italian Petrarch wrote in 1360 that the English 'have reduced the entire kingdom of France by fire and sword to such a state that I, who had traversed it lately on business, had to force myself to believe that it was the same country I had seen before. Outside the walls of towns, there was not, as it were, one building left standing.' A century later French chronicler Thomas Basin wrote:

> From the Loire to the Seine, and from there to the Somme, nearly all the fields were left for a long time ... not merely untended but without people capable of cultivating them, except for rare patches of soil, for the peasants had been killed or put to flight.... We ourselves have seen the vast plains of Champagne, Beauce, Brie, Gatinais, Chartres, Dreux, Mainz and Perche, Vexin, both French and Norman, Beauvais, Caux, from the Seine as far as Amiens and Abbeville, Senlis, Soissonnais, Valois, as far as Laon and, beyond, as far as Hainault, absolutely deserted, uncultivated, abandoned, devoid of all inhabitants, overgrown with brushwood ...

Exaggerations? Probably not, particularly when considered in the context of the Black Death and the slaughter of peasants in putting down the *jacqueries.* When Louis XI ascended the throne in 1461 the waste of the war was such that the desperate need for labour enabled many serfs to win freedom, and many peasants to gain advantageous terms for their tenantry. Many nobles were impoverished, and towns and townsmen had grown stronger (for this was what the insurrections led by Étienne Marcel and the butcher Caboche really signified) relative to the nobility. The age of the bourgeoisie was beginning even as the bonds of feudalism were weakening.

EDUCATION

Meanwhile, the horizons of the intellect deepened and widened during this era of war and devastation, expanding upon foundations laid in the eleventh and twelfth centuries. Primary education was hit and miss: children learnt to read and write at home, in 'dame school' or in chantry, or not at all. Grammar schools were better and more formally organized, and were not uncommon by the fourteenth century. After the manner of Bernard of Chartres, they used Latin in the upper and vernacular in the lower forms, although vernacular was not taught expressly as a subject, whereas Latin was. Universities expanded in number and between 1300 and 1500 13 universities were founded in France beyond the University of Paris, including Caen and Bordeaux in 'English' France, where the idea was to draw students away from Paris.

There was no doubt that Paris was the intellectual centre of Europe, and its university was the reason. The courses were in rhetoric, logic, metaphysics, moral and natural philosophy. The faculties enjoyed great intellectual freedom and were remarkably independent. True, successive kings forbade the discussion of church-state questions and Sorbonne theologians were obliged to argue the king's position in the Great Schism regarding the Avignon papacy; but this was minor secular interference compared to the count of Provence who fined Provençals for attending any university but Aix. Medicine and law, long established at the Montpellier University in Roussillon, were added to the Paris curriculum in the fifteenth century, and the time required to complete the Master of Arts degree was reduced.

In the fourteenth century, Scholasticism promoted fierce debates in Paris between adherents of 'realism' (the real existence of abstractions) and 'nominalism' (abstractions useful only as intellectual devices for speculation). Those who debated were among the finest minds Europe has produced: Thomas Aquinas, Jean Gerson and Roger Bacon, among others. Their intellectual conflicts led directly to the methodological division which has informed western science and philosophy ever since. The French followed 'realism' straight to René Descartes in the seventeenth century, who linked it with modern mathematics to make 'rationalism'; the English endorsed and promoted 'nominalism', which led to Francis Bacon, Descartes's contemporary, who advanced the methodology common to modern science, and known as 'empiricism'.

VERNACULAR LITERATURE

In popular literature the vernacular had been the currency for generations. *Chanson de Roland*, the romance in *Langue d'Oïl* about the betrayed Carolingian hero Roland dying in defence of the pass at Roncesvalles against the Basques, appeared around 1100. It was in the heroic *chanson de geste* tradition. Meanwhile, in *Langue d'Oc* and *Langue d'Oïl* Troubadour poetry, the literature of 'courtly love' – a far cry from the men-only *chanson de geste* – captured the fancy of the literate population of Europe. The Troubadours (among them William IX of Aquitaine and Richard I of England) told of ladies worshipped from afar by knightly lovers who sought their favour by displaying the chivalrous virtues of patience, constancy and prowess in war. The genre was probably instructional, meant to curb the savage behaviour of uncultured knights in eleventh-century Aquitaine. Meanwhile, maidens were exhorted to remain chaste for the marriage bed. The moral lessons of Troubadour writing were clear and so was its earthiness. Jean Gerson thought the poetry encouraged lewd behaviour, and wrote a denunciation of *Roman de la Rose* as engendering lustful thoughts. Professor G.G. Coulton reckons that Gerson failed to understand the mentality of his own age: 'Moral at one moment and immoral at another, without any great effort to paper over the cracks.'

One other vernacular tradition both delighted and irked its public. The goliard poets were 'literary outlaws', roaming France and singing of bawdy subjects: drink, seduction, and corrupt clergy. *Passions of our Lord the Pope of the Romans according to the Gold and Silver Marks* was an outstanding and tasteless example. As often as not goliards ended their days at the end of a rope, or worse.

Prose was also popular by the fifteenth century, particularly in the chronicles of men like Froissart and Chastellain. Vernacular commentaries on religious and political subjects also appeared. Philippe de Commynes's *Memoirs*, for instance. The older forms remained and grew even more popular. In Paris, François Villon carried on the goliardic tradition, and like the goliards, remained just one jump ahead of the law until finally he was destroyed by it.

ART AND ARCHITECTURE

As we have seen, Suger of Saint-Denis introduced Gothic, the architectural style which replaced Romanesque in the twelfth century. It incorporated the pointed arch, cross- or rib-vault, flying buttress and rose window. Churchmen such as Suger and Bishop Maurice de Sully of Notre-Dame inspired the Gothic; less well known are the names of its architects: Pierre de Montreuil for Saint-Denis and Sens, Jean Langlois for Troyes, and Jean de Challes for Notre-Dame. Gothic dominated well into the Renaissance, until Michelangelo and Bramante revolutionized church architecture with Saint Peter's Basilica in Rome.

The Gothic church illuminated the Bible for the illiterate faithful: the church buildings became the Bible of the Poor, as Henry Adams made clear in his famous book *Chartres*. Every statue, window, gargoyle, and carving informed and reminded the worshipper of the essentials of Christianity. St Peter held a key; Christ raised his fingers in benediction; rose windows described in their colours the indescribable beauty of the

The tympanum at Chartres

Divine; other stained glass told biblical and inspirational stories; and the gargoyles reminded the wicked that terrible beasts waited to tear the flesh of the damned. Religious manuscripts were illuminated in order to shed the light of glory on the word of God. François Villon had his illiterate mother say: 'I am a poor, old woman who knows nothing, who cannot read. But in church I see Paradise painted, and Hell where the damned boil.' In time, similar techniques, materials, and probably designers, came to be employed in the construction of châteaux and the decorating of secular windows and manuscripts – Books of Hours in particular – and often for the same purposes.

THE CHURCH

By removing Clement V to Avignon in 1307, Philip IV set in motion events which Gallicanized the fifteenth-century Church in France. French influence at Avignon remained considerable after Clement V. Every pope between Clement, who died in 1314, and Urban VI, elected in 1378, was French; and of 134 cardinals created in those six decades, 116 came from France. The Italians thought they should own the papacy, and when it returned to Rome in the 1370s they determined to remove French influence. The outcome was the Great Schism, with popes elected at both Rome and Avignon. Charles V had the Sorbonne declare for Avignon, while the Holy Roman Emperor backed Rome. All Europe divided over support of the two papacies, and for a time it looked as if the ancient unitary concept of Church and Christian civilization would be broken in Europe. In France it was.

With the tiara restored permanently to Rome, the Conciliar movement (the idea that councils of cardinals are superior to popes) took root in France. Jean Gerson was among the strongest Conciliar advocates. The issue came up in Councils at Constance (1415), Pavia (1423), and Basle (1431); papal bulls were issued and episcopal rebuttals circulated. In the end, papal supremacy triumphed in Europe; but Charles VII issued the Pragmatic Sanction of Bourges in 1438, whereby the French clergy were by law made independent of the papacy. This established Conciliarism in France. Later, Louis XI revoked the Sanction; Gallicanism (the church dependent not on the pope but on the king of France) had triumphed all the same. The tendency was too well-seated to disappear; Gallicans believed that the government was devoted to the Catholic faith, and preferred its suzerainty to Rome's. Gallicanism disappeared only when the state was thoroughly secularized; even then it reappeared on such bizarre occasions as the infamous treason trial of Captain Alfred Dreyfus at the end of the nineteenth century.

'SEE THAT THERE ARE NO SLIP-UPS'

This was the favourite admonition given to his servants by Louis XI, the Spider (1461–1483), probably the greatest of the Valois kings, when he sent them off to execute his policies. Francis I, builder of the fabulous Château Chambord, shone brighter than Louis XI, but with less substance. Louis grew up in the latter days of the Hundred Years War. As dauphin to an impoverished, war-racked crown he acquired a taste for streamlining government, improving the economy and centralizing royal authority – which meant bending the great territorial lords to his will. As king he had the energy to implement these authoritarian tastes.

Louis had no great love for his father, Charles VII, not least because he resented the king's mistress, Agnes Sorel, perhaps the greatest beauty of her era. Louis led an abortive rebellion against Charles when he was only sixteen. Afterward Charles was sufficiently suspicious to deny Louis access to his *apanage* of Dauphiné until the prince was into his twenties. Once in charge there, Louis's 'advanced' ideas of government made enemies for him among the great feudal lords. Charles took their side and Louis fled to the protection of his uncle, Duke Philip the Good of Burgundy. There he remained until the crown was his in 1461.

While at Philip's court Louis became friends with Francesco Sforza, duke of Milan, and Philippe de Commynes, Philip's, and later his own, principal advisor on state affairs. He also made the acquaintance of a future enemy, Charles, count of Charolais, heir to the Burgundian throne. At this court Louis learnt the Machiavellian skills which when he was king would earn for him the sobriquet 'the Spider'. He had to: in Burgundy, at Genappe, he was 'the man without a place', and his uncle Philip's benevolence extended only so far.

Louis XI accomplished many things, but nothing more significant than finally subduing the great feudal lords. After Louis, the French nobility never again dominated the crown as they had in his father's reign. In 1465, after four years of his 'shabby, toilsome, efficient, saddle-hardened' government, carried on by 'fearfully hard-working and fearfully intelligent and disgustingly low-born fellows', the French feudal lords had had enough of Louis.

Led by the duke of Bourbon, they issued a propaganda manifesto on behalf of the great lords, the lesser nobility, the churchmen and the poor, on behalf, in short, of the *bein publique* (public welfare), proclaiming their intention 'to remedy injustices and to sweep away taxes which were driving the realm to perdition'. The collaborators were the dukes of Berry (Louis's brother), Brittany, Nemours and Calabria, the counts of Charolais, Anjou, Armagnac, St Pol and Dunois, and various barons. When Louis discussed their grievances with them, it soon was clear that this, like other noble uprisings, had much less of *bien publique* at heart than it did of *bien particulaire* (private welfare).

Louis met the challenge. Through his intrigues, calculations, manipulations and straight military manoeuvres and battles he put the feudal lords in their place. By his death in 1483 all of France bent the knee to royal authority more completely than ever before: Burgundy, Normandy, even Brittany succumbed in the end; and Louis added Picardy, Anjou and Bar in the north, and Roussillon, Cerdagne and Provence in the south (the latter bringing with it Marseille, a great prize) to the royal holdings. Paul Murray Kendall, Louis's biographer, wrote: 'In the south of France, once swarming with semi-independent lords, there remained no prince to defy royal law.'

Louis used professional civil servants to enhance government administration, tax collection and law enforcement and adjudication. He encouraged trade and new industry, and at his death had far-reaching plans for developing 'famous Marseille', for abolishing the irrational and uneconomic local customs which confounded economic development, and for creating a national standard for laws, regulations, weights and measures.

The king maintained a network of diplomats, special investigators, secret agents and officers of foreign states in his pay throughout his feudality and Europe, through which he was kept informed and on top of the complicated foreign relations which characterized his reign. Through a combination of intimidation, manipulation and warfare (as a last resort), Louis broke the Anglo-Burgundian connection and brought the last great independent territorial princes (Burgundy and Brittany) to heel. Philippe de Commynes recounted Louis's policies in intimate detail. The Emperor Charles V called the Commynes *Memoirs* 'a textbook for kings'.

Louis XI was a bridge between the Middle Ages and the Renaissance. He was a medieval king in that he ruled from horseback, convened his lords as advisors, believed that where possible the king should live on his private revenue, and hunted incessantly during which time he often lived rough. But Louis also was a Renaissance prince. He attended to trade and commercial regulation, made foreign policy into an art, opened government to commoners of ability, exercised his mind vigorously (he corresponded with scholars, and as dauphin enrolled as a student at the University of Louvain), commissioned a 'modern' Loire château (Langeais, designed by Jean Bourré), and may even have learnt the new game of tennis which was all the rage at the court in Burgundy. Louis's 'new' ideas were not altogether new. But in the fifteenth century, for the first time in six centuries, at a time when feudalism was dying of its own decrepitude, they could be implemented. Significantly, in 1484, a year after Louis's death, the Estates met and for the first time included a Third Estate representing the commons of France.

After he died, the nobility tried to overturn Louis's accomplishments. They had only limited success, despite the fact that his son, Charles VIII (1483–1498), ruled neither wisely nor well. On the strength of bad advice and against the urging of his much abler sister, Anne of Beaujeu, Charles embroiled France in the Italian wars. In consequence he lost Roussillon, Cerdagne, Artois, Franche Comté (part of Burgundy), and 'gold by the shovelful'. Charles died unlamented at Amboise, replaced by his distant cousin, Louis XII (1498–1515).

Out of weakness, Louis XII practised docility. 'He had a kind heart,' wrote the historian Albert Guérard. Under Louis 'the country knew internal peace: no "foolish war", no "League for the Public Weal". Prosperity was abounding: his reign and the first decade under Francis I are among the happiest moments in France's chequered life.' Not for nothing was Louis XII known as the Father of his People. Tranquillity reigned along with him; but inevitably it could not last.

CHAPTER FIVE

Renaissance, Reformation and Raison D'État
1515–1661

It is difficult to make sense of France between 1515 and 1661. There seems to be no symmetry, no inner historical logic. The Renaissance (when, according to eighteenth-century writers, France was rescued from barren medievalism) gives way to savage religious civil war which is followed by a cynical and pragmatic opportunism. Apparently, there is only confusion. But appearances can be deceptive.

The Renaissance

The Renaissance, characterized by the rebirth of classical learning and humanism (ancient wisdom allied with human reason) and new forms in art, literature, learning and politics, percolated out of fourteenth-century Italy and climaxed in France during the reign of Francis I (1515–1547). This king seemed the perfect model of a Renaissance prince. In the words of Guillaume Budé, whose patron he was, Francis 'is educated in letters ... and also possesses a natural eloquence, wit, tact, pleasant manners; nature, in short, has endowed him with the rarest gifts of body and mind. ...' Francis possessed *virtu*; he was born to rule; he was, simply, a Renaissance prince.

Francis I

The king patronized Leonardo da Vinci, Andrea del Sarto, Benvenuto Cellini and Jean Clouet, built or remodelled châteaux at Chambord and Blois in the Loire Valley and Fontainebleau near Paris, and commissioned Pierre Lescot to renovate the ancient Louvre in Paris, a palace made by Philip Augustus out of a castle erected by Hugh Capet.

71

The Francis I staircase at Blois

Francis made Budé Master of the King's Library, a collection which formed the foundation of the Bibliothèque Nationale, today one of the great research libraries of the world; set up four regius professorships – the *lecteurs royaux* – at the University of Paris; and encouraged humanism in theology and letters. Francis tried, without success, to lure the great Dutch humanist, Erasmus, to France, and created an atmosphere of sufficient intellectual freedom to encourage Rabelais to produce his humanistic satires, *Gargantua* and *Pantagruel*.

Renaissance 'types' included the prince, artist and scholar, but also the merchant, royal servant (noble or otherwise), courtesan and intellectual. Francis was singularly fortunate in the 'types' around him, some of whom were his relatives and all of whom were useful. Jean de Beaune, Baron de Semblançay, a merchant, directed royal financial administration until his fall from favour. The oddly named Anne de Montmorency, Constable of France, espoused a Machiavellian view of princely power which suited Francis's self-image perfectly. The queen mother, Louise of Savoy, intelligent, educated, even gifted, twice acted as regent for Francis and in 1529 negotiated the Peace of Cambrai on his behalf. She took a 'liberal' view of religious heresy, as did her daughter Marguerite of Angoulême.

Marguerite too was gifted, a writer, foreign-policy formulator, and author of a poem, *Mirror of the Sinful Soul*, which the Sorbonne blacklisted – on a technicality, they hastily assured the king, who resented any apparent affronts to royalty. Anne of Heilly, duchess of Étampes, the most important of several royal mistresses, was described by the imperial ambassador as 'the real president of the king's most private and intimate council'. She played politics with the best of them, and was a patron of the arts despite not being on cordial terms with Cellini. Queen Claude also played her part by providing Francis with abundant heirs. But that was hardly a function of the Renaissance spirit.

PRINCELY STATECRAFT

In 1518 Budé wrote *L'Institution du Prince*, which urged Francis to be an absolute ruler. The king followed this advice, or tried to. The *Parlement* of Paris, a law court and quasi-legislative body and the most important of a number of *parlements* throughout France, was forced to give in to Francis over the Concordat of Bologna. By acquiescing to this agreement with the papacy, the *Parlement* enabled Francis to bend the Gallican church and its theologians of the Sorbonne to his will also. Meanwhile he centralized patronage, which increased royal control over the provincial nobility. They and the higher clergy were thereby made more susceptible to royal pressure. The king relied upon assemblies of notables for counsel and dispensed with the Estates General, a body he considered not only useless but dangerous. The structure of royal government was still too feudal to provide for absolute rule, but Francis at least took a step in that direction.

The king's foreign policy did not quite achieve its aims either, but in form did lay the foundations of the *raison d'état* style of later French statecraft. Francis's policy centred upon rivalry with England (Henry VIII) and Spain and the Holy Roman Empire (Charles V) over Italy and the Low Countries. He fought five wars in 1515, 1526, 1527–29, 1536–38 and 1542, and juggled his rivals diplomatically, seeking alliance with first one and then the other. Francis considered alliance too with German Protestant princes against Charles after 1530, and in

1533 made a treaty with Sultan Suleiman of the Ottoman Empire, Charles's great enemy in the Balkans. This shocked Christian opinion and did Francis no good at home. Other treaties, more acceptable but of no particular advantage – save for the first – included the Concordat of Bologna (1516), the Field of the Cloth of Gold (1520), Cambrai (1529) and Crépy-en-Laonnois (1544).

Francis's constant objectives were control of the duchies of Milan and Burgundy, and, until Charles was elected, of the Holy Roman Empire. What he got was a victory at Marignano in 1515; better relations with the papacy, but also greater control over the Church in France from the Concordat; improved relations with Henry VIII out of his approach to the German princes; brief security for Normandy but the loss of his Italian claims out of Cambrai; and from Crépy-en-Laonnois the promise that through marriage his third son, the duke of Orléans, would inherit the duchy of Milan – which did not happen because Orléans died before the marriage took place.

Otherwise, nothing much came of the treaty with the Sultan, and Francis was captured by Charles at Pavia in 1526 and forced to pay a huge ransom as well as leave his sons in Madrid as hostages. The meeting with Henry VIII at Val Doré near Calais, the Field of the Cloth of Gold, was a great but empty gesture; two Renaissance princes out to cut a figure postured and pranced, erected gorgeous tents, wore dazzling clothes, put on splendid tournaments, and possibly engaged in a royal wrestling match which French records say Francis won handily, but which English records do not mention. Then they went home. Nothing of any lasting significance had taken place.

Meanwhile, the cost to France of having Francis on the throne mounted. There were war debts and general social and economic deterioration, a condition blamed on corruption rather than on the increased taxes, steady inflation and rising population without an attendant increase in productivity which really caused it. Francis borrowed heavily from Parisian and Lyonnais bankers in order to keep going, which mortgaged the throne. By selling revenue-producing offices he created a hereditary bureaucracy and thus mortgaged the future of royal administration. Sale of offices extended patronage and produced revenue in the short run; in the long run it extended 'bastard feudalism' as the fundamental structure of political relationships. This guaranteed the formation of new power blocs across the country.

Francis died in 1547 in debt to the equivalent of nearly a year's royal revenue. By then, too, the peasantry had suffered from general impoverishment, and conflict between royal officials, traditional landed nobles and higher clergy was on the rise.

STATECRAFT AND MARRIAGE

Royal marriage was traditionally an important element of statecraft. Francis continued the tradition. His sister, Marguerite of Angoulême, married Henry of Albret of Navarre, allying that Pyrénéean kingdom to the Valois house. Marguerite's grandson became Henry IV, the first Bourbon king of France. The dauphin (Henry II) married Catherine de Medici, who lived to be queen mother to three kings through whom she virtually ruled France for thirty years. One of the three, Francis II, married Mary Stuart of Scotland, thus linking France with England's most ancient enemy.

After Francis I

Henry II (1547–1559) ruled neither wisely nor well. He kept his father's foreign policy, thus weakening France internally with more war and more debt, and made no more substantive efforts at fiscal reforms than had Francis. In 1559 peace was agreed at Cateau-Cambrésis, ending France's long war with the Empire. But while jousting in the tournament celebrating this peace, the hapless Henry was speared and killed. It was probably an accident rather than the assassination many romanticists later claimed; it was an ill-omen all the same. Henry's limitations were many compared to his father, and that his mistress, Diane of Poitiers, is best remembered as a model for magnificent classic statuary (the duchess of Étampes at least had a brain) may be a more than adequate epitaph for him. Diane occupied the Château Chaumont-sur-Loire, which Catherine de Medici owned. Henry made no contribution to the arts beyond visiting Diane. Francis II (1559–1560) survived little more than a year, and after his death Mary Stuart returned to Scotland to become a thorn in the side of

Elizabeth I of England. Charles IX (1560–1574) then entered upon his reign, just in time for the half-century of religious warfare sometimes called the Era of Politics by Assassination.

The Reformation

The era opened with religious reformation, but religion soon sparked conflict which involved ancient issues of class and politics. With access to the new printing technology, all sides made effective use of propaganda in focusing the views of people of every class and condition. Opinions turned into bigotry; bigotry became persecution; and the wars began. Louis Le Roy, a Parisian humanist writing in the mid-sixteenth century, thought spreading religious sectarianism was a malady worse than venereal disease which was also on the increase.

The Protestant Reformation had many causes, but its catalyst was Martin Luther, Augustinian monk in Wittenburg, challenging Roman orthodoxy and being excommunicated for his pains. This was the work of Pope Leo X, backed by the new Holy Roman Emperor, Charles V. The Empire was mainly German and Italian, and Germany was full of petty principalities and semi-autonomous merchant cities which chafed under papal taxes and interference in their affairs by an absentee ruler who, in any case, was a Spaniard. The princes began it, rebelling in the name of their rights and their nationality (discovered when Luther translated the Bible into German). Their peasants followed suit, which led the princes to conclude that Luther's teachings meant freedom for princes but obedience for peasants. He agreed, and the peasants were put down with great bloodshed in 1525–26. Then the princes organized themselves into a league poised against Charles, and made war against him until the Peace of Augsburg in 1555. Augsburg provided that a prince could decide if his realm would be Catholic or Lutheran. For the first time Christian Europe was divided into two religious parts, both having official status. Soon the French were right in the middle of it.

REFORMATION IN FRANCE

The immediate impact of the Reformation was muted in France. But impact there was all the same. In 1519 the Sorbonne condemned

Luther's writings out of hand; in 1523 the *Parlement* seized all Lutheran books from Paris booksellers; and in 1526 Louise of Savoy ordered the extermination from France of the 'evil and damnable heresy of Luther'. The queen mother's career as a liberal on reform was over. That same year a weaver from Meaux became the first French Protestant martyr. Meanwhile, Bishop Briçonnet of Meaux (Semblançay's nephew) undertook to envangelize his diocese and invited famous preachers like Guillaume Farel to take part in the process. Jacques Lefévre of Étaples translated the scriptures into French and published humanistic textual criticism. Marguerite of Angoulême wrote evangelical verse, corresponded with Briçonnet, and patronized and protected humanists like Étaples. Francis I contemplated an anti-Habsburg alliance with the Protestant princes.

Then, in 1534, the Affair of the Placards produced scurrilous anti-Catholic propaganda in Paris and throughout the country, driving orthodox mobs to frenzy. The king decided that Lutheranism was both heresy and sedition, and a wave of repression and persecution began, involving both the burning of heretics and the censoring of heretical writings. Many French reformers headed for cover. Among them was a humanist evangelical and former University of Paris law student from Noyon, Jean Calvin.

Jean Calvin

In 1536 Calvin published his reformist doctrines in *Institution of the Christian Religion*. In 1541 he was in Geneva undertaking to establish a church according to the sacraments, litany, patterns of worship, catechism and discipline of *Institution*. Within a decade and a half it was achieved and integrated with city government so that Geneva became a theocracy. Once in power, these 'Calvinists' dealt summarily with opposition. (Servetus was condemned and burnt for criticism.) In 1557 French exiles flooded into Geneva; in 1560 they flooded back as Calvinist missionaries. Royal edicts condemning their activities had no effect on the traffic either way.

Persecution produced martyrs, whose blood, Calvin preached, was the seed of the true church. Jean Crespin's *Book of the Martyrs*, periodically updated between 1554 and 1609, was effective propaganda for Calvinism in France. By 1570 twelve hundred Protestant churches dotted France: heavily in Normandy, Poitou (in La Rochelle Protestants actually outnumbered Catholics), Dauphiné and Languedoc; lightly in Picardy, Champagne and Burgundy; and not at all in Brittany and the Vendée where, the local clergy feared, Christianity of any sort was as unknown among the inhabitants as among the natives of the New World.

HUGUENOTS

French Protestants, mostly Calvinist, were called Huguenots. No one seems to know why. Opinion on who they were varied widely. Gaspard de Saulx-Tavannes, Marshal of France, believed they mainly were townsmen, vagabonds, women and children; Jean Michieli, Venetian diplomat and spy, said they were the nobility 'under forty years old'; Blaise of Monluc, ultra-Catholic Lieutenant of Gascony, pointed to royal officials and financiers in his region; Florimond de Raemond, judge, believed schoolmasters had much to answer for, having taught pupils to read, think and act for themselves; in Gaillac, rich merchants were blamed for Protestantism; and in Toulouse, one judge held that it was all the fault of rich young men and beautiful young women – which judgement contains some interesting implications. Clearly Huguenot heresy aroused much excitement and hostility, but it seemed to be a tidal wave which nothing could hold back. In 1560 Charles IX issued a general amnesty to Protestants, mute testimony to the failed legal repression of Huguenots.

CIVIL WAR

By 1561 the Huguenots believed victory for Protestantism in France was imminent. That summer they sang psalms in Rouen, Toulouse, and throughout urban France. Many Huguenots ran printing presses (like Jean Crespin in Paris) and Protestant literature spread widely. It was often vicious and satiric: *Muster of the Archers at the Popinjay* (an attack on the papacy); or the woodcut, widely circulated, called *The Great Marmite Overturned*, which showed the pope and his minions trying to prop up Church wealth (a great stew pot) whilst the light of the Holy Gospel inspired common people to pull it down. This propaganda frightened the orthodox as it revealed the 'menacing public face of the blossoming new faith'. Catholic-Huguenot animosities grew – and provided the perfect arena for old clan feuds and traditions of violence.

Civil war began in 1562 when the prince of Condé raised the Huguenot standard at Orléans, claiming that the fight was for both religious freedom and the political rights of princes of the blood. Calvin approved this. Anne de Montmorency, the Constable, led royal forces against them, aided by his eldest son and his old enemy, the ultra-Catholic duke of Guise. Montmorency's Châtillon nephews (Gaspard of Coligny, Admiral of France, and his brother Odet of Châtillon, count-bishop of Beauvais and a cardinal) and the Constable's younger son were in the Huguenot camp. The war soon became a Montmorency-Guise struggle. The aim of the civil war, whatever justifications were stated, was to seize power.

Catherine de Medici

The queen mother tried to contain the crisis. Intelligent, determined, and politically supple and devious, Catherine was also tolerant and extended the olive branch to Protestants at court and in the country. Nothing worked, and the English (backing the Huguenots from their base at Le Havre) and the Spanish (invading Protestant-held areas of the Low Countries) were soon involved in the civil war. Catherine personally rallied the army to defend their new young king against 'English traitors'.

The battle of Dreux in 1562 was a narrow victory won by the duke of Guise. Catherine thereupon organized a peace which granted some Huguenot demands. Between 1564 and 1566 she took King Charles around the country, reinforcing loyalties and damping down disputes. Unfortunately, she met with the Spanish duke of Alba in 1565, which the Huguenots read as a plot against them. The war resumed in 1567.

SECTARIAN VIOLENCE

Dreux, Jarnac and Montcontour were the only major pitched battles of the civil war, and there were a few sieges: Rouen and Orléans, for

example. Mainly the war was outbreaks of mob violence and acts of
assassination and sabotage, which fed the propaganda of both sides, and
which in turn fed hatred and fuelled the violence.

In 1563 the duke of Guise was assassinated; in 1568 a Huguenot
nobleman was slaughtered by masked men outside his home in Mâcon;
the prince of Condé was killed in 1569 at Jarnac.

In 1562 the *parlement* of Toulouse legalized the slaughter of heretics;
Huguenots everywhere committed sacrilege against the sacred host,
statues of the Virgin, the Crucifix, holy oil and fonts and holy-water
basins; and mobs of the orthodox frequently fell upon Huguenots and
tore them to pieces. All of this was faithfully recorded in pamphlets and
broadsheets. King Charles once rebuked the duke of Guise for reading
such a broadsheet during Mass.

ST BARTHOLOMEW'S DAY

On 18 August 1572, Henry of Navarre, Condé's cousin and a
Huguenot, married Charles IX's sister, Marguerite, at a ceremony in
Paris. Many Protestant leaders attended. On 22 August with the
newlyweds still in Paris, Admiral Coligny was wounded in an assassination attempt. The next day Huguenot nobles threatened retaliation
against the royal family, whom they accused of betrayal. In a panic,
Charles and his mother consented to a scheme to finish off Coligny and
other Huguenot nobles with him. Henry of Navarre saved himself only
by promising to return to orthodoxy, a promise he abandoned once he
was away from Paris.

The scheme was put into play early on 24 August, which was St
Bartholomew's day. A Paris mob got wind of this, took it as a sign, and
began slaughtering every Huguenot they could find. Thousands died in
Paris and elsewhere as the news spread. The result was disastrous. Never
again would Huguenots trust the word of a Valois; and never again
would Paris Catholics offer the olive branch to Protestants.

THE CATHOLIC LEAGUE

When Henry III (1574–1589) succeeded his brother Charles IX, he
reckoned the time had come for concessions to the Huguenots. The
Catholic backlash was immediate and a league was formed to defy the

crown and reopen the war against Protestantism. Henry barely saved the day by naming himself head of the Catholic League and declaring war against the Huguenots. The League was then disbanded.

In the 1580s Henry's questionable court favourites, called sneeringly *les mignons* (literally, 'the sweets', but meant here to imply unnatural sexuality), and economic dislocations and heavy taxes accumulated by the civil war, brought royal prestige to an all-time low. The Catholic League revived and mobilized not only country aristocrats but lower-class fanatics in the towns. The League put forward the cardinal of Bourbon (a Guise) as a rival heir to the throne to Henry of Navarre, and Pope Sixtus V backed them by denying Navarre's right to succeed. This revived Gallican resentment of Roman interference in French affairs, and weakened the cardinal's candidacy.

In 1587 Queen Elizabeth of England, tired of Mary Stuart's continuous intrigues against her, allowed the Scottish queen, who was her prisoner, to be executed. The next year Philip II of Spain, partly in retaliation, launched a massive naval expedition, the Armada, against England. It was wrecked by Admiral John Hawkins, Francis Drake, an English fleet, and a strong wind propitiously blowing eastward so that the duke of Alba could not sail out from the Spanish Netherlands as reinforcement against the English warships. Catherine de Medici died that year, and Henry was murdered in 1589 by the League in revenge for having arranged the death of the duke of Guise and his brother, the Cardinal of Bourbon. Henry of Navarre at once claimed the throne as Henry IV (1589–1610), the first Bourbon monarch. Sitting securely upon it was another matter.

Henry IV

Henry's task was daunting enough: to restore political order, rebuild a war-ravaged country, reconcile contending forces, sort through the foreign-policy complications created by religious war, actually secure his throne, and make himself popular.

The new king was shrewd and able, and above all a pragmatist. He never actually said 'Paris is worth a mass', as older histories maintain, but he did abjure the abjuration of his 'conversion' in 1572. This, and a number of military successes against the Catholic League, finally got him to Paris in 1594. Thereafter he even tolerated the Jesuits, the religious order founded by Ignatius Loyola with the support of François Xavier, as the cutting edge of the Catholic response to Protestantism. Naturally his former Huguenot comrades were not pleased. They distrusted the newly Romanised monarch, and to ease their minds, he arranged the Edict of Nantes in 1598 which gave political and religious protection to Huguenots. Henry also made a Protestant, the duke of Sully, his principal advisor. For a few years something like peace settled over the bitterly divided country.

The depth of Henry's Catholicism is suspect. His foreign policy was pro-Dutch, which is to say pro-Protestant, and anti-Spanish, which is to say anti-Habsburg and anti-Catholic. Throughout he held his cards close to his chest, and with the adept seigneur of Villeroy as his foreign minister, neither Spain nor Rome knew that Henry subsidized the Dutch and their Protestant allies. Meanwhile, he procured a papal sanction for his divorce and his subsequent remarriage to Marie de Medici in 1600.

Henry appeared more forthright on matters touching royal authority. He overrode the *parlements* and other courts regularly, intervened arbitrarily in provincial affairs, dictated marriage alliances among the great houses (thereby keeping the nobility at each other's throats instead of at the king's), and used more 'new' men and fewer old nobles as royal servants than any king before him: Villeroy, Sully and Brulart of Sillery, the chancellor, among others. This practice advanced the *noblesse de la robe*, the clerical and state bureaucracy, which became a mainstay of royal absolutism during his reign. The traditional nobles, who began to fear for their power, prestige and wealth, were therefore

not drawn to Henry. Moreover, as the expanding *robe* nobility had to provide for their progeny just as did their landed counterparts, a new venue was opened for venality which in the long run could only weaken absolutism.

It is not clear that Henry achieved much of lasting value by making royal authority absolute, nor did he make substantive improvements in fiscal or administrative operations. The sale of offices continued as did tax farming, and inflation was still treated as a problem of corruption without considering that economic factors might lie beyond it. Taxes too were increased and their burden distributed without regard for long-term effects. This was not the king's fault alone: the *parlements* and *cours des aides*, courts of registry with power to block tax and other reforms, often did exactly that when class interests were, or appeared to be, threatened. One minor triumph was Sully's success in ensuring that the Dutch subsidies were subtracted from France's debt to England.

Both Henry and Sully undertook economic rebuilding by increasing agricultural production (Sully) and encouraging manufacturing (Henry). The silk industry of Nîmes and Lyon, glass and pottery works in Paris and Nevers, and various metal, tapestry (such as Gobelins in Paris), carpet and linen manufactories were started up with Henry's support. Sully oversaw the recovery of swamplands in Bas-Médoc (the Gironde) and worked to remove export duties on corn to encourage trade.

Perhaps this first Bourbon king was not sufficiently open in the pursuit of his policies. At any rate, in 1610 he was assassinated while his carriage was stuck in Paris traffic. The assassin, François Ravaillac, thought he was performing an act both patriotic and Catholic. At least it was the last such act of great significance in an epoch distressingly full of terrorist acts.

Marie de Medici

Louis XIII (1610–1643) was eight when his father was killed. His mother, Marie de Medici, acted as regent and it was a surprisingly quiet time. She bought off those nobles most likely to be troublesome, arranged marriages for Louis with the Infanta Anne of Austria, and for his sister with the future Philip IV of Spain (only a temporary deviation from France's anti-Habsburg policy). Marie reaffirmed the Edict of Nantes, which helped keep the ever-suspicious Huguenots quiet, and summoned the Estates General in 1614 to help head off a revolt by the prince of Condé. When the Estates had done that, they took issue with the crown over fiscal and other reforms. The session was hastily wound up, and the Estates did not meet again until 1789, when they helped to start a revolution.

In 1617 the duke of Luynes persuaded Louis to cut the apron strings and let him, Luynes, run things. The duke succeeded only in provoking another Huguenot revolt, and was killed trying to put it down. The way to power was open for Marie de Medici's personal chaplain and advisor, Cardinal Richelieu, bishop of Luçon.

The Thirty Years War

This began as a religious war in 1618, but turned into a primarily political struggle long before it ended in stalemate in 1648 and only involved France after 1632. It also was unprecedentedly destructive, a monument to the price central Europe had to pay for the purely dynastic desires of the Holy Roman Emperor, the Habsburg Ferdinand II, who pressed the war as emperor solely in order to re-establish Habsburg rule in Germany. The war began when Protestant Bohemian nobles threw two Jesuits representing Ferdinand (who also was king of Bohemia) from a high window in Hradčany Castle in Prague. A propaganda war ensued. The Catholics claimed that the Jesuits survived because angels caught them up and bore them gently to earth; the Protestants countered that they had survived by falling into a dung heap. Whatever the truth, the war was on, and in 1620 imperial forces crushed the Bohemians at the battle of White Mountain. This should have ended the war. But the mercenaries Ferdinand hired for his huge army had caught the scent of plunder, and they continued the war on their own. The Emperor now used them as an excuse to launch a campaign of reconquest.

White Mountain made the Huguenots feel insecure, and they rose in the rebellion which killed the duke of Luynes. From 1624 onward the war spread, and after the Edict of Restitution in 1629, by which Ferdinand declared his intention to make all Germany bend the knee to the Catholic emperor, France became involved in the war – but only indirectly.

Cardinal Richelieu and Raison d'État

Richelieu, who had dissembled so well that until 1632 it appeared he was willing to give the Habsburgs a free hand in Europe, now unfolded the policy which justly won for him the reputation of the first great exponent in France of *raison d'état*. Everything Richelieu did was meant to further the interests of France abroad, and of the French state, the royal administrative power structure through which government operated. This was *raison d'état*. To implement it Richelieu needed to be a supreme pragmatist and dissembler, and an expert manager of the royal person. He was all of this, and Louis, aware of the cardinal's great gifts, stood loyally behind him even when he chafed at being 'managed'. For his part the cardinal was always straightforward with the king, if with no one else.

FOREIGN POLICY

Richelieu was subtle, even ambiguous. He arranged a marriage between Henrietta Maria, Louis's sister, and Charles Stuart of England, which recognized an Anglo-French anti-Spanish venture in the Netherlands. In 1626 he made a treaty with Spain while Dutch Protestants made peace with Spain through English mediation. Then came the Edict of Restitution, and as Habsburg domination of Europe was not in the French interest, Richelieu offered subsidies to the Lutheran King Gustavus Adolphus II of Sweden, to enter the war and fight against the Emperor. He paid subsidies to other Protestant princes as well after Gustavus was dead, to keep the war going. All the while a Habsburg was queen of France.

In the 1630s, French foreign policy for the future emerged: Balance of Power, that is, the idea that no one state should dominate Europe, and that this might be prevented by juggling combinations of states. Ironically, only the French themselves overturned the balance, or

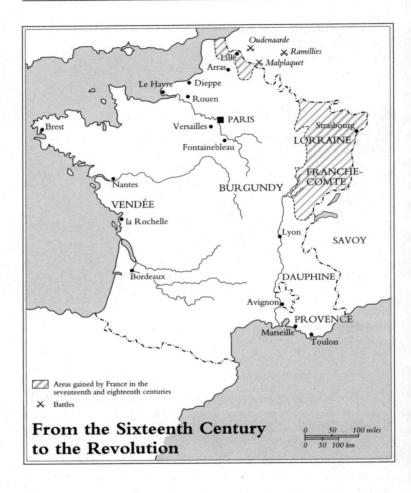

Oudenaarde
✕ Ramillies
✕ Malplaquet
Lille
Arras
Le Havre • Dieppe
• Rouen
Strasbourg
Brest
Versailles • ■ PARIS
LORRAINE
Fontainebleau
FRANCHE-
COMTE
Nantes
BURGUNDY
VENDÉE
• la Rochelle
Lyon
SAVOY
Bordeaux
DAUPHINE
Avignon •
PROVENCE
Marseille •
Toulon

▨ Areas gained by France in the
seventeenth and eighteenth centuries
✕ Battles

From the Sixteenth Century
to the Revolution

0   50   100 miles
0   50 100 km

sought to, between 1648 and 1815. Each time the other powers
employed Richelieu's conception to put things right. The essence of
Richelieu's policy was articulated two hundred years later by the British
foreign secretary Lord Palmerston when he said: 'In foreign policy
there are no permanent alliances, only permanent interests.'

GOVERNMENT

Richelieu was little better here than were his predecessors. He used patronage as a means of control, and once it was distributed used it to squeeze money out of those dependent upon it. This alienated a significant portion of the body politic. Meanwhile, he did little to curb the recalcitrance, or limit the traditions of independence, of the *parlements* and *cours des aides*. Their periodic rebellions against centralized fiscal reforms did not cease. On the other hand, the cardinal raised the *intendants*, servants working directly for the crown and with power to interfere directly in the operations of the regular bureaucracy in any part of the country (not unlike Charlemagne's *missi dominici* in this regard), to new and greater powers. They now became a permanent fixture of government, and by 1642 were responsible for fiscal administration, tax collection and supervising the bureaucracy.

The *intendants'* task, or tasks, required the best and brightest that France could produce. Doors opened wider for talent, strengthening Richelieu by further weakening the traditional nobility, but in turn weakening the cardinal by strengthening the resentments of this nobility and the older elements of bureaucracy. It was no different from Henry IV's time. Nevertheless, through his professionals Richelieu undertook developments in trade and industry, built up the navy and attempted administrative reforms. However, the system of *intendants* fell under Richelieu's concept of patronage, and many of them were his 'creatures', as they came to be called, creating jealousy throughout the government. Eventually the *intendants* became like other *noblesse de la robe:* rigid, self-serving and hereditary. But until then they had much to do with strengthening the qualities of absolutism in the French state.

FRANCE OVERSEAS

In the sixteenth and seventeenth centuries, France joined other European nations in overseas expansion. Jacques Cartier explored eastern Canada; a cartography school was opened in Dieppe; France started trade with Portuguese-claimed areas in southern America; Henry IV established a great naval base at Toulon on the Mediterranean; overseas commercial treaties were made with the Hanseatic League, Denmark and Sweden; and finally, colonies were laid down in

Canada, plantations in the West Indies, and trading factories in India. French colonialism would ebb and flow over the next three and a half centuries. In Richelieu's time its tendency was to flow.

North America was an important beneficiary of the 'flow'. French fur trappers followed Cartier, and soon Québec was established, along with French settlements in the Ohio river valley. Québec became an integral part of Canada, and maintained strong cultural ties with France, even after it was amalgamated into British Canada. Canada is officially bilingual today, as a result. Other French communities did not fare so well at British hands. The British took over Acadia (Nova Scotia) in 1713, and expelled the Acadians, who fled to Louisiana. In time, 'Acadian' was perverted into 'Cajun', by which the descendents of these émigrés are now known. Louisiana was the southern tip of a territory that spread as far as the Pacific Northwest, and which Napoleon Bonaparte sold to the United States in 1803 (the 'Louisiana Purchase'). French traditions remain in the name Louisiana, in *la vieux Carré*, or French Quarter, in New Orleans, and in Cajun culture itself.

REBELLION

Richelieu's years of supremacy also saw sporadic rebellions, of a religious or social nature, against the government. Rebellion was endemic by the early seventeenth century. The Huguenot wars ended finally in the 1640s, but their great cost had forced tax increases which townsmen, peasants and nobles alike frequently rebelled against paying. One element was added, and if it was not new it was at least more prominent than in the past: the urban poor and the peasants were linking up in opposition to nobility and the upper bourgeoisie.

Revolts were endemic, but one deserves special mention simply because of its bizarre ending. In 1641 the count of Soissons led a rebellious army, including some Spaniards, into eastern France, and won an impressive victory at La Marfée. As the smoke cleared, the count paused to survey his triumph. He raised the visor on his helmet with his pistol and accidentally blew his brains out.

AFTER RICHELIEU

Richelieu died in 1642 and Louis XIII in 1643. Louis XIV was only five. Cardinal Mazarin emerged as first minister of the regent, Anne of Austria. They got on well and may even have been secretly married. Louis's uncle, Gaston, duke of Orléans, always a thorn in Richelieu's side, emerged now as a helpful addition to royal administration. Even so, under Mazarin France was afflicted by war and rebellion, and his tenure was only a sort of line-holding. He did successfully negotiate the French position in the Treaty of Westphalia ending the Thirty Years War in 1648, a treaty which firmly established the balance of power principle; but no sooner was it signed than the French nobles were in rebellion behind the prince of Condé (Condé rebellions against central authority had become a family tradition by this time) in an attempt to reverse the absolutist trends of the monarchy.

The Fronde was the most significant rebellion of the seventeenth century. It was also nearly the last; only the Bordeaux and Breton revolts in 1675 approached it in scale. Between 1648 and 1661 the royal army (in the later days with young Louis XIV at its head) ended the Fronde and established a royal control non-existent before in France. Mazarin died in 1661. Louis, who had not forgotten the humiliations he suffered as a boy at the hands of Fronde leaders, threw off all restraint and took France entirely into his own hands. Now the age of French absolutism began in earnest.

Did this epoch lack symmetry? Was there no inner historical logic from the accession of Francis I to the death of Mazarin? Francis I glittered without substance and planted the seeds of political and religious upheaval even as he built the great châteaux and centres of learning. Civil and religious war raged after him. Reforms succeeded only in papering over cracks in the administrative and fiscal systems. Rebels often protested against the administrative corruption and the grinding taxation. Cynical ministers vied with arrogant aristocrats to manipulate government in their own interests. There was symmetry to this era after all: the tension between the whole and its parts which had characterized French history for more than half a millennium was alive and well. There should have been a revolution, all things considered. Instead there was Louis XIV, and that which sometimes is referred to romantically, or at least nostalgically, as 'the glory that was France'.

CHAPTER SIX

'The Glory that was France'
1661–1789

In the seventeenth and eighteenth centuries, the French sought first to explain and then to order the world around them; a legacy of both the Renaissance and the religious wars. Explanation and ordering characterized philosophy and criticism, and influenced art, literature, politics and the social order, at least secondarily. But the French got more than they bargained for. What began as philosophical enquiry ended as revolution – with the aid of economic malaise, corrupt officials, a starving and deprived urban populace, and a grasping and increasingly useless aristocracy. The philosophy, thinking about the relationship – if any – between the moral and physical ordering of things, divided between the Rationalists, who thought that universal systematic knowledge was possible, and the Empiricists, who did not. Rationalism and Empiricism permeated Europe. In France Rationalism held the field, even after the thinking of Isaac Newton, the English empiricist, was distilled into a book, *Newtonisme pour les Dames*, which was read in all of the best Paris *salons*.

RATIONALISM

Michel de Montaigne and other sixteenth-century Sceptics doubted that truth was knowable, arguing that the mind is too dependent on the senses. René Descartes thought otherwise, and in *Discourse on Method* (1637) and *Metaphysical Meditations* (1641) propounded a mathematical equation into a philosophical proposition which distinguished true from false and laid the foundation for a system of universal knowledge. Descartes worked logically through his doubts until he was left with an indisputable single fact which was greater than mere fact: '*Je pense, donc je suis*' (I think, therefore I am).

Descartes left an important legacy. He invented a method by which a multitude of instances of the behaviour of a physical object can be expressed by a single mathematical formulation. Broadly speaking, Einstein owed the Theory of Relativity to Descartes. In his own thinking, however, Descartes preferred to deduce reality from primary intuition, as in 'I think, therefore I am'.

EMPIRICISM

Like the earlier Sceptics, the Empiricists doubted that everything could be known, and argued that what could, would derive from learning, not from speculation. Blaise Pascal, a mathematician like Descartes, was also his most severe empirical critic. The existence of God was the theme: Descartes's system, Pascal argued, led straight to Deism, the unsatisfactory view that God existed only in order to give the universe the initial push to set it in motion. But for Pascal human experience could be explained only through Christian revelation. Pascal was also an experimental scientist far in advance of his time, and by keeping his theology and his science so clearly separated he was adhering to the empirical tradition that not everything can be known. There were Empirical Deists, however, but they came into their own in the eighteenth century as *philosophes* of the Age of Enlightenment, such as the *libertin* (free-thinker) François La Mothe le Vayer.

BAROQUE AND CLASSICISM

These terms denote both ornamentation and refinement, and are commonly applied to the sweep of cultural forms in the seventeenth and early eighteenth centuries. The paramountcy of order and stability is recognized in Fréart de Chambray's observation: 'Proportion, symmetry and agreement of the whole with its parts, taught above all by geometry, the source and guide of all the arts.' The centre was Paris, but Toulouse and Aix-en-Provence were not far behind. The exponents of Baroque and Classicism are legion: Simon Vouet, Sébastien Bourdon, Louis Le Nain, Georges de La Tour and Claude Lorraine in painting; François Girardon, Antoine Coysevox and Pierre Puget in sculpture; Jacques Lemercier, François Mansart (his sloped, flat-topped roof form with dormer windows remains one of the most characteristic architectural features of Paris), Louis Le Vau, André Le Nôtre and Jules Hardouin-Mansart in architecture; Pierre Corneille, François de La Rochefoucauld, Cyrano de Bergerac and Jean-Baptiste Poquelin (Molière) in literature; and Jean-Baptiste Lully, court composer to Louis XIV, Jean-Philippe Rameau and François Couperin in music. There were many others.

They worked mainly because kings, the rich bourgeoisie and nobles patronized them, or hired them to adorn palace, hôtel and château. The *salon* was part of the patronage system for culture, where people such as Madame de Rambouillet, who held the most famous *salon* in Paris, gathered the best of the best, and brought together the upper bourgeoisie and aristocracy to mix in nearly perfect harmony. Later the *philosophes* would dominate the *salons*, and then the tone was less reflective. The *philosophes* wanted their ideas actually to change things.

The Sun King

Political and economic ordering was arranged by the royal government. Under Louis XIV (1643–1715), whose dazzle and grandeur – plus a fanciful costume worn in a ballet – won for him the sobriquet *Roi du Soleil* (Sun King), that government was absolute, or as near as ever it could be. In 1661 he arrested Nicolas Fouquet, superintendent of finance and among the wealthiest and most powerful men in France, on charges of corruption. He wrote to the queen mother: 'I told them that I would not have another superintendent . . . that I would work on the finances myself with the aid of faithful people who would act under my direction.' Reflecting on his kingly role years later, Louis wrote:

> Nothing is so dangerous as weakness, of whatever kind it may be. To command others, one must rise above them; and after having heard all sides, one must decide on what must be done with an open mind, always keeping in view to order or execute nothing unworthy of oneself, of the character one bears, or of the grandeur of the State . . .

He was to keep up these high standards throughout his life.

Louis was hard-working and would accept nothing less from his servants. In 1695 he warned the archbishop of Reims that his nephew, the marquis of Louvois, the war secretary, practised deception, flirted, was never at home and rarely was in his office: '. . . I do not wish to lose the services of your nephew; . . . but that for me, the welfare of the State comes before everything else.' Never had France had such a monarch. Never would it again. He was an absolute prince who believed in the trinity of order, regularity and unity.

Louis was a man for all seasons. Religious and a staunch Catholic, he backed the Church – so long as the Church remembered who ruled in France. His mistresses were numerous (in this he was a true Bourbon). The most important were Louise de La Vallière and Athénaïs de Montespan. Two wives but only one queen shared the royal bed. Marie Thérèse of Austria, who died in 1683, was the queen, and Madame de Maintenon, whom Louis married in secret because she was a commoner, was simply his wife. She was probably also his only true friend. The king was a patron of the arts, a daring, progressive and skilful warlord, an innovator in government, an able and enthusiastic diplomat, popular, courteous (he even touched his hat to chambermaids), a hunter, a gourmand, and a man with a sense of humour. The king loved Molière's comedies (a passion he shared with Madame de Maintenon), which often were performed at court.

Louis was no intellectual, but he possessed a shrewd and astute mind. He believed it was his Godly duty to work for the good of France and the French State – something which thoroughly distinguished him from medieval kings. Louis identified himself with the State and its paraphernalia, not with a personal domain called France. His unofficial motto was: '*l'État, c'est moi*' (I am the State). This was true only at first. By his death the State was able to get on reasonably well no matter what sort of monarch sat on the throne.

Colbert

Jean-Baptiste Colbert was a draper's son, honest, loyal, dedicated, brilliant and capable, and wholly dependent upon the king for his power, wealth and position. Louis described him to his mother in 1661 as the ultimate 'faithful' person. The king 'inherited' Colbert from Cardinal Mazarin, whose secretary he had been, and used him (and

Captain d'Artagnan, a musketeer upon whose character Alexandre Dumas, *père*, based his hero in *The Three Musketeers*) to arrange the downfall of the corrupt Superintendent Nicolas Fouquet.

Colbert then became finance minister. His task (under Louis's supervision) was to make France economically and administratively strong as befitted Europe's most populous nation (20 million in 1661). The minister never doubted who was in charge, once he had received this letter from Louis, sent after Colbert had argued with the king over naval expenditure: '. . . do not risk vexing me again, because after I have heard your arguments and those of your colleagues and have given my opinion on all your claims, I do not ever wish to hear further talk about it.' One warning was enough.

COLBERTISM

Self-sufficiency was widely held to be the key to power and stability. The finance minister set out to achieve it by bending and manipulating economic development. This, in principle, was Mercantilism, or as it was in France, Colbertism. Tax reforms increased revenues over expenditure. Importing textile, metal, glass, leather and other skilled workers, and promoting scientific and technical research (the Academy of Science opened in 1666), improved industry. Lowered tariff barriers improved overseas trade, and new merchant companies exploiting non-European resources (colonial development, particularly in Canada, took off in this era) for a time made France the overseas rival of Holland, Spain, Portugal and England. Such was Colbertism, and by 1671 king and finance minister had set the feet of France on the path to what Colbert, after summing up industrial activity across the country in 1669, rather breathlessly termed: 'Grandeur and Magnificence!'

Meanwhile, king and minister, but principally king, established sound, strong central government well beyond what Henry IV had attempted: a council of state with four ministers; a cooperative Paris *parlement*; provincial *parlements* brought in line with Paris and limited to judicial deliberations. Municipal government was reformed and mayoral power restricted; the nobility were replaced as *intendants* almost entirely by members of the bourgeoisie; and there was uniform administration of the law (on two occasions Louis decided lawsuits against himself).

The army was also important to Louis's concept of glory and the absolute state, and he introduced extensive modernization carried forward by hard-working, competent professionals. Colonel Martinet reformed military discipline; Monsieur de Bayonet invented a long knife which attached to the end of the musket for hand-to-hand combat; standard uniforms were supplied beginning in 1686; and an astute innovator introduced the portable field kitchen, which greatly improved morale. No longer would soldiers have to subsist on the traditional doughnut-shaped hard biscuit while in the field. Meanwhile, Marshal Sébastien Vauban, an engineer, applied scientific principles to tactics, strategy, defence and supply, and the French army, modern and formidable, was ready for war. A strong government and armed forces was part of Colbertism, in that the idea always was to strengthen the state and thereby France.

VERSAILLES

This too was the idea behind Versailles, the magnificent château twelve miles south-west of Paris. With its 10,000 rooms and as many windows, ordered gardens and extensive park lands, Versailles was more than a house for King Louis. It was a symbol of French glory and unity, and of royal mastery over the forces of disorder. It was safe now to have large windows and extensive gardens instead of fortified walls and barbicans; openness overcame the grim seclusion of the Louvre. Versailles became the centre of the nation and Paris was a kind of suburb.

Louis conceived the grand plan in about 1670, and soon as many as 36,000 men and 6,000 horses were at work building, improving, landscaping and terracing. The king moved in, in 1682. Work continued on the château even then and for much of the rest of the reign. Versailles could never be quite grand enough. One example of its splendours, the *Galerie des Glaces* (hall of mirrors), was 80 metres long with 17 huge windows looking out across broad lawns to fountains, statuary, trees and parks; opposite each window was a mirror of equal size. The *Galerie des Glaces* achieved a fame enduring well beyond Louis and the Bourbon monarchy. In 1871 Bismarck proclaimed the new German empire there; and in 1919 the treaty ending the First World War was signed there – a treaty in part made necessary by Bismarck's act in 1871.

The *Galeries des Glaces* at Versailles

Louis in residence was the working king at home, surrounded by officials and courtiers who were kept on their toes by rigid rules of etiquette (though less rigid than in many European capitals of the time), and by their conviction that to be at Versailles was the ultimate privilege of their class. The marquis of Varde, for example, exiled for twenty years for interfering in Louis's love affairs, was finally allowed to return and appeared wearing the now outmoded clothes he had worn on the day he had left Versailles. He knelt before Louis who raised and embraced him. The marquis wept openly and explained: 'To have displeased your Majesty is to be wretched; to be apart from you is to appear ridiculous.' Of course Versailles bred sycophancy, too, which was the point of the reference in François de Fénelon's famous letter criticising Louis's rule: '... truth is free and strong. You have hardly been used to hearing it.'

Within limits, Versailles was open to the public. The populace could come and watch the king dine, and when the dauphin was ill, Paris fishwives came by to kiss him on the cheek. The château was also the centre of French cultural life. Molière plays were performed, as was the music of Lully, Couperin and, in the eighteenth century, Rameau. Le Vau, Le Nôtre and Jules Hardouin-Mansart were its architects, and the best artists were employed in decorating and redecorating. Versailles cost a fortune to maintain, and Colbert disapproved of developing the château instead of the Louvre.

But Versailles cost little compared to warfare. Unfortunately, Louis spent lavishly on both. He was at war with his neighbours for 35 years. The economic and fiscal advantages gained by his reforms were nullified, and the foundations of absolutism he was at such pains to establish were undermined in consequence.

Holland

For most of his reign, Louis was at war with Holland, England and/or the Empire. He disliked Holland because it was republican, Protestant and most of all, because it was in his way. In 1672 he attacked the Dutch with a well-organized, well-armed and disciplined army of 119,000 officers and men.

THE DUTCH WAR

Louis obtained nearly everything he wanted against the Dutch and their allies. English troops fought alongside the French until 1674, and Louis personally commended young John Churchill for bravery at Maastricht. After England left the alliance, Louis effectively neutralized it through secret deals with Charles II. France gained Franche Comté and half of Flanders, and the king won fame as a military leader and in diplomacy. By 1683 he was master of Europe.

But French glory came at a high price. In the first place, the Dutch war cost £30 million a year, and was soon unpopular because taxes rose to meet expenses. In 1675 a rebellion broke out in Brittany, and at the same time Bordeaux, starved of its wine trade with Holland, conspired with the Dutch against Louis. In the second place, although Louis's neighbours were awed by him, they were also made uneasy. After the Peace of Westphalia ended the Thirty Years War in 1648, England and the Habsburg Empire were committed to the balance of power in Europe. Now Louis XIV was upsetting it and neither England nor the Empire were prepared to let this go unchallenged. In the third place, success made Louis arrogant. He committed precipitous acts certain to rouse anti-French feeling in England.

Prince William of Orange, Stadholder of Holland and commander of the Dutch armies, had married Mary Stuart, daughter of the future James II of England and niece of Charles II, in 1677. In 1685 Louis revoked the Edict of Nantes and began systematic persecution of the Huguenots. Between 1677 and 1683 England had passed through the 'Popish Plot' and Succession Crises, and anti-Catholic feeling ran high. Revocation of the Edict simply focused that feeling against Louis. By 1685 England was in a mood for war with France, and had allies in Holland, the Empire and Brandenberg Prussia, ruled by a Calvinist. In 1688 the Glorious Revolution deposed James II, a Catholic, and brought in his son-in-law, William of Orange, a Protestant, to rule England jointly with his wife as William III and Mary II. James fled to France where Louis welcomed him as the rightful king of England and a true son of the Church. In 1689 the first of two long wars began between France and England in alliance with the Empire.

THE GERMAN WAR

Louis planned to expand French territory to the north-east, and made an alliance with the Turks who were to keep Emperor Leopold I distracted while Louis invaded the Habsburg Rhineland. But in 1683 Leopold won a great victory over the Turks outside Vienna, breaking their European strength. (Viennese bakers celebrated by creating a crescent-shaped bun in imitation of the crescent moon of Islam. This bun later became popular in France as the *croissant*.) When war began in 1689, the Empire was ready to counter-attack in alliance with England, Holland, Spain, Savoy, Brandenberg and Bavaria. The 1689 war did not go well for France as a result. In the Treaty of Ryswick in 1697, King Louis gave up most of the occupied territories, plus Lorraine. What he retained was kept mainly because his enemies were as exhausted as himself.

THE SPANISH WAR

After Ryswick, Louis felt surrounded by enemies and had it in mind to make Spain a permanent ally by promoting a Bourbon as heir to the Spanish throne. This he achieved through diplomacy, and when the Habsburg King of Spain, Charles II, died in 1701, Louis's grandson was crowned Philip VI. The Imperial Habsburgs and the English objected, and war broke out again. In 1702 William III died, and was succeeded by Queen Anne. Louis did himself little good by proclaiming for the exiled James II. Meanwhile, the duke of Marlborough, John Churchill, stepped forward as the power behind Queen Anne's throne. If Louis was prepared to go to war on behalf of his grandson and the Stuart claimant, Marlborough and Prince Eugène of Savoy, the Emperor's principal commander and a general the equal of Marlborough, were glad to accommodate him.

The war ended only in 1713. It was filled with famous battles, most of which France lost. Louis's best advisors were gone (Colbert died in 1683), debts sky-rocketed and public disquiet increased. His great reputation bled away at Blenheim, Ramillies, Turin, Oudenaarde, Lille, Malplaquet and Denain. At Utrecht in 1713, Louis ceded terri-tory, much of it in North America, and kept only the Spanish throne for his grandson, with the proviso that no Spanish Bourbon could ever inherit the French throne. With that the war ended. In 1715, aged, disappointed, weary, much of his life's work diminished by this war, Louis died.

The Enlightenment

Louis died and the Age of Reason was born. Seventeenth-century thinkers wanted system; eighteenth-century intellectuals wanted action, enlightened solutions to specific problems born out of reasoned analysis of what was wrong. The life of the mind in France was never livelier. These intellectuals were critics, satirists, materialists, metaphysicians, anti-clericals, republicans, constitutionalists, radicals, rich and poor. Men like Voltaire corresponded with princes and were also exiled by them. Meanwhile, in the arts this was the Age of Rococo, almost frivolous compared to Enlightened thought, but no less innovative and interesting.

Voltaire

Elegant, light and airy, its decorative swirls and curves teased the symmetrical lines of the Baroque and Classical. Rococo was symbolized by a delicate Antoine Watteau painting, a low-relief horse carved by Robert le Lorrain over the stables of the Hôtel de Rohan in Paris, or a harpsichord concerto by Jean-Philippe Rameau, foreshadowing the neo-impressionism of Claude Debussy a century and a half later.

THE PHILOSOPHES

The intellectuals were called *philosophes*, and they wrote and argued about every subject under the sun. In *The Spirit of the Law*, Montesquieu explained how the separation of powers between legislature, executive and judiciary was the secret to political stability. In *The History of the Reign of Louis XIV, Candide*, and other writings, Voltaire criticized society and urged change. He also championed Deism as the only reasonable alternative to the priest-ridden and corrupt Church. Diderot argued for a broader-based science of experimentation and observation, and founded the *Encyclopédie*, wherein the sum of human knowledge would be assembled in rational categories for the enlightenment of humanity. In *Émile* and *The Social Contract*, Rousseau elaborated new concepts in education and an egalitarian society based upon the General Will of the community. Regrettably, he did not leave space for dissent, and Rousseauism led directly to totalitarian concepts of democracy during the Revolution, and again in the twentieth century. The list of contributors to the world of the intellect in eighteenth-century France includes, among others, La Mettrie, Alembert, Maupertuis, Holbach, Condillac, and even de Sade, in his perverse way. They created new expressions for established ideas, and some new ideas of their own. Above all, they created an atmosphere of intellectual ferment in which dissatisfaction with the failings of the *Ancien Régime* was readily expressed and acted upon.

ENLIGHTENED ABSOLUTISM

The Enlightenment appealed to at least some absolutist rulers. Most of the *philosophes* corresponded with princes, and visited them, outside of France. They were less welcome at Versailles, which fact adds credence to the ancient adage that a prophet rarely finds honour in his own land. Voltaire was virtually idolized by Frederick II of Prussia, an intellectual and composer in his own right, despite several disagreements. Catherine II of Russia patronized Diderot so that he would have funds to continue with the *Encyclopédie*. Joseph II of the Habsburg Empire looked for inspiration to the *philosophes* for the reforms he was attempting within his domains. George III of England, though no absolutist, was caught up in the fascination with technics. He dabbled in agriculture and wrote articles about it under the name Ralph Robinson. Frederick, Catherine and Joseph held no brief for democratic principles contained in *philosophe* writings; but they were much interested in the techniques of analysis and reform found there, which were applicable to economics, government or the arts. They reasoned that if properly applied, these techniques would make the state, economy or war machine more efficient and thus would enhance absolutism. They also did not encourage home-grown *philosophes*, despite founding academies right and left; better to import French intellectuals – as Frederick brought in Maupertuis to head the Prussian academy – and send them packing if they became troublesome.

The Ancien Régime

In the period 1715–1789, the social, economic and fiscal failures of the previous two centuries caught up with the Bourbon monarchy. This was the era of the *Ancien Régime*, the 'old order'. Two kings sat on the throne in this period, and neither could come to grips with these failures. Many specific factors led to revolution in 1789, but decades of failing to provide lasting reforms underscored them.

In the eighteenth century the gap between rich and poor, privileged and deprived, town and country, locality and the centre, widened. The provinces defended their rights against royal authority with heightened vigour, and the *intendants* found their jobs ever harder to do. No real improvements were made in the tax system. Tax farmers made hefty profits as always and resentment among ordinary and landed locals towards them increased. *Parlementaire* powers revived, and those of municipalities and guilds expanded. The old nobility lost virtually none of its privileges, regained some of its power, abnegated all sense of responsibility, and concerned itself solely with defending its social exclusivity. Louis XV (1715–1774) ascended the throne as a five-year-old child with a regent, the duke of Orléans, ruling for him. He was Louis XIV's great-grandson; this did not deter the old nobles, who seized this opportunity to stage a 'palace revolution'. Prophetic words.

Louis XV

The Peers of France (the highest of the ancient nobility) took control of the government in 1715, and with the aid of the reviving *parlements* took back the powers the late king had taken from them. But they made a hash of governing and by 1718 the secretaries of state were again running the bureaucracy. Moreover, the arrogance of the peers alienated other ancient nobles, who now placed the protection of their interests in the hands of the *noblesse de la robe* and the *parlement* of Paris (which was also sick of the peers) which the *robe* backed. Their aristocratic leadership remained until the Revolution. Absolutism was being dismantled. The process would take a half-century, but when complete, the full poverty of the system begun by Francis I, enhanced by Henry IV and brought to fruition by the Sun King, would be revealed. It should have been Louis XIV, rather than Madame de Pompadour who said: '*Après nous le déluge.*'

Cardinal Fleury

By 1726 French government settled down under the direction of Cardinal Fleury. Royal finances improved and deficits were reduced. However, there was no corresponding improvement in industry, and the conditions of the peasantry remained the same as in the past, or deteriorated.

The *parlements* and tax farmers opposed any reforms of industrial or agricultural policy, and Louis XV had neither the strength of will nor the confidence to impose himself upon the court and government. He quickly learnt to give his minister the lead, and himself up to hunting and his mistresses, the marquise de Pompadour and Madame Du Barry, who apparently were more entertaining than his Polish queen, Marie Leszczyńska. The marquise adorned the court lavishly with the latest of everything, which invoked popular criticism about extravagance and waste. But – echoes of Louis XIV and Versailles – her spending was as nothing compared to the costs of the wars which began in 1741 and were paid for with tax increases.

THE SEVEN YEARS WAR

In the decade after 1741 the *parlements*, led by Paris, emerged as the principal obstacles to any attempt by the government at fiscal or pro-vincial reform. The *parlements*, usually behind the façade of defending liberty, became reactionary institutions prepared to drag France into oblivion before surrendering privilege. They had their opportunity with the Seven Years War, which began in 1756, the result of machinations between Frederick II of Prussia, and Prince Kaunitz, chancellor of the Habsburg Empire.

A sudden shift in diplomacy, sometimes called the Diplomatic

Revolution of 1756, ranged Britain with Prussia, and France with the Empire and Russia. The war did not go well for France: India, Canada and Louisiana and some islands in the West Indies were lost. The Seven Years War was known by many names, including, in North America, the French and Indian War.

France emerged from the Treaty of Paris in 1763 shorn of empire and heavily in debt. Taxes had to be assessed, and the *parlements* stood foursquare against it, just as they had in 1749 when minister of finance Machault d'Arnouville introduced a tax to pay for the War of the Austrian Succession. In 1763 the provincial *parlements* drew closer to their *confrères* in Paris, and between them they first curtailed government plans to prolong war-time taxes as a way to reduce deficits, and second, in the name of Gallicanism, launched an attack on the Jesuits which finally forced Louis to suppress the order in 1764.

More disputes erupted between king and *parlements* over the next half-dozen years, particularly in Paris and Brittany, and by 1771 the kingdom was on the verge of anarchy. Meanwhile, Madame Du Barry became royal mistress, and persuaded Louis to dismiss his foreign minister, the duke of Choiseul. Choiseul was popular with the nobility, but made no effort to conceal his dislike for Du Barry. At that moment, Chancellor René-Nicolas de Maupeou abolished the *parlement* of Paris; he got away with this dramatic act because noble opposition to the crown was not then certain how much power the crown might display. New courts were set up to handle judicial affairs and plans for fiscal reform were scrutinized, including a plan to put a tax on all classes. But at this point Louis died.

Louis XVI

Louis XV's grandson, Louis XVI (1774–1793), inherited an enormously unpopular throne, a noisy capital of perhaps a half-million inhabitants still crammed into a city of medieval proportions (save for the parks and the suburbs – or *faubourgs* – where the nobility had developed elegant hôtels and squares), an economy inadequate to meet the needs of 26 million French people, of whom 21 million lived on the land, and a deficit of 37 million livres which within 15 years rose to 112 million. The tax reform plans did not survive Louis XV. His grandson had no means for dealing with financial problems, and began to rely on financiers.

Anne–Robert Jacques Turgot, the finance minister, wanted to tax landed wealth; this proved to be impossible. After Louis XV died the *parlements* had recovered their strength. Now they engineered Turgot's dismissal for even thinking such revolutionary thoughts. The peasants approved of Turgot however, especially his abolishing the *corvée* (forced) peasant labour on public roads.

AMERICA

In 1778 the count of Vergennes involved France in the American War of Independence, part of a manoeuvre against Great Britain. He helped the American rebels considerably, and a liberal reputation was acquired by the marquis de Lafayette, who served as *aide-de-camp* to General George Washington for a winter. Also, a French fleet helped the Americans win the battle of Yorktown. However, Vergennes did nothing at all for French solvency. The money which paid for America was borrowed from bankers, one of whom, Jacques Necker, a Swiss, looked after the loans as director of state finance.

Calonne

Charles–Alexandre de Calonne emerged in the late 1780s as financial controller with a scheme to restore confidence in the government by lavish spending on public works. He also planned tax reforms, including a universal tax to be administered by new, local assemblies. Calonne advised Louis to summon a carefully hand–picked Assembly of Notables to put these 'revolutionary' proposals over in the countryside. Louis did, but the Notables were no more sympathetic than the *parlements*. Privilege had won again. Notables, *parlements*, pamphlets and orators haranguing crowds in the Palais–Royal in Paris, all demanded the summoning of the Estates General to deal with the problems of the reign and the country.

Meanwhile there were other difficulties, among them Louis's queen, Marie Antoinette, daughter of Maria Theresa and sister of Joseph II of Austria. While France seethed, she built rustic cottages in the Versailles park lands and played at being a milk-maid. When told the poor of Paris had no bread, she probably did not actually say: 'Let them eat cake'; but she might have, for all the difference it made to her reputation. Moreover, as *l'Autrichienne* (the Austrian) she was suspect in the popular mind. Pamphleteers accused her of heinous things, some of them straining credulity, like the accusation that in a single night she gave her sexual favours to an entire Guards regiment. Anti-royal propaganda was becoming more scurrilous in the 1780s. Furthermore, the court nobles looked down their noses at rustic provincial aristocrats, which isolated the court from the country; nobles keen to make their estates efficient were frequently at odds with those who simply wished to profit by exploiting feudal dues; the upper bourgeoisie had no sympathy with the petty bourgeoisie and the urban worker, who in turn hated rich merchants and bankers; and the humble *curé* and the prince of the church were miles apart. In short, every social category now pursued its own interests, mostly indifferent to any sense of community.

Louis XVI's reign opened with a severe food crisis and grain riots in Paris. Between 1775 and 1788, riots over food shortages and taxes were regular occurrences. In 1788 the Paris *parlement* revolted over Necker's tax plan, and forced the king to summon the Estates General. The *parlement* then demanded that when the Estates met, voting would be equal between the three parts, even though the Third Estate (commoners) would represent 96 per cent of the population. The *parlement* represented privilege, not liberty; they were sowing the whirlwind.

Revolution

Provincial assemblies elected delegates to the Estates General, and in May 1789 these delegates gathered at Versailles. There were alarming developments from the start. The Third Estate rejected aristocratic leadership and insisted on single-member voting in the form of a National Assembly. On 17 June they so renamed themselves, and three days later met at a nearby tennis court where they swore an oath not to participate in any deliberations until their demands were met.

Meanwhile in Paris, radical orators stirred up the *sans-culottes* (the aristocrats' term for the Parisian working people), pamphlets appealed to popular discontents, royal ministers were burnt in effigy, radical newspapers appeared, ideas of the Enlightenment circulated as the revealed wisdom of a new world order, and certain nobles and clergy – Count Mirabeau and the Abbé Sieyès, for example – joined with the Third Estate in demanding the formation of the National Assembly. Louis and his ministers gave in, and on 27 June ordered the abolition of the Estates and official formation of the National Assembly.

On 14 July, a heavy, overcast and muggy day, a crowd gathered in front of the Bastille. They claimed (wrongly) that this old fortress prison was filled with political prisoners. Tension increased and the crowd grew violent. They demanded that the Bastille surrender its prisoners, to which the commandant finally agreed, on the promise of a safe conduct for himself and his men. He opened the gate, and almost at once he and several of the soldiers were killed. The Revolution had now begun in earnest. The fallen Bastille, however, was a disappointment. There were only four prisoners, and none of them were political. Revolutionary propaganda gave the impression later that half the population of Paris was inside. In any event, the fortress, a hated symbol of the old order, was soon razed to the ground, and survives today only in the name of a square, a stop on the Métro, and a new opera house.

History can turn on accidents, or so Voltaire claimed when he speculated that the Roman Republic might have survived had Cleopatra's nose been less seductive to Julius Caesar and Mark Antony. Thus we must also remember the count of Soissons and his hair-triggered pistol after the battle of La Marfée, and the incident of the Locked Door.

On the morning of 20 June 1789, the Third Estate arrived at their hall prepared to press demands for the National Assembly. The door was locked. Suspecting the worst, they went off to the tennis court and swore the famous oath, effectively beginning the Revolution. It is supposed that they were locked out as part of a royal manoeuvre to nip their demands in the bud, and thus reassert government control of the situation. But another version has it that the door was locked because the porters had not finished cleaning, and they refused to open up until they had. Did the porters start the Revolution by default? Probably the Revolution would have occurred whatever the state of the door. No doubt the count of Soissons would have been amused by the question all the same.

CHAPTER SEVEN

The Era of Revolution
1789–1852

In 1789 the dam broke. France entered upon sixty years of social, political, economic and intellectual upheaval. In this era the French nation was born, and Paris emerged as its beating heart.

Paris

In 1789 a half-million Parisians lived in an eight-by-six-kilometre area characterized by poor hovels, rich hôtels and palaces, churches, narrow and crowded streets and only a few avenues. Six bridges crossed the Seine, of which the Pont Neuf was the largest. It offered strollers entertainments, a view of the river (the Pont Neuf had no houses on it), and raised pavements.

New buildings mixed with old: the Louvre and Tuileries, Notre-Dame, Les Halles and the Bastille were old; the École Militaire, next to the Champs-de-Mars, the Invalides, the Palais-Royal (a sort of arcade encompassing such oddities as the Café Américain), and the Panthéon, built over the old church of Sainte-Geneviève and completed only in 1790 (it became a necropolis for heroes, just as Saint-Denis was a necropolis for ancient kings), were new. Mansart roofs were a commonplace. Place Louis XV was at the west end of the Tuileries; two kilometres east on the Ile de la Cité stood the Conciergerie and the Châtelet. In 1793–94 their inmates were brought by tumbrils through mocking, jeering crowds to Place Louis XV, by then called the Place de la Révolution, for execution. Their route was the Rue St Honoré, the very heart of revolutionary Paris.

Parisians, about to become French in the fully modern sense of the

word, were justifiably proud of their city. Often their English neighbours failed to admire Paris for reasons that were perhaps centuries-old:
resentment and jealousy, aimed at the French themselves. William
Cole, a Cambridge clergyman, wrote in 1765 that if only each 'vain and
Fantastical' Frenchman could see London, then 'if Truth will not make
him acknowledge the *Petitesse*, the Littleness, the Nothingness of Paris
in respect to the Beauty, Grandeur & Superiority of London, he must
be ashamed of nothing; indeed a Very Frenchman.'

The Revolution

The storming of the Bastille was followed by an uprising in the
countryside, which created a panic known as the Great Fear. Châteaux
were burnt, tax-collectors murdered and clergy attacked. It soon passed, but meanwhile the National Assembly felt constrained to enact
legislation abolishing feudal dues, serfdom and tithes, and nationalizing
the Church and clergy. Louis XVI approved this legislation in his new
capacity as 'constitutional' monarch. Perhaps to save their necks, landed
aristocrats and higher clerics in the Assembly voluntarily turned over
their estates for redistribution to the peasants. 'They've all gone mad!'
said one startled observer. At the same time, confiscated clerical lands
were made the basis of a new currency, the *assignat*, which solved
neither currency problems nor inflation, and was soon worthless. Most
people continued to deal in *sous* and *livres*.

In October, inspired by radical orators (and *agents provocateurs* of the
duke of Orléans, Louis XVI's cousin, now known as Philippe Égalité),
a crowd of lower-class Parisian women trekked to Versailles with
shouts of '*Vive la Nation!*', and forced the royal family to accompany
them back to Paris. Food and grain shortages, inflation and unemployment were the harsh realities of city life for these women, and they
reckoned the king could better look after them – and himself be kept
free of corrupt advisors – in the Tuileries.

The women were in no mood to argue. Jeanne Martin, a nurse,
reported that she was forced to go with them on pain of being beaten if
she refused. On the return to Paris they had sport with Queen Marie
Antoinette, whom they threatened to butcher and eat, while some of

the men with them fired guns over the queen's head. For the king they still could feel affection; Marie Antoinette was simply *l'Autrichienne*.

The cry '*Vive la Nation!*' indicated a new mentality, soon rooted throughout France. Early on there occurred the inevitable attempts to use the revolution to separate the provinces from Paris. These failed. Federations of villages and towns formed, brought together by the revolutionary spirit behind the slogan '*Liberté, égalite, fraternité*'. Their representatives, called *fédérés*, went to Paris and brought with them a sense that all France was at last a nation united by common popular action to overthrow the old order.

REVOLUTIONARY GOVERNMENT

The National Assembly, now meeting in a hall next to the Tuileries Palace, struggled with a variety of problems in 1789–91. They were frequently intimidated by mobs who believed that now the *nation* had replaced the feudal order, their opinion would be wanted by the legislature and government. The Assembly solved no major problems, although they did hammer out a constitution, completed in September 1791. France was divided administratively into *départments*, the king no longer ruled by divine right nor could he absolutely veto legislation, the Assembly became permanently part of government, and the Rights of Man were formally spelt out. The way was also left open for future change.

That change would include emancipation of women – a century and a half later, at the conclusion of the Second World War. At the time, liberation for women was an unrealized ideal. The revolutionary intellectual, the marquis of Condorcet urged it, pointing out that 'either no member of the human race has any natural rights or they all have the same; and anyone who votes against the rights of another, whatever their religion, their colour or their sex, has from that moment abjured his own'. Madame de Condorcet also urged female emancipation, as did such women as playwright Olympe de Gouges, who wrote the tract *Declaration of the Rights of Women and the Citizen*, Théroigne de Méricourt, often credited with being unofficial leader of those who sat in the gallery at the National Assembly, and Manon de Roland, a major figure in the Girondiste party and later a victim of the guillotine. Méricourt called upon French women to 'rise to the level of our destinies and break our chains', adding that it was high time 'women emerged from the shameful state of nullity and ignorance to which the arrogance and injustice of men have so long condemned them'. French women repudiated the *Ancien Régime*, gave sons to the revolution, and died on the scaffold in its name. However, neither words nor deeds spoken or performed by French women in the revolution had any lasting effect.

Political parties had formed even before the revolution began. Now they filled the Assembly and jockeyed for position. In 1791 the Girondins (liberals) were in power, led by Jacques Brissot. Other parties included the Jacobins (radicals), led by Camille Desmoulins and later by Georges Jacques Danton and Maximilien Robespierre; the Hébertists (socialists) led by Jacques Hébert; and the *enragés* (communists) led by a former priest, Jacques Roux. The marquis of Lafayette fluctuated between moderate monarchism and conservative republicanism, and created the National Guard from among the bourgeoisie of Paris to keep order and protect the revolution from reactionaries. Philippe Égalité (the duke of Orléans) played his own political game until he fell from favour. The duke went to the guillotine, it was reported, with an enigmatic smile on his face.

In the Assembly the basic political designations of subsequent times evolved: the President sat on a dais at the front; on his Left sat the radicals, on his Right the conservatives, and the moderates occupied seats in the Centre.

The Republic

In June 1791, Louis XVI tried to flee France with his family. They were caught at Varenne by the local *procurateur*, a grocer named Sauce, and returned to Paris. Until then Parisians shouted '*Vive le Roi!*' Now they shouted '*Vive la Nation!*' As they saw it, Louis had betrayed them. The proof, if more was needed, came in August when the duke of Brunswick issued the Declaration of Pillnitz, condemning the revolution and vowing revenge if harm befell Louis. French relations with the rest of Europe deteriorated rapidly. The Girondins argued for war as the best way to head off intervention – and to galvanize the nation into unanimous support for Paris and the revolution. After months of debate war was declared in April 1792, and the inclination towards republicanism became a headlong rush.

THE SEPTEMBER MASSACRES

But first the nation had to root out the enemy within. In August a National Convention was summoned to depose the monarch. Then on 2 September a massacre of political prisoners began, carried out by enthusiastic volunteers. They broke into the prisons and began systematically slaughtering the inmates: 1200 in all – priests, royalists, common criminals, and some for whom no actual crime was in evidence. Contemporary accounts describe incredible horrors and bestiality, including cannibalism. Princess de Lambelle was stripped, raped and her body mutilated; some were beheaded, some slashed to death with sabres, and others set on fire. On the other hand, some prisoners were simply released, and even escorted home by people smeared with the blood of others less fortunate. The English ambassador simply commented: 'What a people!'

VALMY

Thus 'secured', the revolutionary army went off to confront their foreign enemies. They were ill-armed but highly motivated. Flushed by the heady idea of belonging to the Nation and of carrying forward a new order, they defeated the professionals of Prussia and Austria at Valmy. A dispirited Prussian officer commented: 'We have lost more than a battle.'

This was 20 September; the next day the Convention proclaimed the Republic and prepared to bring Louis XVI, now called Louis Capet, a symbolic repudiation of the entire monarchial history of France, to trial for conspiracy. In January 1793 he was convicted, condemned and executed. Marie Antoinette followed in October. The dauphin died of illness in 1795, after having been proclaimed in the courts of Europe as Louis XVII.

The *Ancien Régime* thus ended, save for the myth that 'Louis XVII' survived. American humorist Mark Twain 'tweaked' the myth, having one of his characters in *The Adventures of Huckleberry Finn* announce: 'I am the late Dauphin!' The myth ended finally in 2000, when scientists compared DNA from the boy who died in Temple prison with that of Marie Antoinette. It matched.

Meanwhile, there were increased manifestations of egalitarianism: *citoyen* (citizen) became the standard form of address; powdered wigs and fancy clothes disappeared; people gave their children 'revolutionary' names: 'Égalité' and 'Vertu', for example. 1792 was Year I of the First French Republic.

THE TERROR

At first things went well after Valmy, and the Girondins prospered. French armies annexed Nice and Savoy, captured Belgium and invaded the Rhineland. Everywhere they proclaimed the 'sovereignty of the people' and equated it with nationalism. 'Exporting revolution', a common twentieth-century phenomenon, was first practised in 1792 by the French.

Then the Girondins fell behind both in prosecuting the war and dealing with poverty, shortages and inflation. The public became agitated. In April 1793, the Jacobin leaders (called *Les Montagnards* because they sat on the top seats of the tiered Assembly Hall) forced through the formation of the Committee of Public Safety, an organization for centralizing power and keeping order. It was used first to overthrow the Girondins, whose leaders were hurried to the guillotine shortly after. On 17 September the Law of Suspects was established – anyone suspected of betraying the revolution *ipso facto* had done so – and the Terror began.

Danton ran the Committee, but the true architect of the Terror was Robespierre and his principal aides, the cold-blooded Louis de Saint-Just and the wily Joseph Fouché (as bloodthirsty as any *sans-culottes*). They formed a dictatorship based upon popular fear and hatred of 'enemies of the revolution', and used it to save France from enemies abroad.

A revolutionary army of conscripts was formed; supplies were requisitioned; and anyone who objected was executed for treason. Cries of '*La Patrie en danger!*' and '*Aux armes, citoyens!*' were all that was needed for the Committee to justify any action. The marching song of revolutionary cadres from Marseille (*La Marseillaise*) became the hymn of the Jacobin army. The Terror was Rousseau's law of the General Will gone mad.

During a year-and-a-half 20,000 people in Paris and double that in the country died by the guillotine: aristocrats, priests, ordinary people, former royal ministers – even Madame Du Barry, once mistress to Louis XV, was caught up. Thomas Jefferson, the United States ambassador and a staunch friend of France, thought it prudent to slip quietly away during this period. Equality of a sort had been achieved: no one was safe from the guillotine, neither aristocrat nor commoner, guilty or innocent. Meanwhile, Dame Reason was 'enthroned' symbolically at Notre-Dame Cathedral, and churches were pulled down throughout France, including the famous abbey at Cluny.

The Terror saved France from foreign enemies; at home it produced such tension that the populace wearied of it and began to doubt the revolution itself. There was a turn to the Right. The Jacobins, Hébertists, *enragés* and other extremists were brought down in 1795. Saint-Just, Robespierre – all but Fouché who went missing at the opportune moment – made the journey to Place de la Révolution. The prediction of the Assembly's President, Pierre Vergniaud, was realized: the revolution was 'devouring its children'.

THE DIRECTORY

Rule by another committee followed: the Directory. Composed of conservatives, it ruled unsteadily and insecurely through devious compromise, purges, by hitting alternately at Right and Left, and by relying on the army. It condoned squads of bourgeois bully-boys called *jeunesse dorée*, who roamed the streets with clubs looking for 'radicals'. But economic problems defied the Directory, as they had all of its predecessors, and populist protests, led sometimes by the National Guard, became epidemic. On one occasion a young Corsican brigadier in command of artillery used a 'whiff of grape shot' to break up an anti-government riot. His reward was command of the French army in Italy in 1796 – a mistake, warned Dupont de Nemours, an economist who served the Directory. It was.

The Corsican brigadier won stunning victories, made his own treaties with the Habsburg emperor, and conquered Egypt. Alarmed by his brilliance, independent-mindedness and popularity with his troops, the Directory summoned the officer home for disciplining. He came, but under the inspiration of his brother, Lucien, President of the Council of Five Hundred, the lower house of the Assembly, on 9 November 1799 he overthrew the Directory at gunpoint. The Council soon declared him First Consul of the French Republic. Napoleon Bonaparte had arrived.

Napoleon

The First Consul soon brought order out of the chaos. A plebiscite affirmed him in his powers by a large majority. He then declared that the revolution was ended. In the coming months Napoleon confirmed the peasants in their revolutionary gains, restored the Church, established a code of laws (the Code Napoléon) which governed every aspect of life from the law courts to education, and set up a one-man dictatorship based upon the principle of authority: the father over the children, the husband over the wife, the employer over the employee, and himself over everyone.

Although Napoleon talked republicanism and nationalism, he behaved like an eighteenth-century enlightened absolutist bent on the rationalization of power. In 1804 he proclaimed himself emperor; he set aside his wife, the beautiful bourgeoise Josephine de Beauharnais, in order to marry a Habsburg princess; he personally constructed the French constitution to fit his view of the State; propaganda and censorship were constants of his rule; he allied capital with government through the Bank of France; tax collection was reformed, improved, and committed primarily to the maintenance of his armies; rioters were dealt with ruthlessly; prices were carefully regulated; he reinstated slavery in the French colonies after the revolution had abolished it; and he made an agreement with the pope (the Concordat of 1801) which gave the Church protected status, but left it entirely dependent upon the State. Even as First Consul he claimed the right to name his successors; his birthday was celebrated as a national holiday and coins bore his portrait.

MOSCOW ■
✕
Borodino

Tilsa

PRUSSIA

Revolution and Empire

GRAND DUCHY
OF WARSAW

▨ Areas ruled directly by Napoleon

▨ Areas ruled by members of Napoleon's family

✕ Battles

✕ *Leipzig*
Jena

A U S T R I A N   E M P I R E

✕ *Austerlitz*

Wagram ✕

■ VIENNA

*BLACK
SEA*

KINGDOM
OF ITALY

ME

KINGDOM
OF NAPLES

Naples

KINGDOM
OF SICLIY

E A N   S E A

Napoleon continued the principle of exporting revolution. Many Rhenish states were liberated from the oppressive rule of petty princelings, and German intellectuals such as Goethe and Beethoven (at first) regarded Napoleon as the true apostle of the Enlightenment. However, this, like his republicanism, was a sham. Nothing better revealed Bonaparte's disregard for the principles he exported – freedom, rights of man, and rule of law – than the incident of the duke d'Enghien. A French royalist apparently safe in the neutral German state of Baden, d'Enghien was abducted across the border into French-controlled territory, tried by summary court-martial, and shot as a conspirator against Napoleon. The reappearance of Fouché, who had survived office under the Terror and the Directory, as Napoleon's minister of the interior in charge of police, indicates further that Napoleon's rule was ultimately based upon ruthless, limitless and cynical power.

THE EMPIRE

Napoleon's plans included the reordering of Europe, and the overthrow of the balance of power in France's favour. When Louis XIV attempted this, the European powers took up arms to stop him. They did again now, but it took nearly fifteen years for them to succeed.

Napoleon repeatedly defeated the Habsburgs and forced concessions from them by the treaties of Campo-Formio in 1797 and Lunéville in 1801. But in 1798 at Aboukir Bay, at the Battle of the Nile, Admiral Horatio Nelson destroyed a French fleet, thus securing British power in the Mediterranean. In India Sir Arthur Wellesley disrupted French attempts to intrigue with Tippoo Sahib, Sultan of Mysore. The parameters of the Napoleonic wars were established by 1802: Napoleon could have his way on the continent – for the time being; but he could not overcome the British at sea. An invasion of Britain depended upon Admiral Villeneuve neutralizing admirals Nelson, Collingwood, Cornwallis and Pellew, which he could not do. Napoleon had to settle for isolating Britain diplomatically and commercially, but that, too, failed in the long run.

On the continent Napoleon went from strength to strength up to 1807: there were great victories at Marengo, Austerlitz, Jena and

Auerstadt, among others; there were treaties with Denmark, Russia, the United States, Naples, Portugal, Turkey and – a treaty of mutual distrust – with Britain at Amiens in 1802. Napoleon overran the Rhineland in 1803, crowned himself emperor in 1804, became master of Italy in 1805, and in 1806 abolished the Holy Roman Empire (the Habsburgs now simply became Austrian emperors) and set up the Confederation of the Rhine. In 1807 he met Alexander I of Russia at Tilsit in Poland, where they made a secret peace. Napoleon was master of the continent then, his power at its apex. Britain was isolated, Russia neutralized, and the only world still to conquer was the British Empire.

BLOCKADE

The French emperor knew that until he mastered Britain there would be a gap in the solid front of his power. In an attempt to close the gap, he declared a blockade against all commerce with Britain: British goods were denied access to the continent, and no ship could land in both British and French harbours, or any European port under French control. Britain replied with its own blockade, whereby no neutral was permitted to trade with Napoleonic Europe. The emperor could only try to prevent Europeans from trading with England, for it had to be done through customs officials, whereas Britain had the fleet to enforce its blockade – and to run the French blockade. A lively commerce in smuggling soon developed, negating much of Napoleon's effort, while France's port economy fell into depression from lack of use. At the same time, shortages created by the British blockade raised anti-French resentment among dependent territories, despite Napoleon's propaganda which blamed it all on Britain.

DECLINE

Prince Maurice de Talleyrand, Napoleon's foreign minister and as skilled a survivor as Fouché, was in touch with the British in 1807, preparing for what he thought was the inevitable collapse of the Napoleonic empire. This was clearly treason, but when Napoleon learnt of it, far from having Talleyrand shot he merely verbally abused him, and ordered him to be sacked. Talleyrand had the last word. As he withdrew from the audience, the prince remarked loudly enough to be heard: 'How unfortunate that such a great man should be so ill-mannered.'

After this, things went badly wrong for Napoleon. Fouché also conspired with the British, and fled France altogether. The Spaniards were in revolt with British help; Napoleon called Spain the 'thorn in my side'. In 1808 Napoleon occupied Rome and arrested the pope, Pius VII, which cost him his good relations with the Catholic Church. Jean-Baptiste Bernadotte, a former French marshal and now heir to the Swedish throne, intrigued with Austria to overthrow Napoleon, which intrigue was ended only by the emperor's victory at Wagram in 1809.

The next year, Tsar Alexander repudiated the Treaty of Tilsit, and in 1811 France faced an economic crisis brought on by costly attempts to maintain the blockade. In 1812, after a year of skirting around the issue of Russia, the emperor collected his 600,000 strong *grande armée* (far too large actually to manage efficiently under the limited supply and ordinance capabilities of the time) and invaded the Tsar's domain.

AND FALL

As Napoleon advanced, he found the Russians had denuded his path of the supplies so vital to his vast army. Victory at Borodino, 40 miles from Moscow, cost Napoleon tens of thousands of soldiers and many of his best marshals. The emperor occupied Moscow, which was deserted (save for a Russian aristocrat named Pierre Bezukhov, if we are to believe Tolstoy), and waited for Alexander to seek terms. No Tsar was forthcoming. Winter was, however, and the army was ill-prepared to face it. In October the *grande armée* retreated. Winter and Marshal Kutuzov's Cossack cavalry, fighting a form of guerilla warfare, caught up with them, and the retreat became a horror. There were conspiracies in Paris to unseat Napoleon who raced back to France to deal with them. Scarcely 90,000 of the original 600,000 survived to reach Poland.

Now Europe closed in for the kill. The Prussians joined their reformed army to that of the Tsar; the Spanish drove the French out of Spain, and British armies occupied Gascony as far as Bordeaux. Napoleon was heavily defeated at Leipzig in 1813, and the Rhenish states rose against him. On 31 March 1814, Tsar Alexander entered Paris at the head of an army, and Napoleon abdicated a week later.

In May, Louis XVIII, younger brother of Louis XVI, entered France after the victorious coalition had agreed to restore the Bourbon throne. Napoleon was granted a pension for life and tiny Elba off the coast of Italy for a kingdom. It seemed not a bad end to his career.

WATERLOO

But, being Bonaparte, he was not satisfied. In February, 1815, Napoleon returned to France. Louis XVIII fled, and the French cheered their emperor – but not too loudly, just as they had not cheered too loudly for Louis. 'We are not royalists so much as realists,' one former Napoleonic officer remarked. Napoleon was soon on the march. After a few victories, the allied armies, commanded by the Duke of Wellington, lured him into confrontation at Waterloo in Belgium, on 18 June 1815. It was Wellington's battle plan and the timely assault of the Prussians on the French flank which routed the Napoleonic army on that day. This time there were no mistakes. Napoleon was taken by the

Napoleon's bedroom at Malmaison

English under guard to the tiny south Atlantic island of St Helena
which was a British possession.

What was Napoleon Bonaparte? Monarchist, revolutionary, Byronic
hero, mere adventurer, or all of the above? One thing is certain: he was
an egoist who left a psychological mark upon France greater than any
figure before or since. At St Helena, before his death in 1821, he wrote
his *memoirs*. They were the last and greatest piece of Napoleonic
propaganda, and created a legend that endured for more than a century.

THE CONGRESS OF VIENNA

Representatives of all Europe, great states and small, had assembled in
Vienna in the autumn of 1814 to resolve the problems (fill the power
vacuum, in other words) left by Napoleon's departure. The mood had
been exuberant and Vienna a scene of unremitting celebration and
revelry. Everyone who was anyone had been there. Europe had felt
such relief that the treatment of France was to be lenient. Then 'the
monster' escaped Elba. The statesmen panicked. Their *joie de vivre*
vanished, and when Napoleon was again penned up, their mood was
subdued and unforgiving.

Prince Metternich, foreign minister and later chancellor of Austria,
and Lord Castlereagh, British foreign secretary, were the architects of
the treaty of 1815 and the system of international relations by which
Europe was restored, as nearly as possible, to pre-1789 configurations.
France lost territory, paid indemnities, and was occupied by 150,000
allied troops for three years. A system of international congresses was
devised to deal with insurrection and other problems that might arise,
and the balance of power was reaffirmed. The first congress met at Aix-
la-Chapelle in 1818, where France formally became a signatory to the
treaty. This was so that Europe could keep better control of France.
There was to be no more Gallic revolutionary and military fervour.

The Restoration

This was perfectly acceptable to Louis XVIII (1814–1824), who
understood the fragility of his position, and was determined to compromise; not unlike Charles II when he returned to England in 1660. If

the new constitution, the Charter, favoured property and wealth, it also continued parliamentary and administrative institutions left over from the revolution and Napoleon. The Church, the Jesuits, various reactionaries hoping to restore the old order, and *émigrés* demanding compensation returned with Louis. He listened less to them than to the liberal duke of Decazes. Officials were encouraged not to turn back the clock. In one famous instance an *émigré* nobleman, a naval cadet in 1789, demanded to be made a rear-admiral since he might have achieved that rank had not the revolution driven him out. The authorities got around the problem with similar logic: they admitted his claim, but informed him – sorrowfully – that he had been killed at Trafalgar in 1805.

The French economy was in recession, industry was only beginning to modernize, and the common people were none too ecstatic at having the Bourbons back. However, under Louis's prudent rule, recovery began. A cartoon of 1815 showed an eagle (Napoleon) leaving the Tuileries' back door as five fat geese (the Bourbons) waddled in at the front. It was apt; it also missed the point. Neither Louis nor the nation wanted more adventure, at least for the time being. They wanted peace.

Charles X

The Bourbon honeymoon was short, however. Charles X (1824–1830) had none of his brother's intelligence; he had neither forgotten nor learnt anything. The new king was crowned at Reims where he performed the ritual of touching for scrofula, an indication of things to come. He dismissed liberal ministers and raised his reactionary followers, such as the duke of Polignac and the count of Villèle. Both Polignac and the king belonged to the Congregation of the Virgin, a reactionary lay society dedicated to restoring the old Church and old order. Charles intrigued to reduce the powers of the Assembly and alter election laws, so as to render the Assembly almost wholly a province of the landed aristocracy.

Revolution: 1830

It was not to be. The bourgeoisie had prospered under Louis XVIII and were not to be set aside by his reactionary brother. In 1830 a bad harvest, economic crises, intellectuals up in arms, and anti-Bourbon propaganda produced another revolution.

In July the barricades went up in the streets of Paris; on 2 August Charles abdicated, and a week later, the duke of Orléans, son of Philippe Égalité, sponsored by the ageing but still popular marquis of Lafayette, mounted the throne as Louis Philippe (1830–1848), the 'July Monarch'.

INDUSTRIALISM

The industrial revolution, which had begun in England in the eighteenth century, started in France between 1830 and 1848. France expanded its iron and coal production, revolutionized the technology of the cotton industry, and increased the number of its spinning factories, power looms and mechanized paper mills. A national railway scheme was drawn up in 1842. Lille became an industrial city, Lyon was highly capitalized as the silk centre, and bankers and industrialists took the place of landed aristocrats as the important men of the nation. Industrialism informed the socialist writing of Henri Saint-Simon, who romanticized it, and Charles Fourier, who repudiated it in favour of a bucolic communism. Louis Blanc and Auguste Blanqui were advocates of industrial socialism in the Assembly before 1848.

Industrialism contributed to a widening gap between the classes. Tensions rose steadily between landowners and peasants, factory owners and workers; the working conditions for the latter were even more appalling than had been the case among eighteenth-century industrial labourers. There was now more production of crops and goods as improved technology expanded agriculture and industry equally, but rapid population growth increased demand for land, jobs and food.

Bad harvests were more devastating than ever before. Land and factory-owners feared the classes beneath them, and they in turn resented and hated the classes above. In between were the petty bourgeoisie of doctors, lawyers and teachers, often only a generation removed from being peasants or workers. Some of them defended the industrial social system because they profited from it, or hoped to; others wanted to change the system because they felt excluded from it. Discontent and dislocation, endemic to industrialization in any case, was evident on all sides.

ROMANTICISM

Discontent, if not dislocation, was part of the new outlook in art, literature, music and ideas called Romanticism. Both a product of, and a reaction against, the Age of Reason, Romanticism stressed the imagination and emotion, was both reactionary and progressive, and looked for individualistic and non-rationalist solutions to problems. Romanticism included Jules Michelet writing heroic history; Eugène Delacroix painting Turkish Janissaries massacring Greek peasants; Hector Berlioz horrifying Paris audiences with a guillotine sequence in *Symphonie Fantastique*; Chateaubriand finding the 'genius' of traditional Christianity; Stendhal parodying reactionary society; and the image of Napoleon Bonaparte's son dying of tuberculosis. Romanticism was many things with many variations. What it was not was tranquil.

The July Monarchy

Industrialism and Romanticism were both revolutionary, in their way, and revolution defined the parameters of the July Monarchy of Louis Philippe. It began with revolution, ended with revolution, and feared revolution every day of its existence. The régime's members were anti-revolutionary, because all were connected with revolution from earlier days: Louis Philippe fought at Valmy and Jemappes; the duke of Broglie was Madame de Staël's son-in-law (she was a great memoirist of the revolution, and was later persecuted as a critic of Bonaparte); Casimir Periér's father led the revolt of the Dauphiné Estates; Adolphe Thiers' father was ruined by the revolution; François Guizot's father was a Girondin and guillotined; and some of Louis Philippe's generals had served under Napoleon Bonaparte. The July Monarchy was bourgeois and practical, a perfect example of nineteenth-century monarchy, and had no love for the *Ancien Régime*. The king, himself a banker, strolled the avenues of Paris, unattended, umbrella in hand, like any member of the bourgeoisie. Louis Philippe was industrially-minded, progressive, and opposed to sharing power with any but those whom Guizot termed 'men of the rich and enlightened classes'.

There was opposition from the start: from legitimists because Louis Philippe was not a Bourbon; from socialists because they disliked the system; and from Louis Napoleon (who worked hard to cultivate a Romantic image in his early years), one of the nephews of the late emperor, because he aspired to re-establish his uncle's throne. However, no legitimist rising took place, socialist outbreaks usually responded to the resolution of specific grievances, and the only attempted *coup* in 1836 by Louis Napoleon failed utterly. It raised only mild curiosity at the time – except within the government, where fear of revolution was only equalled by fear of Bonapartism. This was not a régime which felt secure. There were 15 governments before Guizot assembled an administration in 1840 that lasted until 1848. More than one attempt was made on Louis Philippe's life.

Like Louis XVIII, Louis Philippe tried to balance between conflicting forces within French society. The July Monarchy retained the basic 1815 Charter, which was revised to nearly double the electorate. At the same time, the Assembly was filled mainly with landowners and industrialists. Royal ministers appeared to be in charge, with the king as a sort of constitutional father-figure. However, in reality Louis Philippe was the power in the State and merely encouraged the appearance that he was not, simply in order to remain above party and politics. He wished to remain above, for example, the continuous controversy over whether the Church or the State should run elementary education, a question which has been either a rallying cry or a political graveyard for French politicians since 1815.

Louis Philippe was unable to maintain his balancing act over foreign policy. Conservatives wanted to stay out of European politics; their memory of anti-French coalitions before 1815 remained keen. Radicals and nationalists wanted an aggressive, interventionist foreign policy – naval rivalry with Britain in the Mediterranean, for instance – in order either to wipe out the 'humiliation' of 1815, or to 'export revolution' once again. Louis Philippe sided with the conservatives. He stayed clear of involvement in Belgium in 1831, and in Egypt in 1840; but the radicals were given a colonial war against Abd-el-Kader in North Africa as a sop, from which France acquired Algeria and the legendary French Foreign Legion. It was not enough. Radical and nationalist opinion became alienated from the government over foreign affairs.

1848: The Revolution of the Intellectuals

Between 1844 and 1847 bad harvests drove up food prices and caused shortages. In 1847 an economic crisis accrued from short-fall in credit, and a business slump followed. The state was overcommitted to expenditure for the size of its budgets, something which raised fears of tax increases or else government bankruptcy. Unemployment increased steadily. Guizot was unpopular both for his pro-Austrian foreign policy and his refusal to reform the electoral system, and charges of corruption were frequently voiced. Anti-régime propaganda was endemic, and usually scurrilous.

When, in February 1848, the government cracked down on public demonstrations, barricades immediately went up in the streets of Paris. Troops fired and people were killed. Insurrection quickly spread through the city. On 24 February Louis Philippe abdicated, and radicals seized the Assembly. They declared the Second Republic and elected the poet Alphonse de Lamartine to lead it.

The new government at once prepared a republican foreign policy – proposed aid to Italian rebels – and set about reforming financial and economic conditions. The first produced mainly impassioned speeches, and the latter National Workshops and a commission to look after the workers' interests; neither of which solved any problems. Meanwhile, the provinces wearied of dictatorship from Paris and revolted on their own. A civil war followed, expanding quickly into the terrible June Days when peasants, who understood little of the Republican rhetoric but a good deal about hunger, rose against landlords and anyone else who stood in their way.

1848 was a revolution of Romantic intellectuals, informed by liberal and constitutional idealism, who could not bring themselves to extend the revolution to the social and economic systems. Therefore they lost control of it, and after the June Days the intellectuals looked to strong men to save them: to the republican General Cavaignac first, then to a representative of that tradition in France which claimed to reconcile revolution, authority, Catholicism, liberalism, external glory and social amelioration. That representative was Louis Napoleon Bonaparte.

THE MAN ON HORSEBACK

In 1848 the electorate was increased from 250,000 to over nine million, but it returned an Assembly of aristocrats and bourgeoisie. Alexis de Tocqueville described this Assembly as merely going through the motions of 1789, and rather pathetically at that.

Then, after the June Days, when conservative deputies demanded monarchy, Lamartine made an impassioned speech demanding a presidency based upon popular sovereignty. 'It is in the nature of democracy to find its personification in a Man,' he said. Doubters feared that such an office might bestow too tempting a degree of personal power. Lamartine carried the day; the doubters carried history. The first national election for a President of France was in December 1848. It returned Louis Napoleon Bonaparte by a 75 per cent margin.

Louis Napoleon spent the next three years gathering his political strength: speaking in republican tones, posing as the friend of the working class, being the hero of liberals by criticizing the pope and subsidizing the press, and currying Catholic approval by favouring religious primary and secondary education. Clearly a Man for All Seasons; clearly, too, a Man on Horseback.

In December 1851, the Assembly played into his hands by trying to remove the vote from some three million Frenchmen. Louis Napoleon executed a *coup d'état*: he arrested the leaders and shut the Assembly down; then, with much fanfare, he restored universal suffrage and submitted the *coup* to a plebiscite. Opposition was light, and that which developed was quickly repressed by military force. The plebiscite overwhelmingly approved the action. Louis Napoleon now held dictatorial power, and by a species of popular approval.

One act remained. For another year, Louis Napoleon consolidated his position. Then, on 2 December 1852, the anniversary of the *coup*, he put on the crown of Bonaparte and as the Man on Horseback rode into Paris as the Emperor Napoleon III. It was curiously anomalous: monarchy enthroned by popular vote. How well would monarchy and democracy cooperate? It remained to be seen. In any event, the era of revolution was at an end.

CHAPTER EIGHT

Second Empire, Third Republic
1852–1914

The era of revolution ended in 1852, but the search for an acceptable political system went on. Significant segments of the population remained politically radical, but a social conservatism emerged during the Second Empire and dramatically affected the Third Republic which followed it. Rumour had it that while the French still wore their hearts on the Left, they now wore their wallets on the Right. It was no rumour.

The Second Empire

Napoleon III traded on his name. But he was nothing like his famous uncle, save that he too was an adventurer in foreign affairs. The new emperor was lazy, quiet, cautious, reluctant to make hard decisions, and liked war only in theory, only when it was absolutely 'safe'. He tried to be all things to all people: liberal, authoritarian, defender of property, friend of the workers, pro-Catholic and anti-clerical. The Empress Eugénie was a Spaniard with a touch of the bohemian; that is, she presided over what the stiff-necked Paris bourgeoisie regarded as a 'loose-mannered' court.

Napoleon III was successful to a remarkable degree, for all of his limitations. He modernized France politically and economically, and made it competitive with its neighbours. After the first dictatorial years of his reign, the emperor moved steadily leftward in domestic affairs. In 1859 he declared an amnesty for his political opponents; in 1860 the powers of the Senate and Assembly were extended, and the next year the press was allowed to publish verbatim accounts of Assembly debates. In 1863 government ministers began explaining policy in the Assembly, and in 1867 the Assembly was granted the right to question the government. A parliamentary opposition emerged as a result of these changes. Napoleon regarded this as a positive step, and in 1870 introduced parliamentary government with Émile Ollivier as the leader of a government majority. A plebiscite approved all of Napoleon's reforms. Once again, he had won a vote of confidence from the public. The Assembly, meanwhile, was less widely based and also less popular. This gave Napoleon a slight edge over the Assembly. He may have been lazy, but he was astute.

The Second Empire encouraged economic enterprise and expansion at every turn. Financiers and speculators had a field day; fortunes were made – and lost – on the Paris Bourse, and French industrialisation hit its full stride. Railroad mileage quadrupled; seaports expanded; mining developed rapidly; French engineers were everywhere, planning, designing and building: a Paris ship canal, an Alpine rail tunnel under Mont-Cenis, and, one of the greatest triumphs of all, Ferdinand de Lesseps' Suez Canal, which opened in 1869. A channel tunnel was

The Opera House, Paris

planned with grudging British approval, but never materialized. Paris was also modernized. Napoleon gave Baron Haussmann, prefect of the Seine, *carte blanche* for 'urban renewal'. The plan was at once to beautify Paris and make it safe from revolutionary barricades. The old, narrow, crowded central city gave way to broad avenues, boulevards and quays, stately and tree-lined, such as the Champs-Élysées which stretched from the Louvre to Napoleon I's Arc de Triomphe. Parks, churches, hospitals, markets, railway stations (the Gare de l'Est and Gare du Nord) and the modern sewage system were Haussmann's work. The Ile de la Cité was swept clean, save for Sainte-Chapelle, Notre-Dame and the Conciergerie, and remodelled. Many elegant old buildings were razed, and many of the new were gaudy and frivolous. Second-Empire France was frankly materialistic and not always tasteful, and Haussmann's Paris boldly asserted the fact.

Napoleon III, always conscious of his populist base, looked after the interests of ordinary people as well as those of the middle and upper classes: 'Saint-Simon on horseback', Sainte-Beuve once called him. He encouraged advances in public health and slum clearance, was responsible for an array of new financial institutions which welcomed small investors as well as large ones: the Société Générale, Crédit Lyonnais and Crédit Foncier – and Crédit Mobilier, before it collapsed amid scandal.

The emperor was a free trader, as the tariff-reducing 1860 Cobden-Chevalier commercial treaty between Great Britain and France attested. But he also espoused the collective rights of workers against exploiting manufacturers. Trade unions and strikes were legalized, and when Napoleon died in 1873, in exile in England, the only Frenchmen at his funeral were trades unionists.

French Colonialism

Colonial expansion was now a regular part of overseas policy. Even Republicans approved it. Napoleon pressed French interests in Indo-China (Cambodia, Laos and Vietnam), Syria, Africa and Mexico; the Suez Canal was both a commercial adventure and a communications link with outposts in India and the Far East. Colonialism had its drawbacks. The other colonial powers were impressed at French achievements, but also feared them. Meanwhile, colonialism gave Napoleon's opponents at home another stick with which to beat him: Republicans, essentially nationalistic at heart, wanted the emperor to go further; conservatives questioned whether he was wise to go as far as he did. Certainly his Mexican adventure did not display much wisdom.

MEXICO

A civil war ended in Mexico in 1860, and the next year the new government of Benito Juárez suspended payment on foreign debts incurred by the deposed President Miramon. Britain, Spain and France jointly occupied Veracruz to protect their investments, and Mexican *émigrés* in Paris – conservative and Catholic – persuaded Empress Eugénie that only a strong monarchy could save the Church and restore order in Mexico. She pressed her husband to intervene. Over-confident after his own success at 'democratic empire', Napoleon decided the concept would work in Mexico as well. He put forward Prince Maximilian von Habsburg, a former viceroy of Lombardy, as emperor of Mexico. In 1862 Spain and Britain withdrew their troops. They knew that the United States' Monroe Doctrine would not tolerate European interference in the Western Hemisphere. Indeed the Americans were furious; but, caught up in a civil war of their own, they could do nothing to stop the French. In 1864, armed with a dubious Mexican plebiscite in his favour – but, more to the point, behind the bayonets of French troops under Marshals Bazaine and MacMahon – Maximilian entered Mexico City.

Napoleon was already having second thoughts about the venture, but Maximilian and his empress, Carlotta, had the bit in their teeth. Theirs, they reckoned, was a holy mission of restoration, and they persuaded Napoleon to continue French military support. He did so, but with declining enthusiasm.

Napoleon's doubts stemmed from the Americans' antipathy to the venture, and from the fact that in Mexico democratic imperialism was not democratic. Maximilian also had hoped for an enlightened régime, but he was supported mainly by reactionaries to whom enlightenment was anathema. They, not Maximilian, ultimately shaped policy.

President Juárez's followers, meanwhile, were finding caches of weapons and ammunition along the banks of the Rio Grande between Texas and Mexico, seemingly misplaced by the United States Army. With these weapons the Juaristas resisted Maximilian with rising success. The emperor was then persuaded to suppress liberal ideas and shoot suspected Juarista sympathizers out of hand.

In 1865 the American Civil War ended. Napoleon saw the writing on the wall and withdrew French support from Mexico. He was encouraged in this by the United States government using language so firm as to be almost threatening. Violation of the Monroe Doctrine was a *causus belli* in American eyes, if it continued. In 1867 the last French troops withdrew from Veracruz. Maximilian declined to go with them, still believing he had the Mexican people on his side. This seems doubtful, but who will ever know for sure? In the event, Mexico City fell, he was captured, and on 19 May 1867 the victorious Juaristas executed him before a firing squad. The Mexican venture was over. It left Napoleon discredited and the treasury depleted. Equally important, France had been humiliated.

FOREIGN POLICY

The Second Empire fared well in foreign policy before the Mexico fiasco. In 1854 Napoleon involved France as an ally of Britain and Turkey in a war against Russia in the Crimea. The clash was classically European: a war to maintain the balance of power by limiting Russian access to the Mediterranean. It ended with the Peace of Paris in 1856, over which the French foreign minister presided, thus allowing Napoleon to appear as the grand arbiter of European destiny. French pride was satisfied, even if little else had been gained.

The Crimean War was on a small scale, more troops died of cholera than in combat, and military competence was at a premium. The most famous episode, the British cavalry charge at Balaclava, was an utter débâcle. The French commander, General Saint Arnaud, said of it: '*C'est magnifique, mais ce n'est pas la guerre.*' (It is magnificent, but it is not war.)

Léon Gambetta supposedly said much the same thing years later about London's newest marvel, the St Pancras railway station: '*C'est magnifique, mais ce n'est pas la gare.*' (It is magnificent, but it is not a railway station.)

ITALY AND AUSTRIA

Napoleon always fancied an Italian confederation allied with France against Austria. In 1858 he met secretly with Camillo Cavour, the prime minister of Piedmont-Sardinia, the most important north Italian state, and they signed the treaty of Plombières, an agreement to drive Austria out of Italy jointly. The alliance was sealed by the marriage of Clothilde, daughter of the Piedmont-Sardinian monarch, to Jérôme, Napoleon's nephew. Dutiful daughter that she was, Clothilde told Cavour: 'Send Prince Jérôme to me, and if he is not actually repulsive, I shall marry him.'

In 1859 the Austrians provided an excuse and war broke out. Marshal MacMahon was victorious at Magenta in June, and Napoleon entered Milan in triumph. Later he personally commanded at Solferino – and was so horrified at the carnage that he offered an armistice, practically on the spot. The peace of Villafranca and the Treaty of Zurich ended the war officially, giving Nice and Savoy to France while Austria gave up Lombardy and kept Venice. The Italians had wanted this war to lead to the unification of Italy and they therefore felt that Napoleon had betrayed them, and his stock plummeted. It fell still further in 1867 when French troops occupied Rome to protect the pope from Garibaldi. On the other hand, the Austrian emperor, Franz Joseph, thought well of Napoleon's generosity after Solferino, and, back in Paris, even Republicans cheered him for the territorial gains. French troops were still in Rome when the Franco-Prussian war began in 1870. Otherwise, after Villafranca, Napoleon left the Italians to their own devices.

THE FRANCO-PRUSSIAN WAR

This war justified Napleon III's fear of war; it cost him everything.

Otto von Bismarck became Prussian prime minister in 1862; his policy thereafter was to enhance Prussian security in Germany and then German security in Europe. The first aim was fulfilled in 1871 when the German Empire was formed, with Berlin its capital and Prussia its heart and soul. By 1867 Bismarck had made Prussia supreme in Germany through successful wars against Denmark (1864) and Austria (1866).

The possibility of German unification was now clear. French nationalists, believing that France's 'natural' eastern frontier was the Rhine, were not pleased. A sizeable portion of the west bank was in German and Prussian hands, and detaching it from a united German state would be next to impossible. On his side, Bismarck regarded France as the only stumbling block in the way of convincing the Rhenish German states to accept Prussian hegemony.

In 1868 a member of a cadet branch of the Prussian ruling family was nominated to take the recently vacated Spanish throne. 'Encirclement!' cried the French nationalists, and the candidate withdrew. It was not enough. Agitation mounted in the Assembly, and in May, 1870, Count Benedetti, the French ambassador to Prussia, approached King Wilhelm at Ems, on the matter of obtaining a guarantee regarding the Spanish candidacy. *'Jamais encore'* (never again) was the promise that France wanted. The interview was peaceable, and Bismarck received an account of it by telegram. He reworked the telegram to make it appear that the king had rebuffed the ambassador, and that the ambassador had insulted the king. The note was then leaked to the press in Paris and Berlin. Sabres were rattled on both sides. Napoleon III faced an irate Assembly, Bismarck an outraged Reichstag – exactly the mood he wanted from them. The nationalist press in Paris and Berlin was in a martial frenzy. Napoleon did not want war – his meeting with Bismarck at Biarritz the year before had been hopeful – but he was left with no choice. War began in July.

For France it was utter disaster. The Prussians outflanked, outgunned and outgeneralled the French. Marshal Bazaine was trapped at Metz, and Marshal MacMahon at Sedan, where his proud regiments were torn to pieces by Prussian artillery. Napoleon was ill and not able to keep up with the deteriorating situation. He tried to stop the slaughter by getting himself killed at the front, but only managed to be captured. This simply enhanced French humiliation. A Prussian photograph depicts Napoleon and Bismarck, in uniform, seated together in campaign chairs outside of Bismarck's tent. Napoleon looks abjectly miserable; Bismarck resembles nothing so much as the cat who has just finished off the canary.

When news of Napoleon's capture reached Paris, radicals seized control of the Assembly, declared a republic, and formed a provisional government. On 27 October Bazaine surrendered Metz, and the Prussians besieged Paris. Léon Gambetta escaped from the city in a hot-air balloon and made his way to the Loire Valley, where he tried unsuccessfully to raise an army in the name of the new republic. On 28 January 1871, Paris capitulated and the war was virtually over – just three days after the Prussians humiliated France still further by having the German Empire proclaimed at a ceremony in the *Galerie des Glaces* at Versailles.

An election in February 1871 returned a National Assembly full of moderates and conservatives; radicals, for the most part, were not elected. The mandate was clearly for peace. The Assembly selected Adolphe Thiers, a conservative, to head the provisional government, which set up its headquarters at Versailles. Thiers then negotiated the draconian treaty of Frankfurt which ended the war. France had to pay five billion francs in indemnities and lost Alsace and part of Lorraine. The Assembly approved it by 546 votes to 107, and the treaty was signed on 10 May.

The Paris Commune

The Assembly outraged Paris by making the château of Versailles, the symbol of the old order, its meeting place. Municipal elections in March 1871 returned a radical council, or commune. (George Clemenceau, a future prime minister, was elected for Montmartre.) This commune rebelled against Versailles. The Paris Commune was never communist, as many at the time – and later – made out; it was, in fact, extremely bourgeois. Nevertheless it was also revolutionary, and after two months an army under MacMahon besieged it. The Tuileries Palace was burnt down in consequence.

The Commune held out for six weeks, but could not withstand MacMahon's peasant soldiers for whom Paris was not sacred. When the city fell, the government took vengeance. All told, twenty thousand were tried and summarily shot, imprisoned or transported to French penal colonies. Thus was born the Third Republic.

The Third Republic

All of the forces which had been factors in French political and social life since 1815 were manifested in the Third Republic: monarchism, republicanism, reaction, radicalism, clericalism and Bonapartism. Nursed along by Thiers and then by the monarchist soldier, Mac-Mahon, the Republic was officially established only in 1875, and then more or less by default. It came about simply because the Assembly accepted the Wallon amendment. Deputy Wallon said:

> My conclusion is that it is necessary to leave the provisional. If monarchy is possible, show that it will be accepted, propose it. If . . . it is not possible, I do not say to you: decide for the Republic, but I say: recognize the government now established, which is the government of the Republic. I do not ask you to proclaim it as definitive – what is definitive? But all the same do not call it provisional.

This was hardly an oratorical *tour de force*, but it was effective. There was no constitution, only laws having constitutional ramifications: a seven-year renewable presidency; a Senate, one-third chosen for life, the rest for nine-year terms, a third to be elected every three years; and a Chamber of Deputies, elected by constituencies. None of it worked quite as expected, but it did survive, right down to 1940.

REPUBLICAN ISSUES

The royalist cause had scant hope of success, but both the Bourbon count of Chambord and the Orléanist count of Paris had followers. So too did the Bonapartists, and when Napoleon III's son died in 1879, fighting in the British army invading Zululand, the *sense* of Bonapartism continued in strongmen – or would-be strongmen – such as General Georges Boulanger. Meanwhile, clericalism and anti-clericalism dominated the politics of Right and Left, and the strength or weakness of the presidency was of concern to all.

GENERAL BOULANGER

A self-advertising soldier, General Boulanger was a useful minister of war who reformed the army. But his ambitions went well beyond that. Early in the game, radical politicians like Clemenceau supported him. Soon Boulanger took for himself the Bonapartist mantle, and made himself a dangerous and popular force on the Right. In 1889 he was overwhelmingly elected to the Assembly for Paris. Huge mobs surrounded him on election night crying '*À l'Élysée!*', the Élysée Palace in the Rue du Faubourg Saint-Honoré now being official residence for the president. A *coup* seemed inevitable.

But the general hesitated. Why is not clear. He did nothing, and when the government moved to arrest him – or appeared to – he fled to Belgium and his mistress. Boulanger faded from French history at that point, appearing only for an instant a few years later to prove that Romance still informed the French mentality: when his mistress died Boulanger lay down across her grave and shot himself.

SCANDAL

The word is almost synonymous with the Third Republic. Even as Boulanger was proving a broken reed, a scandal erupted over Ferdinand de Lesseps' failure to repeat, in Panama, his triumph in Suez. The controversy concerned corrupt officials, and even more corrupt financiers, such as Cornelius Herz. The Republic stumbled grimly through this, and trauma piled upon trauma. Panama drove Clemenceau briefly from public life; public unrest turned into violence, and President Sadi Carnot was assassinated. Meanwhile, Church–State conflict erupted into the infamous Dreyfus scandal.

THE DREYFUS AFFAIR

'Clericalism – there is the enemy!' proclaimed Léon Gambetta, and after he passed from the scene Jules Ferry continued the theme. Republicans felt threatened by the Church, and Catholics felt persecuted by the Republic. Education was increasingly laicized, '*école sans Dieu*', in Albert de Broglie's phrase, and the Republic made no pretence at allowing for equality between lay and religious education. The result was a Church–State dualism in education which persists to the present day.

In the 1880s, a progressive papacy encouraged *railliement*, a policy of reconciliation between Church and Republic. A 'democratized', and even on occasion radicalized, priesthood went into proletarian neighbourhoods and improved the Church's image. *Railliement* had only limited success among traditional secular anti-Republicans, however. They gave up on monarchism, but created a New Right: anti-Semitic, pro-Catholic, and aimed at seizing control of the Republic.

Such was the state of affairs when in 1896 Captain Alfred Dreyfus, the only Jew on the army general staff, was arrested for selling military secrets to the Germans. The evidence against him was worse than spurious; it was non-existent. He was tried because he was a Jew in an army dominated by anti-Semitic aristocrats and Catholics, who regarded the army as their private preserve. For most of them Dreyfus proved his unsuitability for membership in this élite by refusing to commit suicide when confronted with arrest.

At first it was generally believed that Dreyfus was guilty; even by Clemenceau and Jean Jaurès, who also feared that he might escape punishment. Dreyfus should be hanged, said Clemenceau, usually an opponent of the death penalty. The anti-Semitic press, represented by Édouard Drumont's *La Libre Parole*, had earlier built a case against Jews in the army, and now led the public attack on Dreyfus. The captain was convicted without opposition on the strength of forged evidence and shipped to Devil's Island. The case was closed.

MAJOR PICQUART

But not quite. Major Picquart of military intelligence, as anti-Semitic as any other Catholic officer, was curious why Dreyfus, a rich and happily-married man, would sell secrets. Picquart found no reason; but he did find evidence pointing to a transplanted Hungarian officer, Major Esterhazy – profligate, always in debt, notoriously without scruple, but devotedly Catholic and aristocratic – as the guilty man. Picquart had come too close to the truth. Soon he was in Tunis inspecting fortifications. Colonel Henri, the intelligence officer who compromised Dreyfus in the first instance, wanted no one rocking the boat.

DREYFUSARDS AND ANTI-DREYFUSARDS

The Dreyfus family never stopped protesting, and by 1898 important people began to believe them. The novelist Émile Zola published his famous *J'Accuse*; Clemenceau changed his opinion, and came out in support of reopening the case. France was divided between those who thought Dreyfus innocent – or at least saw in this an opportunity to bring down their political enemies – and those who thought him guilty, or at least a convenient scapegoat. The issue was the survival of the Republic, and for a decade the controversy was very ugly.

The Republic survived. Dreyfus was exonerated and returned to his post with a promotion. Strong governments under René Waldeck-Rousseau and Émile Combes brought the most troublesome anti-Dreyfusard elements of Church and army under control. But scars were left, not least among which was open anti-Semitism and a mood and style highly suggestive of fascism.

ACTION FRANÇAISE

After the Dreyfus Affair, the Right regrouped, mostly as conservative Republicans. But early in the twentieth century *Action Française* appeared. Extremist Catholics, aristocrats and even royalists converged into a league built upon the proto-fascist, anti-Semitic theories of Charles Maurras and Léon Daudet. Maurras's journal, called *L'Action Française*, was one propaganda channel for the league; another was a volunteer corps of *Camelots du Roi*, who wore uniforms and were not above using violence against individuals and groups of which the league disapproved. *Action Française* was small and not very influential; but it reflected a disease of the spirit which would greatly affect the ability of France to function democratically in the years to come.

THE LEFT

Meanwhile, the socialist and trade-union Left was beginning to flourish. Jean Jaurès and Jules Guesde led the Socialists, although they did not agree on their Marxism. Jaurès established *L'Humanité* as the leading socialist newspaper, and in 1899 *L'Internationale* replaced *La Carmagnole* as the party song. Labour was grouped largely in the

Confédération Générale du Travail, which was anarchist rather than socialist. By 1909 it had nearly a million members. Among CGT leaders was Aristide Briand, author of the movement's General Strike ideology: shutting down everything through industrial action in order to force social and political change. It was more myth than reality: there were strikes, and they were often violent, but there was never a General Strike.

ECONOMY AND SOCIETY

The French population grew by only three-and-a-half million between 1870 and 1914, rapidly falling behind Britain and Germany. Half of the French people lived in rural areas; half of French labour was agricultural, and half of them worked on farms of less than two-and-a-half acres. This population was relatively prosperous after 1871. France trailed after only the United States and Russia in grain production, and only after Italy in wine. Phylloxera nearly destroyed the French wine trade in the 1860s but grafts from immune American vines revived it, and by 1885 it was again prospering. Farm houses now had wooden floors, and the blue blouse and wooden *sabot* of the peasant was disappearing. Pressure for change was therefore less now than in earlier decades.

Meanwhile, industry expanded rapidly even though raw materials often had to be imported. By 1914 steam-power use had multiplied ten-fold, coal production doubled, cast-iron multiplied by four and steel by twelve. Yet the industrial workforce was only half of the total labouring population, and a majority of these worked in shops with less than five employees. Large enterprises remained relatively less common than in Germany or Great Britain. The reality, if not the concept, of the industrial masses was not so evident in France as elsewhere. Politically radical, socially conservative just about sums up French society under the Third Republic.

COLONIES

The French were frugal, and vast amounts of savings were available to invest abroad in capital loans or for development of territories already acquired as colonies. Despite the unease about overseas ventures that had been inspired by Napoleon's Mexican débâcle, statesmen of the Third Republic expanded French colonialism well beyond Second Empire limits. Some statesmen, indeed, firmly believed in colonialism: for Jules Ferry it was a supply mechanism for the industrial revolution; Gambetta and other Republicans agreed, and also saw the possession of colonies as the measure of being a great power; and the French Catholic Church was a leading exporter of Christianity, and therefore a supporter of colonial expansion. Three-quarters of Catholic foreign missionaries in these decades were French. In 1881 Tunis became a French protectorate; Tonkin (North Vietnam) in 1885, and Laos and Cambodia five years later, fell to France, giving the Republic control of some of the richest areas in south-east Asia. Madagascar became a French possession in 1896, and other parts of Africa soon followed. By 1898 France controlled a colonial empire second only to that of Great Britain, and well ahead of Germany's.

CULTURE

If French colonialism achieved eminence under the Third Republic, French culture achieved pre-eminence. True, bureaucrats and the conservative bourgeoisie attempted to dictate taste as they had done under the Second Empire – it has been said that the Third Republic held advantage over the Second Empire in public building only in that there was less of it – and to some extent succeeded. The Third Republic was responsible for the basilica of Sacré-Coeur, Gustave Eiffel's Tower (for the Paris Exhibition of 1889), and the Statue of Liberty in New York Harbour, all of doubtful artistic merit. But this was a small part of the picture, and after 1870 France again emerged as the cultural inspiration of Europe.

In 1863 Édouard Manet was rejected by the *Salon des Beaux Arts* in Paris, the arbiter of respectability. The *Salon* ran to such refinements as imposing fig leaves on nude statues by Auguste Rodin. The same year, Manet held a rival exhibition with other rejected artists called the *Salon des Refusés*. His painting *Déjeuner sur l'Herbe* was included, shocking Parisians not because it featured a nude woman picnicking with male companions, but because she was depicted as a tart rather than as a Venus.

IMPRESSIONISM AND OTHER STYLES

A revolution was in the making, and the *Salon des Refusés* began it. The Impressionists abandoned strict definition of line and colour in order to achieve new effects with the play of light on objects. The idea soon spread beyond Impressionist purists, who insisted on limiting their work to landscapes and other exteriors, and an entire generation manipulated the Impressionist principle to create their own individual styles. Claude Monet's painting of a water–lily pond was a misty, dreamy experiment with light; Georges Seurat's pointillism – piling different coloured dots on the canvas until they achieved the desired form and value – was an Impressionist extreme; so too was Pablo Picasso's Cubism, though in the opposite direction. Soon every subject was fair game. Revolution in style merged with revolution in subject matter and purpose: Gustave Courbet insisted that his paintings of peasant life embodied Proudhonian socialism; Paul Gauguin's Tahitian motifs incorporated a vague naturalism; and Henri Toulouse-Lautrec applied Impressionist technique to the bohemian life of the Montmartre. Never have so many great names marched through French art together: Camille Pissarro, Edgar Degas, Paul Cézanne, Henri Matisse, Pierre-Auguste Renoir, and Vincent Van Gogh, among others. Paris was their spiritual home, but not their only venue: much of the time Monet was in Normandy, Gauguin in Tahiti and Van Gogh in Provence, when he was not in an insane asylum.

After the *Salon des Refusés*, sculptors, painters, composers and writers moved away more and more from convention into experimentation with impressionism, realism and naturalism. Auguste Rodin and Jules Dalou were leaders in sculpture. With *Carmen* in 1875, Georges Bizet gave France an operatic style which departed from both the Italians and Richard Wagner. He was soon followed in other musical *genres* by Maurice Ravel, Claude Debussy, Camille Saint-Saëns, Erik Satie and Paul Dukas. Gabriel Fauré and Saint-Saëns helped establish a musical theatre at Béziers intended to be a French rival to Wagner's Bayreuth.

Realism and naturalism – the anatomy of life as lived – informed Gustave Flaubert's *Madame Bovary*, Émile Zola's *Nana* and *Thérèse Raquin*, Guy de Maupassant's three hundred short stories, and Charles Baudelaire's *Les Fleurs du Mal*, which linked realism with romanticism through eroticism, lesbianism and other forbidden themes. Six of the poems in *Les Fleurs* were condemned in a court case and stricken from the published volume. In 1913, Paris was shocked again – but by now was more resigned to it – by the erotic and disturbing implications of Igor Stravinsky's ballet *Le Sacre du Printemps*, stage set by the Russian, Nicholas Roerich and with choreography by Vaslav Nijinsky.

Philosophy too was radically alive. Auguste Comte created Positivism, a sort of religion of science based on the laws of social progress, from which evolved sociology. It was fundamentally politically conservative, although methodologically innovative. So too were Hippolyte Taine (also a Positivist), who hated democracy and feared revolution, and Émile Durkheim, whose group, or mass, sociology sought to expose the irrationality of democratic action. By contrast, liberal rationalism was evident in Ernest Renan's 'biography' of Christ – but not among his colleagues at the Collège de France, who deprived Renan of his chair of Hebrew history over the book. Meanwhile, in the field of science, the Third Republic basked in the glow emanating from Henri Poincaré in mathematics, Marie Curie in radiology, and Louis Pasteur in bacteriology.

In this epoch France also contributed to the expanding world of sport, which is an expression of style all on its own, as any cricket enthusiast can attest. In 1896, Pierre, baron de Coubertin inspired the revival of the Olympiad of ancient Greece. The first of these modern Olympic Games was held in Athens; the second, in honour of Coubertin and plagued with all manner of problems, met for 'five chaotic months' in Paris. They came to Paris again in 1924, and went much more smoothly than before. Then, in 1903, Henri Desgrange organized the first Tour de France, an international bicycle race that covers, in several phases, more than 1000 kilometres. The Tour de France is unquestionably the most prestigious sporting event of its kind in the world.

FOREIGN POLICY

After 1870 France recognized that it was not a match for Germany alone. There were years of sabre-rattling ahead, over the indemnity and the loss of territory, and the cry '*revanchisme!*' (revenge) was a part of political rhetoric at the hustings and in the Assembly. But realists saw the way the wind now blew. In the early years, Bismarck, chancellor of the new German Empire, maintained alliances and relationships designed to keep France isolated: the Three Emperors' League (Germany, Russia and Austria), and later the Triple Alliance (Germany, Austria and Italy). He also maintained good relations with Great Britain, whose traditional policy was to keep a watchful eye on the balance of power in Europe and, if possible, to stay out of it. French policy would have to change. No more French mastery over Europe. Even survival might now depend on outside help.

ANGLO-FRENCH RAPPROCHEMENT

Great diplomatist that he was, Bismarck was not infallible. In 1884–85 he revised his basic policy and wooed France with the aim of isolating Great Britain. But France was not to be wooed. The effort resulted in France and Britain together looking distrustfully at Germany. In 1890 Bismarck was dismissed from office by the new emperor, Wilhelm II, who wanted an aggressive, expansionist world policy. In 1894 France made a mutual defence pact with Russia, aimed specifically against Germany, and French isolation was broken.

Théophile Delcassé, foreign minister from 1898 to 1905, was anti-German at heart and wanted to go further than an understanding with the Tsar. His policy was to strengthen the Russian bond and reconcile France to Great Britain. A common enemy, in short, or potential common enemy, achieved a reversal of Anglo-French antagonism that was 900 years old. How long it would last, no one could say. But no matter: for now, Delcassé arrived at amicable solutions to Anglo-French imbroglios in Egypt, the Sudan and Morocco, and in 1904 constructed the Entente Cordiale with Britain.

The Entente in its particulars covered everything from disputes in Egypt and Morocco to Newfoundland fisheries claims, and when the first Moroccan confrontation with Germany occurred in 1905, the agreement was transformed into a mutual Mediterranean defence pact aimed directly at Germany. German Mediterranean policy had worried Delcassé, and the German naval expansion programme had irked Britain, for some time before then. After 1905 Europe was, in effect, divided into armed camps.

Europe Divided

Wilhelm II seemed intent upon stirring every available pot. He publicly proclaimed Germany's sympathy with the Boers in South Africa, and tested the Entente Cordiale by claiming a share in the Moroccan investments in 1905 and again in 1911. Britain and France had shared Morocco between themselves alone, and had no intention of doing otherwise. Wilhelm was rebuffed, but such confrontations as these heightened tensions throughout Europe. Faced with the emperor's posturing, and his aggressive colonial and naval policies, Great Britain joined France and Russia in the Triple Entente, signed in 1907. Europe's six major powers were now grouped in two mutually suspicious and, on occasion, hostile alliance systems.

Tension then piled upon tension: Germany financed a railway system linking Berlin to Baghdad, which was interpreted as a German threat to Britain's control over the Suez Canal; Austria annexed Bosnia on the Adriatic Sea; Russia backed an anti-Austrian *coup* in Serbia; German generals trained Turkish armies; efforts to initiate international disarmament talks fell flat; and Balkan states at war with Turkey in 1912–13 were armed and trained by the French. The Middle East, meanwhile, to which the Balkans were the European gateway, was of rising importance well beyond the need to control the Suez Canal.

The new ingredient was oil. Middle East oil production was still small in 1914, but clearly it would increase. European navies were beginning to transfer from coal to oil-powered engines, and the age of the automobile and oil-powered factories was beginning. Through all of this, Europe's leaders did the routine things and went through the usual diplomatic motions, and pretended that the world could go on as it was forever.

Paris was lovely in the spring of 1914; so too was Provence, the Dordogne, and the beaches of Brittany, where the French would soon spend their summer holidays. Some thought about the disturbing implications of Marcel Proust's *À la Recherche du Temps Perdu* (Remembrance of Times Lost), the first volume of which was published in 1913.

Then the summer came; it was the hottest that anyone could ever remember.

CHAPTER NINE

France in the Century of Total War
1914–1945

In a sense, the European nineteenth century ended with the outbreak of the First World War in 1914. For the next thirty years, Europe was in a state of waging, recovering from or preparing for general war. France was squarely in the middle of it all, and the experience transformed France quite as effectively as had the wars of the Revolution and of Napoleon.

The First World War

Archduke Franz Ferdinand, heir to the Austrian throne, visited Sarajevo, in Bosnia, on 28 June 1914. Gavrilo Princip, a Bosnian nationalist, was one of a half-dozen student terrorists sworn to assassinate him. It was a confused, messy business. The archduke did not appear when or where he was meant to on the route out of the city, and Princip thought he had missed his chance. Disconsolate, he sat at a table in a pavement café. An open car stopped in the square opposite. Incredibly, inside sat the archduke and archduchess. Without hesitation, Princip dashed into the street, leaped onto the running-board, and fired six shots at the pair before the startled bodyguards could move. Both Franz Ferdinand and Sophia died of their wounds. So too, in a manner of speaking, did Princip, who was executed for this murder. But his place in history was assured. His six shots were the first heard in what came to be known as the First World War.

No one expected this event to produce a general war; after all, Balkan crises were nothing unusual. But Austria, seeking to turn the assassination to advantage against Russia in the Balkans, declared war on

Russia's client, Serbia, on 28 July. Russia reacted; Germany reacted to Russia; alliances were invoked and armies mobilized; ultimata flew back and forth; and war began on 3 August, unexpectedly and disastrously. British foreign secretary, Sir Edward Grey, uttered perhaps the most subsequently quoted words from that moment: 'The lights are going out all over Europe. We shall not see them lit again in our lifetime.'

France at War

There was no great agitation for war as in 1870. All the same, nationalism was rampant. Jean Jaurès, the only pacifist voice in the Assembly, was assassinated on 31 July. President Raymond Poincaré called for national unity, and, for once, got it. Every shade of political opinion believed German aggression lay behind the war, and so backed the government. There was no French Fifth Column in 1914.

Unity did not, however, guarantee competence. As in the past, the General Staff set out in 1914 to fight the preceding war instead of the present one. Of course, so did everyone else. The commander-in-chief, Marshal Joseph Joffre, along with the General Staff, expected a short war on the order of 1870, to be decided by a single, sharp offensive.

In the early days of the war – and as in 1870 – it looked as if the Germans were winning. Following the Schlieffen Plan, Germany's order of battle in the west, General von Kluck drove across Belgium, into France and towards Paris. The government withdrew to Bordeaux, just in case, after reorganizing to include Socialists, Radicals and Conservatives in the cabinet. The national union was secure; the nation was not, however, and on 5 September Paris itself seemed likely to fall.

But General Gallieni, commander of the Paris garrison, counterattacked that day on the Marne, with reinforcements sent from Paris literally by taxi cabs. Von Kluck was stopped. Over the next four months, with the help of the British Expeditionary Force, the lines were stabilized with ten *départements* in enemy territory, and the armies in trenches which stretched from the Swiss frontier to the North Sea. In these first four months of war France suffered 850,000 casualties. Sadly, they were only a foretaste of losses to come.

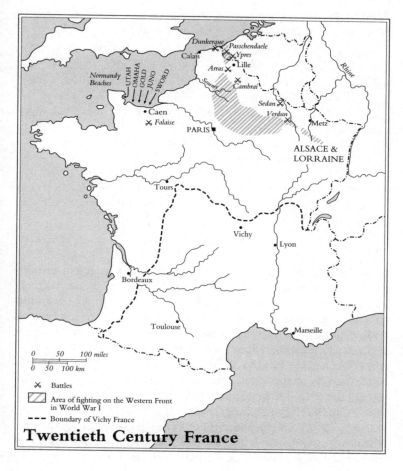

Twentieth Century France

The French command continued committed to the concept of the large offensive, to which soon was added attacks by troops who sallied forth from the trenches in small numbers. The main effect was large-scale slaughter, to little apparent purpose. It was the style on all sides, and casualties mounted steadily through 1915. Political and military nerves grew frayed, hence the symbolic tragedy of Verdun.

VERDUN

In February 1916, the Germans attacked Verdun, near Sedan. Aristide Briand, now premier, knew that if Verdun – strategically unimportant but a symbol of the national will to resist – fell, public morale and his government would fall with it. Verdun had to be held. Briand ordered a counter-offensive, led by General Philippe Pétain. Pétain saved the fortress and made his reputation; but between Verdun and the Somme offensive in July to relieve pressure on the fortress, there were half-a-million French casualties – and Marshal Joffre lost his reputation. Public disillusionment set in, and the government embarked on an extensive propaganda campaign to sustain public support for the war. Joffre was its victim, and was dismissed at the end of the year. His successor, General Nivelle also failed; Marshal Foch played the game better and lasted until 1918.

1917

This year was the turning point in the war and in twentieth-century European and French history. The United States entered the war, and would subsequently play a role in Europe; mutinies broke out in the allied armies, chiefly as protests against the endless slaughter; in France radical journals of Left and Right, *Le Bonnet Rouge* and *L'Action Française*, for example, stirred civilian unrest; first the Briand and then the Ribot and the Painlevé governments fell, the latter caught up in a scandal involving the famous German spy, Mata Hari; strikes, absent in France since the war began, now were widespread, given impetus by the Bolshevik Revolution in Russia in November; and Georges Clemenceau became premier. Like Britain's David Lloyd George, Clemenceau was an able and ruthless politician who would stick at nothing to bring order out of the sudden chaos. The war ground on.

THE VERSAILLES TREATY

The war ended at last on 11 November 1918. The Kaiser was forced to abdicate and a Republic was declared in Germany. At the end, German armies were in full retreat before Allied armies led by British, French and American generals. When the Americans arrived in France early in

1918, General Pershing probably did not actually say: 'Lafayette, we are here!' – a reference to French contribution to American independence. However, American President Wilson did urge upon Europeans the ideals of open diplomacy, national self-determination, and a League of Nations through which nations would arbitrate their differences. Clemenceau remarked: 'God gave us ten commandments we couldn't keep. Now Wilson gives us fourteen!'

In the spring of 1919, the victorious powers met in Paris to work out the peace at a conference which much resembled – or so many historians have thought – the Congress of Vienna a century before. France had been the battleground for much of the war, and had moral force on its side. Behind Clemenceau's leadership, France got most of what it wanted. The treaty returned Alsace and Lorraine, reduced the German military to 100,000 with no air force or submarines, demilitarized the Rhineland (Clemenceau would have preferred a separatist Rhineland, but Lloyd George, looking to the future, would not permit it) and assessed heavy reparations against Germany.

The treaty was signed on 28 June 1919 in the *Galerie des Glaces* at Versailles – sweet revenge for 1871. The Germans had no input; for them the treaty was a 'diktat', and a growing source of resentment in the interwar years which made no small contribution to the rising tide of German fascism and the coming of the next war.

WHAT PRICE GLORY?

The war cost the earth. France had 1,322,000 dead and 3 million wounded soldiers; a quarter of the dead were under 24 years of age. The dead included 81,000 out of the 608,000 colonial troops fighting with the French army. Consequently, the birth-rate plummeted. In 1938 France had only half the number of 19- to 21-year-olds it would have had without the war. In 1919 France was short of 3 million workers, and the gap had to be made up by foreigners, whose mere presence created resentment among French labourers. Ten *départements* had been laid waste by the Germans, including mines, blast furnaces, roads, railways, agriculture, sometimes whole towns. The population of Reims dropped from 117,000 to 17,000, Soissons from 18,000 to 500. The war also played havoc with the nation's finances. The national debt

in 1919 was 175 billion francs, five times greater than in 1913. Prices
had risen 400 per cent since 1914, and the income tax introduced to
pay for the war ate into everyone's income, especially among the
bourgeoisie.

There were advances, too. Mass production was introduced on a large
scale during the war, and many heavy industries expanded to make war
materiél. They cut back in peacetime, but the principle of growth had
been established and the industrial economy was ready for the take-off in
productivity which began in the 1920s. Inflation pushed up farm prices
further than costs, and the peasants were better off than before 1914.
Trade unions at the war's end were accorded more respect than in the
past, and the number of women teaching in schools increased.

WOMEN AND THE WAR

The status of French women hardly altered as a result of participating in
the war. Women entered the war-work force in large numbers: they
comprised 25 per cent of the munitions workers, for example, and at
Renault were 4 per cent of the general work force in 1914, rising to 32
per cent by 1918. But working conditions were appalling. Women
were resented by male workers, who saw to it that they had largely
menial, and even dangerous, jobs. 70,000 industrial accidents reported
in 1917 involved women. Sexual harassment was commonplace. After
the war, the numbers of women in work increased, but shifted into
'light' industry and white-collar, mostly secretarial, jobs.

The sexual division of labour was not altered; and no 'feminist
revolution' was in the offing. If French men could have had their way,
French women would have stayed at home and had babies. French
governments tended to agree: stiff penalties were invoked for dis-
tributing propaganda for birth control through the use of contraceptives,
or in favour of abortion. In 1922 an attempt to give the vote to women
passed the Chamber, but was thrown out by the Senate. French women
would have to wait for their political liberation until 1945.

POST-WAR

Meanwhile, the slaughter of those four years and the horrors of life in
the trenches produced a disillusioned and pacifist generation. Even the

most patriotic of returning soldiers were fervent partisans of peace at any price. Pessimism and malaise: these were the war's legacy.

POLITICS

In the 1920s, French politics operated on the principle of Buggins' Turn. First the *Bloc National* had power; it was a Nationalist–Catholic alliance formed to protect the interests of big business and the Church. It was supported in the pages of *L'Action Française* and other extreme right-wing publications; Léon Daudet, an *Action Française* contributor, was elected to the Chamber for Paris in 1919. For the first time, the Third Republic had produced a Chamber in which the majority of members were practising Catholics. This was known as the 'Sky-Blue Chamber', Conservative and clericist.

The first item on the post-war agenda was reconstruction. But that would cost a great deal, and the *Bloc* had no intention of paying for it by raising taxes. Rather, the Germans could pay through reparations. This idea had wide sympathy on both the Left and the Right. In 1922 Raymond Poincaré, former president, became premier with a specific mandate to enforce reparations.

When Germany defaulted on the payments in January 1923, Poincaré activated a clause in the Versailles Treaty which allowed Marshal Foch to occupy the Ruhr Valley and enforce payment. The occupation force also encouraged Rhenish separatism: 19,000 German state officials were dismissed and replaced by pro-separatist Rhinelanders. The German government responded by flooding the Ruhr with inflated currency. The effect was to ruin the German monetary system and deprive France of the full allotted reparation bill. In 1924 Poincaré was forced to accept an American mediated reduction of reparations. His government fell soon after, and it was the turn of the *Cartel des Gauches* (Left Alliance) to govern, under Radical premier Édouard Herriot.

The *Cartel* was Radical–Socialist, with the Radicals in the majority. As a gesture to the Socialists, Jean Jaurès's ashes were installed in the Panthéon. Otherwise, Radicals and Socialists were miles apart. The Radicals advocated the free-market system, reducing government to a minimum; the Socialists expected the government to run the economy as well as the state. But the Socialists had no real power, and they were at odds with the Radicals over social policy, and with the French Communist Party and its 500,000-member trade union, the Confédération Générale du Travail Unitaire, over the Communists' insistence that political guidance must come from Moscow. The best the Socialists could do was help the Radicals fend off the *Bloc*. The Communists, like *Action Française* (which temporarily lost credibility through a row with the papacy), were mainly a nuisance value in French political life.

THE ECONOMY

The Herriot government gave up only reluctantly on the idea that reparations could pay for reconstruction. But there was no choice. Serious inflation and a fall in the value of the franc came after 1924, and there were signs of incipient public rebellion as confidence waned. The government then forgot artificial solutions to economic problems and simply raised taxes and reduced expenditure. It worked. The economy was fundamentally sound and took off almost at once. Confidence in the government returned; the franc revived, and by 1928 the economy was as prosperous and progressive as it had been before the war.

FOREIGN POLICY

Foreign affairs remained the chief topic of interest throughout the 1920s. From the moment war ended, France looked for security. There seemed none to be had. The United States refused to ratify the Versailles Treaty, which left Europe bearing the responsibility for the League of Nations; in 1922 Britain sided with the Greeks against Turkey, whom France favoured. 'Perfidious Albion', the French cried, grimly assenting to Clemenceau's lament in 1919: 'England is the lost illusion of my life! Not a day passes that I do not receive from one of our agents abroad reports indicating veritably hostile acts.'

Suitable alliances were sought: Belgium in 1920, Poland in 1921, and Czechoslovakia in 1924, the latter associating France with the 'Little Entente' of Czechoslovakia, Rumania and Yugoslavia. France did not wish to distance itself from Britain or from Soviet Russia, despite French antipathy to Bolshevism. Only Germany was a constant negative factor in foreign-policy considerations, and Britain's efforts to ease reparations payments, as at the Genoa Conference in 1921, met with a flat French refusal. France also fared better at the naval disarmament conference in Washington than did Britain; but in 1923 came the disastrous occupation of the Ruhr. French troops stayed on in the Ruhr until 1929 when there was a second mediated reparations reduction.

In 1924, Aristide Briand took over foreign policy. He was flexible, subtle yet idealistic, and took a different tack from his predecessors. He involved France in on-going disarmament talks, and drew upon the Francophilia of British foreign secretary, Austen Chamberlain, to arrange some accommodations with Germany that would recognize French apprehensions. The result was the Locarno meeting between Briand and the German foreign minister, Gustav Stresemann, in 1925, and a general agreement between them, the Treaty of Locarno. While problems were not solved, an atmosphere was created which promised a more constructive approach in the future. For this Briand was a hero in Paris.

The 'Locarno Spirit' operated in foreign policy for four years, during which French economic recovery continued, aided by expanding Franco-German trade. The idealistic high point came in 1928 when the multilateral International Treaty for the Renunciation of War as an Instrument of National Policy was constructed by Briand and the American secretary of state, Frank Kellogg.

The Crash of 1929

For every silver lining there is a cloud, to turn the adage around. In 1930 Briand derived a plan for Franco-German economic co-operation leading towards European integration, and then another for European Union. But Europe was not yet ready for a Common Market, and in any case, events were already in train which would undercut Briand's achievements.

The New York Stock Market crashed in October 1929. Subsequently President Herbert Hoover declared a moratorium on German reparations payments, while insisting that France continue to pay its war debts; in 1930 the Nazis gained 107 seats in the Reichstag, and in 1932 took control of it with 250 seats. In 1933 Adolf Hitler was named chancellor of Germany. In that year too, French unemployment reached 1,300,000, an indication that the general depression triggered by the Stock Market crash had reached France. Illusions of peace and prosperity were shattered. By 1935 production was down by 20 per cent; shares on the Bourse fell by 33 per cent, dividends by 50 per cent; agricultural income had dropped 33 per cent by 1934, and bankruptcy among small businesses had doubled. In 1938 French exports were down by 50 per cent, and the balance of payments was running a 3000 million franc deficit. The government had no idea how to deal with the crisis.

CRISIS POLITICS

Prime ministers came and went after 1924: Herriot, Painlevé, Briand, Poincaré, and in 1929 André Tardieu. Tardieu was a former henchman of Clemenceau, whom Bernhard von Bülow, German chancellor (1900–1909), once called 'the seventh greatest power in Europe'. Superior in every way, Tardieu was trusted by no one. He had sweeping political reforms in mind, including a Five-Year Plan for 'national retooling', but they came to nothing because of opposition from Radicals, Socialists and Conservatives. He left office in 1932.

A new *Cartel des Gauches* then emerged, and having learnt nothing from 1924, it named Édouard Herriot as prime minister. He again demonstrated his inability to grasp economic problems and soon left office. After him came Édouard Daladier and a succession of non-entities, until the formation in 1936 of the *Front Populaire* under the brilliant Jewish Socialist, Léon Blum. Crises continued, and still governments had no idea how to solve them. Extremists of the Right, on the other hand, thought that they did.

THE STAVISKY SCANDAL

Serge Stavisky, a prominent businessman, committed suicide in 1934 when it appeared that the police were closing in on him over some shady financial dealings. Revelation followed revelation, and it emerged that Stavisky was highly connected with the government. The situation was made to order for the extremists, and the journal *L'Action Française* lost no time in alleging in its pages that Stavisky had in fact been murdered to keep him from talking. On 6 February 1934, Right-wing demonstrators congregated outside the Chamber chanting anti-Republican slogans. The scene quickly deteriorated into a riot: 14 people were killed and another 236 were injured. Deputies were manhandled, and the rioting continued on into the night.

Republican politicians were sure all of this was part of a conspiracy to seize the government, that there was a fascist plot. They were not entirely wrong, but were far from correct. *Action Française* was not fascist, but had fascist traits: anti-parliamentarism, anti-Communism, nationalism, xenophobia, anti-Semitism and the cult of violence were part of the outlook of *Action Française, Jeunesse Patriotes, Solidarité Française*, and other extreme groups on the Right in the 1930s. They all had their blue-shirts, or other bully-boys to stir up trouble, do battle with the police and break shop windows in Jewish neighbourhoods. The *Croix de Feu*, run by Colonel de la Rocque, had nearly half-a-million members and was thought by the Left to be the most dangerous extremist group.

The intellectuals of the extreme Right urged what amounted to authoritarian models for government and society. They thought they knew best how to solve French problems; but the Right never came closer to taking control than the attack on the Assembly on 6 February 1934. This incident was not a failed *coup* so much as an indication of growing economic, social and political malaise, discontent with the Republic and successive governments, and exasperation over seemingly irresolvable economic difficulties.

THE FRONT POPULAIRE

The climate of the times was well illustrated by the brutal physical assault by an *Action Française* mob on Léon Blum, just five months before he formed his popular front government in 1936. Charles Maurras, editor of *L'Action Française*, was briefly imprisoned for inciting the attack, which merely heightened his popularity. Blum was not deterred by the assault; but his task was in any case formidable. A massive strike spread through French industry in April and May, in the belief that the election which had brought Blum to power was the start of the revolution. It was not. Blum's government attempted much; it achieved little.

The strike ended with some gains for the workers, and perhaps some increased disillusionment. Extremist Right-wing 'leagues' such as *Action Française* were dissolved (though *Croix de Feu* simply re-formed into a political party, *Parti Social Français*, which soon had 800,000 members). War industries were nationalized. Women were made government undersecretaries of state, even though they did not yet have the franchise. The rest of Blum's plans never went beyond theory. First, the Spanish Civil War began almost as Blum took office, and while he sympathized with the Spanish Republic against General Franco's nationalist rebels, it was not politically expedient to interfere. Second, capital began to flee the country, for investors had no faith in capitalism under a Socialist government. Soon the Blum régime paused, and then retraced its steps away from reform. At once it lost the support of the Left, including the unions. In June 1937 Blum resigned. After another year of nonentity governments, Édouard Daladier took office again as premier.

Under Daladier the Republic shifted permanently to the Right. The 40-hour work-week was extended to 44 hours in order to stimulate production, and the government made it clear that it would back employers against unions in this and other matters. An attempted General Strike in December 1938 fell flat. Daladier, Paul Reynaud and Georges Bonnet, the principals in the government, were Radicals. But French Radicalism had changed its oulook. Now it co-operated with the Catholic Church; Jewish ministers were excluded from a reception for German foreign minister Ribbentrop; foreigners were subjected to strict security controls; the Radicals actively sought support from the provincial bourgeoisie, which once had leaned towards anti-Radical conservative groups and parties; and Radicalism now came to be identified with pacifism.

PRE-WAR

Once again foreign policy became the centre of interest in France. On domestic issues, the years from 1919 to the election of the Popular

Front could be termed 'post-war'; in foreign affairs the years after 1933 were definitely 'pre-war'.

In October 1933, Germany left the Geneva Disarmament Conference and the League of Nations. Thereafter French policy was to search for a European system whereby Germany could be controlled – Collective Security was Stanley Baldwin's term for it – and, failing that, sought to appease Germany as an alternative to risking another general war. In 1934 foreign minister Joseph Paul-Boncour failed in his efforts to construct a Four-Power Pact of France, Italy, Britain and Germany, because France's eastern allies (Czechoslovakia, Poland, Hungary and Rumania) did not trust Italy. The same year, Louis Barthou as Paul-Boncour's successor, tried to create a Franco-Soviet arrangement that would isolate Germany. The Poles objected, and while Barthou was trying to reassure them, he was killed by an assassin's bullet intended for King Alexander of Yugoslavia. Barthou's successor, Pierre Laval, had no liking for Soviet Russia, and while in 1935 he signed a defence treaty with the Russians, he would not follow it up with staff talks and a military convention.

France participated with Britain and Italy in the Stresa Front agreement to guarantee Austria in 1935, and Laval agreed with British foreign secretary Samuel Hoare that Italy should keep its ill-gotten gains in Abyssinia, now modern Ethiopia. That pact was repudiated in Britain and France, but Laval continued wooing Mussolini and also tried to achieve a Franco-German rapprochement.

Until 1935 the Versailles Treaty had defined Germany's position among the European powers. But after a plebiscite in the Saar went overwhelmingly in favour of returning that industrially-rich region to Germany, Hitler threw off Versailles restraints. He announced his rearmament programme in 1935, remilitarized the Rhineland and announced the formation of the Rome-Berlin Axis in 1936. He then united Germany with Austria and incorporated the Sudeten region of Czechoslovakia, with its large German population, into the Reich in 1938 (with the acquiescence of both Britain and France). Throughout these developments, the French did little beyond drawing closer to Britain. General Maurice Gamelin, heard of the General Staff, insisted that nothing could be done to prevent the remilitarization of the

Rhineland; Blum, Ivan Delbos and then Laval refused to consider any serious alliance with the Soviet Union; and they 'watched with interest' in March 1938, when German troops marched into Vienna.

MUNICH

The greatest blow to peace was the Munich Pact of September 1938. Hitler's aim was to create a large, powerful German state that could dominate Europe, without war if possible, with war if necessary. Through 1938 it appeared he could have it peacefully. The Czech Sudetenland was home to three-and-a-half-million Germans, agitating to join the Reich. The Czech government used force to quell riots while Berlin protested and threatened. In response, Prague mobilized the Czech army, assuming it could count on the mutual defence pact of 1924 with France. Immediately, British prime minister, Neville Chamberlain, sought to mediate between Prague and Berlin, and France reneged on its treaty obligations in order to ensure Czech acquiescence. In accordance with German demands, Czechoslovakia was partitioned. Georges Bonnet thereafter claimed that Chamberlain had hamstrung French policy; in fact, the Munich Pact, by which Hitler, Mussolini, Chamberlain and Daladier formalized Czech partition, simply opened the door for France to renege on all of its eastern-European commitments. It was not an unpopular policy; 57 per cent of the French people approved the Munich agreement. Those who were perceptive, however, could read between the lines. Munich was the written evidence that France was no longer a great power.

War

After Munich there was little to do but wait. In December 1938, France signed a declaration recognizing Germany's right to expand in the east. In March 1939, Hitler annexed 'rump' Czechoslovakia and danced a jig on the steps of Hradčany Castle in Prague. Two weeks later the British unilaterally guaranteed the security of Poland. In the summer of 1939, both Britain and France made belated overtures to Soviet Russia, which were rebuffed dramatically in the Nazi-Soviet Non-Aggression Pact of 23 August. A week later, Germany invaded

Poland, and on 3 September, after coordinating the timing, both western democracies declared war on Germany.

THE PHONEY WAR

Nothing much was to happen for the next eight months, save for the war in Poland and a few conflicts at sea. French and German armies looked at each other across fortified frontiers and waited. No bombs fell (except on Warsaw), no tanks roared across fields. It was the period of the 'Phoney War'. It ended as abruptly as a shot from a rifle. In April 1940, the German western offensive began. Belgium, Denmark and Holland fell. In June masses of French and British forces were forced back to the English Channel. 320,000 of these were evacuated successfully from Dunkerque to form the nucleus of an army which in three years' time would invade North Africa and Italy.

But in the meantime, France was beaten by again fighting a war that had been fought a generation earlier. On paper the French army looked at least the equal of the German. But the paper did not take into account *Blitzkrieg*, the armour-air combined assault strategy devised by General Guderian. As they had been in 1870, and nearly were in 1914, the French army was outdone in 1940 by thinking in terms of the last war. The General Staff had not paid attention to such war theorists as the Englishman, Captain Basil Liddell-Hart, who understood the uses of the tank, nor to their own Colonel Charles de Gaulle, who had read Liddell-Hart.

Italy declared war on the Allies on 10 June; the next day the government fled to Bordeaux – again – and the day after, General Weygand ordered a general retreat. Two million Parisians fled the city, joining another 6 million refugees clogging the roads and interfering with the movement of troops. On 14 June the Germans entered Paris, and on 16 June Paul Reynaud resigned as premier, replaced by Marshal Pétain who sued for peace. It was granted on 22 June, effective from 25 June. On 10 July, after having been hounded and harangued by Pierre Laval, the National Assembly voted 468 to 80, with 20 abstentions, to give Pétain full power to revise the constitution.

The Third Republic thus died. In its place was the *État Français*, headquartered at Vichy and subject to the victorious Germans. It would rule directly over about half of the country; the rest, including Paris and all coastal regions, was occupied by the Germans.

Vichy

The story of Vichy France is not a pretty one. It was ruled until 1942 by Marshal Pétain, vainglorious, haughty, using as part of his title the royal *nous*. In 1942 Pierre Laval, whom Pétain did not like, took actual control of the régime as premier. So far as the Germans would allow it, he ruled France on his own. Vichy may not have been a puppet state in the technical sense, but its leaders were sufficiently collaborationist that the difference made small odds. French workers went off to feed the German war economy – three workers sent gained the release of one French prisoner-of-war; French police rounded up Jews for the death camps; and French agents ferreted out members of the *Résistance* and sometimes summarily executed them. Laval claimed that he 'policed' France in order to keep the Germans from doing it, and he and Pétain both claimed that their collaborationist régime 'saved' France from destruction by Germany. The cost of saving France proved to be very high.

The Vichy régime embodied most of what the extremist Right-wing had long advocated. Indeed, Pétain himself was sympathetic to *Action Française*, though he was not strictly a follower of Charles Maurras. Vichy was authoritarian, anti-parliamentary, anti-Semitic, racist, xenophobic, clericist – for a time education was put back into the hands of the Church – and moralistic, in a totalitarian manner. The economy strove for corporatism, as in fascist Italy, but fell short of success. Women were regarded officially as baby machines. Pétain, Laval, Pierre Flandin and Admiral Darlan, the principal officers of the régime at various times, all tried to fit France into Hitler's new European order. They succeeded; by 1944 Vichy existed only in name, and Germany controlled everything.

Sadly, there were many French Nazis ready to applaud: Robert Brasillach, Jean Luchaire and Jacques Doriot, among others; Joseph Darnand's *Milice Français*, a sort of French SS, brought ideological collaboration to its worst depths. Sadly too, Vichy was not an aberration. The roots went deep into the Third Republic. At the same time, having seen the produce of the roots at their ugliest, post-war France would never be content simply with a re-creation of the old order. Interesting times lay ahead.

THE FREE FRENCH

In 1940, Charles de Gaulle was a very minor French general, with a position in the War Office. His major contribution at that point was in refusing to surrender to Germany. He escaped from Bordeaux to England, where over the next three years he persuaded the British, the Americans, and finally the French themselves to recognize him as the symbol of French resistance as head of the Free French Forces. It was not easy. Churchill found him trying (though also a 'man of destiny'), Roosevelt considered him impossible and not altogether trustworthy, and the French, or those prepared to defend Vichy – which in 1940 was a very great many indeed – thought he was a traitor. The Vichy régime sentenced him to death *in absentia*.

Charles de Gaulle

THE RÉSISTANCE

Within France itself, in everything from cold-shouldering Germans to blowing up railway bridges, thousands of French patriots in the occupied areas and Vichy fought back. In the north they fought against an invader; in the south, the *Résistance* struggle had the characteristics of a civil war. Every ideological persuasion from Catholic to Communist, and every social category from peasant to aristocrat, was involved. (Six members of the du Granrut family went to concentration camps for *Résistance* activity, for example.) It was most dangerous in the occupied north; it was most political in the south, where resisters hoped to combine anti-Nazi and anti-collaborationist activity with planting the desire to change France once Hitler was defeated.

The groups included *Combat, Libération, Franc-Tireur, Témoignage Chrétien*, and the essentially guerilla *Maquis*, among others. Jean Moulin, working for de Gaulle, unified them and persuaded them to accept de Gaulle as their symbolic head, regardless of their political or ideological preferences. Moulin established MUR (*Mouvements Unités de la Résistance*) before he was betrayed in 1943 and tortured to death by the infamous Klaus Barbie, the 'butcher of Lyon'. Moulin was replaced by Georges Bidault, later de Gaulle's enemy over independence for Algeria.

Liberation

On 6 June 1944, the allies effected a landing in Normandy and began the operation of liberating France. All *Résistance* groups, Left and Right, agreed that a mass uprising should take place both to throw out the Germans and remove the odour of Vichyism. De Gaulle agreed; but when such a rising occurred, German reprisals were swift, brutal and thorough. The *Parti Communiste de France* was the most firmly committed to a mass rising. The Paris Free French were commanded by Communist Colonel Rol-Tanguy, and key posts within the 'secret army', as the *Résistance* had come to be called, were held by Communists. On 22 August Paris insurgents were at war with the Germans.

De Gaulle despaired at the idea of a Communist takeover of France, and the allies shared his concern. Paris was not strategically important; politically it was a vital symbol, and General Eisenhower dispatched

American and French troops, the latter commanded by General Jacques Leclerc, an officer in the French colonial army in Africa when the war broke out.

The German commander, General von Choltitz, surrendered to Leclerc on 25 August, and de Gaulle entered Paris that afternoon. He drove straight to his old office at the War Ministry, to symbolize that in his view Vichy was an illegal establishment and that officially the Third Republic still existed. On 26 August he led a giant demonstration and parade on the Champs-Élysées, despite the fact that there were still snipers in the city.

The fiftieth anniversary of this moment was celebrated on 25 August 1994. Notre-Dame bells pealed, bicycles and vintage military vehicles paraded along General Leclerc's route into the city, the president and premier made speeches, and the son of the man who had ascended the Eiffel Tower on liberation day in 1944 to hang a huge French flag re-enacted his father's exploit. Some 500,000 people lined the parade route and filled the Place de la Concorde to watch the celebration.

COLLABORATIONISTS

For France it was all over but the shouting – and the revenge. Perhaps 9000 summary executions of collaborators took place. In the Dordogne Valley there was a virtual reign of terror. 'Horizontal collaboration' – liaisons between French women and German soldiers – was dealt particularly severe punishment: the women were publicly humiliated, often paraded naked through the streets with shaved heads. Official purging of collaborators accounted for about 767, including, famously, Pétain and Laval. Pétain's death sentence was commuted to life imprisonment by Charles de Gaulle. The others were shot. Which is not to say that all collaborators were dealt with, such as the chemical manufacturers who, according to historical evidence made public in the late 1990s, helped make the Zyklon-B used in German concentration camp gas chambers.

De Gaulle was no fool. Getting rid of collaborationists did not mean getting rid of every civil servant or official who had served the Vichy régime. Élites were swept away, to be replaced by a new kind of élite, the veterans of the *Résistance*; but left-over officials from the Vichy régime remained in the civil service. In 1948, for example, 97 per cent of *inspecteurs de finance* had been employed by Vichy, and in the 1960s Maurice Couve de Murville, a high civil servant of Vichy, was President de Gaulle's foreign secretary. Couve de Murville was among those who had practised 'wait and see', and skipped out the moment it was clear who was winning.

Post-War

De Gaulle established a provisional government, and later claimed that he had saved France from Communism. This was not true: there was no serious Communist expectation of seizing power in 1944, 1945 or even 1946. For one thing, the Anglo-Americans would never have permitted it. De Gaulle certainly did battle with the Communist party, but more important, he held on to power until some order came out of the chaos. The country was in ruins in 1945, far more than in 1918: 55,000 factories and business houses, 135,000 agricultural buildings and 2,000,000 dwellings were destroyed; 4000 kilometres of railways and 7500 bridges were gone; inflation was rampant; antagonism between town and country operated at a high level of intensity; and industrial production was only 50 per cent that of 1938.

De Gaulle resorted to a time-honoured French tradition and held a plebiscite. On 21 October 1945, 96 per cent of French people voted '*non*' on the Third Republic. At the same time elections to a Constituent Assembly (women voting for the first time) produced a Chamber with few Radicals, slightly more Rightists, and large Socialist, Communist and Christian Democrat (*Mouvement Républicain Populaire*) parties, the latter led by Georges Bidault. De Gaulle remained aloof from party. In January 1946 he resigned his provisional leadership, disgusted because his views on a powerful presidency were not accepted. He would return.

In May, a new constitution was drawn up. It looked remarkably like the old one: a weak presidency, a premier forced to balance parliamentary parties which again were looking like mainly self-interest groups. It was approved by a mere million-vote majority; but approved it was, and the Fourth Republic was born. In 1947 it became as operational as it ever would be.

CHAPTER TEN

Contemporary France

1945 was a crossroads for France. The French could continue to stagnate, the national condition since 1918, or they could, in Charles de Gaulle's words, 'marry their century' and liberate themselves from the decadent aspects of their past, just as they had finally liberated themselves from the Germans. The choice, however, was not so simple as it might appear.

IDEAS

The problem of stagnation and the search for solutions to it began in 1918 and affected both mind and body. Liberation of the one entailed liberation of the other. In 1919 Paul Valéry wrote: 'We civilizations now know that we are mortal ... We see that the abyss of history is large enough for everyone. We feel that a civilization is as fragile as life.' So it was. French intellectuals now believed that traditional civilization had been swept away by war, and searched for new, often perverse and always despairing, alternative values. The Dadaists had celebrated mindless destructiveness in the 1920s; then the Surrealists exalted 'the dream; the subconscious; love, freed from all moral or social fetters; revolutionary fervour; flamboyant atheism'. Marcel Proust had pioneered stream-of-consciousness in the novel, while André Gide, failing to resolve the ambiguities of the universe, experimented with Henri Bergson's concept of the 'gratuitous act', devoid of purpose or meaning. These and the ideas that came after them, found expression not only in literature, but in art, music, theatre and the cinema.

Despair deepened in the 1930s. For artists and writers Paris might be a 'moveable feast', as Ernest Hemingway phrased it, but the fare was sometimes nearly indigestible. Louis-Ferdinand Céline's nihilism revealed 'a satanic vision of the godless world, rolling helplessly through space and infested with crawling millions of suffering, diseased, sex-obsessed, maniacal human beings'.

Despair produced a desire for action, if it could be justified: André Malraux found *engagement* in neo-romantic exploits in Indo-China, the Spanish Civil War and the *Maquis*. Or, if action could not be justified: Jean-Paul Sartre considered the role of Existential Man, alone in an absurd and irrational universe, absolutely free to choose. Existentialism never caught on; the burden of absolute freedom was too heavy. Moreover, it was at odds with Sartre's own Communist beliefs. Meanwhile, Simone de Beauvoir's legendary book *Le Deuxième Sexe* encouraged the advance of feminism within a vaguely Existentialist context.

In the 1950s *engagement* gave way to *dégagement* (disengagement) and an aloof, intellectual élitism. In the 1960s Claude Lévi-Strauss's Structuralism – everything can be understood because societies are collections of simple structures, eternally coherent and much alike – caught on with sociologists, planners and the *Annales* school of historians. Structuralism faded in the 1970s into Post-Structuralism, a loosely-grouped collection of extremely complicated variations of Structuralism. Critics called Post-Structuralism a 'glorious cerebral game', and noted that simple ideas did not become sophisticated merely by dressing them up in unintelligible jargon.

The old, mainstream ideas of the French tradition, Rationalism and Humanism, were not displayed by these fruits of intellectual despair and extremism. Albert Camus cogently illuminated the fact by moving beyond Existentialism toward moral responsibility. If the world seems absurd, he argued, human beings are not thereby excused from trying to make sense of it, or improve it, or from fighting against fanatics, tyrants or saviours who offer themselves as substitutes for God. Frenzied intellectualism from Dada to Post-Structuralism offered no lasting alternative to Voltairian scepticism, Marxist materialism and Christian humanism. On the other hand, it paralleled in time the evolution of twentieth-century politics and society. It was no mere coincidence that Existentialism was in vogue in 1945, at the moment when France faced choosing its path into the future.

The Fourth Republic

In 1947 Communists and Socialists found that they could not co-operate after all, and a centrist 'third force' formed. It allied Socialists, Radicals and the *Mouvement Républicain Populaire* (MRP). In 1948 the Socialists fell back as the political centre of gravity shifted rightward. Charles de Gaulle's *Rassemblement du Peuple Français* and Pierre Poujade's populist shopkeeper and peasant bloc kept the pressure on. The Gaullists had ideas, at least, even if they were vague. Poujadism had 'as much intellectual content as a scream'.

Between 1947 and 1958 governments lasted an average of six months. At best they fended off crises and maintained slim majorities in the lower house, renamed the National Assembly; at worst they tried actually to govern, to meet crisis head on, and were thrown out of office. French government balanced precariously between negative interest groups: the Fourth Republic had died, said one cynic, and had been replaced by the Third.

RECOVERY

While witty enough, this judgement was neither fair nor true. Progress was made in every sphere but the political. Women finally had the vote and constitutional guarantees of equality of rights. Coal, gas, electricity and the four largest deposit banks were nationalized, a comprehensive welfare state emerged with social services far more comprehensive than anything before the war, and the Communist party was now one of the largest political forces in the country – though less effective than its numbers implied. A birth-rate revolution reversed the negative population growth rate, pushing upward the demand for more schools, social services and jobs. Even old Radicals now conceded defeat on the most eternal of education questions, and agreed to schemes which gave state assistance to church schools in order to meet the expanding needs of primary and secondary education.

Meanwhile, forward-looking newcomers to 'social management' had their eyes fixed firmly on economic planning and European integration as the way to the future. Jean Monnet's Planning Commission drew up a series of Four-Year Plans which, fuelled by United

States' Marshall Plan aid, revived industry and technology. Production increased 50 per cent by 1953 over 1938. The Communist party led strikes against this 'American imperialism' in 1947 and 1948. Jules Moch, the Socialist interior minister, blunted them successfully, largely because the public was suspicious of Communist motives.

THE TREATY OF ROME

Robert Schuman was the architect of the European Coal and Steel Community, which linked France, West Germany, Italy, Belgium, Holland and Luxembourg. The Six, as they were known after 1951, formed the basis of the Common Market, founded by the Treaty of Rome in 1957. René Pleven was less successful with his European Defence Community (EDC), which was to include West Germany. (The idea of integrating Germany into western Europe as quickly as possible was in the forefront of all enlightened French political thinking in the first post-war decade, and for obvious reasons.) The EDC died of neglect in 1954. By then defence was in the hands of the North Atlantic Treaty Organization (NATO), which was dominated by the United States and Britain. The Americans believed that European defence was too important to be left to Europeans. Apparently the British felt the same, even with the socialist Labour government in power.

Only agriculture made no significant progress in this period. Inflation wiped out gains made at war's end. Uneconomical small farms and antiquated farming methods, which nevertheless produced an almost constant surplus, kept agriculture in a state of permanent depression. A conservative peasantry resisted modernization: the number of tractors increased from 16,000 in 1938 to 630,000 in 1959, but they apparently were used less for tilling fields than for blocking roads during frequent demonstrations against falling farm prices. Eventually, the national trend towards urbanization reduced the rural population significantly, and those who remained began to prosper. The advent of the Common Market provided an expanded agricultural market, which helped even more.

Decolonization

'Retreat from Empire' was a major theme of European post-war reorganization. The retreat was not without incident. In France it brought down the Fourth Republic.

The French had hoped to retain their empire after the war by democratizing it. Social and economic reforms were introduced; the French Union, an idea not unlike the British Commonwealth but within which the colonies acknowledged that their allegiance was first to France, pretended to integrate the colonies into policy-making. But the Paris government failed to understand the depth of nationalism among most native populations or the extent to which *les colons* (French colonials), particularly in Algeria, were prepared to resist any kind of change, which might take local political and economic power out of their hands.

INDO-CHINA

While Syria and Lebanon became independent during the Second World War, almost by default, the British spearheaded liberation from the Japanese in Indo-China (Cambodia, Laos and Vietnam) in 1945, and handed control back to the French. Indo-China was raised to the status of an Associated State of the French Union in 1949. The Vietnamese were not impressed.

Vietnam claimed independence even as the Japanese withdrew. After that its Vietminh nationalists, led by Paris-educated Ho Chi Minh, waged war against France. Ho was a Communist, as the French rightly understood; he also was a nationalist, which they did not grasp, and had the support of the bulk of the Vietnamese people. The war dragged on, justified as an anti-Communist struggle. The cost was enormous in manpower, money and disillusionment. In 1954 Dien Bien Phu, important strategically and symbolically, fell to the Vietminh after a long siege. Dien Bien Phu inspired a deeply romanticized film, *Jump Into Hell*, in 1955; who knows what impact it may have had on inspiring American intervention in Vietnam a decade later? Pierre Mendès-France, a Radical, was summoned to the premiership specifically to bring an end to the struggle. He arranged an internationally arrived-at settlement, signed in Geneva. That the French were relieved to have the nightmare over was evident when the Assembly voted 471 to 14 in favour of the settlement.

NORTH AFRICA

Mendès-France did not stop with Indo-China. His talks with the Tunisians led to their independence in March 1956. Morocco followed in a few days, which left Algeria. In June 1956 a law passed the Assembly paving the way for future independence for all of France's African colonies.

Algerian nationalists were not prepared to wait. A nationalist uprising and campaign of terrorism, begun at the end of the Second World War, now intensified. By 1955 170,000 French troops, many of them veterans of Indo-China, were in Algeria. In 1956 the Socialist Guy Mollet became premier, was shocked at the *colons'* hostility when he proposed to negotiate with the rebels, and reversed government policy. Reinforcements poured into Algeria, swelling the French army to 350,000 while the rebel FLN numbered perhaps only 15,000. All the same, the French were unable to crush them.

THE SUEZ CRISIS

In 1955, Gamal Abdel Nasser, president of Egypt, nationalized the Suez Canal. The British government feared the effect on Arab nationalism throughout the Middle East; the French believed – or claimed to – that Egypt was arming the FLN. An Anglo-French plot was hatched, with Israel's co-operation, to take the canal back and perhaps overthrow Nasser into the bargain. French interest in this affair was Algeria.

The Suez adventure would have succeeded – the actual invasion did succeed – had not the United States threatened intervention, backed by the American Sixth Fleet, and also declined to support the wavering pound. The United States was fearful of the moral advantage, if nothing else, which the Soviet Union might gain among Arabs (who sat upon much of the world's known oil reserves) from this recrudescence of European imperialism. Anglo-French forces withdrew. Thereafter French policy was more determined than ever to 'keep Algeria French'.

ALGERIA

However, the resolve was not universal. In 1958 matters came to a head. The French public wearied of another costly colonial war, and entertained doubts as to how 'honourable' was the French army's role in it: brutal torture was being employed; a village was bombed against government orders, provoking a furore which bought down the Félix Gaillard government; and on 13 May, when it was rumoured that Premier Pierre Pflimlin intended to negotiate with the FLN, a *colons'* revolt broke out. In Paris, sympathizers took to their cars and began tooting horns to the beat of '*Al-gér-ie-Fran-çaise*'; it was unnerving. Some army units went over to the *colons*, and on 24 May, paratroopers behind General Salan, a rabid supporter of French Algeria, invaded Corsica. A military *coup* seemed to be in the making.

Two things prevented it: the army rank and file, and General Charles de Gaulle. Ordinary French soldiers in Algeria, unlike the paratroopers whose special *esprit* was shaped largely by the 'humiliation' of Indo-China, were not prepared to follow extremist officers into rebellion. De Gaulle, the great hope of the Right, refused to lead a *coup*. Committing himself to no party or faction, he made it widely known that he 'stood ready to serve' should the nation summon him. With no acceptable alternative, the nation – in this case the Assembly and President René Coty – did call him on 29 May. Only the Communists were solidly opposed.

A sense of relief and optimism spread across the nation. At his insistence, de Gaulle was given power to rule by decree as premier for six months rather in the manner of an ancient Roman Consul, or yet another Man on Horseback. He used the time to introduce reforms and a new constitution, drafted by himself and Michel Debré, the justice minister. This constitution was approved in a national referendum by 80 per cent. The Fourth Republic was consigned to oblivion.

The Fifth Republic

The ghost of Louis Napoleon was much in evidence during the autumn of 1958. The new constitution recognized the president as the representative of the national sovereignty. The Assembly continued to function as a parliament, but with its powers over the government curtailed and its sessions limited to six months in the year. Legislative power passed to the premier and cabinet, which was no longer entirely responsible to the Assembly, and the premier was now the choice largely of the president. De Gaulle used national referenda much as had Louis Napoleon, and with similar success: favourable votes of 80 per cent in 1958, 75 per cent in 1961, and 91 per cent in April 1962. At first he was elected president by 80,000 electors chosen by local government units. In 1962 de Gaulle took the step no régime had been willing to take since 1870: he made the presidential election subject to direct universal suffrage. Louis Napoleon had been the last leader selected in such fashion, and scepticism showed in this referendum passing with only 62 per cent in favour.

Meanwhile, Assembly elections gave de Gaulle's *Union pour la Nouvelle République* (UNR) 200 seats, a rightist independent-peasant bloc 118, the MRP 56, the Socialists 44, the Radicals 13 and the Communists a mere ten. The UNR had a plurality rather than a majority, but with de Gaulle's overwhelming popularity there was little chance of conflict between the executive and the legislature, at least for the time being.

THE OAS

One outstanding piece of old business remained before the new Republic could get down to new business: Algeria. In 1959 de Gaulle annouced a policy of Home Rule. In January 1960 a coalition of army officers, *colons*, and such former Gaullists as Georges Bidault and Jacques Soustelle, attempted a further revolt. They naïvely expected it to inspire a popular uprising against the president. Nothing happened and they tried again in April 1961, with General Salan as leader. This time de Gaulle went on radio to appeal for public support. Portable radios had been widely distributed among units of the French army so that ordinary soldiers could hear the speech. They listened, they were moved, and when their officers revolted, they had no stomach for a *coup*.

Thereafter disaffected officers, *colons* and former Gaullists, calling themselves the *Organisation de l'Armée Secrète* (OAS), made war against the régime. It was simple terrorism, and became one of the bloodiest underground conflicts of modern times: there were 12,000 victims in all, and 800,000 embittered *colon* refugees pouring into France, backing the OAS in sympathy if not with action. De Gaulle stood firm, and the

OAS was crushed. The war, in its final phase, became the subject of a highly entertaining novel by Frederick Forsyth, *The Day of the Jackal*.

In March 1962 de Gaulle recognized Algerian independence. The two nations have got along reasonably well since. A film, *The Battle of Algiers*, made jointly by French and Algerian film-makers, celebrated the struggle for liberation realistically, honestly and with compassion, telling both sides of the story with remarkable objectivity. Good relations continued but on a different level when Islamic fundamentalists began working to overthrow the Algerian government. In 1993, the French government ordered a round-up of Algerian Islamic militants living in France, where they propagandized extensively against the Algerian government. Said the interior minister: 'An Islamic State can be established in Algeria only against France.'

Prophetic words. Over the next several years, five French nationals were killed in Algiers by Islamic fundamentalists, attempts were made by Algerian terrorists to hijack an Air France passenger airplane, there were repeated bomb scares on the Paris Metro, and in May 1996 the Armed Islamic Group slit the throats of seven Trappist monks, ostensibly because some 'imagined negotiation process with Paris' had failed. The French response mostly was a police crackdown on suspected Algerian militants in France and a tougher policy on immigration from the former French colony. Despite all of this, French entrepreneurs continued to operate in Algeria and to do very well as a result, despite feeling the pressure of anti-French attitudes.

Indeed, the focus of Algerian-inspired violence seemed to turn more and more inward in the later 1990s, the result, argued anthropologist Gilbert Grandguillame, of Islamic fundamentalists at war with the government, and the government encouraging the population to form armed militias in order to defend itself. As usual, innocent people are caught in the middle, such as in September 1997 when some 300 inhabitants of a rural village were massacred. By whom is not absolutely certain, though Islamic fundamentalists were probably responsible. All the same, Amnesty International had established well before this that the behaviour of the Algerian government was fully as brutal and terroristic as that of the fundamentalist groups, a fact which had an unexpected negative impact on Franco-Algerian relations at the outset of 1998. In

November 1998, a former member of the Algerian *sécurité militaire* revealed that the Paris bombings alluded to above, which had been blamed on Islamic terrorists, actually had been the work of the Algerian government. Needless to say, the Quai d'Orsay was not pleased.

De Gaulle

The president's policy from the start was restoration of French *grandeur*. This was perfectly consistent with his Catholic, royalist, aristocratic and military background. De Gaulle was first and foremost a *patriote* whose refusal to submit either to Vichy or Germany in 1940 made him the symbol of French pride and honour. His dedication to the interests of France informed his politics, and prevented him from trying to cling to power when the will of the nation was against him. De Gaulle came to be known affectionately as *le grand Charlie*. The sobriquet fitted him as well as *le Roi du Soleil* fitted Louis XIV, and for similar reasons. An American cartoon of the 1960s depicted portraits of Joan of Arc, Louis XIV and Napoleon Bonaparte in the Louvre; all wore de Gaulle's face. The metaphor was appropriate. It was around his style that patriotic, political and state activities revolved.

THE ECONOMY

When de Gaulle took office, the economy was in a perilous state: a massive financial crisis threatened the 'economic miracle' of the 1950s. Prices rose, exports fell, gold and capital fled the country, and the franc destabilized. De Gaulle introduced deflation and austerity: tax increases; reduction of state expenditure in veterans' pensions and food subsidies; a wage-price freeze; and devaluation of the franc. Meanwhile, import controls were relaxed in hope that foreign competition would revitalize domestic productivity.

This 'short-sighted archaic liberalism', as de Gaulle's critics termed his economic policies, appeared to work. Exports rose; capital returned; gold and foreign exchange made gains; the franc stabilized, and the modernization process was resumed. The gross national product increased 5 per cent annually from 1958 through 1967, and France turned into a major industrial power with the highest economic growth rate in the Common Market. Appropriately symbolic, the Caravelle jet emerged to lead the European aviation industry. In the Gaullist decade, a majority of French people grew accustomed to the outward manifestations of an affluent society: television, automobiles (by 1973 63 per cent of French families owned a car), refrigerators, decent housing and holidays away from home.

But there was a price to pay. The gap widened between haves and have-nots, and the lowest stratum of society remained as impoverished and hopeless as ever. Modernization drove out marginal operations in business and industry; between 1960 and 1970 France built nearly 1000 supermarkets, while 100,000 small shopkeepers went bankrupt. Official tax, housing, social and credit policies benefited the prosperous strata, but at heavy cost to the rest. Meanwhile, French élitism enlarged rather than disappeared. Without a diploma from the École Polytechnique, the Institut d'Études Politiques, or the École Nationale d'Administration, a hopeful young technocrat could whistle for a place among the country's managers. Stress increased. The Left made steady gains in politics, and the Right protested with obstructionist acts, such as seizing local tax offices and destroying official records. For this they went to prison and Gaullist policies remained unchanged. In the long term, economic growth and stability was only marginally better under de Gaulle than it had been without him.

FOREIGN POLICY

Following the presidential-election referendum of 1962, the UNR won a landslide victory in Assembly elections. Gaullist power was now unshakeable, with a majority of seats in the Assembly and a strong president. As one observer put it, the referendum 'blew up the road back to the Fourth Republic'. De Gaulle could get on with the policy which mattered most to him: restoring French *grandeur* in foreign affairs.

Knowing that France could not compete alone with the post-war superpowers, de Gaulle set out to create a Third Force, a bloc of European and Third World nations, excluding Britain, with France as its leader. In constructing his Third Force, de Gaulle switched sides in the Middle East from supporting Israel to the Arab states (France was concerned over lack of oil resources); recognized the government of mainland China; made a treaty with the West German chancellor, Adenauer, aimed at transforming the old Franco-German enmity into friendship; and approached the Soviet Union amid much fanfare about a continental unity stretching 'from the Atlantic to the Urals'.

Meanwhile, he attacked both NATO and the Common Market, to which the Fourth Republic had committed France. These organizations would destroy French independence, he argued; and anyway, they were unworkable. Moreover, NATO was dominated by the United States and Britain. De Gaulle was not keen on either, lumping the Americans and British together as 'les Anglo-Saxons' and accusing them of conspiring to rule Europe without reference to France. It probably rankled the austere general when the attractive young American president, John F. Kennedy, visited and drew large, enthusiastic crowds which he charmed beyond all reason by introducing himself as 'the man who came to Paris with Jacqueline Kennedy'.

De Gaulle wanted to take France out of both NATO and the Common Market. He succeeded only with the former. First he demanded a triumvirate leadership for NATO of Britain, France and the United States: when the Americans rejected this he began withdrawing French forces. In 1967 he invited NATO to remove itself altogether from French soil. From that point forward France no longer was part of NATO. The public, with five years of Gaullist chauvinism under its belt, heartily approved. Opinion was less keen, perhaps, for the development of the Force de Frappe, an independent French nuclear strike force. Its function was as much diplomatic as military: having 'the bomb' guaranteed French membership in the 'nuclear club', and that France would be consulted whenever there was an international crisis – which simply is one definition of a great power. The first atomic tests were carried out in the Sahara in 1960. Over the years the Force grew more costly, and its benefits are still uncertain. Most recently it has involved France in contretemps with both Australia and New Zealand over testing in the South Pacific.

De Gaulle could not undo the Common Market. It had wide support in France, where membership greatly benefited agriculture. Therefore he decided to make of it another pillar supporting French independence. His policy was, first, to scoff at the notion that the Common Market was aimed at European federation, and then to coordinate the foreign policies of the Six behind French leadership. For example, in 1963 and again in 1967 France vetoed British membership on the pretext that Britain simply was America's 'Trojan horse in Europe'. Actually, he feared that once in the Common Market, Britain would rival France for leadership. So it has come to pass since the British joined in 1969.

De Gaulle's *bête noire* in foreign policy remained *les Anglo-Saxons*, and he missed no opportunity to set France, and where possible other nations, against them. He challenged the world-wide influence of the dollar and sterling; he denounced America's role in Vietnam; and on a visit to Canada in 1967, he ended a speech in Quebec with the words: '*Vive le Québec libre!*' These actions did not endear de Gaulle to the English-speaking world.

1968

In May 1968, a student-worker uprising in Paris shook the foundations of the Gaullist state. Ironically, the president's New Year's Day message that year said: 'Amid so many countries which are being shaken by so many upheavals, our own country will continue to offer an example of effectiveness in the conduct of affairs.'

In 1968, 605,000 students attended higher educational institutions which were equipped to handle about 60,000 comfortably: inadequate classrooms, lack of access to teachers, an administration which treated students like second-class citizens, and at the end, no guarantee of a job. Moreover, there was then a world-wide student protest movement fuelled by the Vietnam War, but aimed against everything associated with traditional values. Paris students were no exception, and the Nanterre campus of the Sorbonne was a particular hotbed. Radical students like 'Danny the Red' Cohn-Bendit, a German national, were disenchanted with the orthodox Left, and embraced Trotskyism, Maoism, anarchism and other extremist, dissident ideologies. An explosion need only an excuse to happen. The arrest of a student terrorist in connection with the bombing of American Express offices in France provided it.

A student strike (the 22 March movement) was called in sympathy for the arrested 'victim of imperialism', and clashes between students and police followed. In May, barricades went up (an old Paris tradition); students threw stones, Molotov cocktails and uncomplimentary epithets at police, who responded by beating them up and anyone else who happened to be handy. Abuse of power under the Gaullist régime thus became an additional protest issue. The trade unions called a General Strike in sympathy with the students, and on 13 May 750,000 students and workers marched through Paris against the régime. Eventually ten million workers joined the strike.

The workers' grievances were genuine: low wages, unemployment and obdurate employers. The students, mostly from the privileged classes, were seen as seeking to outrage civilized values and vent anti-establishment frustrations. The Communist party was dismayed that the workers joined them. Communist party chairman Georges Marchais called the students 'mindless anarchists', 'fascist provocateurs', or 'student adventurers'. Communist opposition to *les événements*, as the May rising was called, both divided and weakened its overall impact.

De Gaulle went on radio on 30 May and rallied support, which was manifested in mass demonstrations in his favour. In June the strikes ended, and Assembly elections gave the Gaullists a massive 291-seat majority. De Gaulle seemed to have won. The new Assembly sought conciliation: there were wage increases for industrial labour and drastic university reforms.

Actually, during the May crisis de Gaulle lost control. His government blundered along, and the Gaullist election sweep afterwards was because there was no viable alternative to the president, not because he had handled the crisis well. Now his judgement failed him, for the first time in his political career. De Gaulle's first act after the elections was to replace a good premier, Georges Pompidou, with a colourless bureaucrat, Maurice Couve de Murville, who had been foreign minister. Then, having toyed with the idea of introducing government reforms (increased regional autonomy and reorganization of the Senate), he decided in 1969 to submit these reforms to a simple 'oui' or 'non' referendum.

The referendum failed by 53 to 47 per cent, and de Gaulle did a completely unexpected thing. He simply walked away: no resignation, no explanation, he simply retired to his home at Colombey-les-deux-

The Pompidou Centre

Églises to resume writing his memoirs. The French nation, loyal to him for so many years, felt betrayed. Gaullism never fully recovered, either from the May crisis or from the General's peculiar exit. But a year later de Gaulle died, and in death France forgave him, his great contributions recalled. It remains to be seen if this forgiveness will continue in the present century. In May 1998 the diaries of Jacques Foccart, an official at the core of Gaullist strategies for France and Africa, were published. They depict de Gaulle as bloodthirsty, petulant, petty, and racist, a politician who practised nepotism and engaged in questionable financial practices – hardly the image of the French hero who liberated Paris in 1944.

After de Gaulle

George Pompidou, *bon vivant*, businessman and language scholar, followed de Gaulle as president and pledged to continue Gaullist policies. But Pompidou was not de Gaulle, and policy soon shifted: opposition to British membership in the Common Market was abandoned, and a classical *laissez-faire* policy was favoured in economics. The latter

development encouraged revival on the Left, and a Socialist–
Communist coalition was formed behind Socialist François Mitterand.
It won impressive gains in Assembly elections in 1973.

In 1974 Pompidou died suddenly of cancer. A new face and party
pushed the Gaullists aside. Valéry Giscard d'Estaing, relatively youthful,
energetic, aristocratic and very reminiscent of John F. Kennedy in style,
led his conservative independent republican party to victory over
Mitterand's coalition. Giscard promised an 'advanced liberal society'
and introduced progressive tax reform, lowered the voting age to
eighteen, relaxed controls on contraceptives and abortion, and
emphasized concern for ecology. But this bright outlook was quickly
marred by a world-wide recession growing out of the oil crisis of 1973,
when drastic increases in Middle East oil prices drove inflation through
the ceiling. For the first time in twenty years, French industrial growth
slowed, unemployment reached serious levels, and the government had
to consider austerity. In 1977 the Left again challenged; and so did a
sparkling young newcomer, Jacques Chirac, Giscard's own premier, for
party leadership.

Giscard led a charmed life. He replaced Chirac with economist
Raymond Barre, the Mitterand coalition suddenly collapsed, he held
his own in the 1977 Assembly elections, and could look optimistically
towards presidential election in 1981. However, the Giscard luck was
fleeting. The recession continued and Barre introduced austerity
measures. He cut government programmes and froze wages and prices.
Almost no relief was forthcoming, from unemployment, inflation or
industrial slowdown as a result. Suddenly Giscard's charm had worn off,
and he could not explain satisfactorily even a gift of diamonds from
Emperor Bokassa, disreputable ruler of a former French African colony.
Mitterand referred to the gift with annoying regularity during the
election campaign, and with his coalition again intact, won the presidency in 1981 by 52 to 48 per cent.

France Today

On election night, thousands of young Parisians congregated spontaneously in the Place de la Bastille (the choice of site was not mere

coincidence), to express their confidence that now things would change. In Assembly elections a few weeks later the Socialists swept to a landslide victory. Gaullist France was completely reversed; Mitterand was free to create a Socialist France, more revolutionary than social democracy, and more respectful of individual liberty than Communism.

In the first year, the régime introduced deficit spending in order to reinvigorate industry and cut unemployment (it was hoped that the other industrial nations would follow suit, thus ending the world-wide recession); nationalized large segments of the economy, and decentralized power from Paris to regional and local authorities; increased the minimum wage, family allocations and old-age pensions; expanded workers' rights and those of the expanding immigrant population; abolished the death penalty; and reduced overcrowding in prisons with a programme of early release. But with all of this, the economy remained sluggish, inflation and unemployment increased, trade deficits rose, capital fled the country, and nationalized industries proved an economic albatross.

In the second year of the régime hope gave way to doubt, and Mitterand began temporizing his 'revolution'. This encouraged Right-wing opposition. In one instance, an Assembly bill to integrate Catholic schools into the national system had to be withdrawn when opposed by a massive popular demonstration. In another, the increased visibility of non-French residents, particularly blacks and Asians, attracted extremists of the Left and Right to Jean-Marie Le Pen's violently zenophobic and racist *Front National*, the ideological heir to *Action Française*. Le Pen was a former paratrooper and admirer of General Salan, the OAS leader in 1962. Assembly elections in 1986, influenced by rising unemployment resentment against Middle East terrorists again using Paris streets for a battleground, and the scandal of French secret-service involvement in sinking the Greenpeace ship *Rainbow Warrior* in a New Zealand harbour, went heavily against the Socialists. Conservatives gained 286 seats to 212 for the Socialists, and 35 each for the Communists and the *Front National*. Mitterand had to select a Conservative, Jacques Chirac, as premier.

Socialist failure between 1981 and 1986 to turn France into a land of harmony, prosperity and social justice disillusioned many French people. At the same time, changes had been accomplished, even if they fell short of expectations. Above all, the myth that only Conservatives could be entrusted with governmental powers was dispelled. If Socialists had failed, they had done so no more dramatically or calamitously than had the Conservatives before them. In any event, the exclusion of the Left from political life was over, at least for the foreseeable future. In 1988, with the Right in shambles owing to Le Pen's rising influence, Mitterand won a second term with a 54 per cent majority, and appointed the moderate Michel Rocard premier, pending Assembly elections in June.

Rocard's was a minority government, and in May 1991, after three years of struggle in which he found himself increasingly stalemated by the opposition parties and unable to force legislation through the National Assembly, he resigned and President Mitterand took the unprecedented step of appointing a woman, Edith Cresson, to the post. The socialist Cresson was the obvious choice, he claimed. An engineer and economist, she was committed to European economic and political unification, set to begin in 1992 and be completed by the end of 1993. Thus Mitterand made clear that the cornerstone of French socialist policy was to see European integration succeed, and with it the French economy strengthened. His policy for the future was Objective 1993, as the president termed it.

In the event, Objective 1993 was only just attained; France voted in favour of European Union by the narrowest of margins, and French complaints against Union economic policies – the Roussillon wine producers protesting at having their acreage reduced by action of the European Community conference in Dublin, for example – grew more frequent.

Meanwhile, the economy declined, unemployment rose, industrial action increased, and Edith Cresson proved no more able than Rocard to overcome parliamentary stalemate. There was also the matter of Eurodisney, the Disneyworld of Europe. Mitterand supported it for economic reasons, and Culture Minister Jack Lang opposed it as being, though this was not his phrase, a 'cultural Chernobyl'. Eurodisney opened in 1992 at Marne la Vallée, which disappointed Lang, and operated at a huge deficit, which disappointed the President. It lost

£614 million in its first year. And, if that was not enough, the French wine trade, for centuries a mainstay of the national economy, now finds its markets being challenged by quite palatable vintages from Australia, Bulgaria, and Oregon in the United States.

Cresson resigned in 1992 and Mitterand appointed Pierre Bérégovoy in her place. Nothing improved as a result, and in April 1993, Bérégovoy had to watch a 'tidal wave' from the Right collect 460 of the 577 National Assembly seats in the general election. Some critics thought this was the end of traditional Socialism in France. Former Socialist premier Michel Rocard seemed to think so when he spoke out for a new left coalition of 'progressive' forces ranging from reform-minded communists to Greens and human-rights activists – not unlike, in principle at least, the Popular Front of the 1930s. The idea was to relight the fire on the Left that appeared to have gone out. Perhaps Bérégovoy agreed, for two months after the election he shocked the nation by committing suicide, ostensibly because he felt responsible for the election disaster. Bérégovoy was replaced by Édouard Balladur, a neo-Gaullist imposed upon Mitterand by the new disposition of assembly seats. Taken together, Balladur the neo-Gaullist, Rocard the neo-Socialist, and Bérégovoy the suicide, seemed a clear indication of the degree to which Mitterand's policies and his party had come unstuck. The decline continued when in June 1994 French Socialists lost six of their 22 seats in the European Parliament.

Balladur was immediately popular when he entered the premiership. However, like his predecessors he was soon under attack. When he rejected an austerity plan for Air France which would have solved some major economic difficulties for the airline albeit at the cost of many jobs, critics charged that Balladur had 'buckled under' to union pressure. Far more damaging was his defence of a Senate amendment that would have allowed the state to subsidize private schools beyond the 10 per cent limit imposed by the 140-year-old Faloux law. At once 600,000 teachers, parents, local government workers, and left-wing politicians from across France poured into Paris to protest, and the premier was forced to back down. Wrote one critic, 'slipping in the polls and not relating well to the French people, it is both a surprise and a paradox that he is still running for the presidency in 1995'.

Actually, his growing unpopularity may have had less to do with Balladur himself than with growing disillusionment, particularly among the young, with traditional politics. Polls in 1994 revealed that among those 16–24 years of age, 61 per cent 'distrust' politics, 63 per cent characterize politics as a 'dishonourable' activity, 43 per cent would not care if political parties were abolished, and 33 per cent abstained from voting in the 1993 General Election. Disillusionment with the political establishment no doubt was contributed to by a rash of scandals in 1994 and 1995 involving ministers in the Balladur government, charges of political 'sleaze' to be found in city halls from Paris to Grenoble, and by the revelations of corruption concerning wealthy businessman and member of parliament, Bernard Tapie. Not that these successors to the 1968 generation are apathetic; far from it. However, their activism is less political than social. Such youth groups as the Droit de Cité work to fight Aids, drug addiction and delinquency, help the sick, handicapped and destitute, defend the environment, and struggle against racism.

Early polls anticipating the presidential election scheduled for April 1995 indicated that Balladur would win a tough race, first in a preliminary against rival Gaullist Jacques Chirac, and then in the election itself against Socialist candidate Lionel Jospin. However, in the end France seemed to be looking for some sort of *Bonaparte redivivus*, and when the electoral dust had settled, Chirac emerged as president of the republic with 52 per cent of the vote. This meant in practice the introduction of policies with a definite Gaullist flavour: renewed nuclear testing in the South Pacific (concluded at least for the moment in early 1996) which provoked animosity towards France within the European Union and elsewhere; tough policies on Islamic immigration accompanied by charges that the Chirac government was racist; governmental structural adjustments which seemed to centralize power in the hands of the president to a degree that had not been seen since the de Gaulle era; and in foreign relations, the appearance of an arrogant French president thumbing his nose at world opinion. Meanwhile, tough economic policies introduced by new premier Alain Juppé led to labour unrest, and in December 1995, a wave of strikes and demonstrations across France involving both trades unionists and students invoked memories of Paris in May 1968. All the same, the new régime's popularity did not seem to suffer overmuch – at least, not at first.

However, more strikes occurred in 1996, along with a spiralling national debt and unemployment, hints at scandal such as questionable Paris housing policies involving President Chirac, a public opinion shift leftward in response to rising right-wing support for Chirac's anti-immigration policies (his approval rating among *Front National* members rose by 28 per cent in August 1996), and various failures of the Chirac government to have its way with the rest of Europe and the United States over Balkan and central African issues. The result was a dramatic victory for the left in a general election in May 1997. Alain Juppé was replaced as premier by Lionel Jospin (Juppé then became mayor of Bordeaux), who was greeted enthusiastically in Britain as the way to 'a unique European alliance' with Britain's new Labour prime minister Tony Blair. Jospin at once announced emergency programmes to put 700,000 young people to work, a halt to privatization, and a rise in the minimum wage. In November his government also decided, over the objections of local developers, to go ahead with European Union environmental legislation to create a 'green zone' in the Loire river estuary. A year into office, the Jospin government was generally reckoned to be if not a complete success, at least an improvement over its predecessor.

However, by the beginning of 2001, despite the improvements Jospin had introduced into French politics and economy, the resurgence of unrest and violence in Corsica, the continuing anti-globalization crusade of traditionalist farmer José Bové, and a flagging economy – flagging despite reductions in the unemployment rate – were cutting into his previously high approval ratings. Strikes continued, ranging from lorry drivers and the unemployed to employees of Air France and even a protest against shortening the hunting season for migratory birds to bring it into line with the rest of Europe.

Meanwhile, relations between Jospin and President Chirac became, and remained, somewhat strained. This became the foundation, so to speak, for the run-up to presidential elections scheduled for May 2002. Even before 1999 ended, the principal candidates were taking shots at each other. Moreover, President Chirac had to confront financial scandals associated with his time as Paris mayor, Premier Jospin faced accusations that he had once been a hard-core Trotskyite who worked against the interests of the Socialist party, and the National Assembly votes to shorten the presidential term from seven to five years (which Chirac first opposed and then supported) and make constitutional reform of the judicial system, proved controversial. And of course there was fear that 'Mad Cow Disease' might migrate from Britain to France, despite the British claim in January 2002 that the epidemic was 'officially over'. But in the April run-off election, to the surprise of everyone, Front National leader Jean-Marie Le Pen defeated Jospin and faced Chirac for the presidency. This indicated, it was thought, a resurgence for right-wing extremism, and when the results of the election were known, a masked protester in Paris held up a sign that read: 'Je pleure ... pleure ... j'ai hontè d'etre Français.' (I cry, I cry, I am ashamed to be French). Then came the day and Chirac was returned with an overwhelming majority; Left joined Centrist and Conservative to assure the defeat of Le Pen.

Given the 2002 election, how odd that the Front National had seemed on the run. In May 1998 it lost its one seat in the National Assembly to a Socialist, and in January 1999 the party split when Le Pen and Bruno Mégret had a falling out. However, at the same time attitudes on race were changing. In June 1998 former premier Édouard Balladur called for the formation of a committee to consider whether French citizens (popularly understood to be white French people) ought to have priority over 'foreigners' (understood to be non-whites) in jobs, public housing, and welfare. Needless to say, Front National welcomed Balladur's proposal. Nor were they alone. In 1999 66 per cent of the French admitted to being 'quite' or a 'little bit' racist, and 51 per cent said there were 'too many Arabs' in France.

FOREIGN AFFAIRS

In foreign affairs, beyond promoting European Union, Mitterand's France joined the rest of western Europe in trying to find a solution, short of direct military involvement, to the Bosnian crisis. France balked at air strikes until the Serbs shelled a Sarajevo market in February

1994. Then, foreign minister Alain Juppé and defence minister François Léotard urged issuing a joint American-European ultimatum to the Serbs, which though considered, was never acted upon. The French role in the Bosnian crisis was significant all the same. In 1993, General Philippe Morillon, head of the United Nations peace-keeping force in Bosnia, brought a kind of glory to himself and to France. When Bosnian Serbs laid siege to Srebrenica, this 'unpredictable, impulsive, eccentric, a "loose cannon"' character refused to leave the Muslim inhabitants to their fate and withdraw, as he was ordered to do. 'Yes, I am a shield,' he said, and established his headquarters at a post office and raised the UN flag. In due course, in the glare of world attention which Morillon's action focused on the besieged city, the Serbs were forced to reconsider their policy. Not long after this, he was succeeded by another French officer, General Jean Cot, who demonstrated an equal penchant for defying orders. France continues to play a central role in United Nation's efforts in Bosnia, including a controversy in 1995 over General Bernard Janvier's role in negotiating an end to NATO air strikes on Serb positions in exchange for a release of Serb-held hostages and an even bigger one in late 1997 between France and the Yugoslav War Crimes Tribunal after chief prosecutor Louise Arbour charged that French NATO forces in Bosnia were harbouring war criminals. France worked closely with Britain and the United States in the Balkans, but was divided from them over sanctions against Iraq. Also, French political opinion outside of government criticized French support for air strikes during the Kosovo conflict, a policy it blamed on the United States. Chirac and Jospin were accused by *Front National* leaders of being 'President Clinton's lapdogs'. French policy was not significantly affected by this charge, and France again joined with the United States in prosecuting a 'war on terrorism' following the 11 September 2001 attack on the World Trade Center in New York City.

In the spring of 1994, French forces joined with Belgians in 'Operation Turquoise' to play a rescuer role in the African nation of Rwanda when a vicious civil war broke out. Rwanda was not a former French colony, but the French government had played a part there in establishing a government several years before, consisting mainly of members of the Hutu tribe. Premier Balladur insisted that the intervention in the civil war was purely humanitarian; the Tutsi tribe, which bore the brunt of Hutu violence in the civil war, insisted that the French had a political motive. Whether they did or not remains unclear, but after several months, the government declared Operation Turquoise a success and by 21 August had withdrawn the last French forces from Rwanda. That was not the end of it, however, for soon after some United Nations peacekeepers in Rwanda were claiming that the French had protected Hutus guilty of committing atrocities against Tutsis.

French involvement in African affairs, sometimes criticized as 'neocolonialism', continued in the later 1990s, but with limited success or no success at all. In 1996 the Chirac government stood by helplessly while Zairian rebels backed by Rwandan and Ugandan troops took control of part of Zaire. French efforts to gain United Nations backing for an international peace-keeping force for Zaire were rejected in March 1997 by UN members who distrusted French motives. By June French influence in Zaire had been replaced by that of the United States, which with other western nations suspected that there was substance to allegations of French complicity in Hutu atrocities committed in Rwanda in 1994. Even so, the French government continued to pursue a role in Africa including economic and cultural involvement in Nigeria which is bordered by several francophone nations, and helping to train and finance a multinational African peace-keeping force in and around Senegal.

As to the conflict in Iraq which reached crisis proportions in 2002 and became a war involving primarily the United States and Great Britain in 2003, President Chirac, backed by German Chancellor Schröder, refused to vote for a United Nations Resolution to back the war. This had a negative affect upon Franco-American relations, symbolized perhaps by US Secretary of State Donald Rumsfeld referring to France and Germany as 'the old Europe'. For the next two years Franco-American relations remained strained; as Rumsfeld's successor as Secretary of State Condoleeza Rice is reputed to have remarked regarding American European policy: 'Forgive Russia. Ignore Germany. Punish France.' Then, in 2005, Rice went to Paris to lay the groundwork for a George W. Bush presidential tour of Europe.

French Foreign Minister Michel Barnier urged a 'new start' in Franco-American relations, and President Bush and President Chirac sat down together in Brussels for a 'fence-mending' dinner. Still, while relations were improved, the French government did not then, nor has it since, changed its anti-war position on Iraq, and even with the 2007 French presidential election victory of pro-American Nicolas Sarkozy, they still won't.

SOCIETY AND ECONOMICS

What had it all amounted to? Had the French 'married their century? Unequivocally the answer is yes. Since 1945 France has been heavily urbanized; the population of Paris and its surrounding conurbation is 12 million, a fifth of the population of the country. The divorce rate has risen steadily, and a growing number of French people live alone, which suggests some major and fundamental alterations in values. Credit card and hire purchase are a way of life now (as is McDonald's and its French equivalents), and autoroutes are crowded on Friday afternoons with traffic heading for beach, mountains or countryside for 'le weekend', as it has come to be called. A higher percentage of French people than either Americans or British own a 'getaway' place outside their normal urban environment.

The gross national product of France is five times greater than in 1950 – aided certainly by such economic coups as the £1.5 billion Airbus deal with China made in April 1996 – and despite the economic slump that surfaced in 2001; since 1960 the buying power of the average French person has doubled. High tech has replaced the dominance of traditional industry – the 'post-industrial revolution' – and there are now more white- than blue-collar workers. Correspondingly, only 12 per cent of the work-force belong to unions. Women are 43 per cent of the work-force, representing 72 per cent of women aged 25–49. Women sit in the Assembly; Pierre Mauroy's 1982 cabinet included five women; there were two women candidates for president in 1981; Edith Cresson became France's first woman premier a decade later; the general election in 1997 increased female membership in the National Assembly from 33 to 100; in 1998, Elisabeth Guigou was in office as France's first female justice minister;

and in 1999, Martine Aubry was being touted as likely to become the first woman president of France. Of course, a significant percentage of French men would still prefer that French women find fulfilment in fecundity.

In due course, 'marrying their century' also included coming to grips with the other side of France's role in the Second World war and its behaviour during the Algerian War. It has not been easy. In October 1997, Cardinal Jean-Marie Lustiger at a ceremony at Drancy, from where French Jews had been transported to extermination camps, made apology on behalf of the French Church for failing to act in defence of Jews during the war, and symbolically shook hands with Rabbi Joseph Sitruk. Meanwhile, evidence presented in the trial of Maurice Papon for complicity in 'crimes against humanity' in co-operation with the Nazi occupation forces in France, made it abundantly clear that those who resisted were vastly out-numbered by those who either stood aside or actually abetted the occupiers. This has not been easy for many French people to accept, and it is the opinion of some that the relatively light sentence handed down to Papon (ten years in prison) indicates that 'the jury was afraid of public opinion'. Even so, it seems clear that the French will never again look at the war years as an epoch when all Frenchmen were heroes. And, in December 2000, Jospin responded to increasing demands from French historians and others that the government 'come clean' over abuses the French military practised against Algerian rebels, promising to help historians gain access to relevant government records. Meanwhile, President Chirac admitted that 'nothing could ever justify' the atrocities committed during the Algerian war.

EUROPEAN RELATIONSHIPS

Franco-German relations continue to be close, within the Common Market and on defence matters. Some strain emerged over matters concerning the German idea of 'federalizing' Europe in the context of European Union (the presidency of which France took over in June 2000), but, early in 2001, the issue was set aside and the two countries mended fences. Franco-British relations are more erratic, perhaps, owing in no small part to the furore over British beef exports to France and 'Mad Cow Disease'; but the joint Concorde SST project disrupted for a time after July 2000 when an Air France Concorde crashed near Charles de Gaulle airport, and the cross-channel tunnel popularly known as the 'Chunnel', indicate more Anglo-French co-operation than since 1918, and perhaps yet more to come in the new millennium. This ends hundreds of years of English insularity from France and Europe, and becomes the perfect symbol for the European economic integration that began in 1992.

The 'Chunnel' (Eurotunnel) is a case in point. When Queen Elizabeth and President Mitterand took the inaugural journey through the Eurotunnel on 6 May 1994, their trip covered 32.3 miles at a depth of 131 feet beneath the English Channel. Regular passengers were using the tunnel after 14 November 1994 (more than a year later than original estimates). The November opening trip between Paris and London was reported by two journalists, one of whom took the channel train and the other by airplane. To their mutual surprise, they arrived at Trafalgar Square at exactly the same moment. Despite an £8 billion debt reported the following April, the tunnel continued to function and it was estimated that Eurotunnel would carry 44 million passengers annually beginning in 2000. That level of success was achieved, in spite of occasional disruptions such as the fire that briefly closed the tunnel in 1996 (which officials concluded likely was the result of arson) and non-European asylum seekers trying to walk through the tunnel into Britain in 2001. Eurotunnel carried 486,359 passengers in April 1997 alone.

With a market of 350 million consumers, a pan-European network of high-tech trains, including in France 5000 kilometres of lines for the futuristic *le Train à Grande Vitesse*, among other developments, and the possibility of including eastern European states in the community in future, European Union may mean a dramatically new European order and perhaps a new French order as well. In the former case, according to Jacques Delors, European Commission president, that could mean a 'European president', an elected leader who would be a public figure to represent the Union in its relations with non-European states. Meanwhile, under single currency commissioner Yves Thibault de Silguy, the European Union produced the Euro. It was officially launched in December 1996, decorated with 'vague architectural motifs' – in an effort to appear completely neutral and thus avoid upsetting any national sensibilities. Unfortunately, some of these motifs were famous European bridges that were easily recognizable, and even a pontoon bridge from India, 'not known to be applying for EU membership'.

PRINCESS 'DI'

On 30 August 1997, an event occurred which the French likely wish they could forget. Just after 1 a.m. on that day Diana, Princess of Wales, was involved in a car crash in Paris along the voie Georges Pompidou near the Pont de l'Alma. Also involved were the driver, Henri Paul, bodyguard Trevor Rees-Jones, and film producer Dodi Al Fayed, Diana's lover and son of the owner of London's fashionable Harrod's department store. It was rumoured that she and Dodi were to be married. Driver and lover were killed outright; the princess died at 4 a.m. Only the bodyguard survived, though so badly injured that he was unable to shed light on what actually had happened. While accounts were varied and often contradictory, it appeared that Diana was killed while being pursued by motorcycle-riding 'paparazzi', photographers who make their living taking unauthorized pictures – the more sensational the better – of the rich and famous. In June 1998 a French court was convened to try to reconcile the contradictory accounts of what had actually happened.

Seven paparazzi were arrested by Paris police soon after the event on charges of forcing the driver, who it was later revealed had consumed at least a bottle of wine before taking the wheel, to drive at speeds as high as 125 mph in an effort to escape their pursuit. A total of nine paparazzi and a press motorcyclist eventually came to trial on charges of manslaughter; a French court acquitted them in April 2002.

The paparazzi were not the only source of controversy. Dodi Fayed's father made public his view that a 'racist British establishment' objected to Diana's relationship with the Egyptian-born Dodi and had them both murdered. The fatal crash was a tragic event with an ugly aftermath which Paris, France and the rest of the world would long remember.

Change and Continuity

France celebrated New Year's 2000 with a spectacular light display in Paris that featured the Eiffel Tower seeming to 'explode' with fireworks. Does the new millennium mean a genuinely 'new France' or a France in which change and continuity blend in history as they have always done? The latter, obviously. France today is different from the France of a hundred, or even fifty years ago. But there are similarities, if only symbolic. The Fifth Republic presidency has monarchial characteristics. Regional power bases compete with Paris. An *International Herald Tribune* headline in 1987 referred to mayors of regional cities who 'Reign like Omnipotent Dukes'. In similar vein, Bretons, Corsicans and Basques agitate for ethnic autonomy, with ever increasing militancy. Indeed, in 1996, Corsican separatists carried out bomb attacks on symbols of the French state, Breton separatists were accused of harbouring Basque terrorists, and in their turn, Basque separatist group ETA went so far as to threaten violence against participants in the Tour de France as they cycled through Basque country. In 1999 protesting French farm and vineyard workers demonstrated that France's perennial struggle against Americanization and globalization is as lively as ever. Elements of racial and sexual discrimination remain: ethnic minority barristers, particularly Africans, find it difficult to gain acceptance in the French legal system, while women in politics – as in the case of Elisabeth Guigou – are judged more by their looks than their ideas. (Who can say whether that was a factor in Ségolène Royal's defeat in the 2007 presidential election). On the other hand, France not only embraced the Euro but as of 1 January 2002 joined twelve other EU members in making it the official currency. For tourists the advantage lies in having to change currency only once when travelling in these countries.

Over the past four years France has both changed and remained the same. The 2007 presidential election was a competition between a reformist-minded centre-right politician, Nicholas Sarkozy, who has included both a black woman and a man of North African birth in his government, and a woman, the first in history to stand for president of France. Ségolène Royal is a socialist and working-mother of four who wanted to install a government that supported both socialist and capitalist programmes. Old and new certainly, on both sides. Meanwhile: trades unions and university students continue staging protest marches and strikes. sometimes together; gangs, welfare 'fraudsters,' and illegal immigrants continue to create unrest in Paris *banlieues* for which newly elected president Sarkozy promises 'zero tolerance'; French public opinion remains reluctant towards full and equal participation in the EU, even after Sarkozy on the night of election proclaimed: 'Tonight, France is back in Europe'; and in 2006 a burgeoning economy that had for several years surpassed even Germany, began to lag as unemployment and poverty figures rose along with deficits in the national budget.

And, though more involved in international organizations than ever in its history, France continues to look after French interest first. French opposition to the Uruguay GATT (General Agreement on Tariffs and Trade) in 1993, for example, was described by Jacques Delors as France building a new Maginot Line. In 1995, President Jacques Chirac backed away from participating in the 1985 Schengen agreement under which seven European Union countries committed to ending their internal border controls by January 1996. A *Le Monde* editorial described this as 'an unfortunate step backward'. On the other hand, France not only embraced the Euro but as of 1 January 2002 joined twelve other EU members in making it the official currency. For tourists the advantage lies in having to change currency only once when travelling in these countries.

In the Pompidou Centre, France has a high-tech architectural monument which equals the symbol of industrializing France, the Eiffel Tower, in artistic bad taste. Moreover, major restoration of the structure had to be undertaken beginning in the mid-1990s. Owing to fading colours, bird droppings on the escalator tubes, and grimy, scuffed and shabby carpets, the Centre had begun to look like 'the rusting hulk of a starship that has crash-landed into the Marais'. The traffic in Paris moves today at about the same rate of speed that it did in 1900 – and produces sufficient air pollution to envelope the Eiffel Tower in a haze of smog, as was the case on 1 October 1997 – and only slightly faster than in 1610. Perhaps it should be no surprise that traffic congestion in central Paris, which today brings curses to the lips of frustrated motorists, in 1610 brought Henry IV within range of his assassin.

This 'change and remain the same' pattern is actually a reflection of long standing traditions; therefore it is neither new nor surprising. Sociologists argue that certain elements in French national behaviour are as old as France itself: the regionalism which contributes to a French tendency to denigrate foreigners and each other, which may explain President Chirac's refusal to modify the constitution to allow official recognition of France's seven regional languages; and the undercurrent of individuality, perhaps also a product of ancient regionalism, which 'can't tolerate authority, yet at the same time ... considers it indispensable'. The sum of French history would seem to be this: *plus ça change, plus c'est la même chose*. 'The more things change, the more they remain the same.'

Chronology of Kings of the Franks and France

(Merovingian)

Merovich 447–458
Childeric I 458–482
Clovis I 482–511
Childebert I 511–558
Clothaire I 558–562
Caribert 562–566
Chilperic 566–584
Clothaire II 584–628
Dagobert I 628–637
Clovis II 637–655
Clothaire III 655–668
Childeric II 668–674
Thierry III 674–691
Clovis III 691–695
Childebert II 695–711
Dagobert III 711–716
Chilperic II 716–721
Thierry IV 721–737
(interregnum)
Childeric III 743–751 (died 754)

(Carolingian)

Pepin the Short 751–768
Charlemagne 768–814
Louis I, the Debonair 814–840
Charles I, the Bald 840–877
Louis II, the Stammerer 877–879
Louis III 879–882
Carloman 882–884
Charles II, the Fat 844–888
Odo, count of Paris 888–898
Charles III, the Simple 898–929
(interregnum)
Louis IV, the Foreigner 936–954
Lothaire 954–986
Louis V 986–989

(Capetian)

Hugh Capet 987–996
Robert II, the Pious 996–1031
Henry I 1031–1060
Philip I 1060–1108
Louis VI, the Fat 1108–1137
Louis VII 1137–1180
Philip II, Augustus 1180–1223
Louis VIII, the Lion 1223–1226
Louis IX (Saint-Louis) 1226–1270
Philip III, the Bold 1270–1285
Philip IV, the Fair 1285–1314
Philip V, the Tall 1316–1322
Charles IV, the Fair 1322–1328

(Valois)

Philip VI *1328–1350*
John II, the Good *1350–1364*
Charles V, the Wise *1364–1380*
Charles VI, the Fool *1380–1422*
Charles VII, the Victorious *1422–1461*
Louis XI, the Spider *1461–1483*
Charles VIII *1483–1498*
Louis XII, Father of his People *1498–1515*
Francis I *1515–1547*
Henry II *1547–1559*
Francis II *1559–1560*
Charles IX *1560–1574*
Henry III *1574–1589*

(Bourbon)

Henry IV *1589–1610*
Louis XIII *1610–1643*
Louis XIV, the Sun King *1643–1715*
Louis XV *1715–1774*
Louis XVI *1774–1793*
(interregnum)
Louis XVIII *1814–1824*
Charles X *1824–1830*

(Orléans)

Louis Philippe *1830–1848*

(Bonaparte Emperors)

Napoleon I *1804–1815*
Napoleon III *1852–1870*

Presidents and Heads of Government

THIRD REPUBLIC

Presidents:

ADOLPHE THIERS, 1871–1873
PATRICE DE MACMAHON, 1873–1879
JULES GRÉVYM 1878–1887
SADI CARNOT, 1887–1894
JEAN CASIMIR-PÉRIER, 1894–1895
FÉLIX FAURE, 1895–1899
ÉMILE LOUBET, 1899–1906
ARMAND FALLIÈRES, 1906–1913
RAYMOND POINCARÉ, 1913–1920
PAUL DESCHANEL, February–September 1920
ALEXANDRE MILLERAND, 1920–1924
GASTON DOUMERGUE, 1924–1931
PAUL DOUMER, 1931–1932
ALBERT LEBRUN, 1932–1940

Heads of Government:

LOUIS-JULES TROCHU, 1870–1871
EUGÈNE CHEVANDIER DE VALDRÔME, 1870–1871 (The Bordeaux
    Government)
ADOLPHE THIERS, February 1871–February 1875
LOUIS BUFFE, March 1875–February 1876
JULES DUFAURE, February–December 1876
JULES SIMON, December 1876–May 1877
ALBERT DE BROGLIE, May–November 1877

GAËTAN DE GRIMAUDET DE ROCHEBOUET, November–December 1877

JULES DUFAURE, December 1877–January 1879

WILLIAM H. WADDINGTON, February–December 1879

CHARLES DE FREYCINET, December 1879–September 1880

JULES FERRY, September 1880–November 1881

LÉON GAMBETTA, November 1881–January 1882

CHARLES DE FREYCINET, January–July 1882

CHARLES DUCLERC, August 1882–January 1883

ARMAND FALLIÈRES, January–February 1883

JULES FERRY, February 1883–March 1885

HENRI BRISSON, March–December 1885

CHARLES DE FREYCINET, January–December 1886

RENÉ GOBLET, December 1886–May 1887

MAURICE ROUVIER, May–November 1887

PIERRE TIVARD, December 1887–March 1888

PIERRE-EMMANUEL TIRARD, December 1887–April 1888

CHARLES FLOQUET, April 1888–February 1889

PIERRE-EMMANUEL TIRARD, February 1889–March 1890

CHARLES DE FREYCINET, March 1890–February 1892

ÉMILE LOUBET, February–November 1892

ALEXANDRE RIBOT, December 1892–April 1893

CHARLES DUPUY, April–November 1893

JEAN CASIMIR-PÉRIER, December 1893–May 1894

CHARLES DUPUY, May 1894–January 1895

ALEXANDRE RIBOT, January–October 1895

LÉON BOURGEOIS, November 1895–April 1896

JULES MÉLINE, April 1896–June 1898

HENRI BRISSON, June–October 1898

CHARLES DUPUY, October 1898–June 1899

RENÉ WALDECK-ROUSSEAU, June 1899–May 1902

ÉMILE COMBES, June 1902–January 1905

MAURICE ROUVIER, January 1905–March 1906

FERDINAND SARRIEN, March–October 1906

GEORGES CLEMENCEAU, October 1906–July 1909

ARISTIDE BRIAND, July 1909–February 1911

ERNEST MONIS, March–June 1911

JOSEPH CAILLAUX, June 1911–January 1912

RAYMOND POINCARÉ, January 1912–January 1913

ARISTIDE BRIAND, January–March 1913

LOUIS BARTHOU, March–December 1913

GASTON DOUMERGUE, December 1913–June 1914

RENÉ VIVIANI, June 1914–October 1915

ARISTIDE BRIAND, October 1915–March 1917
ALEXANDRE RIBOT, March–September 1917
PAUL PAINLEVÉ, September–November 1917
GEORGES CLEMENCEAU, November 1917–January 1920
ALEXANDRE MILLERAND, January–September 1920
GEORGES LEYGUES, September 1920–January 1921
ARISTIDE BRIAND, January 1922–January 1922
RAYMOND POINCARÉ, January 1922–June 1924
FRÉDÉRIC FRANÇOIS-MARSAL, June 1924
ÉDOUARD HERRIOT, June 1924–April 1925
PAUL PAINLEVÉ, April–November 1925
ARISTIDE BRIAND, November 1925–July 1926
RAYMOND POINCARÉ, July 1926–November 1929
ANDRÉ TARDIEU, November 1929–February 1930
CAMILLE CHAUTEMPS, February 1930
ANDRÉ TARDIEU, March–December 1930
THÉODORE STEEG, December 1930–January 1931
PIERRE LAVAL, January 1931–February 1932
ANDRÉ TARDIEU, February–May 1932
ÉDOUARD HERRIOT, June–December 1932
JOSEPH PAUL-BONCOUR, December 1932–January 1933
ÉDOUARD DALADIER, January–October 1933
ALBERT SARAUT, October–November 1933
CAMILLE CHAUTEMPS, November 1933–January 1934
ÉDOUARD DALADIER, January–February 1934
GASTON DOUMERGUE, February–November 1934
PIERRE-ÉTIENNE FLANDIN, November 1934–May 1935
FERDINAND BOUISSON, June 1935
PIERRE LAVAL, June 1935–January 1936
LÉON BLUM, June 1936–June 1937
CAMILLE CHAUTEMPS, June 1937–March 1938
LÉON BLUM, March–April 1938
ÉDOUARD DALADIER, April 1938–March 1940
PAUL REYNAUD, March–June 1940
PHILIPPE PÉTAIN, June–July 1940

VICHY

PHILIPPE PÉTAIN, 1940–1944
PIERRE LAVAL, 1942–1944

FOURTH REPUBLIC

Presidents:

VINCENT AURIOL (Soc.), 1947–1954
RENÉ COTY (Cons.), 1954–1958

Heads of Government:

CHARLES DE GAULLE (provisional), September 1944–January 1946
FÉLIX GOUIN (Soc.), January–June 1946
GEORGES BIDAULT (Chr. Dem.), June–November 1946
LÉON BLUM (Soc.), December 1946–January 1947
PAUL RAMADIER (Coalition), January–November 1947
ROBERT SCHUMAN (Coalition), November 1947–July 1948
ANDRÉ MARIE (Coalition), July–August 1948
ROBERT SCHUMAN (Coalition), August–September 1948
HENRI QUEILLE (Coalition), September 1948–October 1949
GEORGES BIDAULT (Coalition) October 1949–June 1950
HENRI QUEILLE (Coalition), June–July 1950
RENÉ PLEVEN (Coalition), July 1950–February 1951
HENRI QUEILLE (Coalition) March–July 1951
RENÉ PLEVEN (Coalition) August 1951–January 1952
EDGAR FAURE (Coalition) January–February 1952
ANTOINE PINAY (Cons.), March–December 1952
RENÉ MAYER (Coalition), January–May 1953
JOSEPH LANIEL (Coalition), June 1953–June 1954
PIERRE MENDÈS-FRANCE (Coalition), June 1954–February 1955
EDGAR FAURE (Coalition), February 1955–January 1956
GUY MOLLET (Socialist), January 1956–May 1957
MAURICE BOURGÈS-MANOURY (Radical), June–September 1957
FÉLIX GAILLARD (Radical), November 1957–April 1958
PIERRE PFLIMLIN (Chr. Dem.), May 1958

FIFTH REPUBLIC

Presidents:

CHARLES DE GAULLE (Gaullist), 1959–1969
GEORGES POMPIDOU (Gaullist), 1969–1974
VALÉRY GISCARD D'ESTAING (Cons.), 1974–1981

FRANÇOIS MITTERAND (Soc.), 1981–1995
JACQUES CHIRAC (Gaullist), 1995–2007
NICHOLAS SARKOZY (Cons.), 2007–

Heads of Government:

CHARLES DE GAULLE (Gaullist), June 1958–January 1959
MICHEL DEBRÉ (Gaullist), 1959–1962
GEORGES POMPIDOU (Gaullist), 1962–1968
MAURICE COUVE DE MURVILLE (Gaullist), 1968–1969
JACQUES CHABAN-DELMAS (Gaullist), 1969–1974
JACQUES CHIRAC (Cons.), 1974–1976
RAYMOND BARRE (Cons.), 1976–1981
PIERRE MAUROY (Soc.), 1981–1984
LAURENT FABIUS (Soc.), 1984–1986
JACQUES CHIRAC (Cons.), 1986–1988
MICHEL ROCARD (Cent.), 1988–1991
EDITH CRESSON (Soc.), 1991–1992
PIERRE BÉRÉGOVOY (Soc.), 1992–1993
ÉDOUARD BALLADUR (Gaullist), 1993–1995
ALAIN JUPPÉ (Gaullist), 1995–1997
LIONEL JOSPIN (Soc.), 1997–2002
JEAN-PIERRE RAFFARIN (Cons.), 2002–2005
DOMINIQUE DE VILLEPIN (Gaullist), 2005–2007
FRANÇOIS FILLON, (Cons.), 2007–

Chronology of Major Events

B.C.

153	First Roman soldiers enter Gaul
52–51	Vercingetorix revolt

A.D.

262	Saint-Denis martyred in Paris
313	Emperor Constantine embraces Christianity as the Roman state religion
406	German tribes invade Gaul
451	The Huns are stopped at Châlons
486	Clovis defeats Syagrius at Soissons
507	Clovis defeats the Visigoths at Vouillé
507–11	Salic Law drawn up
534–36	Franks conquer Burgundy and acquire Provence
732	Charles Martel stops the Moors at Tours
751	Pepin crowned first Carolingian king of the Franks
800	Charlemagne, king of the Franks, crowned Holy Roman Emperor
843	Treaty of Verdun divides Charlemagne's empire into three parts
885–86	Viking siege of Paris
909	The Abbey of Cluny founded by Bruno of Baume
911	Rollo the Viking granted the fief of Normandy
987	Hugh Capet crowned first king of France
994	'Truce of God' Council at Limoges seeks to curb feudal anarchy
1066	William, duke of Normandy, conquers England
1095	Pope Urban II preaches the first crusade at Clermont

1100	Peter Abélard begins teaching in Paris
1122	Suger becomes abbot of Saint-Denis and advisor to King Louis VI
1130–60	Chrétien de Troyes and Marie de France write Arthurian stories
1152	Louis VII divorces Eleanor of Aquitaine, who then marries Henry II of England
1154	Henry II becomes King of England and establishes the Angevin Empire: Britain and western and southern France
1186	Philip II paves the streets of Paris
1200	Philip II codifies the study of medicine, civil and canon law; student riots at the University of Paris
1210	The Pope officially recognizes the University of Paris
1259	Henry III of England abandons Normandy, Maine, Anjou and Poitou, and recognizes French overlordship in Aquitaine
1280	Chartres Cathedral completed
1302	First meeting of the Estates General
ca.1310	*Parlement* of Paris established as judicial court apart from *Curia Regis*
1339	Beginning of the Hundred Years War
1346	French defeat at Crécy
1348	The Black Death
1356	French defeat at Poitiers
1358	Paris uprising and *jacquerie*
1411	Paul and Jean de Limbourg: *Les Très Riches Heures du duc de Berry*
1415	French defeat at Agincourt sounds death knell of chivalry
1420	Treaty of Troyes makes Henry V of England heir to the French throne
1429	Joan of Arc raises the siege of Orléans; Charles VII crowned at Reims
1431	Joan of Arc burnt at Rouen as a heretic
1435	Reconciliation of France and Burgundy at Arras
1438	Pragmatic Sanction of Bourges establishes the Gallican church
1453	French victory at Castillon virtually ends the Hundred Years War
1465	Rising of the League of the Public Weal against Louis XI
1484	The Third Estate recognized as part of the Estates General
1515	French victory at Marignano at the outset of the Italian wars
1516	Francis I persuades Leonardo da Vinci to settle at Amboise
1518	Budé's *L'Institution du Prince*
1523	Failed attempt of the duke of Bourbon to overthrow Francis I
1525	Battle of Pavia; Francis taken prisoner by Emperor Charles V

1529	Peace of Cambrai – 'Peace of the Ladies', Franco-Imperial alliance arranged by Louise of Savoy and Margaret of Savoy
1534	'Affair of the Placards', Protestant outburst in Paris
1536	Calvin's *Institution of the Christian Religion*
1544	Anglo-Imperial invasion of France
1554	Crespin's *Book of Martyrs*
1562–98	Wars of Religion between Huguenots and Catholics
1572	St Bartholomew's Day massacre and climax of Huguenot persecution
1576	Bodin's *De la République*
1588	Spanish Armada threatens England and Catholic League of Sixteen seizes control of Paris
1593	Henry IV converts to Catholicism at Saint-Denis
1598	Edict of Nantes grants religious toleration to Huguenots
1614	Last meeting of the Estates General until 1789
1618–48	The Thirty Years War
1628–29	Hugeunots defeated at La Rochelle; Edict of Nantes reaffirmed
1630	Cardinal Richelieu, first minister of Louis XIII, subsidizes Sweden in the Thirty Years War
1635	*Académie Française* established
1635,40,45,70	Anti-tax riots
1637	Descartes's *Discourse on Method*
1638	Swedish-French alliance
1648	Peace of Westphalia establishes the principle of the European Balance of Power
1648–60	The Fronde and other rebellions against Louis XIV
1665	Colbert appointed first minister
1670	Molière's *Le Bourgeois Gentilhomme*
1675	Breton uprising against Louis XIV's Dutch War
1677	Racine's *Phèdre*
1682	The court moves officially to Versailles
1683	Death of Colbert
1685	Edict of Nantes revoked
1689	Grand Alliance of England and the Empire against France
1701–13	War of the Spanish Succession; the French are defeated at Chiari, Blenheim, Ramillies, Turin, Oudenaarde, Lille and Malplaquet
1713	Peace of Utrecht ends the War of the Spanish Succession
1717	Watteau paints *L'Embarquement pour l'Ile de Cythère*
1740–48	War of the Austrian Succession
1748	Montesquieu's *L'ésprit des Lois*
1751	Diderot's *Encyclopédie*, first volume

1756–63	Seven Years War
1757–59	French lose India and Canada
1762	Rousseau's *Émile* and *Social Contract*
1763	British take over Québec and Louisiana passes from France to Spain
1778	France supports the Americans against England
1781	French navy help Americans win the Battle of Yorktown
1785	David paints *Oath of the Horatii*
1788	Paris *Parlement* forces summoning of the Estates General
1789	Declaration of the Rights of Man, Storming of the Bastille, and formation of the National Assembly
1792	Victory of revolutionary armies at Valmy: first victory of the Revolution against external enemies
1793	The Terror: Rule of the Committee of Public Safety
1796	Napoleon defeats the Austrians at Lodi and Arcola
1799	Napoleon's *coup d'état*
1802	Peace with Britain at Amiens
1803	France sells the Louisiana Purchase to the United States
1804	Napoleon crowns himself French Emperor
1805	Lord Nelson crushes Franco-Spanish fleet at Trafalgar
1806	Confederation of the Rhine formed by Napoleon; Holy Roman Empire abolished
1807	Treaty with Russia at Tilsit
1812–13	French driven out of Russia and Germany
1814	Napoleon abdicates; Bourbon monarchy re-established
1815	Napoleon returns; Battle of Waterloo; Congress of Vienna partially restores the Old Order in Europe
1816	Saint-Simon's *Industry and Society*
1818	Occupation armies withdraw from France
1824	The newspaper *Le Globe* founded
1830	Reactionary policies of Charles X foment revolution; first performance of Berlioz's *Symphonie Fantastique*
1830–81	Building the African and Indo-China empires
1839	Stendhal's *La Chartreuse de Parme*; Daguerre introduces photography
1841	Child Labour law passed
1848	Revolution overthrows the July Monarchy
1851	*Coup d'état* of Louis Napoleon, Napoleon's nephew
1852	Louis Napoleon is crowned Napoleon III
1852–65	Baron Haussmann rebuilds Paris
1854–56	Crimean War
1859	Italian War of Unification; Peace of Villafranca
1860	Cobden-Chevalier free-trade treaty with Britain

1862	Hugo's *Les Misérables*
1863	Renan's *La Vie de Jésus*; Manet exhibits *Déjeuner sur l'Herbe* at Salon des Refusés
1864–67	Napoleon III's Mexican Empire experiment
1869	Suez Canal opens; Flaubert's *L'Éducation Sentimentale*
1870–71	Franco-Prussian War, Napoleon III captured at Sedan
1871	Paris Commune
1874	Monet paints *Impression: Soleil Levant* – one critic mockingly dubs Monet and his friends the Impressionists
1875	Third Republic established
1876	Mallarmé's *L'Après-midi d'un Faune*; Renoir's *Moulin de la Galette*; France makes a gift of the Statue of Liberty to the United States
1880	Zola's *Nana*
1884	Trade unions legalized
1886	Seurat exhibits *Dimanche à la Grand Jatte* at the last Impressionist exhibition
1892	Panama Canal scandal
1892–94	Monet paints *Rouen Cathedral* series
1894–1906	Dreyfus Affair
1894	Franco-Russian alliance
1895	*Confédération Générale du Travail* formed; Lumière introduces cinematography; Cézanne given one-man show by the dealer Vollard
1896	Pierre, baron de Coubertin inspires the first modern Olympic Games in Athens, which except for years when the world was at war, has met every four years since. The centennial of Coubertin's effort was celebrated in Atlanta, Georgia in the United States of America, in July 1996
1902	First performance of Debussy's *Pelléas et Mélisande*
1903	Henri Desgrange founds the Tour de France cycling race
1904	*Entente Cordiale* with Britain
1905	Legal separation of church and state
1907	Triple Entente with Britain and Russia; Bergson's *L'Évolution créatrice*
1908	Sorel's *Réflexions sur la violence*; *L'Action Française* becomes a daily newspaper
1909–10	Matisse paints *La Danse* and *La Musique*
1913	First performance of Stravinsky's *Le Sacre du Printemps*; Proust's first volume of *À la recherche du temps perdu*
1914	First World War begins; battle of the Marne saves Paris

1916	Struggle for Verdun, battle of the Somme; Sykes-Picot agreement divides the Turkish Empire between Britain and France
1918	Armistice
1919	Versailles Treaty ending the war
1920–26	Alliances formed with Belgium, Poland, Czechoslovakia and Rumania
1922	Valéry's *Le Cimetière marin*
1923	French occupy the Ruhr
1925	Locarno agreements
1930	French troops leave the Rhineland
1932	The Crash of 1929 catches up with France; non-aggression treaty with Soviet Russia
1932–34	Failed disarmament conferences
1935	Franco-Russian mutual assistance pact
1936–37	Léon Blum's Popular Front
1938	Munich agreement dismembers Czechoslovakia, Daladier signs for France
1939	Anglo-French guarantee of Poland; Germany invades Poland
1940	Fall of France to Germany; Vichy state formed under Marshal Pétain
1943	Free French formed under General de Gaulle
1944	Allies land in Normandy; Sartre's *Huis Clos*; Paris liberated
1945	Third Republic ends; French women vote for the first time
1947	Camus's *La Peste*
1949	Organization of NATO
1951	European Coal and Steel Community treaty
1954	Fall of Dien Bien Phu, and France leaves Indochina; Algerian revolt
1956	Suez Canal invasion
1957	Treaty of Rome founds the Common Market
1958	*Colons* revolt in Algiers; Fifth Republic forms
1959	De Gaulle proclaimed first president of the Fifth Republic
1960	First French atom bomb tested
1962	Algeria becomes independent
1963	Anglo-German treaty of mutual cooperation
1966	Anglo-Russian rapprochement
1967	France leaves NATO
1968	Student-worker uprising in Paris
1969	De Gaulle withdraws from public life. He dies a year later
1974	Valéry Giscard d'Estaing and conservatives push Gaullists aside
1981	Left coalition elects François Mitterand president
1984	Jean-Marie Le Pen forms the ultra-right National Front

1984–87	France extends military assistance to former African colonies; Mitterand favours US military presence in Europe; terrorist activities associated with Middle Eastern extremists; strikes and protests reminiscent of 1968
1988	François Mitterand re-elected president
1991	Edith Cresson appointed first woman premier of France
1992	Eurodisney open as Marne la Vallée, near Paris; General Philippe Morillon named to head United Nations peace-keepers in Bosnia
1993	Premier Pierre Bérégovoy commits suicide; France narrowly votes approval of the Maastricht agreement on European Union; Oscar de la Renta becomes the first American to head a French fashion house, the House of Pierre Balmain; General Jean Cot replaces General Morillon as head of UN forces in Bosnia
1994	The Eurotunnel, connecting England and France under the English Channel, opens for business; France continues to advocate a policy of ethnic partition in Bosnia; French send peace-keeping force to Rwanda; French secret service arrest 'Carlos', the notorious terrorist known also as 'the Jackal'
1995	France resumes nuclear weapons testing against world-wide protest; Marie Curie becomes the first woman to be entombed in the Panthéon among the 'great men' of France; the French army officially admits that Captain Alfred Dreyfus was framed in 1895 on charges of spying for imperial Germany
1996	François Mitterand, the longest-serving president in French history, dies; Jacques Delors steps down as European Commission chairman; ashes of André Malraux (died 1976) deposited in the Panthéon
1997	Britain's Princess Diana dies after car crash in Paris; at Drancy near Paris, Cardinal Jean-Marie Lustiger makes public apology on behalf of the French Church for its attitude towards French Jews during the Second World War
1998	Maurice Papon is convicted of crimes against humanity in the Second World War and sentenced to 10 years in prison; the Football World Cup is held in France, which wins the title against previous champions Brazil; the 35-hour standard work week becomes official

1999	Henri d'Orléans, pretender to the French throne, and Maurice Couve de Murville, foreign minister under General de Gaulle, die; thirty-five people die in a fire in the Mont Blanc tunnel between France and Italy; French ban import of British beef owing to fear of 'Mad Cow Disease'
2000	More than 100 million trees felled by massive storms that rip across France; France wins the European Football Championship; the Holocaust becomes a subject of study in French secondary schools for the first time
2001	France joins other NATO members in waging a war on terrorism in the wake of the terrorist attack on the World Trade Center in New York
2002	The Euro replaces the franc as France's official currency; in the first round of the election the far right-wing party of Le Pen defeats the Socialist Lionel Jospin, however on 6 May Jacques Chirac is re-elected with a huge majority; Henri Rol-Tanguy, leader of French resistance who helped liberate Paris from the Germans in 1944, dies; neo-Nazis attempt to assassinate President Chirac
2003	President Jacques Chirac and German Chancellor Gerhard Schröder commemorate the 40th anniversary of the Elysée Treaty, and refuse to vote for a UN Security Council Resolution backing an Anglo-American war against Iraq; Students in 18 French universities strike against a new diploma system; more than 3,000 die in the worst heat waves in French history
2004	President Jacques Chirac joins Chancellor Gerhard Schröder at Caens in Normandy for a ceremony of reconciliation on the 60th anniversary of D-Day; left-wing parties won an absolute majority in regional elections for the first time since 1988; former prime minister Alain Juppé found guilty of corruption during his time as prime minister; Lance Armstrong becomes the first ever to win a sixth Tour de France; compensations will be paid to the children of French resistance fighters killed by Germans in World War Two
2005	The French government takes steps to ban all neo-Nazi groups in France in light of the number of their violent attacks having doubled since 2004; trades unions strike across France in protest of new labour laws; more than 70,000 outbreaks of urban violence occur across France by year's end; 66 residents of Angers are brought to trial on charges of sexually abusing their own children; the French electorate vote against the new EU constitution

2006   Student and trades unions protests involving up to 3 million people are called by some the 'new French revolution'; Ségolène Royal, the Socialist party candidate, is the first woman put forward to run for president of France; the French economy shows signs of improvement after several years in the doldrums

2007   Ségolène Royal is defeated in her run for president by Nicolas Sarkozy; the new president's party wins only 345 seats in the National Assembly after expecting to win 500; the French government works to improve its relations with the United States

2008   President Sarkozy orders television news channel France 24 to drop English and broadcast only in French; Lazare Ponticelli, France's last surviving First World War veteran, dies at age 110; pirates seize a French luxury liner off the Somalia coast, taking 30 crew members prisoner; President Sarkozy's popularity rating drop from 65 per cent in 2007 to 37 per cent in March 2008, the result of his presidential style and that his economic reforms did not yield results as expected; Yves Saint Laurent, French fashion legend, dies at age 72; a Moroccan woman married to a French man is denied citizenship because she wears a burka

2009   Union and student street protests over employment and pay cuts spread across France; the French Socialist party falls well behind other parties for failing to adjust to economic changes across Europe; former prime minister Dominque de Villepin goes to court in the Clearstream trial, accused of participation in making false accusations, forgeries, receipt of stolen goods, and 'breach of trust'; President Sarkozy works with USA President Barack Obama to improve Franco-American relations

2010   Facing financial downturns in the French economy, President Sarkozy increases government involvement in French business; 4 books are published on the 50th anniversary of the death of Albert Camus, honouring the writers' great contributions to French literature; former Prime Minister Dominique de Villepin is acquitted of all charges in his trial; President Sarkozy visits Port au Prince, Haiti in the aftermath of the disastrous earthquake; Socialist Party defeats President Sarkozy's party in regional elections; German Chancellor Angela Merkel and Sarkozy cannot agree on what is the future of Europe; the police raise the terror security as they conclude France is a primary al-Qaida target

2011   France imports "Green electricity" from Spain: Dominique Strauss-Khan is named Socialist Party candidate for President of France in 2012 elections; Jean-Marie Le Pen at age 82 says farewell to Front National leadership, and is succeeded by his daughter, Marine

Major Universities and Founding Dates

Aix-en-Provence, 1409
Besançon, 1691
Bordeaux, 1441
Bourges, 1463
Caen, 1432
Clermont-Ferrand, 1854
Dijon, 1722
Lille, 1887
Lyon, 1896

Montpellier, 1289
Nantes, 1461 (transferred to Rennes
  in 1735)
Orléans, 1305
Paris, 1200
  The Sorbonne, 1253
  Collège de France, 1530
Strasbourg, 1566
Toulouse, 1299

Select List of Religious Buildings
(from the oldest dated remains)

LUÇON (Vendée), Notre-Dame, 14th century
LYON (Rhône), Saint-Jean, 12th century
MARSEILLE (Bouches-du-Rhône), Notre-Dame-de-la-Major, 11th century
MEAUX (Seine-et-Marne), Saint-Étienne, 12th century
METZ (Moselle), Saint-Étienne, 13th century
MONTPELLIER (Hérault), Saint-Pierre, 16th century
NANTES (Loire-Atlantique), Saint-Pierre, 15th century
NARBONNE (Aude), Saint-Just, 13th century
NEVERS (Nièvre), Saint-Cyr-et-Sainte-Juliette, 12th century
NOYON (Oise), Notre-Dame, 12th century
ORLÉANS (Loiret), Sainte-Croix, 8th century
PARIS, Notre-Dame, 12th century
PÉRIGUEUX (Dordogne), Saint-Étienne-de-la-Cité, 11th century (replaced
    in the 17th century by Saint-Front)
POITIERS (Vienne), Saint-Pierre, 12th century
PONTOISE (Val-d'Oise), Saint-Maclou, 12th century
REIMS (Marne), Notre-Dame, 13th century
RODEZ (Aveyron), Notre-Dame, 13th century
ROUEN (Seine-Maritime), Notre-Dame, 12th century
SENLIS (Oise), Notre-Dame, 12th century
SENS (Yonne), Saint-Étienne, 12th century
SOISSONS (Aisne), Saint-Gervais-et-Saint-Protais, 12th century
STRASBOURG (Bas-Rhin), Notre-Dame, 11th century
TOULON (Var), Sainte-Marie-Majeure, 11th century
TOULOUSE (Haute-Garonne), Saint-Étienne, 11th century
TOURS (Indre-et-Loire), Saint-Gatien, 13th century
VANNES (Morbihan), Saint-Pierre, 13th century
VERDUN (Meuse), Notre-Dame, 11th century

Abbeys and Churches

AMBOISE (Indre-et-Loire), abbey church of Saint-Denis, 12th century
CAEN (Calvados), Abbaye-aux-Dames, 11th century
CERNAY (Yvelines), abbey, 12th century
CHÂALIS (Oise), abbey, 12th century
CHARLIEU (Loire), abbey, 10th century
CHATEAUBRIANT (Loire-Atlantique), church of Saint-Jean-de-Béré, 11th
    century; Abbaye-de-la-Meilleraye-de-Bretagne, 12th century
CÎTEAUX (Côte-d'Or), abbey, 12th century
CLAIRVAUX (Aube), abbey, 12th century
CLUNY (Saône-et-Loire), abbey, 11th century
CONQUES (Aveyron), abbey, 11th century

FÉCAMP (Seine-Maritime), abbey, 7th century
FIGEAC (Lot), Abbaye-de-Saint-Sauveur, 11th century
FONTENAY (Côte-d'Or), abbey, 12th century
FONTEVRAULT (Maine-et-Loire), abbey church of Notre-Dame, 12th century
GORDES (Vaucluse), Abbaye-de-Sénanque, 12th century
GRANDE-CHARTREUSE (Isère), abbey, 11th century
GUINGAMP (Côtes-du-Nord), Abbaye-de-Sainte-Croix, 12th century
JUMIÈGES (Seine-Maritime), abbey, 11th century
LA CHARITÉ-SUR-LOIRE (Nièvre), abbey, 11th century
LANDÉVENNEC (Finistère), abbey, 10th century
LA SAUVE-MAJEUR (Gironde), abbey church, 12th century
LAVAL (Mayenne), Abbaye-de-Clermont, 12th century
LE BEC-HELLOUIN (Eure), Abbaye-de-Bec, 11th century
LE MANS (Sarthe), Abbaye-de-Notre-Dame-de-la-Couture, 11th century
MARMOUTIER (Indre-et-Loire), abbey, 4th century
MOISSAC (Tarn-et-Garonne), abbey, 11th century
MONCONTOUR (Côtes-du-Nord), Abbaye-de-Bouquen, 12th century
MONT-SAINT-MICHEL (Manche), abbey fortress, 8th century
NANT (Aveyron), Abbaye-de-Saint-Pierre, 12th century
NARBONNE (Aude), Abbaye-de-Fontfroide, 11th century
NEVERS (Nièvre), church of Saint-Étienne, 11th century
NOIRLAC (Cher), abbey, 12th century
NOYON (Oise), Abbaye-d'Ourscamp, 12th century
PARAY-LE-MONIAL (Saône-et-Loire), abbey, 10th century
PARIS: churches
   Sacré-Coeur, 19th century
   Saint-Étienne-du-Mont, 15th century
   Saint-Germain-des-Prés, 7th century
   Saint-Julien-le-Pauvre, 12th century
   Saint-Sulpice, 17th century
   Sainte-Chapelle, 13th century
PLOUGASTEL-DAOULES (Finistère), Abbaye-de-Daoules, 12th century
POITIERS (Vienne), Abbaye-de-Ligugé, 4th century
PONTIGNY (Yonne), abbey, 12th century
PONT-SAINT-PIERRE (Eure), church of Fontaine-Guérard, 12th century
PRADES (Pyrénées-Orientales), Abbaye-de-Saint-Michel-de-Cuxa, 11th century
REIMS (Marne), abbey, 12th century
ROMANS-SUR-ISÈRE (Drome), abbey, 9th century
ROUEN (Seine-Maritime), church of Saint-Ouen, 14th century
ROYAT (Puy-de-Dôme), church of Saint-Léger, 11th century
ROYAUMONT (Val-d'Oise), abbey, 13th century

SAINT-DENIS (Paris), abbey and cathedral, 3rd century
SAINT-GILLES (Gard), abbey, 8th century
SAINT-GUILHEM-LE-DÉSERT (Hérault), abbey, 9th century
SAINT-JEAN-DE-CÔLE (Dordogne), abbey church, 11th century
SAINT-MARTIN-DU-CANIGOU (Pyrénées-Orientales), abbey church, 11th century
SAINT-PHILBERT-DE-GRAND-LIEU (Loire-Atlantique), abbey, 9th century
SAINT-PIERRE-SUR-DIVES (Calvados), abbey, 11th century
SAINT-SAVIN-SUR-GARTEMPE (Vienne), abbey, 9th century
SAINT-SEINE-L'ABBAYE (Côte-d'Or), abbey, 13th century
SAINT-WANDRILLE (Seine-Maritime), abbey, 7th century
SAINTE-MÈRE-ÉGLISE (Manche), village church, 12th century
SILVACANE (Vaucluse), abbey, 12th century
SOISSONS (Aisne), abbeys:
    Saint-Jean-des-Vignes, 11th century
    Saint-Léger, 12th century
    Saint-Médard, 6th century
SOUILLAC (Lot), abbey, 11th century
THORONET (Var), abbey, 12th century
TOURNUS (Saône-et-Loire), abbey church of Saint-Philibert, 10th century
VALMONT (Seine-Maritime), abbey, 12th century
VÉZELAY (Yonne), abbey, 9th century
VIENNE (Isère), church of Saint-André-le-Bas, 9th century

Selected Reading on French History

ARDAGH, JOHN *France in the 1980s* (London, 1982)

BATES, DAVID *Normandy before 1066* (London, 1982)

BERNSTEIN, RICHARD *Fragile Glory: A Portrait of France and the French* (New York, 1990)

BRIGGS, ROBIN *Early Modern France* (Oxford, 1977)

CHAMBERLIN, E.R. *Life in Medieval France* (London, 1967)

COBDEN, ALFRED *A History of Modern France*, 3 vols. (London, 1965)

CRONIN, VINCENT *Louis XIV* (London, 1964)

DRUON, MAURICE *The History of Paris from Caesar to Saint-Louis* (London, 1962)

FEBVRE, LUCIEN *Life in Renaissance France* (Cambridge, 1977)

GIES, FRANCES *Joan of Arc: The Legend and the Reality* (New York, 1981)

GREENGRASS, MARK *France in the Age of Henry IV* (London, 1984)

HALLAM, ELIZABETH *Capetian France* (London, 1980)

HIBBERT, CHRISTOPHER *The French Revolution* (London, 1980)

JAMES, EDWARD *The Origins of France* (London, 1982)

KENDALL, PAUL MURRAY *Louis XI* (London, 1971)

KNECHT, R.J. *Francis I* (Cambridge, 1982)

LACOUTURE, JEAN *De Gaulle* (London, 1970)

LADURIE, EMMANUEL LE ROY *Montaillou* (London, 1978)

MARKHAM, FELIX *Napoleon* (London, 1963)

MCMILLAN, JAMES *Dreyfus to De Gaulle* (London, 1985)

SCARRÉ, CHRISTOPHER, ed. *Ancient France* (Edinburgh, 1983)

WRIGHT, LOUIS *France in Modern Times* (New York, 1987)

Historical Gazetteer

Numbers in bold refer to the main text

Aachen *(Aix-la-Chapelle)* The Rhineland city from which Charlemagne ruled his empire. Now part of Germany. **25–26, 122**

Aix-en-Provence One of the principal cities of Provence and site of a medieval university. Paul Cézanne and Émile Zola were born here, and Count Mirabeau, an architect of the French Revolution, was elected from here to the Third Estate in 1789. **8–9, 17, 64, 91**

Albi A Languedoc bishopric, Albi was the centre of the Albigensian heresy (anti-Roman, anti-clerical) in the thirteenth century. It also is the birthplace of Impressionist painter Henri Toulouse-Lautrec, in whose honour the Musée Toulouse-Lautrec was established within the walls of the Palais de la Berbie. **45**

Amboise (Château) Mainly the work of Charles VIII and Francis I, this Loire château hosted Leonardo da Vinci in 1516, among other masters of the Renaissance. **70**

Arles A city in Provence of Greek, Roman and French antecedents, Arles has been, variously, the capital city of the early Burgundian-Provençal kingdom and part of the Holy Roman Empire. It was joined to France only in 1481. Roman-style bull fights are still staged in the second-century Roman arena, and Vincent Van Gogh did much of his painting in Arles. **3, 8–10, 17**

Arras The capital of the Artois region and the scene of some of the most bitter fighting in the First World War. Arras also is famous for its tapestries and as a centre of economic and industrial activity since the Middle Ages. **147–151**

Autun This Burgundian city was a great educational centre in Roman times. Prince Talleyrand, Napoleon's foreign minister and a renegade churchman, was bishop of Autun just before the Revolution. Napoleon himself, and Lazare Carnot, a Revolutionary general, were pupils in the lycée. Marshal and president of the Third Republic, Patrice de Mac-Mahon, was born at nearby Château de Sully. **9**

Avignon The city on the Rhône where for seventy years (1307–77) the papacy was held 'captive' by the French crown. A locally-produced wine was specially favoured by the papal palace, and has been named

Chateauneuf-du-Pape ever since. Avignon was annexed to France in 1789. The Palais des Papes is a magnificent example of Gothic architecture. The English philosopher, John Stuart Mill, died in Avignon in 1873 and is buried in the Cimetière Saint-Veran. **10, 51, 64, 67**

Battles

AGINCOURT *(Artois)*, 1415: The English under Henry V destroyed the pride of the French aristocracy. **59–60**

BOURGES *(River Yèvre)*, 52 BC: Julius Caesar conquered this last Gallic stronghold. **9**

BOUVINES *(Flanders)*, 1214: Philip Augustus defeated John I of England, forcing him to give up most of England's French holdings. **43**

CASTILLON *(Gascony)*, 1453: A French victory here brought the Hundred Years War effectively to an end. **62**

CHÂLONS *(Champagne)*, 451: The Roman general, Aetius, stopped the advance of Attila the Hun towards Paris. Merovech, first king of the Salian Franks, was allied with Aetius. **10**

CHAMP-DE-MARS *(Paris)*, 52 BC: Julius Caesar defeated the Parisii and secured Roman power in the Paris Basin. **12**

CLERMONT *(Auvergne)*, 52 BC: Roman legions defeated rebel Gauls under Vercingetorix. **9**

CRÉCY *(Artois)*, 1346: The first major English victory in the Hundred Years War. **55–56**

DREUX AND ROUEN *(Loire and Normandy)*, 1562: Simultaneous sieges of Protestant strongholds by Catholic forces, opening the wars of religion in France. **79–80**

DUNKERQUE *(Artois)*, 1940: The Germans failed to prevent the evacuation of more than 300,000 British and French soldiers. **161**

FALAISE *(Normandy)*, 1944: The allied victory in the 'Falaise Pocket' was decisive in opening the way to the liberation of Paris. Appropriately, one of the greatest French warriors of all time, William the Conqueror, was born here in 1027. **164**

FORMIGNY *(Normandy)*, 1450: Dunois defeated English reinforcements. The most important French victory in the Hundred Years War, paving the way for Castillon three years later. **62**

JEMAPPES *(Flanders)*, 1792: French revolutionary armies defeated the Dutch and became the masters of Belgium. A future king, Louis-Philippe, fought in the Revolutionary army. **125**

LILLE *(Artois)*, 1708: The Anglo-Imperial armies of the duke of Marlborough defeated Louis XIV here. **99**

MALPLAQUET *(Artois)*, 1709: The French fought Marlborough to a draw; it was nearly the last gasp for France in the War of the Spanish Succession all the same. **99**

MARNE *(Champagne)*, 1914: Marshal Joffre rushed troops from Paris by bicycle, in taxis and on foot, to stop the German advance. They did, Paris was saved, and the First World War then settled into the long stalemate in the West which ended only in August 1918. **148**

MONT AUXOIS *(Cote d'Or)*, 52 BC: Julius Caesar won another victory over the rebellious Gauls, bringing ever closer the final triumph of the Roman Empire. **9**

NORMANDY INVASION *(Normandy)*, 1944: In June, allied landings on beaches between Cherbourg and Harfleur opened the final phase of the Second World War in the West. **164**

POITIERS *(Poitou)*, 1356: Edward the Black Prince led the English to their second major victory in the Hundred Years War. **57**

RONCESVALLES *(Pyrénées)*, 778: The Basques defeated the Franks, and the epic poem, *Chanson de Roland*, was inspired by the death here of the Frankish leader. **65**

SAINTE-MÈRE-ÉGLISE *(Normandy)*, 1944: On 6 June, units of the American 101st Airborne overshot their drop zone and landed in the very centre of this tiny village. The Germans shot them as they came down. Most of the company were killed. **164**

SEDAN *(Ardennes)*, 1870: This battle opened the Franco-Prussian War. Emperor Napoleon III was taken prisoner. **135**

SOISSONS *(Champagne)*, 486: Clovis overthrew Syagrius, the last Roman ruler in Northern Gaul. **19**

SOMME *(Picardy)*, 1916: This bloody battle was fought to relieve pressure on the fortress at Verdun. **150**

TOURS *(Loire)*, 732: Charles Martel, grandfather of Charlemagne, defeated an advance party of Moors (Moslems). The Moors penetrated no further into France. **22**

VALMY *(The Argonne)*, 1792: Revolutionary armies defeated the duke of Brunswick, ending for the moment the threat of a counter-revolutionary invasion of France. **112–113**

VOUILLÉ *(Poitou)*, 507: Clovis defeated the Aquitanians, establishing once and for all the supremacy of the Franks in western and southern Gaul. **19**

WATERLOO *(Belgium)*, 1815: The duke of Wellington led an allied army to victory over Napoleon, ending his efforts at reestablishing his empire. Napoleon then was exiled to St Helena, a British-held island in the South Atlantic. **121–122**

WATTIGNIES *(Flanders)*, 1793: A reorganized Revolutionary army defeated the Austrians. **112–113**

YORKTOWN *(America)*, 1781: Admiral Count Grasse and General Count Rochambeau commanded French forces which backed George Washington against the British, and effectively ended Britain's hope of defeating the rebellious American colonists. **105**

Bayeux A Norman town where hangs the famous Bayeux Tapestry, which tells the story of the Norman conquest of England. It was commissioned in the eleventh century by bishop Odo of Bayeux, William the Conqueror's half-brother. **37**

Besançon This city near Dijon in Burgundy, once a free city of the Holy Roman Empire, is the birthplace of Victor Hugo, Charles Fourier, Joseph-Pierre Proudhon, and Auguste and Louis Lumière, inventors of cinematography. The citadel fortifications were designed by Louis XIV's military engineer,

Vauban. Besançon is the centre of the French watch and clock-making industry. **95**

Blois (Château) Francis I's favourite Loire château, and where Henry III summoned two meetings of the Estates General and plotted the assassination of the duke of Guise and his brother, the cardinal of Bourbon. **52, 71–72**

Bordeaux An ancient Roman town, now capital of the Aquitaine region and an important port, Bordeaux produces some of the finest red wines in the world. Always closely associated with England, which possessed the region during much of the Hundred Years War. On three occasions, 1870, 1914 and 1940, French governments withdrew to Bordeaux in time of war when Paris was threatened. The philosopher Michel de Montaigne was mayor in the sixteenth century. **4, 7, 9, 14, 21, 45, 55, 89, 97, 120, 148, 161–162**

Bourges A Roman town, an archbishopric in the 3rd century, a ducal capital, and finally, briefly, capital of France under Charles VII when the English held Paris. Joan of Arc came here in 1429 to persuade Charles VII to drive the English out. Jacques Coeur, Charles's banker and one of the richest men of the age, was born here, as was Louis XI. Jean Calvin attended university at Bourges. **9, 60**

Cahors This city in the Lot Valley was briefly in Moorish hands in the eighth century, was governed by Thomas à Becket in 1159–60, and was nearly destroyed during the Hundred Years War. Pope John XXII and Léon Gambetta, a prime minister in the Third Republic, were born here. **63**

Calais A town in the Artois region through which many English tourists enter France, Calais was an English possession for centuries. In 1347 Edward III captured it after six of its citizens gave themselves up for execution so that the town might be spared a siege. Auguste Rodin immortalized their sacrifice in sculpture. Calais was the last English possession to be recovered by the French, in 1558. **54, 56, 58**

Carcassonne For centuries a crossroads of trade between Aquitaine and the Mediterranean, this city in Roussillon was constantly under attack and, consequently, heavily fortified. Visigoths, Moors and Simon de Montfort during the crusade against the Albigensian heresy in the thirteenth century, attacked the city. The old town is probably the finest example of medieval fortification extant. **50**

Carnac This Breton coastal village is the centre of one of the most famous areas in France for Neolithic remains. **5**

Chambord (Château) Francis I built it, Louis XIV visited often, and Molière created *Monsieur de Pourceaugnac* and *Le Bourgeois gentilhomme*

here; in appearance the most medieval of Loire châteaux. **68, 71, 82**

Champ-sur-Marne (Château) Built in the eighteenth century by a wealthy army contractor who collapsed and died on the front steps when he was about to be arrested, probably for defrauding the government. The most famous resident was Madame de Pompadour. **103**

Chantilly (Château) Built near Paris by Louis XI, it later housed Anne de Montmorency, Constable of France and friend of Francis I. **68–70, 72**

Chartres Fifty miles south-west of Paris, Chartres is famous only for its cathedral, which is the most important Gothic church in France. It is the subject of the most extensive explanation of the symbolic importance of cathedral decoration ever written, Henry Adams's *Chartres*. **66–67**

Châteaudun (Château) This northern Loire château was rebuilt in the fifteenth century, when it housed its most noteworthy owner, Dunois, bastard of Orléans and companion in arms of Joan of Arc. **61**

Chaumont-sur-Loire (Château) Queen mother Catherine de Medici forced Henry II's mistress, Diane de Poitiers, to trade it for Chenonceaux. Diane presumably modelled for her classic sculptures elsewhere, for, not liking Chaumont, she rarely went there. **75**

Chenonceaux (Château) Henry II gave this Loire château to Diane de Poitiers, who lost it to Catherine de Medici. In the eighteenth century Jean-Jacques Rousseau stayed here as 'the cosseted guest of Mme Dupin, wife of a rich tax farmer'. It was built by Thomas Bohier, a tax farmer of the early sixteenth century. **75, 79, 81**

Chinon A small town in the Berry region, Chinon was where Henry II of England died in 1189, and Richard I may have done in 1199. Many Templars were imprisoned here during the suppression in 1308, Joan of Arc met with Charles VII here, and the region around Chinon inspired Rabelais' *Gargantua* and *Pantagruel*. **61**

Clermont-Ferrand The capital of the Auvergne region since Roman times, a bishopric since the fifth century and an industrial town since the nineteenth. Pope Urban II both preached the first crusade and excommunicated Philip I here in 1095. Blaise Pascal, Bishop Gregory of Tours, the chronicler, and Pierre Teilhard du Chardin, the Jesuit thinker, were from Clermont. **9, 17, 39**

Cluny This Burgundian town contains the ruins of what was once the greatest abbey in France, founded by Bruno of Baume in 909. Its greatest abbot, Hugh, orchestrated the famous reconciliation between Pope Gregory VII and Henry IV of Germany at Canossa in 1078. Peter Abélard died at Cluny. **38–39, 114**

Colmar One of the most fought-over towns in France, having belonged to both France and Germany on several occasions. In 1945 the retreating Germans put up stiff resistance here, leaving the town badly damaged. Sculptor Frederic Auguste Bartholdi was born in Colmar. **164**

Compiègne In this village north of Paris, Joan of Arc was captured by the Burgundians in 1430; in a railway car here in 1918 the Germans signed the armistice; as a symbolic gesture of retaliation, Hitler made Marshal Pétain sign the armistice of 1940 in the same railway car. Louis XV built a château here as an escape from Versailles; it is often described as a fine example of neo-classical decadence in design. **61, 150–151, 161**

Corsica   An island off the south coast of France acquired from Italy in the eighteenth century, just in time to make Napoleon Bonaparte, who was born in the town of Ajaccio, a French subject. **114–5, 173**

Dauphiné   This Alpine province was autonomous until 1349, when it became an *apanage* of the crown prince, who was thereafter known as the dauphin. The first stirrings of the French Revolution were felt in Dauphiné. The winter Olympic games were held at Grenoble in 1960. **48, 57–68, 125**

Dijon   The capital and principal city of Burgundy, and seat of its dukes for centuries. It also is the centre of one of France's richest wine-producing areas, and is known for its mustard. Famous Dijonnais include: Bishop Bossuet, the apologist for absolutism; Jean-Philippe Rameau, the composer; Gustav Eiffel; and Bernard of Clairvaux was born nearby. **59**

Domrémy-la-Pucelle   The birthplace of Joan of Arc, near Nancy on the River Meuse. **60–61**

Étampes   One of the oldest towns in the Ile de France, it was annexed by Hugh Capet, who maintained a palace there. Diane de Poitiers also lived there part of the time, and Ravaillac, Henry IV's assassin, was born there. **31, 36–37, 46**

Foix   The stronghold of the Albigensian heresy in the foothills of the Pyrénées. The village of Montaillou is in this region. **52**

Fontainebleau   (Château)   Northeast of Paris and the most famous château in France, Fontainebleau was started in the Middle Ages and expanded in the sixteenth century by Francis I. At Fontainebleau Philip IV was born and died, Louis XIII was born, Louis XIV signed the Revocation of the Edict of Nantes, Pope Pius VII, who excommunicated Napoleon, was imprisoned, and Napoleon signed his abdication. **71**

Fontevrault   Isabella of La Marche, widow of King John of England, was incarcerated in the abbey here after she organized resistance to the French king in Poitou. Many Plantagenet kings of England were buried there. **37, 49**

Gaillard   (Château)   Now a ruin on the Seine, this château was built in only two years by Richard I of England about 1190. It is one of the finest examples of High Medieval castle building. **43**

Gisors   This Seine château was the favourite retreat of Henry II of England in his Norman duchy. It provided the setting for his Christmas meeting in 1182 with Philip Augustus. Eleanor of Aquitaine, Henry's wife, probably was there, and their four sons may have been. In any case, it was assumed that they were for purposes of making Gisors the backdrop of the film *The Lion in Winter*, which dramatized the tense relationship of Henry with his family and the king of France. **43**

Grenoble　Famous for ski-ing, this city in Dauphiné also is the birthplace of Stendhal, Condillac, Casimir Periér, whose father led the revolt of the Third Estate in Dauphiné in 1788, and the seigneur de Bayard, the peerless knight of romantic song from the reign of Francis I. **68**

Grotte-de-Cougnac　Cave paintings from the Neolithic age. **4, 5**

Grotte-de-Lascaux　The most famous Neolithic-age cave paintings, but not open to the public. **4**

Le Creusot　One of the earliest French industrial towns. The famous Le Creusot metal works helped spark French industrialization in the early nineteenth century. **124**

Lille　This commercial and industrial centre from the sixteenth century was the capital of ancient Flanders, until France took it in 1667. Lille also is a military crossroads. Louis XIV laid siege here in 1667, after which Vauban built the *citadelle*, one of the finest examples of military architecture anywhere. The Germans occupied Lille in 1914–1918. Charles de Gaulle was born here. **99, 124**

Loches　(Château) Louis XI and Louis XII used this Loire château as a prison. It contains the tomb of Agnes Sorel, Charles VII's mistress, and the famous portrait of her with one exposed breast. **62**

Lourdes　In 1858 a vision of the Virgin Mary reputedly appeared to Bernadette Soubirous several times, and a spring appeared in the Grotte de Massabielle where she saw the vision. The Catholic Church ruled that she had seen what she claimed, and Lourdes became the largest centre of

pilgrimage in the Christian world. Bernadette became a nun at Saint-Gildard, where she died in 1873.

Lyon　The capital of Roman Gaul, then the kingdoms of Burgundy and Provence. It now is the third largest city in France, and the centre of one of France's richest agricultural regions. Thomas Aquinas died here, and Édouard Herriot, the Third Republic prime minister, was mayor in 1905. One of the first national financial institutions began here, Crédit Lyonnais. Famous Lyonnais include two Roman emperors, Claudius and Caracalla, the poets Sidonius Apollinaris and Louise Labé, the economist Jean-Baptiste Say, the physicist André-Marie Ampère, and the aviation pioneer and writer, Antoine de Saint-Exupéry. **3, 9, 11, 17, 20, 83, 124**

Maintenon　(Château) Set in an extensive park on the Eure, Maintenon was given to Madame de Maintenon, Louis XIV's second wife, by her royal husband, when she was governess to his children. She derived her last name from the château. **93**

Malmaison　(Château) Famous as the place where Napoleon, Empress Josephine de Beauharnais and their intimates held lively parties. She kept this retreat on the Seine as part of the divorce settlement, and died there in 1814. Napoleon III bought it, then sold it again. **115, 121**

Marseille　The oldest city in France, dating to Phoenician times, it passed successively through Greek and Roman hands, and then was independent until it became French in the late fifteenth century. In the Revolution, city radicals sang Rouget de Lisle's *Chant de Guerre pour L'Armée du Rhin*, which, rechristened the *Marseillaise*, is the national anthem of France. The Château d'If in Marseille harbour, a sixteenth-century fortress, was the prison setting in Alexandre Dumas' *Count of Monte Cristo*. Desirée Clary, queen of Sweden as wife of Bernadotte, Adolphe Thiers, Émile Ollivier, statesmen, Honoré Daumier the cartoonist, and dramatist Edmond Rostand were born there. *Bouillabaisse* (fish soup) is the most famous dish served here. **6–7, 17, 69, 114**

Montlhéry The most troublesome royal fief in the Ile de France in early Capetian times. Its châtelains inspired Philip I's comment that the Montlhéry tower had 'made me old before my time'. **35**

Mont-St-Michel The fortified abbey on a tiny island off the Norman coast was begun in 706. Over the centuries the Benedictines took it over, and it became so strong that Viking raiders could never sack it. At high tide it is completely surrounded by water; at low tide a sandy isthmus connects it to the mainland. Mont-Saint-Michel was suppressed during the Revolution and turned into a prison afterward. **32**

Nantes This Breton city always has been a commercial centre, strategically located for trade. Henry IV issued the edict granting toleration to Huguenots there. Gilles de Rais, the infamous Bluebeard, was hanged and burned here in 1440. Jules Verne, René Waldeck-Rousseau and Aristide Briand came from Nantes. **82, 98**

Nîmes A Roman town first, this Languedoc community still stages bull fights in the Roman manner in a Roman arena. It suffered at the hands of Simon de Montfort during the Albigensian Crusade. Its most famous landmark is the Pont du Gard, a Roman aqueduct which still functions. **8, 83**

Noyon Charlemagne was crowned king of Neustria here in 768, and Jean Calvin was born here. Hugh Capet was elected King of France at Noyon in 986. Eligius, Dagobert I's relentless tax collector, was bishop of Noyon in the seventh century. **21, 31, 77**

Orléans The road from Orléans to Paris was among the first major Roman highways in Gaul, an indication of the importance of this Loire city from the beginning. Early Capetian kings spent as much time in Orléans as in Paris. The city was besieged by Attila, Clovis and the English. Joan of Arc relieved the English siege in 1429, which was the turning point in the Hundred Years War. Orléans suffered from war also in 1594, 1870, and 1940–44. Jean Moulin, the legendary *résistance* leader was killed there by the Gestapo in 1943. Notable Orléannais include poet Charles Péguy. Marcel Proust did his military service in Orléans. **13, 14, 19, 23, 31, 46, 61, 79–80**

Paris

ARC DE TRIOMPHE: Built to glorify Napoleon Bonaparte, it was completed only in 1836. It houses the tomb of the Unknown Soldier from the First World War. **131**

BIBLIOTHÈQUE NATIONAL: One of the world's great libraries,

founded in the nineteenth century but based upon the royal library assembled by Guillaume Budé in the reign of Francis I. **72**

BOULEVARD DU MONTPAR-NASSE: In the 1920s and 1930s, this Left-Bank street was the centre of Parisian literary and intellectual life. Ernest Hemingway wrote much of *The Sun Also Rises* in the Café Closerie des Lilas. **167–168**

AVENUE DES CHAMPS-ÉLYSÉES: Built at the end of the seventeenth century, it connects the Arc de Triomphe with the Place de la Concorde. German troops staged a triumphal parade along this avenue following the armistice in 1940; four years later Charles de Gaulle led a march of jubilant Parisians along the Champs-Élysées in celebration of liberation from the Germans. **131, 165**

COLLÈGE DE FRANCE: Part of the University of Paris which grew out of the regius lectureships established in 1530 by Francis I. **72, 144**

THÉÂTRE FRANÇAIS (COMÉ-DIE-FRANÇAISE): Opened in 1790, and the principal venue since for classical French theatre. Molière, Racine, Corneille and Voltaire are regularly performed there. **92, 99**

CONCIERGERIE: Here in 1792, on the Ile de la Cité, opposite the Châtelet, prisoners were dragged out and slaughtered in the September massacre. In 1793 their successors were taken to the Place de la Révo-lution (Concorde) to be guillotined, notably Queen Marie Antoinette. **108, 131**

ÉCOLE MILITAIRE: Completed in 1774 to house the new Military Academy, it was built near the site of Caesar's victory over the Parisii in 52 BC. In 1880 it became the École Supérieure de Guerre, a school for staff officers. **108**

GOBELINS FACTORY: Founded by Henry IV to house the Royal Tapestry workshops. **83**

HÔTEL DES INVALIDES: Built by Louis XIV as a hospital for wounded soldiers in 1671, designed by Libéral Bruant. In 1836 it became the house for Napoleon's tomb; also, Napoleon II, Vauban, Marshals Turenne, Foch and Lyauty, and Jérôme and Joseph Bonaparte, Napoleon's brothers. The Invalides actually is a complex, con-taining with the Hôtel a church, Saint-Louis-des-Invalides, also by Bruant, and the Dôme des Invalides by Jules Hardouin-Mansart. **108**

HÔTEL DE VILLE: City Hall; here Blanqui, Blanc, Lamartine and others made the impassioned speeches, and were censored for them, which sparked the Revolution of 1848. The present building dates from 1882; that which served in 1848 dated from the fifteenth century. It is on Place de l'Hôtel de Ville, opposite the Ile de la Cité, which, as Place de Grève, was used for public executions from 1310 to 1832. **126, 127**

ILE DE LA CITÉ: The place where Paris began, where Caesar camped in 53 BC, where Odo defended the city against the Vikings in 885–86, and where the first Capets lived (occa-sionally) in a palace on the site of the Palais de Justice. Notre-Dame Cathedral is the most famous building on the island, followed by the Gothic

square at the foot of the Champs-Élysées held the guillotine to which most of the principal actors in the Revolution sooner or later bent their knee: Louis XVI, Danton and Robespierre, to name but three. In Dickens's *A Tale of Two Cities*, Madame La Farge sat knitting while she watched the executions. **108, 114**

PLACE PIGALLE: During the last decades of the nineteenth century, the Café Le Rat Mort in Place Pigalle in Boulevard de Clichy was a recognized meeting place for lesbians. The writer Colette and her lover 'Missy', the marquise de Belbeuf, frequented the café. The area figured as a location in Zola's *Nana*. **142–143**

PLACE VENDÔME: Proust dined here almost nightly to observe the decadence about which he wrote in *À la Recherche du Temps Perdu*. Chopin died in a house in this square. **146**

PONT NEUF: Completed early in the seventeenth century, this was the first Seine bridge in Paris not to be lined with houses. Connecting the Ile de la Cité with both Left and Right Banks, Pont Neuf quickly became the heart of Paris. French literary heros – and anti-heros – often paused on the Pont Neuf to stare at the Seine's dark waters and contemplate suicide, as in the case of Sartre's Mathieu Delarue in *L'Âge de Raison*. **108**

QUARTIER LATIN: One of the oldest parts of the city, it has been a student and scholarly area since the second century. Abélard founded his school there in the cloisters of Sainte-Geneviève, a century before the University of Paris, also in the Quartier Latin. **13**

SAINT-DENIS: The abbey church, a cathedral since 1966, was built by Suger beginning in 1136. It was the model for Gothic church architecture. Built on the site of churches dedicated to Saint-Denis since the third century, Suger's church continued the tradition of royal necropolis. Saint-Denis contains the remains of most French monarchs from Dagobert I to Louis XVII. **11, 13, 24, 38, 41, 53, 108**

SAINTE-CHAPELLE: The exquisite Gothic church on the Ile de la Cité built in the thirteenth century by Louis IX. **48, 131**

THE SORBONNE: The theology faculty established in 1253 by Robert de Sorbon, Louis IX's confessor. In 1544 its faculty rather unwisely censored writings on religion by Francis I's sister, Marguerite of Angoulême. They quickly recanted. The Sorbonne is now part of the University of Paris. **64, 73, 76–77, 179**

TOUR EIFFEL: This symbol of industrial culture, standing at the northwest end of the Champs-de-Mars, was built in 1889 by Gustav Eiffel for the Paris Exhibition. **142, 165, 194**

UNIVERSITÉ DE PARIS: Founded by Philip Augustus about 1200, formally recognized by the pope in 1210, and a centre of intellectual ferment ever since, this is one of the great universities in the world. In the thirteenth century it led the Christian world as a centre of theological and philosophical innovation and speculation. In 1968 its students seemed likely to start a revolution. There are campuses spread throughout the Left Bank. **47, 64, 73, 77**

Pau   The capital of Béarn, Queen Jeanne d'Albret of Navarre lived there in the sixteenth century, and her son, Henry IV, was born there. So too was Jean Bernadotte, who grew up to be first a Napoleonic marshal and then king of Sweden. **80, 83**

Plessis-les-Tours   (Château) Louis XI's favourite residence on the Loire, where he died in 1483. **70**

Plombière-les-Bains   This Vosges spa was a favourite watering place of Napoleon III, where he met Camillo Cavour, the Piedmontese prime minister in 1858 to plot the War of Italian Unification – which did not achieve that result, of course. **134**

Le Puy   This small city in the Auvergne, surrounded by extinct volcanic cones, seems dedicated to religion as no French community has ever been: Bishop Adhémar of Le Puy joined Bernard of Clairvaux to preach the crusades; Louis IX brought the statue of the famous Black Virgin in 1254; and Le Puy lay across the route of pilgrims on their way to worship at the shrine of Santiago de Compostela in Spain. A rather pretentious statue of the Virgin and Child stands on a ridge outside of the town. **39–40**

Rambouillet   (Château) Near Paris, this château is the summer residence for presidents of France. It has had a chequered career: Francis I died there, and in 1783 Louis XVI bought Rambouillet with the intention of making an experimental dairy farm. **75**

Reims   The coronation city of

Reims Cathedral

French monarchs. Clovis was crowned there in 496; Joan of Arc brought Charles VII there in 1429; and in 1824, Charles X resurrected the old régime, at least symbolically, by being crowned at Reims and by touching to cure scrofula, a power attributed to French monarchs since Robert II (996). Reims also is the 'champagne capital' of France. **9, 14, 38, 41, 61, 92, 123, 151**

Rennes   The capital of Brittany, the last of the great territorial principalities to be reconciled to rule from Paris. As there is now a Breton separatist movement (mostly limited to demands that the Breton language be recognized), it may be said that reconciliation is not altogether complete. General Boulanger was from Rennes. **51, 185**

La Rochelle One of the great French maritime cities and the first to trade with America, La Rochelle was also the central stronghold and last refuge of the Huguenots. It held out against the Catholics from 1573 to 1628, when a siege engineered by Cardinal Richelieu brought submission. Jean-Paul Sartre attended lycée in La Rochelle. **2, 78**

Rouen The capital of Normandy and William the Conqueror's seat until 1066. Joan of Arc was tried, condemned and burnt there in 1431; Corneille and Fontenelle were born there; and Flaubert was born, lived much of his life, and died in Rouen. The surrounding countryside was the setting for his *Madame Bovary*. **13, 21, 32–33, 61, 143**

Senlis A few miles outside Paris, Senlis was where Hugh Capet was crowned, and remained a royal residence from then until Henry IV. In 1352 a *jacquerie* massacred noble hostages, and in 1418 the Burgundians, and in 1914 the Germans, also massacred hostages in this town. **31, 63**

Sens Near Paris, Sens was one of the earliest French archbishoprics, to which even Paris was subject until 1627. By the ninth century its prelates were titled Primate of the Gauls and Germania, and dominated the Ile de France. Here Archbishop Saint-Loups condemned Abélard's writings and had them burnt, in 1140. Its inhabitants enthusiastically supported the Catholic League during the religious wars of the sixteenth century. **38, 47, 66**

Strasbourg One of Europe's oldest cities, Alsatian Strasbourg was an episcopal city-state until the seventeenth century, when it was joined to France. For a time its religious climate was very congenial for French Protestants. Rouget de Lisle composed what became the *Marseillaise* here, and Strasbourg has been the Council of Europe headquarters since 1949. Famous Strasbourgeois include Gottfried de Strasbourg, author of *Tristan und Isolde*, Raimond de Charbonnière, the geologist, and sculptor Jean Aup. Gutenberg worked on his printing press in Strasbourg. **76, 113**

Toulon France's most important Mediterranean naval base, and a site of naval activities since the Romans used it for the same purpose. French royalists handed it to the British in 1791, and Napoleon took it back in 1793. The French fleet here was scuttled by its sailors in 1942 when the Germans occupied Vichy France. **87**

Toulouse Capital of the old Languedoc region, this city on the River Garonne was first Roman, then Alaric the Visigoth made it his capital, in 419. Its independence later was crushed when the counts of Toulouse were caught up in the Albigensian heresy. Toulouse was the centre of 'Troubadour literature', of which Eleanor of Aquitaine was so fond. Jean Bodin and probably Michel de Montaigne attended the university here in the sixteenth century. Presently, Toulouse is headquarters of the French aviation industry, the home of *Caravelle*, *Concorde* and *Airbus*. **1, 8, 9, 17, 29, 34, 42, 45, 50–51, 78, 80, 91**

Tours This Loire city is famous for the purity of its French and the quality of its food. Gregory of Tours, the first French chronicler, was bishop here in the sixth century, and Alcuin of York made it one of the great centres of learning in the early Middle Ages. Charles Martel defeated a party of Moors nearby in 732. Famous inhabitants include François Clouet, portraitist of Francis I, Louise de la Vallière, mistress of Louis XIV, and Honoré Balzac, the writer. **14**

Valençay (Château) Located in the Berry region, the château was built by the d'Étampes family in the sixteenth century, one of whom was mistress to Francis I. Prince Talleyrand bought the château in 1805 and remodelled it according to his own highly refined and imaginative tastes. **71–75, 119**

Valenciennes Once called the 'Athens of the North', despite being in the centre of a heavily industrialized region, Valenciennes suffered heavy damage in the First World War. Its most famous product was Antoine Watteau, France's greatest rococo painter. **100**

Vaucouleurs Joan of Arc set out from this Meuse village on her mission of national liberation. Madame Du Barry, prostitute, mistress of Louis XV and victim of the guillotine, was born here. **60–62, 103, 104**

Vercors This region of western Dauphiné was the centre of *Maquis* resistance to the Germans and to the Vichy régime during the Second World War. The National Cemetery of Vercors located in Vassileux-en-Vercors commemorates the achievements of the *Maquis*. **164, 168**

Vichy Located in the Auvergne region, this spa is famous for its water which was prized from Roman times to the present. Unfortunately, Vichy is also infamous as the seat of the collaborationist government of Marshal Pétain and Pierre Laval between 1940 and 1944. The town has lived down that episode and remains the most popular spa in France. **161–165, 176**

Villefranche (Villafranca) In 1859 Napoleon III and Franz Joseph, Emperor of Austria, negotiated an end to the War of Italian Unification, after the Franco-Piedmontese alliance won victories at Magenta and Solferino. This small city on the Côte d'Azur provided the venue. **134**

Index